S0-BAP-839

Understanding
Early Adolescent
Self and Identity

SUNY Series, Studying the Self
Richard P. Lipka and Thomas M. Brinthaupt, editors

Understanding Early Adolescent Self and Identity

Applications and Interventions

Edited by

Thomas M. Brinthaupt and Richard P. Lipka

State University of New York Press

Published by

State University of New York Press, Albany

© 2002 State University of New York

All rights reserved

Printed in the United States of America

No part of this book may be used or reproduced in any manner whatsoever without written permission. No part of this book may be stored in a retrieval system or trans-mitted in any form or by any means including electronic, electrostatic, magnetic tape, mechanical, photocopying, recording, or otherwise without the prior permission in writing of the publisher.

For information, address State University of New York Press,
90 State Street, Suite 700, Albany, NY 12207

Production by Christine L. Hamel
Marketing by Michael Campochiaro

Library of Congress Cataloging-in-Publication Data

Understanding early adolescent self and identity : applications and interventions /
edited by Thomas M. Brinthaupt and Richard P. Lipka.
    p. cm. — (SUNY series, studying the self)
  Includes bibliographical references and index.
    ISBN 0-7914-5333-2 (alk. paper) — ISBN 0-7914-5334-0 (pbk. : alk. paper)
      1. Identity (Psychology) in adolescence. 2. Self-esteem in adolescence.
  I. Brinthaupt, Thomas M., 1958- II. Lipka, Richard P. III. Series.

BF724.3.I3 U53 2002
155.5 182—dc21

                                                              2001049473

10 9 8 7 6 5 4 3 2 1

CONTENTS

CONTRIBUTORS

Françoise Alsaker
Institute for Psychology
University of Berne
Berne, Switzerland

Margarita Azmitia
Psychology Department
University of California
Santa Cruz, CA

Thomas M. Brinthaupt
Department of Psychology
Middle Tennessee State University
Murfreesboro, TN

Gilbert Botvin
Institute for Prevention Research
Weill Medical College of Cornell University
New York, NY

Carol Burk-Braxton
Department of Psychology

University of Missouri
Columbia, MO

Peggy Clements
Center for Community Research and Action
New York University
New York, NY

Nancy Deutsch
Program in Human Development and Social Policy
Northwestern University
Evanston, IL

David L. DuBois
Department of Psychology
University of Missouri
Columbia, MO

Rutger C. M. E. Engels
Department of Child and Adolescent Studies
Utrecht University
Utrecht, The Netherlands

Catrin Finkenauer
Department of Social Psychology
Free University
Amsterdam, The Netherlands

Barton J. Hirsch
Program in Human Development and Social Policy
Northwestern University
Evanston, IL

Michael H. Kernis
Department of Psychology & Institute for Behavioral Research
University of Georgia
Athens, GA

Shun Lau
School of Education
Stanford University
Stanford, CA

Richard P. Lipka
Special Services and Leadership Studies
Pittsburg State University
Pittsburg, KS

Wim Meeus
Department of Child and Adolescent Studies
Utrecht University
Utrecht, The Netherlands

Dan Olweus
Research Center for Health Promotion
University of Bergen
Bergen, Norway

Annerieke Oosterwegel
Department of Child and Adolescent Studies
Utrecht University
Utrecht, The Netherlands

Robert W. Roeser
School of Education
Stanford University
Stanford, CA

Lawrence M. Scheier
Institute for Prevention Research
Weill Medical College of Cornell University
New York, NY

Edward Seidman
Center for Community Research and Action
New York University
New York, NY

Randall G. Starling
Department of Family and Community Medicine
University of New Mexico
Albuquerque, NM

Heather D. Tevendale
Department of Psychology

University of Missouri
Columbia, MO

Lily Dow Velarde
Department of Health Science
New Mexico State University
Las Cruces, NM

Nina B. Wallerstein
Department of Family and Community Medicine
University of New Mexico
Albuquerque, NM

1

Understanding Early Adolescent Self and Identity: An Introduction

Thomas M. Brinthaupt & Richard P. Lipka

Early adolescence is a time of change, challenge, and potential. The cognitive, social, and physical changes experienced by early and later adolescents have been well documented (e.g., Graber, Brooks-Gunn, & Petersen, 1996; Johnson, Roberts, & Worell, 1999; Lerner, 1993; Montemayor, Adams, & Gullotta, 1990; Schulenberg, Maggs, & Hurrelmann, 1997). The effects of these changes on self and identity have also been of interest to theorists and researchers (e.g., DuBois & Hirsch, 2000; Harter, 1999; Lipka & Brinthaupt, 1992; Rosenberg, 1979, 1986). However, whereas some have addressed the effects of specific changes on self in early adolescence, there are no previous books that are devoted exclusively to the self- and identity-related issues of this developmental period and that focus on applications and interventions related to these issues.

In this book, we have assembled leading contributors to issues of self and identity pertaining to early adolescence. They provide a broad and interdisciplinary approach to studying the self in early adolescence. Throughout the book, the contributors emphasize the practical implications of their work for understanding early adolescent self and identity and for designing interventions that facilitate early adolescent development and adjustment. Recent theory and research on adult self and identity (e.g., Baumeister, 1999; Hoyle, Kernis, Leary, & Baldwin, 1999) have focused on topics such as possible selves, self-discrepancies, the stability of self-esteem, self-efficacy, self-related motives, and self-regulation. The contributors to this book utilize several of these topics as they help us to understand early adolescent self and identity.

A Brief Review of Pre-Adolescent Self and Identity Development

Most research on the development of the self has been concerned with the self in infancy, childhood, and adolescence (e.g., Cicchetti & Beeghly, 1990; Lipka & Brinthaupt, 1992). Traditionally, researchers and theorists have assumed that it is during these years when most of the "action" regarding the development of self and identity is occurring. The changes prior to adolescence are dramatic and important, and they set the foundation for later developments. Without the groundwork for self-awareness, self-conscious emotions, and self-evaluation, the concerns of the adolescent and adult self would be nonexistent. As Harter (1999) notes, cognitive and social changes complement and mutually affect each other at all stages of development.

Cognitive Changes

Among the first major developments in infancy and very early childhood is the awareness of the self-as-agent (the "I" or private, subjective sense of self) and the self-as-object (the "me" or public, objective self-as-known). Related to this basic distinction, Lewis (1990) proposed three broad levels of identity development in early life. These include the ability to differentiate self from others, a sense of self-permanence or conservation of self over time and place, and (by 15-18 months of age) the initial aspects of self-awareness or self-consciousness.

From Lewis' (1990) perspective, the development of social relationships and the experience of particular emotional states arise out of this newly developed sense of self or identity. Beginning at around 2 years of age, the child's emerging facility with language allows him or her to begin constructing a "verbal self" (e.g., Bates, 1990). It is during this time that the self-as-object emerges more fully. These children also begin to show anxiety over their failures. For the first time, we see children responding to outcomes with specifically self-evaluative emotions, such as pride, shame, envy, and guilt. The younger child of one and a half years does not experience these emotions.

As the child enters middle childhood, he or she begins to develop the abilities to reason, take the perspective of others, and develop social skills (Harter, 1999). These new abilities have important implications for the self. As we might expect, children in middle childhood must deal with their relatively recent discoveries of a public and a private self, as well as the difference between real and ideal selves. Increasingly, the possibility that the different parts of oneself are not consistent with one another must be addressed.

According to Rosenberg (1986), there are several developmental trends that characterize the shift from middle childhood to adolescence. One change is in the content of the child's self-conceptions over time. Rosenberg describes this transition as the shift from an emphasis on the social exterior to an emphasis on the psychological interior. In particular, the younger child tends to think of the self in terms of overt, external dimensions, such as personal attributes and possessions, features of the bodily or categorical self, and typical and preferred activities. The older child tends to emphasize more internal, covert, psychological dimensions (such as traits and attitudes).

A related developmental shift is from what Rosenberg (1986) calls percept to concept. That is, the self-descriptions and self-perceptions of the child change from the primarily visual and observable to a more abstract and conceptual trait system. In addition, he argues that the developing child shows a self-concept that changes from a simple, global construct to one that is increasingly differentiated. That is, the ways we think of ourselves begin to become more complex and multidimensional.

According to Harter (1999), early and middle childhood are characterized by unrealistically positive self-representations and an inability to distinguish between one's real and ideal selves. Research has shown that, during middle to late childhood, children's self-evaluations become much more realistic and accurate (e.g., Harter & Pike, 1984). Interestingly, as children move into later childhood, they also show greater differentiation (and discrepancies) between the real self and the ideal self (see Shirk & Renouf, 1992). As we noted earlier, one of the changes during this period is that the self becomes less global and more differentiated. The self-image disparity findings reflect this increasing differentiation.

As the child approaches early adolescence, he or she begins to show higher-order reasoning about the self and its qualities (Harter, 1999). According to Damon and Hart's (1982) developmental model of self-understanding, by late childhood and early adolescence, the physical aspects of the self become relatively less important than the psychological aspects. In addition, the self is increasingly experienced as a subjective psychological phenomenon. Early adolescents now have a more important inner life and they begin to introspect about it. As Harter (1999) points out, whereas early adolescents are able to consider separate parts of their self and begin a superficial integration of their self-facets, they have yet to organize those facets into a coherent, internally consistent and realistic self-system. This is likely to be a major reason why fluctuations in the level and stability of self-evaluations reach their peak during early adolescence (Demo & Savin-Williams, 1992).

Social Changes

At the same time as these cognitive shifts are occurring, changes in social relations are having strong effects on the lives of children. According to Harter (1999), very young children respond to adult reactions and are primarily concerned with meeting the external standards of others. However, their lack of social comparison skills inhibits their ability to think of themselves in more complex ways. In early to middle childhood, children learn to anticipate others' reactions and internalize behavioral standards. Self- and social-comparison information is more influential, as these children begin to compare their performance to their own past and to other children. However, it is not until late childhood and early adolescence that self and identity most fully reflect the interpersonal domain, including selves that differ depending on the social context (see Harter, 1999). This is a time when children begin to show greater independence from their families and when peer relations increase in importance and intensity, particularly with regard to assessments of personal competence. Within these peer relations, children learn a great deal about social and group conformity, deviancy, and what it means to be included or excluded (Dishion, McCord, & Poulin, 1999; Gavin & Furman, 1989).

In a detailed study of peer relations and culture among a group of predominantly white, middle-class U.S. children and pre-adolescents, Adler and Adler (1998) explored the effects of friendship, popularity, and social status on self and identity. As children move from early to later elementary school, social relations are increasingly characterized by dynamics of inclusion and exclusion. For instance, the most popular cliques were found to have a hierarchical structure, with one or two leaders. These leaders required members to subjugate and stigmatize other children who were not clique members, while at the same time showing their subservience to the leaders and the group. Membership in these popular groups was marked by continual social uncertainty and fragility. Adler and Adler suggest that clique dynamics of inclusion and exclusion are likely to foster unstable self-esteem, especially among popular pre-adolescents.

Adler and Adler (1998) found that, by the fourth or fifth grade, around one third of students belonged to one of the (fairly large) popular cliques. The members of these groups tended to feel best about themselves and were seen most favorably by the other children. Below the popular cliques was a smaller set of students (around 10%) falling into a "wannabe" group, continuously striving for inclusion in the most popular cliques. These wannabes experienced strong status insecurity, low self-esteem, and a lack of identity clarity. Roughly half of the students fell into a middle status level, characterized by smaller, independent friendship circles. These students were subjected to status derogation from the popular cliques, but they also experienced high levels of loyalty, security, and support from their friendships. Finally, 5-10% of students were social isolates, languishing at the bottom of the status hierarchy. These children had the lowest self-esteem and frequently experienced degradation and ostracism from their peers.

Research has also found interesting patterns of cross-gender relations from the early to later elementary years. In their study, Adler and Adler (1998) identified three distinct stages of gender relations. After passing through stages of integration and separation, cross-gender friendships re-emerged in early adolescence and initial romantic relations were cultivated. As Adler and Adler describe, for boys and girls alike, this cross-gender reconnection is characterized by feelings of awkwardness, misunderstanding, and anguish. Behaviorally, these relations are characterized by gossip, speculation, and sexual flirting and exploration.

Physical Changes

Early adolescence is also a time when new physical developments begin to occur (e.g., Gunnar & Collins, 1988). Hormonal changes cause the growth spurts and development of primary and secondary sexual characteristics associated with puberty. During early adolescence, the body therefore intrudes upon one's sense of self and identity to a greater extent than in earlier years. The physical self becomes an "insistent presence" for the child (see Toombs, 1994).

Researchers have found large individual differences in the timing of puberty (e.g., Ellis & Garber, 1999) and these physical changes affect early adolescent self and identity (Brooks-Gunn & Graber, 1999; Simmons & Blyth, 1987). According to Simmons' (1987) "arena-of-comfort" hypothesis, if physical changes are too sudden, too early, or too extensive compared to one's age cohorts (i.e., outside of the "arena of comfort"), then the transition to adolescence and early adulthood can have negative effects on how one evaluates oneself. Simmons found that the timing of one's transition to puberty (relative to one's peers) has a greater, negative impact on self-esteem than the experience of puberty itself, particularly for girls.

It should be noted that there is a significant lag time between biological and social adulthood, at least in western cultures. This reflects the ambiguous and poorly defined social status of adolescence. In the United States, adults discourage developing adolescents from acting on their new physical and sexual status, even though these changes have important implications for self and identity (Brooks-Gunn & Graber, 1999). This state of affairs explains in part why peers have such an influence on adolescent sexual activity (e.g., Udry, 1990).

It is also well documented that adolescents (of many species) show increases in novelty seeking, sensation seeking, and risk taking behaviors (Arnett, 1992). Spear (2000) argued that several areas of the brain are transformed during the transition to adolescence. For example, changes have been found in neurotransmitter input to the adolescent prefrontal cortex (associated with goal-directed and self-regulatory behavior) as well as to areas of the limbic brain (associated with emotional reactions and responses to stress). She suggests that such changes in neural mechanisms are closely related to typical adolescent behaviors, such as increased drug use and greater negative reactions to stress.

Summary

As the child enters early adolescence, the stability of the self is threatened. There are several reasons why self and identity may become less stable at this time. The "true" attributes of oneself and others become or remain ambiguous. In addition, early adolescents are likely to receive different pictures of themselves depending on who is providing that picture. For instance, the self-related observations and opinions of one's parents are unlikely to be the same as those of one's peers. At this time, efforts at impression management and self-presentation become more important and focused. To the extent that the child experiments with different roles, this may convey the sense that the self is an amorphous, mutable construct. Of course, all of these changes are occurring at the same time that the child is becoming a young adult, with the bodily and other physical changes that make up puberty.

The early adolescent is subjected to multiple changes and developments, which do not necessarily occur at the same time or complete their trajectories at the same rate. While he or she is equipped with an increasingly complex sense of self or identity, the early adolescent has yet to fully live in these "new clothes." As our brief review shows, this period is characterized by increased self-consciousness, introspection, inner conflict, stress, uncertainty, and disorientation. Taken together, the combination of cognitive, social, and physical changes makes early adolescence a critical time for the consideration of self- and identity-related applications and interventions.

This book illustrates these applications and interventions in four major sections. In the first section, contributors address some of the major conceptual issues for studying the self in early adolescence, including how early adolescent changes relate to self and identity, and why self-esteem must be understood as a multifaceted construct. In the second section, contributors address transitions to new schools and school structures, the self and identity needs of early adolescents, and how these often are in conflict with one another. The third section addresses negative peer relationships and other behavioral problems that commonly affect the early adolescent and some of the ways that these problems can be lessened. Finally, the last section of the book presents case examples of specific self-related applications and interventions as well as a comprehensive review of the effectiveness of self-esteem enhancement interventions.

Conceptual Issues

The contributors to the first part of the book provide some conceptual clarity to the question of what constitutes self and identity in early adolescence. Two major questions are addressed here. First, what are the major changes that early adolescents undergo and what impact do these changes have on self and identity? Second, what is self-esteem and how do its many facets relate to early adolescent adjustment?

In the first chapter, Finkenauer, Engels, Meeus, and Oosterwegel provide a very useful introduction to the major changes and transitions during early adolescence and how these affect self and identity. Their overview touches on many of the issues and topics that are the focus of the other contributors to this book. Finkenauer and colleagues emphasize how early adolescence is a period of heightened stress vulnerability, and they describe some of the ways that this vulnerability can be reduced. In the first part of their chapter, they distinguish between "self" (the relatively stable knowledge and feelings about oneself as a whole, across time and situation) and "identity" (the specific self-aspects that vary in salience as a function of social and environmental factors). Next, they review some of the major problems, difficulties, and stressors associated with early adolescence. They note that, as a period of sometimes extreme discontinuities, early adolescence is filled with both challenges and opportunities.

Among the significant early adolescent changes they review are biological (pubertal and other physical changes), academic (transitions to new schools and school structures), and social and psychological (especially the increasing importance of social relationships). After describing these changes briefly, Finkenauer and colleagues analyze the extent to which they affect the development of early adolescent self and identity, particularly with regard to possible self-discrepancies (Higgins, 1987). For example, discrepancies between actual and ideal body awareness and physical appearance are strongly linked to negative early adolescent self-esteem. Physical changes also seem to be associated with an intensification of one's own and others' gender-related norms and expectations for oneself. The transition to junior high (and possibly middle school) is associated with drops in self-esteem, perceived competence, and academic performance. In addition, researchers have found that this transition is associated with decreased feelings of personal autonomy, less support from teachers, and greater competition and school-related anxiety. Early adolescents also attach a good deal of importance to their social relationships. In particular, status and approval concerns, social rejection, conflicts, unmet expectations, and relationship self-discrepancies can create a variety of problems for early adolescent self and identity (a situation that will not be helped by an increased emphasis on high stakes testing).

In the final section of their chapter, Finkenauer and colleagues discuss the practical implications that these many changes have on early adolescent self and identity. They focus on the steps that parents (and others who play a significant role in the lives of early adolescents) can take to ease some of the pains experienced by these children. Among their recommendations are for parents to provide early adolescents with more realistic and attainable standards for self and identity, to facilitate their planning and self-regulation, and to empathize better with the inevitable worries and concerns that arise in early adolescence.

In the next chapter, Kernis argues that self-esteem is a multifaceted construct, involving much more than the typical high or low levels of self-esteem considered by researchers and the lay public alike. Defining self-esteem as a person's feelings of self-worth, liking, and acceptance, he reviews three recent areas of research that illustrate the multiple facets of the construct. According to the idea of implicit or nonconscious self-esteem, one's explicit, conscious self-esteem may or not be congruent with one's implicit esteem. As the incongruence between these two levels increases, defensive and self-serving actions become more likely. The notion of contingent self-esteem refers to the extent to which one's feelings of self-worth are tied to the outcomes of everyday activities. Such self-esteem needs continual validation by self and others. Kernis describes research indicating that, as contingency increases, self-esteem levels decrease and anger proneness increases. This research raises questions about how contingent self-facets for early adolescents, especially social acceptance and physical appearance, relate to their feelings of self-worth and to their responses to threats and negative feedback.

Self-esteem stability has received a good deal of recent attention, and Kernis is the major contributor to this literature. Unstable self-esteem refers to relatively high levels of day-to-day fluctuations in one's feelings of self-worth. In his review of this literature, Kernis points out that compared to stable self-esteem, unstable esteem is associated with numerous negative outcomes, including greater overall self-esteem fragility, increased vulnerability to depressive symptoms, lower intrinsic motivation, and poorer adjustment and well-being. Then he describes an intriguing study of parent–early adolescent communication patterns and their relation to self-esteem stability. Self-esteem instability was more likely to be shown by children who perceived their parents (especially their fathers) as being insulting or critical, using guilt-inducing control tactics, and employing negative problem-solving styles. This relationship raises the questions of whether and how relationships at home and school contribute to the development of unstable self-esteem. This possibility is addressed by those contributors who examine the effects of school structure and school transitions on early adolescent identity development (see the following section). As Kernis notes in closing, there is a real danger that interventions designed to promote positive self-esteem may be inadvertently promoting unstable or contingent self-esteem among early adolescents.

School and the Sense of Self

How much attention should be spent on self and identity concerns in the schools continues to be a controversial question (e.g., Beane, 1994). Despite the controversy, recent work has illustrated the importance of self and identity concerns for teacher development, from initial training to later career issues (Lipka & Brinthaupt, 1999). The chapters in this section of the book examine how the school context and the academic environment can help and hurt early adolescent identity formation. The major argument is that efforts and activities of schools must be centered around the identity needs of the early adolescent in order for successful development to be fostered.

In their chapter, Roeser and Lau emphasize the importance of the relationship between early adolescent needs for competence, autonomy, and relatedness and the educational environment. How does formal schooling help and hinder academic identity formation? Roeser and Lau review several approaches to human motivation and identity development. Using Eccles and Midgley's (1989) stage-environment fit theory, they illustrate how the lack of fit between early adolescents' needs and their school environments can negatively affect their developing identities. They cite evidence that mismatches between developmental stage and academic environment continue to characterize middle schools.

Theory and research on academic identity development highlight the importance of developing personal goals, acquiring perceptions of self-efficacy, and experiencing positive emotions. Whether these needs are fulfilled or frustrated depends in large part on experiences in the classroom and in the school setting. Roeser and Lau note that, whereas schools can facilitate identity development by providing structure, supporting autonomy, and creating supportive relationships, many schools continue to fall short in these regards. After reviewing some of the long list of don'ts for schools and educators, Roeser and Lau direct their discussion toward those "best practices" that can promote positive academic identity formation. Among these practices are providing challenging and meaningful work in the curriculum that will allow students to link class content with their emerging needs, encouraging a task-mastery orientation as opposed to an emphasis on relative ability, using cooperative and heterogeneous grouping practices, and creating "schools-within-schools." Using the analogy of the individual and group elements of jazz music, Roeser and Lau argue that the key to successful identity formation is to strike a balance between the individual's needs and the collective goals of the school. In essence, schools need to allow early adolescents to "practice improvising" with their emerging academic identities in a context that offers autonomy and care. As Kernis suggests in his chapter, this approach is likely to be associated with increased self-esteem stability and more positive adjustment among early adolescents.

In their chapter, Clements and Seidman focus on the immediate and longer-term effects of transitions to middle grades schools on early adolescent academic identity. Emphasizing the "possible selves" that are being developed for the first time by early adolescents, they describe some of the lasting negative effects of middle grades schools' organizational and social regularities on academic achievement and attitudes. According to the possible selves idea (see Markus & Nurius, 1986), future-oriented aspects of identity can serve both motivating and evaluative purposes. A person's possible academic self could be negative and undesirable (such as when a student comes to believe that he or she is incapable of doing math or science and therefore that he or she cannot seriously consider related career options) or positive and desirable (such as when one acquires strong efficacy beliefs about one's skills or abilities which allow the consideration of new career and occupational possibilities).

Clements and Seidman review many of the features of middle grades schooling (e.g., larger classes, less autonomy and support, increased performance orientation) that are associated with negative identity development. The key concern for them is how such features constrain students in the exploration and development of their positive possible academic selves. Can schools promote such positive possible selves in a way that will encourage a lifelong interest in and enthusiasm for learning and thinking? The physical, social, and cognitive changes in the early adolescent often conflict with the structure of middle grades schooling in ways that discourage such interest and enthusiasm. One of the major ways that school structure and teacher interactions undermine interest and enthusiasm is by fostering the unstable or contingent self-esteem described by Kernis. Nevertheless, the results of research on some major middle grades school reform programs give Clements and Seidman some reason to be optimistic that positive developmental outcomes are possible.

Peer Relationships and Behavioral Problems

One of the most important changes in early adolescence is the increasing importance of friendships and peer relationships. For instance, social comparisons are applied to a greater number of the early adolescent's daily activities than in earlier years and peer relationships begin to have both positive and negative effects on self and identity (Adler & Adler, 1998; Harter, 1999; Juhasz, 1992). Being popular with and accepted by one's peers is associated with high self-esteem in both preadolescence and adolescence (Adler & Adler, 1998; Parker & Asher, 1987; Savin-Williams & Berndt, 1990). Peer relations are sources of both teasing and ridicule for children. Demo and Savin-Williams (1992) noted that, whereas teasing by one's friends and peers is an indication of liking and acceptance, ridicule is an indication of dislike, hostility, and rejection by one's peers.

In her chapter, Azmitia addresses the role that friendships, especially conflicts within friendships, play in the examination and evaluation of the early adolescent self. Given that early adolescence is an important time for the development and revision of self-views, peer friendships are likely to have a strong influence on self-esteem and self-definitions. By having early adolescents provide narratives about their friendship conflicts and "infractions," Azmitia illustrates how self-esteem can act as a filter in the interpretation of such episodes. She suggests that one factor contributing to why some boys and girls show drops in self-esteem in early adolescence is how these children work through their friendship problems.

On the one hand, there is a good deal of evidence that early adolescent friendships can facilitate positive self-exploration and self-evaluation. On the other hand, Azmitia points out that these friendships can also contribute to, confirm, or reinforce negative self-views. In fact, early adolescence is likely to be a critical period for both positive and negative influences on the self, given the emotions, ambivalence, and pressures associated with these friendships. Azmitia's narratives suggest that, compared to high self-esteem children, low self-esteem children tend to avoid talking to their friends about their conflicts and infractions, while at the same time ruminating more about these events. Such a pattern may serve to preserve or even intensify one's already fragile and insecure sense of self.

In addition to the conflicts that arise in their friendships, early adolescents must frequently deal with the possibility of victimization or bullying by their peers. In their chapter, Alsaker and Olweus examine the effects of bullying within the broader question of stability and change in global self-esteem. They describe three longitudinal studies dealing with experiences that can negatively affect self-esteem in both the short and long terms. In the first study, they find that global negative self-esteem shows lower stability over long time periods (e.g., 3 years) compared to shorter periods as well as compared to aggression and other social behaviors. Despite this lower stability, overall changes in global self-esteem during early adolescence tend to be small and gradual.

In their Study 2, Alsaker and Olweus directly examine some of the effects of negative peer interactions on early adolescent self-esteem. These include direct (verbal or physical attack) and indirect (social exclusion and isolation) forms of victimization, both directed at the individual and as part of the broader classroom climate. This study also assessed a school-based intervention program against bullying and other antisocial behaviors, which they describe in some detail. Among the findings in this study was that changes in individual victimization were associated with changes in self-esteem over time. In particular, increased victimization led to lower self-esteem, whereas reduced victimization caused increases in esteem. In addition, victimization problems dropped dramatically following the implementation of the anti-bullying intervention program.

In their third study, Alsaker and Olweus search for some of the long-term effects of victimization on subsequent adjustment in young adulthood. Their focus is on a sample of males who were subjected to intense and repeated harassment and bullying in early and middle adolescence. Encouragingly, they find these victims were no more likely to experience harassment or social isolation in their early twenties than was a non-victimized comparison group of males. However, the victimized young men did report greater levels of depressive symptoms and lower levels of global self-esteem. Thus, there appear to be lasting negative effects of early adolescent victimization on the sense of self. This important research highlights the need for attention to and intervention in bullying and other forms of victimization in the middle grades schools. The anti-bullying intervention program shows much promise in preventing the short-term and long-term effects of these peer behaviors.

Early adolescence is also a significant risk period for alcohol and other drug use (e.g., Newcomb & Bentler, 1986; Spear, 2000). In their chapter, Scheier and Botvin examine the role of competence in preventing and reducing early alcohol use. They propose that competence may be an essential link between early alcohol use and later self-esteem. A good deal of research has shown that high levels of competence (or the personal senses of self-efficacy and mastery) are associated with positive peer relations, personal adjustment, academic performance, and so on (see Masten & Coatsworth, 1998). For purposes of their research, Scheier and Botvin define competence as consisting of high problem-solving efficacy, high (internal) perceived control, and well-defined self-reward systems. Using latent growth curve modeling analysis, they examine both static and dynamic influences on competence, self-esteem, and alcohol use. These include how individual differences in the rate of growth of one construct affect the rate of growth in the other constructs, such as how one's initial level of perceived competence is related to levels of alcohol use. Their major concern is to identify those conditions that enhance competence and lead to a positive sense of self.

Scheier and Botvin's study is a longitudinal analysis of the links between competence, alcohol use, and self-esteem among a large number of students followed from 7th to 10th grade. Reflecting other research, they find that competence tends to decrease over time and alcohol use tends to increase over time for these early adolescents. More importantly, they find that high initial levels of alcohol use were associated with a faster rate of alcohol involvement over time than lower initial levels. In addition, those with high initial levels of competence showed smaller relative drops in competence over time compared to those with lower levels of initial competence. Analysis of the combination of these two growth processes revealed that lower levels of early competence were associated with a much faster pace of alcohol involvement than were higher levels of initial competence. In general, lower levels of initial competence and self-esteem were associated with increased alcohol use over time. Finally, they find that students who reported greater increases in their alcohol use over time also reported higher self-esteem in the 10th grade, a relationship that may reflect the influence of positive social skills and peer associations. Scheier and Botvin finish their chapter by discussing some of the ways that intervention efforts might be useful for preventing and reducing alcohol use and for increasing competence and self-esteem among early adolescents.

Early Adolescent Interventions

A crucial question for those who work with early adolescents is what can be done to facilitate positive outcomes and prevent negative outcomes (see Harter, 1999, for possible therapeutic interventions related to self and identity). In earlier sections of the book, our contributors suggested several possible foci for interventions. These included identifying individuals with self-esteem instability (Kernis), establishing more accurate fits between students' needs and their school environments (Roeser and Lau), developing positive possible selves (Clements and Seidman), attending to conflicts in friendships (Azmitia), reducing bullying and other antisocial behaviors (Alsaker and Olweus), and preventing alcohol abuse (Scheier and Botvin). The contributors to the final section of the book present detailed examples of specific early adolescent interventions and their effects on early adolescent self and identity.

Dow Velarde, Starling, and Wallerstein describe the Adolescent Social Action Program (ASAP), a structured-curriculum prevention program used for several years in the state of New Mexico. The goal of the program is both to reduce early adolescents' alcohol and drug use and to facilitate their development as social change agents who can make positive contributions to society. The program allows predominantly minority early adolescents to meet drug-related hospital patients and detention center residents and to interview them about the harmful consequences of their drug use. A key component of the approach is that students develop, as a result of their interviews and experiences, social action projects designed to improve the health conditions of their schools or communities. In other words, the ASAP aims to help at-risk youth develop and clarify their own identities by facilitating the kinds of positive possible selves described by Clements and Seidman.

As Dow Velarde and colleagues note, the ASAP program is designed to reduce early adolescent inner conflicts and insecurities. It carefully and systematically integrates both threat appraisals (through the interactions with patients and detention residents) and coping appraisals (by guiding the students toward self-protective and socially responsible behaviors). In this way, student self-efficacy is increased. Dow Velarde and colleagues provide detailed descriptions of several of the social action projects initiated by ASAP students, pertaining to drug use, teen pregnancy, violence prevention, and so on. Finally, they discuss research on the effectiveness of the ASAP. This research shows that the program has been successful in increasing self-efficacy, decreasing alcohol use, and increasing early adolescents' perceptions of the riskiness and severity of problems due to drug use.

In the next chapter, Deutsch and Hirsch examine how the social climate of youth organizations can promote positive development in early and later adolescence. These organizations can provide young people with emotional support, companionship, and feelings of self-worth. Deutsch and Hirsch describe how inner-city Boys & Girls Clubs can provide these benefits, by serving as a nonfamilial "home-place" that facilitates the development of self and identity. During interviews, many early and later adolescent club members viewed the club as their "home-away-from-home." From these interviews, Deutsch and Hirsch attempt to identify the qualities that led to this perception of attachment and bonding. Among those qualities are that the club fosters a sense of a reliable physical place attachment, the youth come to see the club as supporting their own identity needs and personal values, and it provides the opportunity for the development of self-regulation and identity maintenance.

How do youth transform a club's physical *space* into a *place* that begins to hold personal meaning for them, and ultimately into a *home* that holds deep personal significance for them? Through their interviews with club members, Deutsch and Hirsch note that there are both psychosocial and physical qualities of the clubs that make them feel like a home for these early and later adolescents. A major psychosocial quality of the clubs are the positive and supportive interactions with other members and with the adult staff. In particular, perceiving the club as a home-place seems to be associated with feeling cared for and accepted and believing that the club provides important help and advice. The major physical quality of the clubs is their ability to serve as a safe boundary from the outside world. Across both psychosocial and physical categories, activities that provide social interaction and relationship building were frequently given by members as reasons for why the clubs "feel like home."

In the next section of their chapter, Deutsch and Hirsch describe two case studies that illustrate nicely the process by which the clubs can become home-places that foster the development of self and identity. In the final section of the chapter, they discuss some of the implications of their research. Clearly, the social climate of the clubs has a strong impact on youth development, above and beyond the specific programs and interventions that are used. In addition, they argue that more attention needs to be given to staff training and retention, since staff play a critical role in creating a positive social climate and developing supportive bonds with young people. Finally, Deutsch and Hirsch note that clubs can allow members the opportunity to take on new roles that reflect and change with their developing identities and needs.

The success of efforts to enhance the self in early adolescence is the focus of the final chapter by DuBois, Burk-Braxton, and Tevendale. They address four fundamental questions. First, to what extent are esteem-enhancement interventions needed? Second, is it even possible to enhance self-esteem and, if so, under what conditions and with what limitations? Third, if self-esteem can be enhanced, to what extent are such enhancements associated with positive outcomes and adjustment? Finally, should time and resources be spent on disseminating esteem-enhancement interventions in the schools and, if so, how?

Regarding the need for esteem-enhancement interventions in early adolescence, DuBois and colleagues note that whereas the majority of children have high self-esteem, there are significant subgroups who develop low self-esteem. One such subgroup reflects some children in early adolescence who show large and lasting drops in self-esteem. In addition, conceiving of self-esteem as a multifaceted construct (as Kernis argues) reveals several self-esteem aspects that can suffer in early adolescence. They point out that significant adjustment problems are associated with drops in overall and other aspects of self-esteem in early adolescence. For example, the excessive use of self-enhancing or self-protective strategies in self-presentation is associated with several problem behaviors.

In the next section of their chapter, DuBois and colleagues examine the question of whether it is possible to increase self-esteem through intervention programs. Reviews of the effectiveness of the few programs that have been assessed show that moderate increases in self-esteem are produced by general self-esteem interventions. In addition, there is some support for the effectiveness of interventions dealing with specific self-facets (such as academic or physical self-esteem). Among those factors associated with greater intervention success are efforts directed toward youth who are at risk or who have preexisting problems and efforts aimed directly (rather than indirectly) at enhancing self-esteem. Finally, studies of the follow-up effects of interventions, while limited in number and scope, are generally supportive of the possibility that lasting effects can be achieved.

Regarding the effects of esteem-enhancement interventions on other domains of adjustment, DuBois and colleagues report that positive associations have been found. However, whether self-esteem changes are responsible for changes in other areas, or vice versa, has yet to be determined. Given these results, is there sufficient justification for the wide-scale use of esteem-enhancement interventions? DuBois and colleagues describe several important considerations that need to be addressed before the widespread implementation of these interventions can be recommended. Whereas there are many reasons to remain cautious, they express optimism about the potential benefits of these programs and they offer several suggestions for enhancing the success of implementation and dissemination efforts.

In the final part of their chapter, DuBois, Burk-Braxton, and Tevendale present an integrative model for esteem enhancement. This model targets contextual opportunities, the processes of esteem formation and the multifaceted aspects of self-esteem, and how these relate to adjustment. To illustrate their thinking, they demonstrate how this model can be used to design better esteem-enhancement interventions for early adolescents. In the process, they offer a crucial outline for anyone considering either the development of a new or the implementation of an existing self-esteem enhancement intervention.

In summary, what are the major self and identity concerns for early adolescents that researchers and practitioners should be aware of? What are the interventions and applications that will address those concerns, helping to smooth the transition into early adolescence and into later adolescence and eventually adulthood? This book addresses these questions.

References

Adler, P. A., & Adler, P. (1998). *Peer power: Preadolescent culture and identity.* New Brunswick, NJ: Rutgers University Press.

Arnett, J. (1992). Reckless behavior in adolescence: A developmental perspective. *Developmental Review, 12,* 339-373.

Bates, E. (1990). Language about me and you: Pronominal reference and the emerging concept of self. In D. Cicchetti & M. Beeghly (Eds.), *The self in transition: Infancy to childhood* (pp. 165-182). Chicago: University of Chicago Press.

Baumeister, R. F. (Ed.) (1999). *The self in social psychology.* Philadelphia: Psychology Press.

Beane, J. A. (1994). Cluttered terrain: The schools' interest in the self. In T. M. Brinthaupt & R. P. Lipka (Eds.), *Changing the self: Philosophies, techniques, and experiences* (pp. 69-87). Albany, NY: State University of New York Press.

Brooks-Gunn, J., & Graber, J. A. (1999). What's sex got to do with it? The development of sexual identities during adolescent. In R. J. Contrada & R. D. Ashmore (Eds.), *Self, social identity, and physical health: Interdisciplinary explorations* (pp. 155-182). New York: Oxford University Press.

Cicchetti, D., & Beeghly, M. (Eds.) (1990). *The self in transition: Infancy to childhood.* Chicago: University of Chicago Press.

Damon, W., & Hart, D. (1982). The development of self-understanding from infancy through adolescence. *Child Development, 53,* 841-864.

Demo, D. H., & Savin-Williams, R. C. (1992). Self-concept stability and change during adolescence. In R. P. Lipka & T. M. Brinthaupt (Eds.), *Self-perspectives across the lifespan* (pp. 116-148). Albany, NY: State University of New York Press.

Dishion, T. J., McCord, J., & Poulin, F. (1999). When interventions harm: Peer groups and problem behavior. *American Psychologist, 54,* 755-764.

DuBois, D. L., & Hirsch, B. J. (2000). Self-esteem in early adolescence: From stock character to marquee attraction. *Journal of Early Adolescence, 20,* 5-11.

Eccles, J. S., & Midgley, C. (1989). Stage-environment fit: Developmentally appropriate classrooms for young adolescents. In C. Ames & R. Ames (Eds.), *Research on motivation in education: Goals and cognitions* (Vol. 3, pp. 13-44). New York: Academic Press.

Ellis, B. J., & Garber, J. (1999). Psychosocial antecedents of variation in girls' pubertal timing: Maternal depression, stepfather presence, and marital and family stress. *Child Development, 71*, 485-501.

Gavin, L. A., & Furman, W. (1989). Age differences in adolescents' perceptions of their peer groups. *Developmental Psychology, 25*, 827-834.

Graber, J. A., Brooks-Gunn, J., & Petersen, A. C. (Eds.) (1996). *Transitions through adolescence: Interpersonal domains and context*. Mahwah, NJ: Lawrence Erlbaum Associates.

Gunnar, M. R., & Collins, W. A. (Eds.) (1988). *Development during the transition to adolescence*. Hillsdale, NJ: Lawrence Erlbaum Associates.

Harter, S. (1999). *The construction of the self: A developmental perspective*. New York: Guilford Press.

Harter, S., & Pike, R. (1984). The pictorial scale of perceived competence and social acceptance for young children. *Child Development, 55*, 1969-1982.

Higgins, E. T. (1987). Self-discrepancy: A theory relating self and affect. *Psychological Review, 94*, 319-340.

Hoyle, R. H., Kernis, M. H., Leary, M. R., & Baldwin, M. W. (1999). *Selfhood: Identity, esteem, regulation*. Boulder, CO: Westview Press.

Johnson, N. G., Roberts, M. C., & Worell, J. (1999). *Beyond appearance: A new look at adolescent girls*. Washington, DC: American Psychological Association.

Juhasz, A. M. (1992). Significant others in self-esteem development: Methods and problems in measurement. In T. M. Brinthaupt & R. P. Lipka (Eds.), *The self: Definitional and methodological issues* (pp. 204-235). Albany, NY: State University of New York Press.

Lerner, R. M. (Ed.) (1993). *Early adolescence: Perspectives on research, policy, and intervention*. Hillsdale, NJ: Lawrence Erlbaum Associates.

Lewis, M. (1990). Self-knowledge and social development in early life. In L. A. Pervin (Ed.), *Handbook of personality: Theory and research* (pp. 277-300). New York: The Guilford Press.

Lipka, R. P., & Brinthaupt, T. M.(Eds.) (1992). *Self-perspectives across the lifespan*. Albany, NY: State University of New York Press.

Lipka, R. P., & Brinthaupt, T. M.(Eds.) (1999). *The role of self in teacher development*. Albany, NY: State University of New York Press.

Markus, H., & Nurius, P. (1986). Possible selves. *American Psychologist, 41*, 954-969.

Masten, A. S., & Coatsworth, J. D. (1998). The development of competence in favorable and unfavorable environments. *American Psychologist, 53*, 205-220.

Montemayor, R., Adams, G. R., & Gullotta, T. P. (Eds.) (1990). *From childhood to adolescence: A transitional period?* Thousand Oaks, CA: Sage Publications.

Newcomb, M. D., & Bentler, P. M. (1986). Frequency and sequence of drug use: A longitudinal study from early adolescence to young adulthood. *Journal of Drug Education, 16,* 101-120.

Parker, J. G., & Asher, S. R. (1987). Peer relations and later personal adjustment: Are low-accepted children at risk? *Psychological Bulletin, 102,* 357-389.

Rosenberg, M. (1979). *Conceiving the self.* New York: Basic Books.

Rosenberg, M. (1986). Self-concept from middle childhood through adolescence. In J. Suls & A. G. Greenwald (Eds.), *Psychological perspectives on the self* (Vol. 3, pp. 107-135). Hillsdale, NJ: Lawrence Erlbaum Associates.

Savin-Williams, R. C., & Berndt, T. J. (1990). Friendship and peer relations. In S. S. Feldman & G. R. Elliott (Eds.), *At the threshold: The developing adolescent* (pp. 277-307). Cambridge, MA: Harvard University Press.

Schulenberg, J., Maggs, J. L., & Hurrelmann, K. (1997). *Health risks and developmental transitions during adolescence.* New York: Cambridge University Press.

Shirk, S. R., & Renouf, A. G. (1992). The tasks of self-development in middle childhood and early adolescence. In R. P. Lipka & T. M. Brinthaupt (Eds.), *Self-perspectives across the lifespan* (pp. 53-90). Albany, NY: State University of New York Press.

Simmons, R. J. (1987). Self-esteem in adolescence. In T. Honess & K. Yardley (Eds.), *Self and identity: Perspectives across the lifespan* (pp. 172-192). New York: Routledge and Kegan Paul.

Simmons, R. J., & Blyth, D. A. (1987). *Moving into adolescence: The impact of pubertal change and school context.* Hawthorne, NY: Aldine de Gruyter.

Spear, L. P. (2000). Neurobehavioral changes in adolescence. *Current Directions in Psychological Science, 9,* 111-114.

Toombs, S. K. (1994). Disability and the self. In T. M. Brinthaupt & R. P. Lipka (Eds.), *Changing the self: Philosophies, techniques, and experiences* (pp. 337-357). Albany, NY: State University of New York Press.

Udry, J. R. (1990). Hormonal and social determinants of adolescent sexual initiation. In J. Bancroft & J. M. Reinisch (Eds.), *Adolescence and puberty* (pp. 70-87). New York: Oxford University Press.

Author Note

Preparing this chapter and conducting the editorial duties for this book were greatly facilitated by a Faculty Research and Creative Activity Grant awarded to Tom Brinthaupt from Middle Tennessee State University.

I

CONCEPTUAL ISSUES

2

SELF AND IDENTITY IN EARLY ADOLESCENCE

The Pains and Gains of Knowing Who and What You Are

Catrin Finkenauer, Rutger C. M. E. Engels,
Wim Meeus, and Annerieke Oosterwegel

Introduction

Few questions have been able to continue to intrigue human beings more than questions surrounding the self and identity. Who am I? What am I? and What will I be? are some of the enduring questions people ask themselves and others. While these questions preoccupy almost all people at certain moments in their lives, they are particularly acute in adolescence.

The neo-Freudian psychoanalyst Erik Erikson (1959, 1968) coined adolescence as the period that focuses on the search for identity. To form their identity, adolescents must release the safe hold on childhood and get a firm hold on adulthood. The formation of identity can move in a positive direction when a stable sense of self is developed that provides adolescents with a sense that they know who and what they are and where they are going. Put differently, a sense of self provides them with a sense of meaning and purpose. The formation of identity can also move in a negative direction when the sense of self remains diffused, blurred, or confused. In this case, adolescents are bewildered and doubtful about who and what they are and where they are going. They are unable to commit themselves, cannot define themselves and, hence, lack meaning and purpose in their lives.

Forming a stable identity does not happen overnight but constitutes a long-lasting process. It starts in early adolescence, when young people explore their opportunities and different roles. It finishes when adolescents are able to synthesize a variety of roles and form a self that provides them with a sense of well-being with who and what they are (e.g., Erikson, 1959, 1968; for reviews see Bosma, Graafsma, Grotevant, & de Levita, 1994; Grotevant & Cooper, 1986; Marcia, Waterman, Matteson, Archer, & Orlofsky, 1993; Meeus, Idema, Helsen, & Vollebergh, 1999). Thus, adolescence poses identity tasks whose accomplishment plays an important role in the successful transition into adulthood.

This chapter aims to provide an overview about self and identity in early adolescence. It begins by defining self and identity. For a comprehensive understanding of self and identity in early adolescence, it is then necessary to describe the period of early adolescence, which is a period of multiple, ongoing changes and personal transitions. Subsequently, the chapter will highlight how these changes and transitions in early adolescence impinge on adolescents' self and identity. Although extreme stress and crisis are the exception rather than the rule, early adolescence is a period of heightened vulnerability about the self and identity. The chapter will conclude by describing the practical implications of how this vulnerability can be diminished.

Definitions

Self and identity in adolescence have been the topic of a considerable literature (e.g., Blos, 1967; Erikson, 1968; Marcia, 1976; Waterman, 1982), underlining the importance of this area of research. Between 1974 and 1993 there were 31,550 publications in psychology that (more or less directly) concerned the self (Ashmore & Jussim, 1997). This magnitude of research and theories on the topics of self and identity obviously leaves room for interpretation, choice, and preferences. To make matters even more difficult, self and identity have been defined in numerous ways. In this chapter, we will attempt to sketch one perspective on self and identity, but want to point out that other perspectives are possible (e.g., for reviews see Baumeister, 1998; Kroger, 1996; Marcia et al., 1993).

Defining the Self

Who am I? Many people have thought and continue to think about this question, and many answers have been suggested. When someone asks, "Who am I?" it is soon clear that there is no simple answer. Everybody is different. One person may answer "I am me," another person may answer "I am an honest, outgoing person," another may answer by giving her name, and children tend to point to themselves and touch their body when asked who they are (Damon & Hart, 1988). If the answers to the question Who am I? differ for every single person, we must look more closely at whether they have some common ingredient. One common ingredient is the self.

The self can be thought of as a global, overall sense of being. It constitutes one's "feeling of being at home in one's body, a sense of 'knowing where one is going' and an inner assuredness of anticipated recognition from those who count" (Erikson, 1968, p. 165). The self includes self-knowledge; beliefs and ideas that people hold about themselves that are (relatively) stable across different situations and contexts (e.g., "I can't help it, it is in my nature," "this is who I am, always was, and always will be"). One's self-knowledge covers a large variety of issues, such as attributes (e.g., I'm good-looking), characteristics (e.g., I'm generous), capacities (e.g., I'm dexterous), and preferences (e.g., I love vacations), all of which contribute to a person's sense of self and may be part of the answer to the question "Who am I?" (Campbell & Lavallee, 1993; Oosterwegel, 1992). Despite their diversity, all issues pertain to the person as a whole, which is inherently linked to the body (e.g., Baumeister, 1995). The self also includes self-esteem; the way people globally evaluate and feel about themselves (e.g., "I'm a good person," "I'm proud of myself"). Self-esteem comprises a sense of self-worth and self-respect that is based on one's self-knowledge (Baumeister, 1998). Thus, the term self is used here to indicate knowledge about and esteem for oneself that, although they may not be fixed but undergo continual changes, refer to the entire person and the same entity across different situations, contexts, and circumstances.

Defining Identity

What am I? Again there is no single answer to this question. Many people have many different answers to this question. In fact, they may have as many answers as they have different roles in specific domains of their lives, such as school, work, religion, relationships, family, or politics (cf. Harter, 1982, 1993; Linville, 1987; Oosterwegel & Oppenheimer, 1993). An answer to the question "What am I?" may hence be multifaceted in that a person can be an athlete, a pupil, a friend, a son, and an environmentalist, all at the same time.

The person is committed to each domain-specific role (Marcia, 1966; Waterman, 1982). Marcia (1994) defines commitment as the choice of one among several alternatives in a particular domain. Put differently, I do not throw a coin to decide whether I am the best friend of X but rather choose to be the best friend of X over being the best friend of Y. I am hence committed to the particular relationship and being the best friend of X is one of my roles in everyday life. It defines what she stands for and thereby plays an important role in guiding my behavior, thoughts, and feelings. These roles a person is committed to refer to what we want to call a person's identity.

Identity, as it will be used in the chapter, represents the aspect of the self that is accessible and salient in a particular context, that interacts with the environment, and to which the person is committed. At school, for example, an adolescent may have the identity of a hardworking pupil, while at home she may be a rebellious daughter, a supporting sister, or a responsible older sibling. When playing in the street she may be a best friend, a punk, or a popular (cf. Brown, Mounts, Lamborn, & Steinberg, 1993). When playing with other adolescents of her own race that aspect of her identity may not be salient. Yet, when her race is in the minority, she may become quite aware of her racial or cultural identity (e.g., McGuire, McGuire, Child, & Fuijoka, 1978). Thus, in contrast to the self that refers to the person as a whole and encompasses knowledge and feelings that are relatively stable, identity refers to specific aspects of the self that are salient and activated by the social and environmental context in which a person functions. As we see it, then, a person has one self and may have different identities that can (but do not have to) vary across situations and contexts.

Different identities add up to an overall identity (Bourne, 1978). Overall identity theoretically overlaps with what we have defined as the self. For example, comparable with our definition of the self, overall identity is assumed to provide individuals with a sense of continuity and consistency (Bourne, 1978; Erickson, 1968). Empirical evidence on the properties of overall identity, however, is scarce. A discussion of the similarities and differences between overall identity and self would exceed the scope of this chapter. The interested reader is referred to the literature in this domain (e.g., Bosma et al., 1994; Bosma & van Halen, 1999; Kroger, 1996). For reasons of clarity, we will use the term *self* to refer to the person as a whole and the term *identity* to refer to one aspect of the self to which the person is committed. To illustrate, an adolescent girl may be a student, a daughter, a girlfriend, and a chum. If she splits up with her boyfriend or changes schools, she remains her*self* but the constellation of her *identities* is transformed (cf. Baumeister, 1998).

Taken together, we propose that the answer to the question "who am I?" pertains to a person's self, her/his knowledge and feelings about her/himself as a whole. The answer to the question "what am I?" pertains to a person's identity(ies) and may depend on the context, the time frame, and the situation in which one asks the question. The two concepts hence clearly differ in their scope. They have in common, however, that they help people to define themselves, thereby providing them with one source of meaning and purpose (Baumeister, 1991).

Having defined self and identity, the question arises how early adolescents see themselves and their identity(ies) and how they feel about them. To develop an understanding of adolescents' self and identity, it is necessary to first paint a brief picture of the period of early adolescence.

Early Adolescence

In recent years there has been some discussion as to whether or not adolescence is a period of crisis. In the beginning of this century, Hall (1904) proposed that adolescence is a period of "storm and stress." Empirical studies throughout this century, however, seemed to disconfirm his suggestion and showed that most adolescents survive adolescence without noticeable problems (e.g., Offer & Schonert-Reichel, 1992). Rather, adolescence is seen as a period of exploration (e.g., Grotevant & Cooper, 1986; Marcia, 1966; Meeus, 1996). While excessive storm and stress indeed seem to be the exception rather than the rule, nowadays most researchers agree that adolescence, compared to other periods in life, involves more acute problems and daily difficulties (for reviews see Arnett, 1999; Eccles et al. 1993). The exploration of different identities, the search for self, and the experience of a large variety of life changes and personal transitions all contribute to rendering adolescence a potentially stressful period of life.

Adolescence is an emotional roller-coaster that is marked by fascinating and exciting discoveries concerning the self and identity as well as frightening and disappointing discoveries (Baumeister, 1995; Baumeister, Shapiro, & Tice, 1985). It is characterized by emotional ups and downs with extremes of both immense joy and misery (Arnett, 1999; Larson & Richards, 1994). To illustrate, Larson and Richards (1994) conducted an elegant study on the daily emotional life of adolescents. They asked older children (5th-grade), adolescents (9th-grade), and their parents to wear a beeper throughout the day and record their thoughts, behavior, and emotions when they were beeped at random times during the day. Compared to their parents and younger counterparts, adolescents reported experiencing more extreme emotions both positive and negative. They reported feeling more ignored, lonely, awkward, and nervous than their parents and felt twice to three times more embarrassed and self-conscious than their parents. The proportion of time experienced as "very happy" by adolescents, as compared to older children, declined by 50%. Larson and Richards (1994) also found a similar decline for reports of feeling "great," "proud," and "in control." The authors conclude that as childhood ends and adolescence begins "daily life gets more difficult" (p. 85).

This suggestion appears to be particularly true for early adolescence. "Early adolescence, ages 10 to 15 years, is a time of drastic and superimposed changes in all spheres of functioning (biological, social, and academic). As such it is a time of maximal discontinuity with the past. Therefore, it represents the developmental period of highest stress and challenge but also a time of maximal opportunity. It is a time of heightened susceptibility to influence and there are possibilities for better or for worse, to change the developmental trajectory in ways that can be sharply different from the past" (Hamburg, 1990, p. 116).

In the following, we will briefly describe some of the normative changes and transitions that take place in early adolescence, before turning to evidence showing that these changes play an important role for early adolescents' self and identity.

Biological Changes

Early adolescence is the period in life where biological changes are most intense. It is the period where the human organism becomes reproductively mature and where this sexual and reproductive maturation becomes evident. At puberty some of the changes in boys and girls are similar. Marshall (1978) identified five major biological changes in puberty. First, young adolescents experience a rapid acceleration in growth, affecting both weight and height. Second, primary sex characteristics develop, including, for example, the testes in boys and the ovaries in girls. Third, secondary sex characteristics emerge, causing changes in the genitals and breasts and the growth of pubic, facial, and body hair. Fourth, changes in body shape and composition occur as a consequence of the changing quantity and distribution of fat and muscle cells. And fifth, the circulatory and respiratory systems change so as to increase physical strength, fitness, and tolerance for exercise.

That these biological changes in adolescence are dramatic is reflected, for example, in the fact that, on average, during early adolescence (10-15 years) boys and girls grow between 6 and 12 cm in one year (!). As Tanner, Whitehouse, and Takaishi (1966, p. 466) aptly put it "some adolescents get a nasty and unavoidable shock" when their growth spurt arrives. The bodily capacity for physical exertion increases at a remarkable rate. The strength of the muscles is associated with their size, which shows an increase by a factor of 14 between the ages 5 and 16 for males and a tenfold increase for females (Cheek, 1968). Among boys, testosterone concentration can increase as much as 20 times between 10 and 17 years (Faiman & Winter, 1974). Among girls, the onset of the menarche occurs on average at around 13 to 14 years, although its timing can greatly vary (Brooks-Gunn, 1987). Other changes are equally dramatic and signal that children become adults (Brooks-Gunn, Warren, Russo, & Gargulio, 1987). Girls develop breasts and pubic hair. Boys begin to have "wet dreams," develop facial hair, and experience voice changes. Thus, biological changes in adolescence are not a single event but indicate a complex and long-lasting process that physically transforms the child into an adult. It starts with the appearance of secondary sexual characteristics in early adolescence and finishes when full reproductive capacity is achieved.

Academic Changes and Transitions

Early adolescence is also a period where important school transitions take place. Children change from elementary school to junior high school or high school. These school transitions may place serious stress on young adolescents (e.g., Cotterell, 1992; Eccles, et al., 1989;

Isakson & Jarvis, 1999; Simmons, Rosenberg, & Rosenberg, 1973). To illustrate, in a study among 373 Australian adolescents, Cotterell (1992) found that feelings of anxiety concerning school procedures and the presence of older students were greatest in the immediate aftermath of the transition from elementary school to high school and decreased over a period of 4 months.

Junior high school and high schools markedly differ from elementary school. Simmons and Blyth (1987), for example, draw attention to changes on the macro-level that greatly affect the early adolescent individual, such as increased school size, decreased contact between individual student and teacher, and increased bureaucratic organization. Higgins and Parsons (1983) point to the disruption of adolescents' peer networks that accompanies school transitions. Eccles, Lord, and Buchanan (1996) provide an elegant overview over micro-level changes in the classroom that are associated with school transitions. For example, junior high school classrooms, as compared to elementary school classrooms, are less personal and are organized to enhance teacher control. High school teachers are reported, both by students and independent observers, as being less friendly, less supportive, and less caring than teachers of the last year in elementary school. The teaching in high school classes is mostly directed toward the whole group, while teaching in elementary schools frequently mixes teaching addressing the whole group with teaching addressing small groups or individuals. Finally, junior high school teachers encourage competition in the classroom much more than elementary school teachers.

Taken together, academic transitions in early adolescence bring about a large number of changes at the macro- and micro-level. The school as a whole, the classroom, the teacher, and the teaching change to become more competitive and individualistic.

Social and Psychological Changes

Early adolescence is also a period of social change. Adolescents spend more time with friends and peers and less time with their families, parents in particular (Larson & Richards, 1991). Romantic and sexual relationships gain importance (Paul & White, 1990). Belonging to a popular group becomes an important goal for adolescents, especially in early adolescence (Berndt, 1996). Having at least one friend to confide in becomes a social achievement for adolescents and an indicator of social competence (Hartup, 1996).

With their increasing concern for social relationships outside the family, adolescents become vulnerable to feelings of social inadequacy and failure (Seiffge-Krenke, 1998). Their concern for social adequacy is reflected in their struggle to control the image they convey to others. They become "sometimes morbidly, often curiously, preoccupied with what they appear to be in the eyes of others" (Erikson, 1959, p. 80). Adolescents' struggle for social recognition is depicted in a study by Roscoe, Diana, and Brooks (1987). In their study, they compared early (6th grade), middle (11th grade), and late (college) adolescents on their reasons for dating and their concerns in the selection of a dating partner. Concerns included, for example, personality characteristics or prestige factors. The results indicated that early and middle adolescents were concerned with self-focused, immediate gains of the dating relationship, with recreation having the highest priority, closely followed by intimacy and social status. Late adolescents, on the contrary, focused more on reciprocity in the dating relationship, their priority being intimacy, followed by companionship and recreation. Early adolescents' concerns in the selection of the dating partner further underlined a need for social status (i.e., gaining status by dating a "highly desirable" person) and other's approval, while late adolescents' concerns dealt with independence from parents, development of techniques for interaction with the opposite sex, and future relational concerns (e.g., marriage).

Thus, early adolescence is a period of social turmoil. Social relationships outside the family become more important. Relationships with others undergo dramatic transformations. Social recognition and approval by others become a major concern for young adolescents.

The increasing impact of others' perception of the self is partly due to the psychological changes and transitions that take place in adolescence (Keating, 1990). In contrast to children who think about things that are real and concern their immediate situation, adolescents become able to think about possibilities. They start thinking about their future and can form hypotheses about what may or may not change in their personalities, behavior, education, family, and relationships with friends and intimate partners (Schaffer, 1996). As a consequence of their increased facility with abstract thinking, adolescents are able to see things as being relative, rather than as absolute. They are able to plan ahead, to anticipate the potential consequences of their behavior, and to provide alternative explanations for things happening to them (Keating, 1990). Also, their social perspective taking improves considerably. Young adolescents become able to engage in "mutual role taking" (Selman, 1980). They can be an observer of others and discern how the thoughts and behavior of one person can affect those of another person. This improvement in thinking has immediate consequences for adolescents' relationships with others. It affects their communication with others, because it is directly related to their ability to take another person's perspective. This ability, in turn, increases their understanding for another person's situation and their ability to adequately respond to others' needs (if they want to). While these psychological changes increase adolescents' awareness of others, their ability to think abstractly also increases their ability to reflect about themselves and on others' perception of the self.

All in all, the evidence is fairly clear and unanimous in indicating that early adolescence is a period of major changes and personal transitions. Such changes impinge on virtually every aspect of young adolescents' lives, from daily interactions to broad patterns, from emotions to biology, and from school to relationships with parents and friends. Although the reputation of extreme storm and stress may not be warranted, these changes are likely to render early adolescence a period of heightened stress and vulnerability.

Self and Identity in Early Adolescence

Because most of the described changes are dramatic, it is immediately tempting to assume that they impact on early adolescents' self and identity. Put differently, they should affect how adolescents see themselves and how they feel about themselves. In the following, we will examine this suggestion.

We want to point out that although it is theoretically and practically important to pinpoint the differences between self and identity, very few studies differentiated between the two concepts but used self and identity interchangeably. While self and identity are closely intertwined, we made an attempt to separately address the two concepts where this was possible.

Biological Changes and Self and Identity in Early Adolescence

In our definition of the self, we underlined that people's sense of self is inextricably intertwined with their body (e.g., Baumeister, 1995; Damon & Hart, 1988). Changes of the body should therefore be experienced as a change of the self. Given that bodily changes indicate a transition from childhood to adulthood, young people's gender identity should also change from the identity of a child to the identity of a young woman or man.

Consistent with the suggestion that biological changes are associated with the experience of the self, many adolescents indicate that their physical characteristics and appearance are among the problems that concern them most (e.g., Richards, Boxer, Petersen, & Albrecht, 1990). In this context, it is important to point out that it is less the "objective" biological change that preoccupies adolescents than their subjective appraisal of this change. Their concerns do not arise because they are inaccurate in their perception of their body. On the contrary, most of them are quite capable of identifying, from a group of body profiles, the profile that is most similar to their own (Clifford, 1971). Rather, as is expressed in the idiom "beauty lies in the eyes of the beholder," adolescents subjectively appraise and evaluate their body and bodily changes. They do not merely notice these changes but compare them to cultural and social standards to judge their own physical attractiveness and adequacy. These standards are mostly unrealistic. To illustrate, in order to have the same figure as a Barbie doll, the average woman (who weighs about 56-60 kg) would have to increase her breasts by 30 cm, reduce her waist 25 cm, and become 2 m 16 cm tall (Moser, 1989)!

In light of the unrealistic ideals for physical attractiveness, most adolescents come to the conclusion that their body and physical appearance fall short of the ideal. This conclusion is often accompanied by feelings of low self-esteem (Friedman & Brownell, 1995). Both early adolescent boys and girls (i.e., around 6th grade) show significant drops in self-esteem, feeling bad about who they are (for a review see Harter, 1993). Because boys' biological changes move toward the cultural ideal (e.g., broad shoulders, narrow hips), while girls' biological changes move away from the cultural ideal (e.g., weight gain), drops in self-esteem generally are steeper for girls than for boys (Simmons et al., 1973; Harter, 1993). Especially during early adolescence, when girls' body-fat increases about 27%, young girls struggle to counteract biological changes that remove them from their physical ideal. More than half of American female adolescents say they are on a diet (Felts, Tavasso, Chenier, & Dunn, 1992). Among fifth- to eighth-grade girls, 31% reported being on a diet, 9% said they sometimes fasted, and 5% had deliberately induced vomiting (Childress, Brewerton, Hodges, & Jarrell, 1993). Pubertal changes in girls, in particular when they have an early onset, are related to less positive body images and self-esteem (Simmons & Blyth, 1987). In comparison to other girls, they find themselves fat and ugly. Worse, they find themselves fatter and uglier than anybody else and may, at times, be convinced that there is no one in the world who would be willing (or stupid enough) to marry them. Early maturing boys, on the contrary, show a drop in self-esteem only in the short run. It commonly does not persist beyond early adolescence (Simmons & Blyth, 1987; for a review on the psychosocial effects of pubertal timing see Graber, Brooks-Gunn, & Petersen, 1996).

Biological changes and physical appearance show an important link with early adolescents' self-esteem. While some adolescents (boys and girls) endorse the fact that changes in their body cause them to feel bad about themselves, others report that when they feel good about themselves they also feel good about their body (Harter, 1993). Thus, physical appearance is clearly related with how early adolescents feel about themselves.

With respect to identity, biological changes accentuate the physical indicators of being a woman or being a man. During adolescence, they thereby enhance the differentiation of gender identity, including gender-specific behavior and gender-related expectations held by adolescents themselves and by their social environment (Sandberg, Meyer-Bahlburg, Ehrhardt, & Yager, 1993; Savin-Williams & Weisfeld, 1989).

The so-called gender intensification hypothesis (Galambos, Almeida, & Petersen, 1990; Hill & Lynch, 1983) suggests that pubertal changes (e.g., breast development in girls and facial hair in boys) signal socializing agents (parents, teachers, peers) that the adolescent is approaching adulthood and should therefore begin to behave accordingly (i.e., in ways consistent with expectations surrounding gender). For example, during early adolescence, parents encourage their daughters to be dependent, affectionate, and gentle, while they encourage their sons to be assertive, competitive, and independent (Hill & Lynch, 1983).

Consistent with their view of males and females, parents behave toward adolescents in a ways that reinforce behavior that is consistent with gender roles. Boys are punished more often and more severely, while girls are restricted in their actions but are punished less and treated with more warmth and physical closeness (Rapoport, 1991). Gender intensification is also reflected in early adolescents' relationships with peers. Girls develop more intimate friendships than boys. As compared to boys, they engage in greater self-disclosure, greater sharing of ideas and feelings, and are more accepting and supportive. Conversely, boys, as compared to girls, engage in more active behavior with their relationships focussing on doing things. In their relationships with others, girls tend to be more compliant and strive for harmony, while boys tend to take greater risks and are more aggressive (Hill & Lynch, 1983). Biological changes thus seem to contribute to adolescents' gender identity in that they facilitate identification with a particular gender for both adolescents and their social environment.

Biological changes not only compel adolescents to develop a sense of being a woman or a man, they also trigger questions concerning gender adequacy, that is an adolescent's self-judgment of her / his sufficiency as a woman or a man. Different researchers (Aubé & Koestner, 1992; O'Heron & Orlofsky, 1990) suggest that deviating from gender-related norms may lead to psychosocial problems, particularly for females. In their study on the relations among gender identity, gender adequacy, and psychological adjustment, for example, O'Heron and Orlofsky (1990) found that perceived gender inadequacy, for both women and men, was associated with depression and anxiety. Additionally, gender identity and gender adequacy were positively correlated. Men who perceived themselves as less masculine tended to feel less adequate as men. Similarly, women who perceived themselves as less feminine felt less adequate as women. A longitudinal study by Aubé and Koestner (1992) suggests that gender-atypical interests and the possession of gender-undesirable traits among 12-year-old adolescents predicts poor adult adjustment and low life satisfaction at a 20-year follow-up. It thus seems that perceiving oneself to deviate from (perceived) gender-related norms is not only associated with psychosocial problems at the time but leads to psychosocial problems in the long run.

Thus, there is an assortment of evidence that biological changes in early adolescence affect adolescents' self and identity. They contribute to adolescents' sense of self and gender identity but they also render them vulnerable to feelings of inadequacy. Adolescents become self-conscious about their body and physical appearance. They do not merely state that their body is changing but evaluate these changes against culturally and socially accepted standards and norms. Early adolescents are quick in rejecting themselves when they think their physical appearance or gender-related behavior deviates from what they think is the norm. Perceived discrepancies between what they are and what they want to be, physically or as a man or as a woman, negatively affect their self and identity (cf. Higgins, 1987) and may give rise to psychosocial problems and painful negative emotions, such as depression, anxiety, and low self-esteem.

Academic Changes and Self and Identity in Early Adolescence

Academic changes and transitions in early adolescence are yet another sphere that is likely to affect adolescents' self and identity. Some work reviewed earlier already underlined the massive school-related changes that are associated with the transition from elementary school to junior high school or high school (e.g., Eccles et al., 1996; Simmons & Blyth, 1987). These changes encourage adolescents to compare themselves, their skills, abilities, and behavior, to others, especially their peers (e.g., Eccles et al., 1996; Harter, Whitesell, & Kowalski, 1992). With this focus on the comparison of oneself against others, academic changes should affect early adolescents' self and academic identity.

Early adolescents show increased anxiety in the immediate aftermath of a transition from elementary school to high school (Cotterell, 1992; Harter et al., 1992). This increased anxiety is partly due to the new social position in which young adolescents find themselves. In elementary school, 12-year-olds are the eldest and have the highest status and peer prestige (Bosma, 1993). After the transition to junior high school, however, they are the youngest and find themselves lowest on the hierarchical ladder. Thus, as compared to their earlier social status, they lose part of their privileges and may become targets of older adolescents' bullying and intimidation: While they were looked up to in elementary school, they are now looked down upon.

The drop in social status and increase in social comparison (cf. Festinger, 1954) associated with academic changes may have considerable impact on early adolescents' self and academic identity. Two longitudinal studies by Susan Harter and her colleagues (Harter et al., 1992) found that a majority of early adolescents who made the transition from elementary school to middle school (6th grade) perceived the new educational environment to greatly emphasize evaluation and performance. The perception of social comparison was associated with considerable amounts of scholastic anxiety and a deterioration of academic identity. A substantial number of adolescents felt threatened and were well aware of differences between their own scholastic abilities and those of their peers. They felt increasingly anxious about their performance at school, fearing that they would not be able to be as good as their peers. At the same time, their motivation to be successful at school increased. Harter et al. (1992) suggest a vicious circle: After a school transition, adolescents lose confidence in their scholastic abilities; they form a low academic identity and lose confidence in themselves, because everybody else seems to do well and they alone are failing (cf. Pines & Aronson, 1981); adolescents' bad feelings about their self and academic identity, in turn, may lead to a further deterioration not only of their perceived scholastic competence (Harter et al., 1992), but also of their actual academic performance (Newbegin & Owens, 1996; Rosenberg, 1965). A cross-sectional study by Simmons et al. (1973) showed that, compared to the older and younger children, the group that had just made the transition into junior high school (i.e., 11-year to 14-year-old children) was the most self-conscious and had a lower self-esteem. Also, suggesting that the new academic environment promotes an aversive focus on the self, children in this group were more aware of their shortcomings, weaknesses, and flaws. They also showed less confidence in their academic abilities than older and younger children. Eccles et al. (1989) conducted a two-year longitudinal study among 1,450 sixth- and seventh-graders who twice a year completed questionnaires that assessed how they felt about themselves. Consistent with the above-reported results, many children felt least positive about themselves immediately after the transition to junior high school.

Comparable to biological changes, academic changes force early adolescents to re-evaluate themselves and their competence. This re-evaluation may, especially in an educational environment that promotes social comparison, cause adolescents to be painfully aware of their academic shortcomings, thereby undermining their academic identity and their self-esteem. If adolescents perceive a gap between known standards (e.g., I was among the popular children) or ideal standards (e.g., I want to be the best in class) and their actual academic performance and abilities, they will experience negative feelings about the self and will be painfully aware of their shortcomings (cf. Duval & Wicklund, 1972). They may feel anxious and uncertain in the new environment, because they do not know whether or not they will be able to re-establish their performance level and compete with others so as to decrease the discrepancies between what and who they are immediately following the academic transition and what and who they want to be.

Social and Psychological Changes and Self and Identity in Early Adolescence

Few situations in adolescence are more powerful in determining adolescents' sense of self and identity than social situations (e.g., Sullivan, 1953; Hartup, 1996). To illustrate, social rejection, in particular by peers, is associated with loneliness, anxiety, and low self-esteem, even among adolescents who have good friendships (Coie, 1990; Renshaw & Brown, 1993). Adolescents in steady romantic relationships have a higher level of self-esteem and a more stable gender identity than those who do not have a steady partner (Samet & Kelly, 1987). Thus, having trusting, long-lasting, harmonious relationships with others is a major determinant of early adolescents' self and identity.

Others' evaluation and recognition constitutes another source of influence on adolescents' self and identity (e.g., Cooley, 1902; Mead, 1934; for a review see Harter, 1998). Others' appraisal of the self, which transpires through their behavior toward us, is reflected in adolescents' appraisal of their self and identity. Through others' feedback toward the self, adolescents not only construct an image of their self and identity, they also create an image of what they should be like, of who and what (they think) others expect them to be (Harter, 1998). In early adolescence, young people develop clear representations of what others expect them to be and to do that render them vulnerable to psychosocial distress (Oosterwegel & Oppenheimer, 1993). Paralleling observations concerning the effects of biological and academic changes on adolescent self and identity, when adolescents perceive a real or imagined discrepancy between their actual self and identity and others' expectations, psychosocial problems (e.g., depression, aggression, excessive worrying), negative self-related emotions (e.g., self-blame, hopelessness), and aversive other-related emotions (e.g., disappointment, guilt, shame) may emerge (Higgins, 1991; Oosterwegel & Oppenheimer, 1993).

In early adolescence, social and psychological changes affect and transform adolescents' relationships with others (e.g., Berndt, 1996; Collins & Repinski, 1994). Developmental changes include an increase in social comparison (see above), growing sex differences, greater intimacy, greater awareness of the others' feelings and thoughts, and the realization that these feelings and thoughts can differ from one's own (e.g., Youniss & Smollar, 1985). These changes affect adolescents' relational identity, which, as a function of changes in social relationships and environment, expands and becomes increasingly complex (Collins & Repinski, 1994; Harter, 1998). The expansion of identities from childhood to adolescence is, for example, reflected in instruments that serve to assess adolescents' perceived competence (Harter, 1982, 1988). Questionnaires for children encompass five domains, namely school, sports, peers, physical appearance, and behavior. Questionnaires for adolescents add three social domains, namely close friendships, romantic relationships, and job competence, reflecting the increasing complexity of adolescents' identity.

Early adolescents express more insecurity about their social position and acceptance among peers than younger children (e.g., Gavin & Furman, 1989). They spend considerable amounts of time, energy, and thought to protect their social status in their peer group and protect themselves against social rejection (e.g., Parker, Rubin, Price, & DeRosier, 1995). While younger children compare their social status and social behavior to absolute standards, early adolescents are more likely to compare their social status and behavior to peers (e.g., Markus & Nurius, 1986; for a review see Parker et al., 1995). To illustrate, in their study, Gavin and Furman (1989) compared preadolescents' (5th and 6th grade), early adolescents' (7th and 8th grade), middle adolescents' (9th and 10th grade), and late adolescents' (11th to 12th grade) perceptions of their (same-sex) peer group. Early and middle adolescents rated membership of a popular group as much more important than pre- or late adolescents. Also, they perceived more peer group conformity within their peer groups than pre- and late adolescents. Gavin and Furman suggest that being in a popular peer group in early adolescence provides young people with a sense of belonging. It allows them to feel secure and bolsters their relational identity in a period in which they loosen their ties with their family. By belonging to a popular peer group they assert their independence and form their own relational identity.

Social relationships and their maintenance in early adolescence are not child's play but require hard work. Adolescent peer groups handle strict normative codes, including group members' clothing and behavior (Berndt, 1979; Sherif & Sherif, 1964). Because peer rejection is such a painful experience, adolescents go to great lengths to prevent deviation from what they believe is the social norm (e.g., Hirsch & Renders, 1986). Most of them become preoccupied by striving to fit in (see also biological changes). They worry about their complexions, are mortified at discovering pimples, are concerned about wearing braces or glasses, or worry about their clothing and haircuts, because these factors may lead to social rejection and ridicule. It is therefore not surprising that adolescents, especially early adolescents, show greater conformity (i.e., adopt the same behavior as others, even if the adopted behavior is erroneous) than school children (ages 7-8) and young adults (ages 19-20) (e.g., Constanzo, 1970). Thus, social relationships in early adolescence may come at a price, a price that may cost adolescents part of their self and relational identity.

Taken together, empirical evidence on social changes in early adolescence suggests that social relationships have a powerful impact on adolescents' self and relational identity. Having intimate relationships and belonging to a popular peer group makes adolescents feel good about themselves. Others' opinions are incorporated in adolescents' self and identity, giving rise to positive emotions about the self when others' expectations can be met, but giving rise to aversive emotions when adolescents perceive a discrepancy between who and what they are and what they believe others expect them to be. Adolescents increasingly compare themselves to their peers. To ensure others' approval, they are willing to disguise and sacrifice parts of their self and identity.

Comment

In the previous section, we tried to paint a brief picture of the development and formation of self and identity in early adolescence in light of normative changes that characterize this period. There is no doubt that other developmental changes with implications for self and identity can be specified, such as changes in adolescents' sexual behavior (e.g., Katchadourian, 1990) and ego control (e.g., Kremen & Block, 1998). It should be noted that we are not arguing that our overview is exhaustive. Rather, we want to point to the important links between changes in early adolescence and early adolescents' self and identity. Despite its limitations, we believe our overview is sufficient to serve as a first basis for practical implications.

Practical Implications

All presented evidence converges to suggest that discrepancies between what adolescents perceive to be their actual self / identity and what they consider the ideal self / identity render early adolescents vulnerable to psychosocial problems. Discrepancies may occur when adolescents compare who and what they are with (a) who and what they want to be or (b) who and what they think others want them to be. The relatively better off adolescents perceive themselves to be in comparison with these standards, the more they are satisfied with their self and identity and the more they experience positive emotions (Harter, 1998). Conversely, perceiving a discrepancy is associated with psychosocial problems and dissatisfaction with self and identity. An attainable standard is thus important for adolescents to develop a stable sense of self and identity. It provides them with a sense of knowing who and what they are and where they are going.

While parents undoubtedly constitute the most influential source of social support for adolescents (e.g., Furman & Wehner, 1997), research also draws attention to the important role teachers play in this regard. To illustrate, in a high-risk inner city sample of 250 adolescents, Felner, Aber, Primavera, and Cauce (1985) found that the level of teacher support perceived by adolescents was not only positively associated with grades and school attendance, but was also strongly related to adolescents' self-esteem. Similarly, Ryan, Stiller, and Lynch (1994) found that 7th and 8th graders' positive representation of teachers significantly and positively predicted their self-esteem, academic performance, and school functioning. Because supportive relationships with both parents and teachers are important for adolescent development, and because both relationships may function as protective factors in time of stress (Rutter, 1987), the practical implications we will discuss in the following are relevant for parents as well as teachers.

The practical implications that can be derived from our overview of self and identity in early adolescence are threefold. First, self and identity in early adolescence need to be distinguished to obtain a complete picture of adolescents' self and identity that includes both their strengths and weaknesses. Second, parents and teachers can take steps to reduce the experienced discrepancy between adolescents' actual self and identity and their ideal self and identity. Finally, because some pain surrounding early adolescent self and identity appears to be inevitable, parents and teachers can take steps to ease adolescents' painful awareness of their shortcomings. In the following we will address these three implications separately.

Painting a Picture of Adolescent Self and Identity

Early adolescents' self and identity are closely related to each other. That the distinction between these two concepts is useful and meaningful, however, is reflected in the following adolescent narrative: "I look in the mirror and most days I don't like what I see, I don't like how I look (*physical identity*), I don't like myself as a person (*self*). So I get depressed and bummed out. Plus my family has rejected me (*relational identity*) and that makes me feel pretty lousy about myself (*self*). My mother is really on my case because I'm not living up to what she wants me to be. If I get A's in school, she's nice and is proud of me, but if I don't, she doesn't approve of me (*academic and relational identity*). . . . Mostly she tells me that I'm a failure, and I'm beginning to believe it (*self*). Doing well in school has always been important to me (*academic identity*), but now I feel like I'll never amount to anything (*self*)" (Harter & Marold, 1994, pp. 343-344, italics added). While self and identity are closely intertwined, the adolescent's narrative shows that self and identity can refer to quite distinct aspects of a person. Identity typically refers to specific, circumscribed areas of a person's life. In contrast, self as we defined it indicates how a person evaluates and describes her- or himself as a whole.

Once these distinct definitions are clarified, it is easy to see how it is possible for various configurations of self and identity to arise: an adolescent boy could feel good about himself but bad about his academic identity; he could feel good about his relational identity and bad about his academic identity; he could feel good about himself and good about his gender identity and relational identity; or he could feel bad about himself and bad about all his identities. The differentiation between self and identities may hence help to clarify the image adolescents have of themselves. More importantly, it provides parents and teachers with a useful tool to diagnose not only adolescents' perceived shortcomings but also their strengths, thereby obtaining a comprehensive picture of the adolescent's self and identity. Based on the configuration of self and identity, parents and teachers can identify the aspect of adolescents' self or identity that is most painful and that shows the greatest discrepancy between actual and ideal self or identity. Once this discrepancy has been identified, they can take steps to reduce excessive discrepancies between actual self / identity and adolescents' ideals.

Steps to Reduce Excessive Discrepancies

Emphasized by biological, academic, social, and psychological changes, early adolescents frequently set themselves unattainable standards for their self and identities that lead to negative emotions, dissatisfaction, and psychosocial problems (Larson & Richards, 1994). Also, they often feel that others, especially parents, set unattainable standards for them (Higgins, Loeb, & Moretti, 1995). To diminish early adolescents' perceived discrepancies between actual and ideal self or identity, parents and teachers can take steps to shift adolescents' focus from unattainable standards toward achievable standards (Harter & Marold, 1994; Locke, Shaw, Saari, & Latham, 1981).

Some steps to optimize adolescents' self and identity focus on the adolescent. Parents and teachers may raise adolescents' confidence by identifying the aspect of the adolescent self or identity that is most discrepant with their ideals and then bolster this aspect. For example, an adolescent girl who goes on a rigorous diet because she wants to improve her physical appearance runs the risk of failure. Indeed, often dieting is unsuccessful leaving the person with a sense of failure and a residue of anger at oneself (Heatherton & Ambady, 1993). Helping the adolescent to increase her acceptance of her physical identity, thus decreasing her perceived discrepancy between actual and ideal physical identity, may contribute to making her not only feel good about her body and physical appearance but also about herself (Harter,

1993). Another step to optimize adolescents' self and identity consists in validating and reinforcing the strengths of adolescents' self and identity. Adolescents tend to dwell on their weaknesses and fears surrounding their self and identity. With a little help from their parents and teachers, they may shift their focus from who and what they are not to who and what they are, thereby emphasizing their strengths and accepting their shortcomings (Harter, 1993). Finally, parents and teachers may help adolescents to differentiate between ultimate standards and intermediate and immediate goals. Most early adolescents think in terms of ultimate standards (e.g., I want to be as good in class as X). However, as a Chinese proverb states "every long journey starts with a single step." Adolescents hence need to learn that if they want to achieve these ultimate standards, they first have to think in terms of intermediate (e.g., in the next six months, I will improve my grades) and immediate goals (e.g., next week I'll do all my homework). This also implies working on the prioritization and integration of competing standards, and, if necessary, the abandonment of irreconcilable and unrealistic standards (Greenberg & Safran, 1987). These steps may help to provide adolescents with more realistic standards that are somewhat higher than their actual perception of their self and identity. They may help early adolescents to develop a sense of control, self-efficacy, and optimism, thereby reducing their vulnerability about self and identity (Harter, 1998; Hattie, 1992).

Other steps to optimize adolescents' self and identity directly focus on parents and teachers. Much of what adolescents want or desire results from social modeling or observational (vicarious) learning (e.g., Bandura, 1977). Adolescents often observe significant adults in their environment and imitate or adopt their behavior or attitudes. Put differently, if adults have unattainable standards for their self or identity, chances are high that adolescents develop unattainable standards for their self or identity. An adolescent girl, for example, who observes her mother dieting and talking about her weight is more likely to become alert and vulnerable about her body and gender identity than an adolescent girl whose mother is content with her physical appearance. It is hence important for parents and teachers surrounding adolescents to monitor their own behavior, expectations, and standards so as to convey standards concerning self and identity that are realistic and attainable. To do so, parents and teachers need to be aware of the messages and signals about what is "good or bad" they convey to young adolescents. Also, parents and teachers will have to realize that it makes little sense to engage in a particular behavior (e.g., dieting, smoking, drinking alcohol) while telling their children that this behavior is bad for them.

While the mentioned steps may be helpful in diminishing the experienced discrepancies between adolescents' actual and ideal self or identity, times where early adolescents experience a discrepancy between who and what they are and who and what they would like to be seem inevitable. However, parents and teachers can take steps to ease adolescents' painful awareness of their shortcomings.

Easing Pain

Adolescence is an emotional roller-coaster and (short or long) periods of deep despair about who and what one is appear to be the rule rather than the exception (Larson & Richards, 1994). Despite the inevitable emotional hazards of early adolescence, most adolescents go through most days feeling good about who and what they are. They quickly recover from setbacks in their physical, academic, or social lives. The most important factors helping adolescents to overcome the many challenges early adolescence poses for self and identity are the social reactions of significant others, especially adults, toward early adolescents' worries, concerns, and doubts concerning their self and identity. One of the most important reactions that may ease the pain caused by discrepancies in adolescent self or identity is empathy (Holdstock & Rogers, 1977). It is essential for parents and teachers to listen to adolescents and try to understand their point of view. To illustrate, although a mother may think her daughter totally unreasonable for thinking that she is ugly and fat, the daughter's feelings are real. Only by trying to put herself in her daughter's shoes and to understand what she is thinking and feeling can the mother succeed to convey support and acceptance to her daughter. Similarly, a teacher may think an adolescent boy to be bright, while the boy is eaten up by the fear of failing every exam. Again, only by carefully listening to the boy and taking his perspective (however distorted it may seem), the teacher will be able to provide the support the boy may need to overcome his fear of failure. Another powerful reaction that may ease adolescents' pain concerning their self and identity is positive regard or respect (Rogers, 1957). Parents and teachers need to treat adolescents with warmth and dignity. It is important that they express appreciation and treat the adolescent as a unique, loveable, and trustworthy person (Bowlby, 1973). They need to show that they care, rather than dismissing adolescents' fears with comments like "You are still young," "When I was your age," or "But dear you are beautiful." Through parents' and teachers' empathy and positive regard for their self and identity may adolescents come to accept who and what they are and learn to deal with the challenges that biological, academic, and social changes pose for their self and identity.

To conclude, during early adolescence the emergence of biological, academic, and social changes, personal transitions, heightened self-consciousness, and increased social comparison force early adolescents to evaluate their self and identity. Because early adolescents often set themselves unattainable standards for their self and identity, early adolescence runs the risk of becoming an emotional roller-coaster and a potentially stressful period of life. With a little help from their friends, parents, teachers, and professionals, adolescents may be able to distinguish between their real and ideal self / identity and begin the process of resolving discrepancies so as to ensure their psychosocial well-being and successful adaptation to the challenges for self and identity posed by early adolescence.

References

Arnett, J. J. (1999). Adolescent storm and stress, reconsidered. *American Psychologist, 54,* 317-326.

Ashmore, R. D., & Jussim, L. (1997). Toward a second century of the scientific analysis of self and identity. In R. D. Ashmore and L. Jussim (Eds.), *Self and identity: Fundamental issues* (pp. 3-22). New York: Oxford University Press.

Aubé, J., & Koestner, R. (1992). Gender characteristics and adjustment: A longitudinal study. *Journal of Personality and Social Psychology, 63,* 485-493.

Bandura, A. (1977). *Social learning theory.* Englewood Cliffs, NJ: Prentice Hall.

Baumeister, R. F. (1991). *Meanings of life.* New York: The Guilford Press.

Baumeister, R. F. (1995). Self and identity: An introduction. In A. Tesser (Ed.), *Advanced social psychology* (pp. 51-97). New York: McGraw-Hill.

Baumeister, R. F. (1998). The self. In D. T. Gilbert, S. T. Fiske, & G. Lindzey (Eds.), *The handbook of social psychology* (pp. 681-740). Boston, MA: McGraw-Hill.

Baumeister, R. F., Shapiro, J. J. & Tice, D. (1985). Two kinds of identity crisis. *Journal of Personality, 53*, 407-424.

Berndt, T. J. (1979). Developmental changes in conformity to peers and parents. *Developmental Psychology, 15*, 608-616.

Berndt, T. J. (1996). Transitions in friendship and friends' influence. In J. A. Graber, J. Brooks-Gunn, & A. C. Petersen (Eds.), *Transitions through adolescence: Interpersonal domains and context* (pp. 57-84). Mahwah, NJ: Erlbaum.

Blos, P. (1967). The second individuation process of adolescence. *The Psychoanalytic Study of the Child, 22*, 162-186.

Bowlby, J. (1973). *Attachment and loss: Vol. 2. Separation: Anxiety and anger.* New York: Basic Books.

Bosma, H. A. (1993). De ontwikkeling van persoonlijkheid en identiteit. [The development of personality and identity.] In W. Meeus (Ed.), *Adolescentie: Een psychosociale benadering* (pp. 100-149). Groningen, The Netherlands: Wolters-Noordhoff.

Bosma, H., & van Halen, C. (1999). Identiteitsproblemen in de menselijke ontwikkeling: Een intergerend perspectief. [Identity problems in human development: An integrative perspective.] *Psychologie en Maatschappij, 88*, 259-271.

Bosma, H. A., Graafsma, T. L. G., Grotevant, H. D., & de Levita, D. J. (1994). *Identity and development: An interdisciplinary approach.* London: Sage.

Bourne, E. (1978). The state of research on ego identity: A review and appraisal: II. *Journal of Youth and Adolescence, 7*, 371-392.

Brooks-Gunn, J. (1987). Pubertal processes and girls' psychological adaptation. In R. M. Lerner and T. T. Foch (Eds.), *Biological-psychosocial interactions in early adolescence* (pp. 123-153). Hillsdale, NJ: Lawrence Erlbaum.

Brooks-Gunn, J., Warren, M. P., Rosso, J., & Gargiulo, J. (1987). Validity of self-report measures of girls' pubertal status. *Child Development, 58*, 829-841.

Brown, B. B., Mounts, N., Lamborn, S. D., & Steinberg, L. (1993). Parenting practices and peer group affiliation in adolescence. *Child Development, 64*, 467-482.

Campbell, J. D., & Lavallee, L. F. (1993). Who am I? The role of self-concept confusion in understanding the behavior of people with low self-esteem. In R. F. Baumeister (Ed), *Self-esteem: The puzzle of low self-regard* (pp. 3-20). New York, NY: Plenum Press.

Cheek, D. B. (1968). *Human growth, body composition, cell growth, energy, and intelligence.* Philadelphia: Lea and Febiger.

Childress, A. C., Brewerton, T. D., Hodges, E. L., & Jarrell, M. P. (1993). The Kids' Eating Disorders Survey (KEDS): A study of middle school students. *Journal of the American Academy of Child and Adolescent Psychiatry, 32*, 843-850.

Clifford, E. (1971). Body satisfaction in early adolescence. *Perceptual and Motor Skills, 33,* 119-125.

Coie, J. D. (1990). Toward a theory of peer rejection. In S. R. Asher, & J. D. Coie (Eds.), *Peer rejection in childhood* (pp. 365- 401). Cambridge, England: Cambridge University Press.

Collins, W. A., & Repinski, D. J. (1994). Relationships during adolescence: Continuity and change in interpersonal perspective. R. Montemayor, G. R. Adams, & T. P. Gullotta (Eds.), *Personal relationships during adolescence.* (Vol. 6, pp. 7-36). Thousand Oaks, CA: Sage.

Constanzo, P. (1970). Conformity development as a function of self-blame. *Journal of Personality and Social Psychology, 14,* 366-374.

Cooley, C. H. (1902). *Human nature and the social order.* New York: Charles Scribner's Sons.

Cotterell, J. L. (1992). School size as a factor in adolescents' adjustment to the transition to secondary school. *Journal of Early Adolescence, 12,* 28-45.

Damon, W., & Hart, D. (1988). *Self-understanding in childhood and adolescence.* New York: Cambridge University Press.

Duval, S., & Wicklund, R. A. (1972). *A theory of objective self-awareness.* New York: Academic Press.

Eccles, J. S., Lord, S., & Buchanan, C. (1996). School transitions in early adolescence: What are we doing to our people? In J. A. Graber, J. Brooks-Gunn, & A. C. Peterson (Eds.), *Transitions through adolescence: Interpersonal domains and context* (pp. 251-284). Mahwah, NJ: Erlbaum.

Eccles, J. S., Midgley, C., Wigfield, A., Buchanan, C. M., Reuman, D., Flanagan, C., & Mac Iver, D. (1993). Development during adolescence: The impact of stage-environment fit on young adolescents' experiences in schools and in families. *American Psychologist, 48,* 90-101.

Eccles, J. S., Wigfield, A., Flanagan, C. A., Miller, C., Reuman, D. A. & Yee, D. (1989). Self-concepts, domain values, and self-esteem: Relations and changes at early adolescence. *Journal of Personality, 57,* 283-310.

Erikson., E. H. (1959). Identity and the life cycle. *Psychological Issues* (monograph no. 1).

Erikson, E. H. (1968). *Identity: Youth and crisis.* New York: Norton.

Faiman, C., & Winter, J. S. D. (1974). Gonadotropins and sex hormone patterns in puberty: Clinical data. In M. M. Grumbach, G. D. Grave, & F. E. Mayer (Eds.), *Control of the onset of puberty* (pp. 32-61). New York: Wiley.

Felner, R. D., Aber, M. S., Primavera, J., & Cauce, A. M. (1985). Adaptation and vulnerability in high-risk adolescents: An examination of environmental mediators. *American Journal of Community Psychology, 13,* 365-379.

Felts, M., Tavasso, D., Chenier, T., & Dunn, P. (1992). Adolescents' perceptions of relative weight and self-reported weight loss activities. *Journal of School Health, 62,* 372-376.

Festinger, L. (1954). A theory of social comparison processes. *Human Relations, 2,* 117-140.

Friedman, M. A., & Brownell, K. D. (1995). Psychological correlates of obesity: Moving to the next research generation. *Psychological Bulletin, 117,* 3-20.

Furman, W., & Wehner, E. A. (1997). Adolescent romantic relationships: A developmental perspective. In S. Shulman & W. A. Collins (Eds.), *Romantic relationships in adolescence: Developmental perspectives. New directions for child development* (pp. 21-36). San Francisco: Jossey-Bass.

Galambos, N. L., Almeida, D. M., & Petersen, A. C. (1990). Masculinity, femininity, and sex role attitudes in early adolescence: Exploring gender intensification. *Child Development, 61,* 1905-1914.

Gavin, L. A., & Furman W. (1989). Age differences in adolescents' perceptions of their peer groups. *Developmental Psychology, 25,* 827-834.

Graber, J. A., Brooks-Gunn, J., & Peterson, A. C. (1996). Pubertal processes: Methods, measures, and models. In J. A. Graber, J. Brooks-Gunn, & A. C., Petersen (Eds.), *Transitions through adolescence: Interpersonal domains and context* (pp. 23-53). Mahwah, NJ: Erlbaum.

Greenberg, L. S., & Safran, J. D. (1987). *Emotion in psychotherapy.* New York: Guilford Press.

Grotevant, H. D., & Cooper, C. R. (1986). Individuation in family relationships: A perspective on individual differences in the development of identity and role-taking skill in adolescence. *Human Development, 29,* 82-100.

Hall, G. S. (1904). *Adolescence: Its psychology and its relation to physiology, anthropology, sociology, sex, crime, religion, and education* (Vols. 1 & 2). Englewood Cliffs, NJ: Prentice Hall.

Hamburg, B. A. (1990). *Life skills training: Preventive interventions for young adolescents. Report of the Life Skills Training Working Group, Carnegie Council on Adolescent Development.* Washington, DC.

Harter, S. (1982). The perceived competence scale for children. *Child Development, 53,* 87-97.

Harter, S. (1988). *The self-perception profile for adolescents.* Unpublished manual, University of Denver, Denver, CO.

Harter, S. (1993). Causes and consequences of low self-esteem in children and adolescents. In R. F. Baumeister (Ed), *Self-esteem: The puzzle of low self-regard* (pp. 87-116). New York: Plenum Press.

Harter, S. (1998). The development of self-representations. In W. Damon & N. Eisenberg (Eds.), Handbook of child psychology: Social, emotional, and personality devlopment (Vol. 3, pp. 553-617). Chichester, UK: Wiley.

Harter, S. & Marold, D. B. (1994). The directionality of the link between self-esteem and affect: Beyond causal modeling. In D. Cichetti & L.T. Sheree, (Eds.), Rochester Symposium on Developmental Psychopathology: Disorders and dysfunctions of the self (Vol. 5, pp. 333-369). Rochester, NY: University of Rochester Press.

Harter, S., Whitesell, N. R., & Kowalski, P. S. (1992). Individual differences in the effects of educational transitions on young adolescents' perceptions of competence and motivational orientation. American Educational Research Journal, 29, 777-807.

Hartup, W. W. (1996). The company they keep: Friendships and their developmental significance. Child Development, 67, 1-13.

Hattie, J. (1992). Self-concept. Hillsdale, NJ: Erlbaum.

Heatherton, T. F., & Ambady, N. (1993). Self-esteem, self-prediction, and living up to commitments. In R. F. Baumeister (Ed), Self-esteem: The puzzle of low self-regard (pp. 131-145). New York, NY: Plenum Press.

Higgins, E. T. (1987). Self-discrepancy: A theory relating self and affect. Psychological Review, 94, 319-340.

Higgins, E. T. (1991). Development of self-regulatory and self-evaluative processes: Costs, benefits, and trade-offs. In M. R. Gunnar & L. A. Sroufe (Eds.), Self processes and development: The Minnesota Symposia on Child Development (Vol. 23, pp. 125-168). Hillsdale, NJ: Erlbaum.

Higgins, E. T., & Parsons, J. E. (1983). Social cognition and the social life of the child: Stages as subcultures. In E. T. Higgins, D. N. Ruble, & W. W. Hartup (Eds.), Social cognition and social development (pp. 15-62). Cambridge, England: Cambridge University Press.

Higgins, E. T., Loeb, I., & Moretti, M. (1995). Self-discrepancies and developmental shifts in vulnerability: Life transitions in the regulatory significance of others. D. Cicchetti & S. L. Toth (Eds.), Rochester Symposium on Developmental Psychopathology: Emotion, cognition, and representation (Vol. 6, pp. 191-230). Rochester, NY: University of Rochester Press.

Hill, J.P., & Lynch, M. E. (1983). The intensification of gender-related role expectations during early adolescence. In J. Brooks-Gunn & A. C. Petersen (Eds.), Girls at puberty: Biological and psychosocial perspectives (pp. 201-228). New York: Plenum.

Hirsch, B. J., & Renders, R. J. (1986). The challenge of adolescent friendships: A study of Lisa and her friends. In S. E. Hobfoll (Ed.), Stress, social support, and women (pp. 17-27). Washington, DC: Hemisphere.

Holdstock, T. L., & Rogers, C. R. (1977). Person-centered theory. In R. J. Corsini (Ed.), *Current personality theories* (pp. 125-151). Itasca, IL: Peacock.

Isakson, K., & Jarvis, P. (1999). The adjustment of adolescents during the transition into high school: A short-term longitudinal study. *Journal of Youth and Adolescence, 28*, 1-26.

Katchadourian, H. (1990). Sexuality. In S. Feldman & G. Elliot (Eds.), *At the threshold: The developing adolescent* (pp. 330-351). Cambridge, MA: Harvard University Press.

Keating, D. (1990). Adolescent thinking. In S. Feldman & G. Elliott (Eds.), *At the threshold: The developing adolescent* (pp. 54-89). Cambridge, MA: Harvard University Press.

Kroger, J. (1996). *Identity in adolescence, the balance between self and other.* London: Routledge.

Kremen, A. M., & Block, J. (1998). The roots of ego-control in young adulthood: Links with parenting in early childhood. *Journal of Personality and Social Psychology, 75, 1062-1075.*

Larson, R., & Richards, M. H. (1991). Daily companionship in late childhood and early adolescence: Changing developmental contexts. *Child Development, 62,* 284-300.

Larson, R., & Richards, M. H. (1994). *Divergent realities: The emotional lives of mothers, fathers, and adolescents.* New York: Basic Books.

Linville, P. W. (1987). Self-complexity as a cognitive buffer against stress-related illness and depression. *Journal of Personality and Social Psychology, 52,* 663-676.

Locke, E. A., Shaw, K. N., Saari, L. M., & Latham, G. P. (1981). Goal setting and task performance: 1958-1980. *Psychological Bulletin, 90,* 125-152.

Marcia, J. E. (1966). Development and validation of ego-identity status. *Journal of Personality and Social Psychology, 3,* 551-558.

Marcia, J. E. (1976). Identity six years after: A follow-up study. *Journal of Youth and Adolescence, 5,* 145-160.

Marcia, J. E. (1994). The empirical study of ego identity. In H. A. Bosma, T. L. G. Graafsma, H. D. Grotevant, & D. J. de Levita (Eds), *Identity and development: An interdisciplinary approach* (pp. 67-80). London: Sage.

Marcia, J. E., Waterman, A. S., Matteson, D. R., Archer, S. L., & Orlofsky, J. L. (1993). *Ego identity: A handbook for psychosocial research.* New York: Springer Verlag.

Marshall, W. (1978). Puberty. In F. Falkner & J. Tanner (Eds.), *Human growth* (Vol. 2). New York: Plenum Press.

Markus, H., & Nurius, P. (1986). Possible selves. *American Psychologist, 41,* 954-969.

McGuire, W. J., McGuire, C. V., Child, P., & Fujioka, T. (1978). Salience of ethnicity in the spontaneous self-concept as a function of one's ethnic distinctiveness in the social environment. *Journal of Personality and Social Psychology, 36*, 511-520.

Mead, G. H. (1934). *Mind, self, and society from the standpoint of a social behaviorist.* Chicago: University of Chicago Press.

Meeus, W. (1996). Studies on identity development in adolescence: An overview of research and some new data. *Journal of Youth and Adolescence, 25*, 569-598.

Meeus, W., Idema, J., Helsen, M., & Vollebergh, W. (1999). Patterns of adolescent identity development: Review of literature and longitudinal analysis. *Developmental Review, 19*, 419-461.

Moser, A. (1989). Die Faszination des "Falschen." / The fascination of "falseness." *Sigmund Freud House Bulletin, 13*, 29-39.

Newbegin, I., & Owens, A. (1996). Self-esteem and anxiety in secondary school achievement. *Journal of Social Behavior and Personality, 11*, 521-530.

Offer, D., & Schonert-Reichel, K. A: (1992). Debunking the myths of adolescence: Findings from recent research. *Journal of the American Academy of Child & Adolescent Psychiatry, 31*, 1003-1014.

O'Heron, C. A., & Orlofsky, J. L. (1990). Stereotypic and nonstereotypic sex role trait and behavior orientations, gender identity, and psychological adjustment. *Journal of Personality and Social Psychology, 58*, 134-143.

Oosterwegel, A. (1992). *The organization of the self-system: Developmental changes in childhood and adolescence.* Unpublished doctoral dissertation, University of Amsterdam, Amsterdam, The Netherlands.

Oosterwegel, A., & Oppenheimer, L. (1993). *The self-system: Developmental changes between and within self-concepts.* Hillsdale, NJ: Erlbaum.

Parker, J. G., Rubin, K. H., Price, J. M., & DeRosier, M. E. (1995). Peer relationships, child development, and adjustment: A developmental psychopathology perspective. In D. Cichetti & D. J. Cohen (Eds.), *Developmental psychopathology* (Vol. 2, pp. 96-161). New York: Wiley.

Paul, E. L., & White, K. M. (1990). The development of intimate relationships in late adolescence. *Adolescence, 25*, 375-400.

Pines, A., & Aronson, E. (1981). *Burnout: From tedium to personal growth.* New York: Free Press.

Rapoport, T. (1991). Gender-differential patterns of adolescent socialization in three arenas. *Journal of Youth and Adolescence, 20*, 31-51.

Renshaw, P. D., & Brown, P. J. (1993). Loneliness in middle childhood: Concurrent and longitudinal predictors. *Child Development, 64*, 1271-1284.

Richards, M. H., Boxer, A. W., Petersen, A. C., & Albrecht, R. (1990). Relation of weight to body image in pubertal girls and boys from two communities. *Developmental Psychology, 26,* 313-321.

Rogers, C. R. (1957). The necessary and sufficient conditions of therapeutic personality change. *Journal of Consulting Psychology, 21,* 95-103.

Roscoe, B., Diana, M. S., & Brooks, R. H. (1987). Early, middle, and late adolescents' views on dating and factors influencing partner selection. *Adolescence, 22,* 107-121.

Rosenberg, M. (1965). *Society and the adolescent self-image.* Princeton, NJ: Princeton University Press.

Ryan, R. M., Stiller, T. D., & Lynch, T. H. (1994). Representations of relations to teachers, parents, and friends as predictors of academic motivation and self-esteem. *Journal of Early Adolescence, 14,* 226-249.

Rutter, M. (1987). Psychological resilience and protective mechanisms. *American Journal of Orthopsychiatry, 57,* 316-331.

Samet, N., & Kelly, E. (1987). The relationship of steady dating to self-esteem and sex role identity among adolescents. *Adolescence, 22,* 231-245.

Sandberg, D. E., Meyer-Bahlburg, H. F. L., Ehrhardt, A. A., & Yager, T. J. (1993). The pervalence of gender-atypical behavior in elementary school children. *Journal of the American Academy of Child and Adolescent Psychiatry, 32,* 306-314.

Savin-Williams, R. C., & Weisfeld, G. E. (1989). An ethological perspective on adolescence. In G. R. Adams, R. Montemayor, & T. B. Gullota (Eds.), *Biology of adolescent behavior and development* (pp. 249-274). Newbury Park, CA: Sage.

Schaffer, H. R. (1996). *Social development.* Malden, MA: Blackwell Publishers.

Seiffge-Krenke, I. (1998). Geheimnisse und Intimität im Jugendalter: Ihre Bedeutung für die Autonomieentwicklung. [Secrets and intimacy in adolescence: Their implications for the development of autonomy.] In A. Spitznagel (Ed.), *Geheimnis und Geheimhaltung* (pp. 257-266). Göttingen, Germany: Hogrefe.

Selman, R. (1980). *The growth of interpersonal understanding: Developmental and clinical analyses.* New York: Academic Press.

Sherif, M., & Sherif, C. (1964). *Reference groups.* Chicago, IL: Regnery.

Simmons, R. G. & Blyth, D. A. (1987). *Moving into adolescence: The impact of pubertal change and school context.* Hawthorne, NY: Aldine de Gruyter.

Simmons, R. G., Rosenberg, F., & Rosenberg, M. (1973). Disturbance in the self-image at adolescence. *American Sociological Review, 38,* 553-568.

Sullivan, H. S. (1953). *The interpersonal theory of psychiatry.* New York: Norton.

Tanner, J. M., Whitehouse, R. H., & Takaishi, M. (1966). Standards from birth to maturity for height, weight, height velocity and weight velocity; British children, 1965. *Archives of the Diseases of Childhood, 41*, 455-471.

Waterman, A. S. (1982). Identity development from adolescence to adulthood: An extension of theory and a review of research. *Developmental Psychology, 18*, 341-358.

Youniss, J., & Smollar, J. (1985). *Adolescent relations with mothers, fathers, and friends.* London: University of Chicago Press.

Author Notes

Address correspondence to: Catrin Finkenauer, Department of Social Psychology, Free University, van der Boechorststraat 1, 1081 BT Amsterdam, Tel. 0031-(0)20-4448857, Fax: 0031-(0)20-4448921, Email: C. Finkenauer @psy.vu.nl

3

SELF-ESTEEM AS A MULTIFACETED CONSTRUCT

Michael H. Kernis

The importance of self-esteem in early adolescence is undeniable. At a time when youth are undergoing immense change, both physically and psychologically, their feelings of self-worth have generally been accorded great importance by parents, teachers, clinicians, researchers, and theorists. This importance seems well placed, as self-esteem has been implicated in a vast array of phenomena among adolescents, including depression and suicidal ideation (Rosenberg, 1985; Harter, 1993), loneliness and peer rejection (Ammerman, Kazdin, & Van Hasselt, 1993; East, Hess, & Lerner, 1987), academic achievement (Hattie, 1992), and life satisfaction (Huebner, 1991) (for a review, see DuBois & Tevendale, 1999). As Susan Harter, a leading developmental psychologist and self-esteem theorist, notes: "Self-evaluations, including global self-worth, are very salient constructs in one's working model of self and, as such, can wield powerful influences on affect and behavior" (1999, p. 315).

However, despite this presumed centrality of self-esteem to various aspects of adolescent functioning, its precise role, more often than desired, remains unclear. In their review of the self-esteem literature, DuBois and Tevendale (1999) note that researchers have found self-esteem to relate positively (Hattie, 1992), as well as negatively (Skaalvik & Hagtvet, 1990), to academic achievement. As well, DuBois and Tevendale note that conflicting findings have emerged in studies predicting delinquent behavior and gang involvement (Baumeister, Smart, & Boden, 1996; Wang, 1994). In addition to self-esteem research being plagued by inconsistent findings, the predictive utility of self-esteem with respect to psychological health, well-being, and (mal)adaptive behavior generally is modest, with the majority of variance in these indices left unaccounted (DuBois & Tevendale, 1999).

In many respects, then, there is ample reason to bemoan the state of the self-esteem literature. Fortunately, recent advances in self-esteem theory and research hold a great deal of promise. Although much of this work is still in its infancy, its impact has already been felt. The overarching goal of this chapter is to review these recent advances, which, although they differ in their particulars, converge in one, very important way: *they all support the view that self-esteem is best understood as a multifaceted construct.* This view stands in direct contrast to a long-standing tradition that holds that what is critical about self-esteem is whether it is high or low. Until recently, virtually all self-esteem theory and research focused exclusively on self-esteem level. As I describe in this chapter, incorporating aspects of self-esteem other than its level has the potential to significantly advance our understanding of the role of self-esteem in various aspects of psychological functioning.

I begin by defining self-esteem and distinguishing it from the related concept of self-evaluations. Following this, I focus on three aspects of self-esteem that have sparked substantial interest and that have challenged traditional views of self-esteem. These aspects are the following: (1) *implicit self-esteem*—nonconscious feelings of self-worth that may or may not match conscious, explicit feelings of self-worth; (2) *contingent self-esteem*—the extent to which self-esteem depends upon specific outcomes or achievements; and (3) *self-esteem stability*—the magnitude of short-term fluctuations in individuals' immediate, contextually based feelings of self-worth. Most of the research dealing with these other aspects of self-esteem has utilized samples of young adults (i.e., college students). Of necessity I present this research in some detail, but I give special attention to research that focuses on young adolescents. Also, I draw connections between findings obtained with adults and matters of significance to young adolescents.

Distinguishing Self-esteem From Self-evaluations

Self-esteem refers to individuals' feelings of self-worth, liking, and acceptance. *Self-esteem level* refers to individuals' general or typical feelings of self-worth, liking, and acceptance, which are thought to be relatively stable across time and context (Rosenberg, 1986; Savin-Williams & Demo, 1983). In contrast, *self-evaluations* refer to specific assessments of the positivity of one's physical and psychological characteristics (e.g., I am very pretty), or of one's skills and abilities in particular domains (I am good at math but I am a poor musician).

Some theorists (e.g., Harter, 1999; Pelham, 1995) assert that self-evaluations are the building blocks of self-esteem, particularly if these self-evaluations are in domains of high importance. Brown (1993) refers to this as a "bottom up" perspective. Others, notably Brown (1993), favor a "top down" perspective in which global feelings of self-worth are thought to "color" specific self-evaluations. Empirically, it is very difficult, if not impossible, to determine which perspective is more correct. One way to resolve this dilemma is to take the position that both perspectives are correct in that each characterizes some people (Harter, 1999; Hoyle, Kernis, Leary, & Baldwin, 1999). I return to this issue in greater detail in the section on contingent self-esteem. I raise it here because, regardless of one's position, it is important to maintain a distinction between self-esteem and self-evaluations. To appreciate the value of this distinction, consider those people who do not like and value themselves despite being highly competent and physically attractive. If self-evaluations and self-esteem were the same thing, there would be no basis for these people to have anything but high self-esteem.

Explicit and Implicit Self-esteem

Typically, self-esteem level is assessed by obtaining individuals' responses to a set of items that tap how much they like themselves, how satisfied they are with themselves, and so forth. Consider, for example, Rosenberg's (1965) Self-esteem Scale, one of the most widely used and well-validated measures of self-esteem (Blascovich & Tomaka, 1991). Respondents indicate their extent of agreement with such statements as: "I feel that I have a number of good qualities; I feel that I am a person of worth, at least on an equal basis with others; and I feel that I do not have much to be proud of" (reverse scored). High self-esteem is reflected by strong agreement to the first two statements and strong disagreement to the last statement.

Responses to statements such as these reflect the self-feelings that people are aware of, or that they are willing to report. In other words, they reflect people's *conscious* feelings of self-worth. These conscious feelings certainly are important, as documented in literally hundreds of studies that have employed self-report measures of self-esteem. Nonetheless, there is a growing sentiment that people also possess feelings of self-worth that are not readily accessible to conscious awareness (Farnham, Greenwald, & Banaji,1999). These nonconscious feelings of self-worth may or may not be congruent with individuals' conscious feelings of self-worth. For example, some people may report possessing high self-esteem, yet simultaneously hold negative self-feelings of which they are unaware (and not just unwilling to report). The idea that people may possess nonconscious feelings of self-worth is not a new one. However, it has received empirical examination only recently, aided by the development of sophisticated computer-based methodologies.

Epstein and Morling (1995) discuss conscious and nonconscious self-esteem within the framework of Cognitive Experiential Self Theory (CEST), which holds that people possess two separate, but interacting, psychological systems. One system, called the rational system, operates at the conscious level according to linguistic and logical principles. Explicit self-esteem resides in this system, reflecting as it does the feelings of self-worth that people consciously hold. The second system, called the experiential system, operates at the nonconscious level, guided in large part by significant affective experiences and heuristic principles. Implicit self-esteem resides here, reflecting as it does feelings of nonconscious self-worth that nonetheless "seep through" to affect peoples' thoughts, feelings, and behaviors.

Epstein and Morling (1995) suggest that high explicit self-esteem that is coupled with low implicit self-esteem is *fragile* and that it relates to heightened use of defensive and self-aggrandizing strategies, perhaps even in the absence of explicit threat. That is, fragile high self-esteem must be continually validated through achievements, praise, or other positive self-relevant outcomes, while vigilantly protected from the potentially threatening implications of negative outcomes or evaluative information (Hoyle et al., 1999; Kernis & Goldman, 1999; Kernis & Paradise, in press; see also Deci & Ryan, 1995; Epstein & Morling, 1995). In short, individuals with fragile high self-esteem are thought to be especially preoccupied with how they feel about themselves and to do whatever it takes to bolster, maintain, and enhance these self-feelings.

In contrast, when explicit and implicit self-esteem both are favorable, one's high self-esteem is *secure*, making it less necessary to defend against real or imagined threats or to flaunt one's strengths. Secure high self-esteem individuals like, value, and accept themselves, "warts and all." They do not feel a need to be superior to others. Instead they are satisfied with being on an "equal plane with others" (Rosenberg, 1965). Attempts to bolster feelings of worth through self-promoting or self-protective strategies will be rare, given that secure feelings of self-worth are not easily challenged (for further discussions of the distinction between fragile and secure high self-esteem, see Hoyle et al., 1999; Kernis & Goldman, 1999; Kernis & Paradise, in press).

One way to protect fragile high self-esteem against threats is to aggressively lash out at others who pose threats to one's vulnerable feelings of worth (Baumeister, Smart, & Boden, 1996; Felson, 1984; Feshbach, 1970; Kernis, Grannemann, & Barclay, 1989). An instance of adolescents who possess discrepant explicit and implicit self-esteem may be adolescent "bullies," who psychologically and physically torment their victims over extended periods of time. Olweus (e.g., 1994) reports that bullies report feeling self-assured, confident, and worthy, yet there is a nagging doubt about whether these self-reports represent the true state of affairs (see Baumeister et al., 1996). One possibility is that bullies may have high explicit self-esteem, while simultaneously possessing low implicit self-esteem.

Recently, several approaches have been used to examine implicit self-esteem and its implications for psychological functioning. One approach developed by Greenwald and colleagues (e.g., Farnham et al., 1999) measures the positivity of implicit self-esteem that individual possess. Called the Implicit Association Task (IAT), it involves the use of reaction time methods to assess the strength of associative links between self-defining terms and various positive and negative stimuli. The greater the relative strength of positive-self to negative-self associations, the higher one's implicit self-esteem (for a review of this work, see Farnham et al., 1999).

An alternative approach involves situationally activating implicit self-esteem by exposing people to positive or negative self-esteem relevant stimuli (e.g., words such as worthless, capable, likeable, insecure) at speeds too fast to be consciously recognized. Abend, Kernis, and

Hampton (1999) recently employed this strategy to examine whether discrepant explicit and implicit self-esteem increases self-serving responding (responding in a way that reflects positively on the self) among college students. In the first of two laboratory sessions, participants completed Rosenberg's (1965) Self-esteem Scale (to assess explicit self-esteem) and a "background survey" in which they indicated whether or not a wide range of characteristics were self-descriptive (e.g., I have a close relationship with my mother; I have good social skills; I am a leader; I regularly read books for pleasure).

Approximately one or two weeks later, participants returned to the lab to perform several different "tasks." The first task was described as a "visual perception task," but, in actuality, it was designed to situationally activate either positive or negative implicit self-esteem. Participants were seated in front of a computer screen and asked to indicate whether each of a series of "flashes" appeared to the left or the right of a fixation point (which was the words "I AM" in the center of the screen). Depending upon the condition, the "flashes" were self-relevant words that either were all positive (e.g., capable, talented, likable, worthwhile) or all negative (e.g., cruel, insecure, worthless, inconsiderate), each of which was followed by a mask of random letters.

Following another task, participants read a description of a fictitious college student and then rated the extent to which various attributes contributed to her successful graduation from college. These were the same attributes that participants previously indicated were or were not self-descriptive. A measure of self-serving responding was created by computing the average importance rating given to those attributes previously deemed non-self-descriptive and subtracting it from the average importance rating of self-descriptive attributes. Computed this way, higher scores reflect the self-serving judgment that successful college performance depends relatively more on those attributes that one possesses than on those attributes that one does *not* possess. This judgment task has been used to assess self-serving responses by Dunning and his colleagues in a number of studies (e.g., Dunning, Leuenberger, & Sherman, 1995).

As anticipated by our characterization of fragile high self-esteem, as well as by Epstein and Morling's theorizing, self-serving responses were greater among those high self-esteem individuals who were presented with negative self-relevant words (*high* explicit, *low* implicit self-esteem), compared to those who were presented with positive self-relevant words (*high* explicit, *high* implicit self-esteem). To our knowledge, these findings represent the first demonstration that the combination of *high* explicit and *low* implicit self-esteem is associated with heightened self-serving responses. Although we are excited about their potential implications, much more work needs to be done. Nonetheless, they provide initial empirical support for the utility of examining both explicit *and* implicit self-esteem.

Implications for Young Adolescents

The discussion of implicit self-esteem suggests that defensiveness is heightened among high self-esteem individuals who possess negative self-feelings of which they are unaware. For young adolescents, available defensive or self-serving behaviors include the following: verbal and physical aggression ("bullies"), prejudice; vandalism; defacing school property (e.g., spray-painting one's nickname in hard to reach, but highly visible, places); self-handicapping (creating or claiming the existence of factors that interfere with good performances); and excluding others from one's clique. Behaviors such as these are especially hard to understand when they are exhibited by youth who are popular, do well in school, and seem, on the surface, to be happy with themselves. However, frequent display of these behaviors may provide clues about the existence of coexisting negative self-feelings that are not readily accessible to conscious awareness. As methods to measure these non-conscious feelings become available, they will provide important assessment tools that can be used in conjunction with traditional, self-report measures of self-esteem level.

Contingent Self-esteem

Another aspect of self-esteem that recently has received attention is the extent to which individuals' self-esteem is contingent upon certain outcomes and achievements. In the words of Deci and Ryan (1995): "Contingent self-esteem refers to feelings about oneself that result from—indeed, are dependent on—matching some standard of excellence or living up to some interpersonal or intrapsychic expectations" (p. 32). For people with contingent self-esteem, preoccupations with how they are performing in particular domains (e.g., Am I popular enough? Pretty enough?) and how they are evaluated by others (Do my teachers think I am smart?) are integral aspects of daily life.

People with contingent self-esteem invest their feelings of self-worth in the outcomes of their everyday activities. When they do well or are positively evaluated, they feel "wonderful and special." Conversely, when they do poorly or are negatively evaluated, they feel "worthless and stupid." People with contingent self-esteem are highly motivated to avoid these painful experiences, so they are prone to distort or rationalize poor performances and to belittle or lash out at negative evaluators (Deci & Ryan, 1995). On the other hand, they eagerly seek out positive performances and may even fabricate such occurrences in order to validate their self-esteem.

It is important to bear in mind that self-esteem that is contingent also is *fragile*, because for it to be high, the person must be continually successful at satisfying relevant criteria. These successes may create the appearance that high self-esteem is secure and well anchored, but it is not. People with contingent self-esteem need continual validation, for they are not satisfied with themselves. This vulnerability is unearthed when success is replaced by failure, which may cause their self-esteem to plummet unless they take defensive measures (Deci & Ryan, 1995).

In contrast, true high self-esteem is not "earned," nor can it be "taken away," by specific outcomes. Rather, true high self-esteem reflects feelings of self-worth that are well anchored and secure—they neither depend upon the attainment of specific outcomes, nor require continual validation. People with true high self-esteem choose activities and undertake goals because they find them interesting or personally important. Doing well is valued because it signifies effective expression of one's core values and interests and it is this effective expression that is valued, not high self-esteem per se (Deci & Ryan, 1995). Directly pursuing high self-esteem reflects contingent, not true, high self-esteem. Individuals with true high self-esteem are unlikely to interpret poor performance as reflecting their incompetence or worthlessness. Instead, they are comfortable enough with themselves to nondefensively use poor performance as a source of information to guide their future behavior. Lest I be misunderstood, I am not suggesting that people with true high self-esteem react unemotionally to poor performances. As Deci and Ryan (1995) note, they may feel disappointed and perhaps somewhat sad or irritated, but they are unlikely to feel devastated or enraged, reactions that become more likely when one's self-esteem is invested in the outcome.

Recently, research has shown that people vary in what their self-esteem is contingent upon. Crocker and Wolfe (1998) reported that common domains of contingency among college students include competence, social acceptance, physical appearance, God's love, power over others, and self-reliance. Among children and young adolescents, common contingency domains include physical appearance, social acceptance, and competence (Harter, 1999). Importantly, across these different age groups, the more contingent individuals' self-esteem, the lower their level of self-esteem (with the possible exception of God's love, see Crocker & Wolfe, 1998). Harter (1999) notes that "Adolescent females who report that appearance determines their sense of self-worth as a person (1) feel worse about their appearance, (2) have lower self-esteem, and (3) also report feeling more affectively depressed compared to females for whom self-esteem precedes judgments of appearance (Harter, 1993; Zumpf & Harter, 1989)" (p. 163). Likewise, Harter, Stocker, and Robinson (1996) found that adolescents whose self-esteem is dependent upon the approval of others were especially preoccupied with the opinions of others, thought that they were receiving relatively low and fluctuating levels of social support, and reported relatively low and fluctuating feelings of self-worth. Additionally, in a study on contingent self-esteem and self-reported anger, Kernis, Paradise, and Goldman (1999) found that college students whose self-esteem is highly contingent on having power over others (using Crocker & Wolfe's measure) reported especially high tendencies to experience anger.

In recent years, we have witnessed a spate of highly violent activities committed by adolescents against their peers. The tragedy at Columbine High School in Littleton, Colorado is one of several tragedies that have resulted in deaths or severe injuries to school-aged victims. A great deal of social commentary appeared shortly thereafter that included considerable speculation about what might cause adolescents to engage in such desperate and antisocial acts of violence. For example, an article in *Time* magazine (December, 1999) documented the perpetrators' anguish over being rejected and ridiculed by their peers. Rather than engage in socially appropriate behaviors that may have fostered their greater acceptance, these teenage outcasts resorted to violence through which they could at least claim notoriety. The present analysis of contingent self-esteem raises the possibility that the intense anger and hatred they felt for their peers may have been fueled, at least in part, by thwarted contingent self-esteem that was based on social acceptance. Reaching this conclusion would in no way justify the heinous crimes they perpetrated. In any case, for this interpretation to have any credence whatsoever, it must first be demonstrated that contingent self-esteem is associated with heightened anger in response to threat.

Paradise and Kernis (1999) recently examined this hypothesis with a sample of women undergraduates. We reasoned that participants with highly contingent self-esteem would be easily threatened by an insulting evaluation and that they would deal with this threat by becoming especially angry and hostile. To test this hypothesis, we first developed a measure of contingent self-esteem (the Contingent Self-Esteem Scale), which consists of 15 items, each of which is rated on 5-point Likert scales (ranging from "Not at all like me" to "Very much like me"). Sample items include "An important measure of my worth is how well I perform up to the standards that other people have set for me" and "Even in the face of failure, my feelings of self-worth remain unaffected" (reverse-scored). The scale is internally consistent (alpha = .85) and shows considerable test-retest reliability (r = .77). Rather than focus on a wide range of possible contingencies (as do Crocker & Wolfe, 1998), we concentrated primarily on contingencies related to meeting expectations, matching standards, and performing competently.

Within several weeks of completing the Contingent Self-esteem Scale, participants attended a laboratory session in which they were led to believe that their "presentational skills" were being rated by an unseen observer in another room. Through random assignment, some women received an evaluation that contained highly insulting statements about their appearance and mannerisms, whereas other women received a generally positive evaluation. Immediately following, they indicated how angry and hostile they felt using a modified version of a state hostility measure developed by Anderson et al. (1995). Our results indicated that the more contingent participants' self-esteem, the more intense their anger in response to the insulting treatment. This effect occurred after controlling for the effect of self-esteem level, supporting the assertion that contingent self-esteem reflects a form of fragile self-esteem that is associated with heightened vulnerability and reactivity to self-esteem threats.

Several weeks later, these same participants (as well as participants in other experimental conditions) also completed the Anger Response Inventory (ARI; Tangney et al., 1996). The ARI is a self-report instrument that taps various aspects of the experience and expression of anger, including anger intensity, intentions for expressing anger, and tendencies to engage in physical or verbal aggression. Consistent with the laboratory findings, the more contingent women's self-esteem, the (marginally) greater the intensity of anger they reported they would feel in response to a range of hypothetical events. Additionally, the more contingent women's self-esteem, the more malevolent their intentions for expressing their anger (i.e., they wanted to get back at or hurt the instigator), and the greater their desire to "let off steam." However, rather than attack the instigator directly, highly contingent self-esteem women, relative to women with less contingent self-esteem, were more likely to focus their anger inward and stew about it, chastise themselves for not doing anything, and lash out at innocent others and things (i.e., displaced verbal, or indirect, aggression). These findings fit with the prevailing characterization of women as being conflicted over their angry feelings and being more likely to express these feelings in indirect ways, rather than directly toward the anger instigator. In future research, it would be desirable to examine if men with highly contingent self-esteem likewise report a heightened intensity of anger, yet display a different pattern of anger expression than women, one that included direct expression toward the anger instigator.

Implications for Young Adolescents

Research with young adolescents should begin by determining which contingencies are most prevalent among people of this age group. Once this is done, a number of interesting and important questions can be addressed. For example, are young adolescents who possess contingent self-esteem easily threatened? Do they resort to aggression as a way of dealing with such threats? Do young women with self-esteem that is contingent on their physical attractiveness develop unhealthy eating habits that eventuate in eating disorders? Are youth with contingent self-esteem likely to be "sun worshipers," excessively exposing themselves to the suns' rays in attempts to enhance their attractiveness? More benignly, does possessing self-esteem that is contingent upon social acceptance predict membership in organized social groups such as the boy and girl scouts, and later, sororities and fraternities? These are but a few of the ways that contingent self-esteem may relate to the psychological and social functioning of adolescent boys and girls.

Stability of Self-esteem

As noted earlier, self-esteem *level* represents people's general or typical feelings of global self-worth and self-liking. These typical feelings of self-worth represent a baseline that is likely to change only slowly and over an extended period of time (Rosenberg, 1986; Savin-Williams & Demo, 1983). In contrast, self-esteem *stability* reflects the magnitude of short-term fluctuations that people experience in their immediate, contextually based, feelings of self-worth (see also Rosenberg, 1986). The most common way to assess self-esteem stability is to have respondents complete a self-esteem measure once or twice daily over a 4-7 day period under instructions to base their responses on how they feel at the moment they are completing each form. The standard deviation of each individual's total scores across these multiple assessments then is computed; the greater the standard deviation, the more unstable one's self-esteem. Correlations between level and stability of self-esteem generally range from the low teens to the low 30s, suggesting that they are relatively independent dimensions of self-esteem. Invariably, the direction of the correlation indicates that more unstable self-esteem is associated with lower levels of self-esteem. However, it is incorrect to presume that only low self-esteem individuals possess unstable self-esteem. In fact, self-esteem stability sometimes has stronger effects among high, not low, self-esteem individuals (e.g., Kernis, Grannemann, & Barclay, 1989).

Perhaps an example would be useful here. Consider Lynn who reports that she typically holds highly positive feelings of self-worth (i.e., she has a high level of self-esteem). However, when she responds to the question "how worthy a person do you feel at this moment?" each morning and evening for five days, her answers vary considerably from "I feel very worthy" to "I feel useless." Beth also reports that she typically has very positive feelings of self-worth. In contrast to Lynn, however, Beth's multiple responses to the question "how worthy a person do you feel at this moment?" remain essentially the same (I feel very worthy). Whereas Lynn's response pattern indicates that her high self-esteem is *unstable* (i.e., her current feelings of self-worth substantially fluctuate across time), Beth's response pattern indicates that her high self-esteem is *stable* (i.e., her current feelings of self-worth remain constant across time). The point to be made here is that although two people may have the same *level* of self-esteem, they can differ very much in the *stability* of their self-esteem.

Unstable self-esteem reflects fragile, vulnerable feelings of immediate self-worth that are influenced by potentially self-relevant events that are externally provided (e.g., a compliment or insult) or self-generated (reflecting on one's appearance) (Kernis et al., 1998; Kernis & Waschull, 1995; Kernis & Paradise, in press). One core characteristic of people with fragile self-esteem is that they are highly responsive to events that have potential relevance to their feelings of self-worth—in fact, they may interpret events as being self-esteem relevant even when they are not (cf. Greenier et al., 1999). For example, a nonreturned phone call may be viewed as reflective of one's own unlikeableness and not the recipient's busyness. Individuals with fragile self-esteem may respond by completely accepting, even exaggerating, an event's evaluative implications (e.g., they may feel incompetent and demoralized following a specific failure; Kernis et al., 1997). At the other extreme, they may respond very angrily and defensively by attacking the validity of the threatening information or the credibility of its source (Kernis et al., 1989). In contrast, people with stable self-esteem typically have less extreme reactions to potentially evaluative events, precisely because these events have little impact on their immediate feelings of self-worth.

As in Deci and Ryan's conceptualization of contingent high self-esteem, people with unstable high self-esteem are thought to be highly ego-involved in their everyday activities. Elsewhere, we (Greenier et al., 1999; Kernis et al., 1997) have portrayed this heightened ego-involvement as an "evaluative set" comprised of several interlocking components. First, an *attentional* component involves "zeroing in" on information or events that have potentially self-evaluative implications. Second, a *bias* component involves interpreting ambiguously or non-self-esteem relevant events as self-esteem relevant. Finally, a *generalization* component involves linking one's immediate global feelings of self-worth to specific outcomes and events (e.g., a poor math performance is taken to reflect low overall intelligence and worth). Each of these components may operate outside of one's awareness or be consciously and deliberately invoked.

Recent research provides support for the assertion that unstable self-esteem reflects heightened ego-involvement and fragile, vulnerable feelings of self-worth. According to a number of clinical theorists (e.g., Chodoff, 1973; Jacobson, 1975; for a review, see Tennen & Affleck, 1993), people who are vulnerable to depression are susceptible to substantial downward fluctuations in their feelings of self-worth, particularly in response to negative events. Consistent with this reasoning, Kernis et al. (1998) tested the hypothesis that having unstable self-esteem would increase individuals' vulnerability to depressive symptoms if they experienced considerable daily hassles. Participants in this study were college students who first completed measures of depressive symptoms and self-esteem level. The following week they completed multiple measures of current self-esteem (to assess self-esteem stability). Approximately 4 weeks later, they returned to complete the same depression scales and a measure of daily hassles calibrated for the intervening time period. The results offered strong support for our hypothesis. Specifically, increases in depressive symptoms were greatest among individuals who experienced considerable daily hassles *and* who possessed unstable self-esteem. Importantly, self-esteem level did not predict increases in depressive symptoms, either alone or in combination with daily hassles (for conceptually similar findings, see also Butler, Hokanson, & Flynn, 1994; Roberts & Monroe, 1992).

Other findings indicated that, compared to participants with stable self-esteem, participants with unstable self-esteem were more prone to overgeneralize the negative implications of failure (Carver & Ganellen, 1983). That is, whereas people with unstable self-esteem react to a specific failure by feeling incompetent and stupid (the generalization component of the evaluative set just described), people with stable self-esteem have more localized reactions (i.e., if they question anything, it may be their ability to succeed at the task at hand). Moreover, these feelings of incompetence appear to contribute to a vicious cycle characterized by a lack of motivation and subsequent additional failures (Kernis, Brockner, & Frankel, 1989).

Most depression research involving children and adolescents focuses on low self-esteem as the critical aspect of self-esteem that is a vulnerability factor for depression (for a summary, see Harter, 1999). However, the findings of Kernis et al. (1998), Butler et al. (1994), and Roberts and Monroe (1992) offer an important alternative. Specifically, each of these studies indicates that it is not low self-esteem per se that is a potent vulnerability factor for depression, but rather *unstable* self-esteem. Given that each of these studies examined young adults and not youth, research involving young adolescents is critical.

Greenier et al. (1999) sought more direct evidence of the heightened ego-involvement thought to characterize individuals with unstable self-esteem. Specifically, these researchers tested the hypothesis that everyday positive and negative events would have a greater impact on the self-feelings of college students with unstable as opposed to stable self-esteem. For two weeks, men and women college students wrote descriptions of their most positive and negative experience each day, Monday through Thursday. They also indicated the extent to which each event made them feel better or worse about themselves (on a scale ranging from "made me feel considerably worse about myself" to "made me feel considerably better about myself"). The results indicated that the more unstable individuals' self-esteem, the worse they reported feeling about themselves in response to negative events and the better they reported feeling about themselves in response to positive events. In both cases (i.e., for reactions to positive and to negative events), the greater reactivity associated with unstable self-esteem remained when the effects of self-esteem level were controlled.

Research with children has also yielded findings relevant to the assertion that unstable self-esteem reflects heightened ego-involvement and vulnerable self-feelings. Waschull and Kernis (1996) examined how self-esteem level and self-esteem stability relate to children's intrinsic motivation in the classroom. Prior research indicates that situational factors that emphasize the link between specific outcomes and self-esteem often undermine intrinsic motivation (Ryan, 1993). This research suggests that heightened concerns about one's self-esteem may undermine the desire to take on challenges and instead promote a more cautious, but safer route to positive outcomes. Given that unstable self-esteem reflects a heightened tendency to link one's self-esteem to specific events and outcomes, we expected that it would relate to lower levels of intrinsic motivation in children.

We administered Harter's (1981) Intrinsic vs. Extrinsic Orientation in the Classroom Scale to fifth-grade children whose self-esteem level and stability had been previously assessed (using the global self-worth subscale of Harter's Perceived Competence Scale for Children). As expected, analyses controlling for self-esteem level showed that unstable self-esteem was related to lower Preference for Challenge

(Does the child prefer challenging tasks or those that are easy?) and Curiosity/Interest scores (Is the child motivated by curiosity or to get good grades and please the teacher?). These findings suggest that unstable self-esteem in children is linked to a relatively cautious or strategic self-esteem focused orientation toward learning rather than to an intrinsic orientation involving learning for learning's sake.

We also examined whether self-esteem stability related to children's reasons for becoming angry at their peers. Participants were presented with five hypothetical vignettes depicting aversive interpersonal events, each of which constituted an instrumental thwarting as well as a potential self-esteem threat (e.g., "You are really thirsty after playing outside with your classmates. Just when you are next in line to get a drink from the fountain, another boy (girl) pushes ahead of you, making you wait"). The results (controlling for self-esteem level) indicated that, compared to children with stable self-esteem, children with unstable self-esteem were more likely to indicate that they would become angry because of the self-esteem threatening aspects of the events depicted in the vignettes.

A final aspect of this study was to examine the extent to which fluctuations in children's global feelings of self-worth related to fluctuations in perceived competence and social acceptance. Evaluative information pertaining to specific self-aspects (e.g., one's academic competence) has direct implications for one's self-evaluations of these self-aspects (cf. Kernis & Johnson, 1990). To the extent, then, that unstable self-esteem is associated with (a) placing substantial weight on specific evaluative information or (b) generalizing the implications of specific evaluative information to one's feelings of self-worth, the magnitude of day-to-day fluctuations in perceived competence and social acceptance should be related to the magnitude of fluctuations in global feelings of self-worth. To address this issue, Waschull and Kernis (1996) had participants indicate their felt competence and social acceptance each time they rated their current self-esteem (to assess self-esteem stability). Findings indicated that the magnitude of daily fluctuations in perceived competence and social acceptance each correlated with the magnitude of daily fluctuations in global self-esteem ($r = .59, .62$, respectively).

In related research involving college students, Kernis et al. (1993, Study 2) tested the hypothesis that variability in specific evaluations and global self-esteem would relate more strongly if the self-evaluative dimension is high rather than low in importance. As was found by Waschull and Kernis (1996), the magnitude of day-to-day variability along each dimension was significantly correlated with the magnitude of self-esteem instability. Additional analyses indicated that the relation between greater variability in perceived competence and self-esteem instability was especially strong among people who viewed competence as an important determinant of their overall self-worth. This pattern also emerged for the dimensions of physical attractiveness and social acceptance, but only among people who generally rated themselves relatively favorably along these dimensions. For people who generally rated themselves unfavorably on these dimensions, high daily variability was related to highly unstable self-esteem regardless of the dimension's importance. Kernis et al. (1993) suggested that the impact of personal importance may have been overridden by the substantial interpersonal consequences associated with low social acceptance and physical attractiveness.

A number of other studies have documented the role of self-esteem stability in various aspects of psychological functioning, including: psychological adjustment (Paradise & Kernis, in press; Tevendale, Dubois, Lopez, & Prindiville, 1997); self-regulatory processes (Kernis, Paradise, Whitaker, Wheatman, & Goldman, 2000); reactions to success and failure (Kernis,Greenier, Herlocker, Whisenhunt, & Abend, 1997); excuse-making (Kernis, Grannemann & Barclay, 1992); and anger and hostility proneness (Kernis, Grannemann, & Barclay, 1989). For example, Kernis et al. (2000) reported that unstable self-esteem in college students was associated with relatively impoverished self-concepts (low self-concept clarity) and with self-regulatory styles characterized by low self-determination (i.e., doing things to please others or to avoid feelings of guilt and anxiety rather than because the activities were fun, interesting, or personally important). Kernis, Grannemann, and Barclay (1989) found that unstable self-esteem (particularly among individuals with high levels of self-esteem) was associated with especially high tendencies to become angry and hostile. Along with the research reported here, these studies support the conclusion that unstable self-esteem reflects fragile feelings of self-worth that are associated with heightened reactivity to potentially self-esteem relevant events and to relatively poor psychological adjustment. Thus, one key to obtaining a better understanding of psychological well-being and adjustment may rest in identifying the factors in childhood and early adolescence that promote unstable and fragile, as opposed to stable and secure, self-esteem.

As a first step toward identifying such factors, Kernis, Brown, and Brody (2000) examined how stability of self-esteem in children relates to their perceptions of how their parents communicate with them. Participants in this study consisted of 174 11-12-year-old children (80 boys, 94 girls), all of whom resided with both of their biological parents. Families were recruited using a telephone-directory-based random sampling strategy that targeted households with at least one child between 10 and 15 years old. Seventy-nine percent of this sample (N = 137) identified as Caucasian; twenty-one percent identified as African-American (N = 37). Ninety-five percent of mothers and ninety-one percent of fathers had graduated from high school, the majority of whom pursued further education. Mother's mean age was 39; father's mean age was 41.

We focused on several aspects of parent-child communication that we thought were especially important with respect to fostering unstable self-esteem in children. First, we examined the extent to which parents were perceived as *being insulting or critical* toward their children. Parental expressions of disapproval need not be experienced as insults or criticism, particularly if they focus on the child's behaviors rather than on his or her personal characteristics. However, insulting communications by parents toward their children may promote not only chronic feelings of relative inferiority and inadequacy, but a heightened tendency to link these feelings to specific negative evaluative events. Consequently, we anticipated that, compared to children with stable self-esteem, children with unstable self-esteem would perceive their parents as being more critical and insulting toward them.

Second, we examined parents' perceived use of various *guilt-inducing or psychologically controlling* techniques to shape their children's behaviors. Guilt-inducing techniques (e.g., "If you loved me, you would not do that") are a form of psychological control in that they are experienced as "pressure to think, feel, or behave in specified ways" (Deci & Ryan, 1987, p. 95). From a child's perspective, success in meeting these contingencies implies worthiness whereas failure implies unworthiness. That is, children's exposure to guilt-inducing techniques is likely to promote considerable daily fluctuations in their feelings of self-worth. Therefore, we predicted that, compared to children with stable self-esteem, children with unstable self-esteem would perceive their parents as more frequently using guilt-inducing techniques.

Third, we focused on communications revolving around the frequency and methods by which parents conveyed *approval* of their children. Expressing approval generally serves to affirm children's positive behaviors and qualities, so we expected its frequency to be related to children's possession of more stable self-esteem. In addition, we suspected that some types of expression would be more effective in this regard than others. We referred to such expressions as *value-affirming*. Ideally, expressions of approval should convey that parents love, value, and accept their children. For example, doing things together, hugs and other forms of physical affection, and verbal encouragement all signal to the child that he or she is valued and loved. Moreover, they serve to foster positive affective bonds and authenticity in parent-child relationships, which contribute to more stable and secure feelings of self-worth (Ryan, 1993). Consequently, we predicted that, compared to children with stable self-esteem, children with unstable self-esteem would perceive their parents as using less value-affirming communications.

However, other modes of displaying approval may be less strongly linked to children's feelings of self-worth. Specifically, giving material rewards like money, or extending special privileges, to children, may be experienced by children as attempts to control their behavior (Deci & Ryan, 1985). In addition, communications involving *tangible rewards* do not necessarily signal parental involvement and caring. Rather, they can serve to distance the child from the parent, if, for example, the parent feels too busy to attend to child and gives money for the movies instead. In essence, rewards and privileges may provide conflicting messages to the child (e.g., I like what you did, but you are not worthy enough for my time or affection), which may serve to cancel each other out. Consequently, we expected little or no relation between parents' use of rewards and privileges and their children's self-esteem stability.

Fourth, we examined the *problem-solving* styles of the parents. Seeking children's input, recognizing their feelings, and working together toward a solution (*positive problem solving*) help create a family atmosphere that fosters children's autonomy, competence, and relatedness (Ryan, 1993). In contrast, when parents tend to get angry and refuse to acknowledge or accept a solution other than their own (*negative problem solving*), children may be left feeling controlled, incompetent, and potentially unloved, all factors that undermine a stable and secure sense of one's self-worth (Deci & Ryan, 1995). Consequently, we predicted that, compared to children with stable self-esteem, children with unstable self-esteem would perceive their parents as lower in positive problem solving and higher in negative problem solving.

In sum, we predicted that, compared to children with stable self-esteem, children with unstable self-esteem would perceive their parents as *more* critical, psychologically controlling, and negative in their problem solving, but as *less* likely to acknowledge their children's good behaviors, less value-affirming when demonstrating their approval, and less positive in their problem solving.

The data were collected in two home visits conducted by trained research assistants. The visits were scheduled approximately one week apart and each lasted two to three hours. At each home visit, questionnaire items (except for the self-esteem stability measures) were administered to the target child on a laptop computer privately, with no other family members present. Each individual item and its response set appeared on the screen until the child entered an answer on the keypad. Cardboard shields prevented the research assistant from seeing any respondent's answers.

At the end of the first home visit, the interviewer provided the child and his or her parents with instructions for completing the stability of self-esteem measure. A packet of self-esteem measures (Rosenberg's Self-esteem Scale, with added instructions to base their responses on how they feel "right at this moment") were left with the child. Participants were asked to complete one form before bedtime and one before leaving for school in the morning for a period of five consecutive days. If a scheduled time was missed, they were asked to complete the measure at the next scheduled time. The completed packet was collected at the beginning of the second home visit. For each child, self-esteem stability was computed as the standard deviation of his or her total scores on these multiple assessments; the greater the standard deviation, the more unstable the child's self-esteem.

The findings offered strong support for our hypotheses. That is, children's perceptions of many aspects of parent-child communication patterns (especially fathers') were linked to how much they fluctuated in their contextually based feelings of self-worth (i.e., possessed unstable self-esteem). For example, children who perceived their fathers to be highly critical, to engage in insulting name calling, and to use guilt arousal and love withdrawal as control techniques had more unstable (as well as lower) self-esteem than did children who did not perceive their fathers in this manner. Moreover, compared to children with stable self-esteem, children with unstable self-esteem indicated that their fathers less frequently talked about the good things that they (the children) had done and were less likely to use value-affirming methods when they did show their approval. Still other findings indicated that, compared to fathers of children with low self-esteem, fathers of children with *stable high, but not unstable high,* self-esteem were perceived as using better problem-solving methods to solve disagreements with their children. Interestingly, perceptions of mothers' communication styles were more consistently related to children's self-esteem level than to their self-esteem stability. The findings for self-esteem stability that did emerge, however, were largely consistent with those that emerged for fathers.

To our knowledge, these findings are the first to relate parental communication styles to the instability of their children's self-esteem. It is disconcerting, though not entirely surprising, that derogatory name calling and criticism by parents appears to undermine both the stability and level of their children's self-esteem. Children tend to be very sensitive to evaluative information conveyed about them by parents and other significant individuals in their lives (Dweck & Goetz, 1978; Rosenberg, 1986). When this information is clearly and frequently negative, it is very difficult for children to avoid questioning their own value and worth (Harter, 1993). Once the foundation for feelings of self-worth is shaken, a vicious cycle of negativity and self-esteem instability may become self-perpetuating (Kernis, Brockner, & Frankel, 1989). For example, children may place more weight on negative than positive evaluative information and they may overgeneralize the implications of negative self-relevant information (e.g., they may think that they are a stupid person after doing poorly on a test). In fact, recent data indicate that among young adults, unstable self-esteem is associated with heightened tendencies to overgeneralize the implications of failure (Kernis et al., 1998).

When fathers attempt to control children's unwanted behaviors by arousing guilt or withdrawing their love, they may set up contingencies whereby children feel worthy and valuable when they act appropriately, but useless and unworthy when they act inappropriately. Called *conditions of worth* a number of years ago by Rogers (1959), such contingencies are likely to promote self-regulatory styles that are *external* and *introjected* rather than *identified* and *intrinsic* (Deci & Ryan, 1985). External regulation involves engaging in activities to obtain a reward or because someone else requires it. Introjected self-regulation involves pressuring oneself to do something because one "should," or because not doing the behavior will cause one to feel guilty, anxious, or unworthy (Ryan, Rigby, & King, 1993). External and introjected self-regulation are characterized by low amounts of choice and self-determination. Identified and intrinsic self-regulation, in contrast, are characterized by high choice and self-determination, in that actions are freely chosen and personally valued for their importance (identified) or enjoyment (intrinsic). A growing body of research demonstrates that identified and intrinsic self-regulation are positively related to psychological adjustment and well-being, whereas the opposite is true for external and introjected self-regulation (Ryan & Connell, 1989; Ryan et al., 1993; Sheldon & Kasser, 1995). Importantly, among college students, unstable self-esteem is related to stronger external and introjected regulatory styles and weaker identified and intrinsic regulatory styles (Kernis et al., 2000).

On a more positive note, the more value-affirming ways that fathers reportedly showed approval of their children, the more stable and higher was their children's self-esteem. Spending time together, displaying physical affection, and so forth, provide opportunities to deepen the affective bonds between parent and child and they signal to children that they are valued and appreciated. Instead of promoting an external or introjected self-regulatory style in children, value-affirming methods promote identified and intrinsic self-regulation (Ryan, 1993). In short, value affirmation encourages children to trust, value, and utilize their own internal states as guides for action, as well as to feel likeable.

Finally, fathers of children with stable (but not unstable) high self-esteem were perceived as being especially high in positive problem-solving behaviors (e.g., considering child's feelings, listening to child's viewpoint) and especially low in negative problem-solving behaviors (e.g., get angry and criticize child's ideas, insist on getting his way). Importantly, the problem-solving style of these fathers is very similar to the authoritative parenting style described by Baumrind (1971). In fact, previous research has linked authoritative parenting styles to high self-esteem in children (Coopersmith, 1967; Buri et al., 1988). Kernis, Brown, and Brody's findings suggest that as far as fathers' problem-solving style is concerned, this relationship may be limited to promoting stable high self-esteem in children. Specifically, we found that children with unstable high self-esteem did not differ from children with (stable or unstable) low self-esteem in how they characterized their fathers' problem-solving styles.

Implications for Young Adolescents

Considerably more research exists on self-esteem stability than on either implicit self-esteem or contingent self-esteem. Several conclusions can be drawn from this research. First, unstable self-esteem reflects fragile and vulnerable immediate feelings of self-worth that are responsive to self-generated and environmentally based positive and negative events. Second, unstable self-esteem is related to relatively poor psychological adjustment and well-being. Third, parental communication patterns appear to be vital in promoting unstable self-esteem in children.

Future research with young adolescents should examine the links between unstable self-esteem and deficits in psychological adjustment. For example, is unstable self-esteem a vulnerability factor for severe depression among young adolescents? Does rejection from one's peers have a greater adverse impact on youth with unstable as compared to stable self-esteem? Are youth with unstable self-esteem especially likely to give up and respond helplessly to failure in a given academic domain? Also, school and home environments should be examined as factors that may precipitate the development of unstable self-esteem, especially in combination with children's qualities (e. g., temperament).

Summary and Final Observations

The overarching theme of this chapter is that there is more (much more!) to self-esteem than whether it is high or low. Two people may obtain the same score on a self-report measure of self-esteem, but the nature of their self-esteem and how it relates to psychological functioning may be quite different. In some instances, a high score may mask negative feelings that a person has about himself. In the case of high explicit/low implicit self-esteem, for example, the individual is unaware of the existence of negative self-feelings. Despite this unawareness, implicit self-esteem may influence people's thoughts, feelings, and behavior. For example, research reviewed in this chapter suggests that people who possess discrepant explicit and implicit self-esteem will be more self-promoting than people who possess congruent implicit and explicit self-esteem.

In other instances, people's self-esteem may be dependent upon the achievement of certain goals, matching particular standards, or obtaining specific outcomes (contingent self-esteem). When things are going well, self-esteem will be high. However, the fragility of contingent self-esteem is readily unmasked, because when things are not going well, self-esteem will be low. True self-esteem, in contrast, is secure, well anchored, and resilient. Finally, people may experience considerable short-term fluctuations in their contextually based feelings of self-worth (unstable self-esteem), or they may experience little or no fluctuations (stable self-esteem). This tendency to experience (or to not) short-term fluctuations is relatively independent of whether people have high or low self-esteem.

Though not identical, contingent and unstable self-esteem share important features, as do true and stable self-esteem. First, both contingent and unstable self-esteem involve linking feelings of self-worth to specific outcomes (i.e., heightened ego-involvement). Second, both contingent and unstable self-esteem reflect enhanced tendencies to be caught up in the processes of defending, maintaining, and maximizing one's positive, though tenuous, feelings of self-worth. Conversely, both stable and true self-esteem reflect secure, well-anchored feelings of self-worth that do *not* need continual validation. Pleasure following success and disappointment following failure characterize people with either stable or true self-esteem, but these reactions are not tinged with defensiveness or self-aggrandizement (Deci & Ryan, 1995; Kernis et al., 1997).

The constructs of contingent (versus true) and unstable (versus stable) self-esteem have important implications for how we conceptualize high self-esteem. Specifically, they suggest that it is important to distinguish *secure* from *fragile* forms of high self-esteem (Kernis & Goldman, 1999; Kernis & Paradise, in press). *Secure* high self-esteem reflects positive feelings of self-worth that are well anchored and secure, and that are positively associated with a wide range of psychological health and well-being indices. Individuals with secure high self-esteem like, value, and accept themselves, "warts and all." They do not feel a need to be superior to others, nor do they feel a great need to self-promote or to defend against threats. In contrast, people with *fragile* high self-esteem are very proud of whom they are, they feel superior to most other people, and they are highly attuned to defend against possible threats to their positive self-view. In addition, people with fragile high self-esteem frequently engage in self-promoting activities and they constantly seek validation of their worth.

Secure high self-esteem (whether labeled true or stable) emerges when one's actions are self-determined and congruent with one's inner, core self, rather than a reflection of externally imposed or internally based demands (Deci & Ryan, 1995; Kernis et al., 2000). Secure high self-esteem is not *earned*, nor can it be *taken away*. In contrast, directly pursuing high self-esteem reflects fragile high self-esteem (whether labeled contingent or unstable), because feelings of self-worth and value are subject to the vicissitudes of internally generated and externally provided positive and negative events (Deci & Ryan, 1995; Greenier et al., 1999; Kernis et al., 1998). In other words, when individuals strive to have high self-esteem, their self-worth is continually "on the line" as they go about their everyday activities.

In short, the quest for high self-esteem may foster the development of *fragile* as opposed to *secure* high self-esteem. Lest I be misunderstood, I am not intimating that there is something wrong with wanting to feel good about oneself. Rather, what I am suggesting is that when feeling good about oneself becomes a *prime directive*, excessive defense and self-promotion are likely to follow and the resultant self-esteem is likely to be fragile rather than secure. To the extent that striving for high self-esteem promotes fragile and not secure high self-esteem, this suggests that some recent attempts in schools to directly raise children's self-esteem may be ill-conceived. Rather than promoting secure high self-esteem, programs that focus directly on self-esteem, may, in fact, be fostering fragile high self-esteem. It may be more fruitful, then, to foster the emergence of secure high self-esteem by promoting the satisfaction of one's fundamental psychological needs and the development of one's true or core self. Toward this end, creating autonomy supportive environments that foster creativity, self-expression, competence, and caring relationships with one's peers and teachers is critical (Deci & Ryan, 1995).

These are bold assertions, in that they challenge the unequivocal "good" associated with possessing high self-esteem. As such, they deserve careful scrutiny by both educators and researchers in the years to come. Working together to optimize self-esteem among young adolescents will be beneficial to all.

References

Abend, T., Kernis, M. H., & Hampton, C. (2000). Discrepancies between explicit and implicit self-esteem and self-serving responses. Manuscript under review.

Ammerman, R. T., Kazdin, A. E., & Van Hasselt, B. (1993). Correlates of loneliness in nonreferred and psychiatrically hospitalized children. *Journal of Child and Family Studies, 2,* 187-202.

Anderson, C. A., Anderson, J., & DeNeve, K. (1995). Competitive aggression without interaction: Effects of competitive versus cooperative instructions on aggressive behavior in video games. *Personality and Social Psychology Bulletin, 21,* 1020-1030.

Baumeister, R. F., Smart, L., & Boden, J. M. (1996). Relation of threatened egotism to violence and aggression: The dark side of high self-esteem. *Psychological Review, 103,* 5-33.

Baumrind, D. (1971). Current patterns of parental authority. *Developmental Psychology Monographs, 4,* (1, Pt. 2), 1-103.

Blascovich, J., & Tomaka, J. (1991). Measures of self-esteem. In J. P. Robinson, P. R. Shaver, & L. S. Wrightsman (Eds.), *Measures of personality and social psychological attitudes* (Vol. 1). New York: Academic Press.

Brown, J. D. (1993). Self-esteem and self-evaluation: Feeling is believing. In J. Suls (Ed.), *Psychological perspectives on the self* (Vol. 4, pp. 27-58). Hillsdale, NJ: Erlbaum.

Buri, J. R., Louiselle, P. A., Misukanis, T. M., & Mueller, R. A. (1988). Effects of parental authoritarianism and authoritativeness on self-esteem. *Personality and Social Psychology Bulletin, 14,* 271-282.

Butler, A. C., Hokanson, J. E., & Flynn, H. A. (1994). A comparison of self-esteem ability and low self-esteem as vulnerability factors for depression. *Journal of Personality and Social Psychology, 66,* 166-177.

Campbell, J. D., Trapnell, P. D., Heine, S. J., Katz, I. M., Lavallee, L. F., & Lehman, D. R. (1996). Self-concept clarity: Measurement, personality correlates, and cultural boundaries. *Journal of Personality and Social Psychology, 70,* 141-156.

Carver, C. S., & Ganellen, R. J. (1983). Depression and components of self-punitiveness: High standards, self-criticism, and overgeneralization. *Journal of Abnormal Psychology, 92,* 330-337.

Chodoff, P. (1973). The depressive personality: A critical review. *International Journal of Psychiatry, 11,* 196-217.

Crocker, J., & Wolfe, C. T. (1998). Determining the sources of self-esteem: The contingencies of self-esteem scale. Manuscript submitted for publication.

Coopersmith, S. (1967). *The antecedents of self-esteem.* San Francisco: W. H. Freeman.

Deci, E. L., & Ryan, R. M. (1985). *Intrinsic motivation and self-determination in human behavior.* New York: Plenum.

Deci, E. L., & Ryan, R. M. (1987). The support of autonomy and the control of behavior. *Journal of Personality and Social Psychology, 53,* 1024-1037.

Deci, E. L., & Ryan, R. M. (1991). A motivational approach to self: Integration in personality. *Nebraska symposium on motivation: Vol. 38. Perspectives on motivation* (pp. 237-288). Lincoln: University of Nebraska Press.

Deci, E. L., & Ryan, R. M. (1995). Human agency: The basis for true self-esteem. In M. Kernis (Ed.), *Efficacy, agency, and self-esteem* (pp. 31-50). New York: Plenum.

DuBois, D., & Tevendale, H. D. (1999). Self-esteem in childhood and adolescence: Vaccine or epiphenomenon? *Applied and Preventive Psychology, 8,* 103-117.

Dunning, D., Leuenberger, A., & Sherman, D. A. (1995). A new look at motivated inference: Are self-serving theories of success a product of motivational forces? *Journal of Personality and Social Psychology, 69,* 58-68.

Dweck, C., & Goetz, T. E. (1978). Attributions and learned helplessness. In J. Harvey, W. Ickes, & R. F. Kidd (Eds.), *New directions in attribution theory* (Vol. 2). Hillsdale, NJ: Erlbaum.

East, P. L., Hess, L. E., & Lerner, R. M. (1987). Peer social support and adjustment of early adolescent peer groups. *Journal of Early Adolescence, 7,* 153-163.

Epstein, S., & Morling, B. (1995). Is the self motivated to do more than enhance and/or verify itself? In M. H. Kernis (Ed.), *Efficacy, agency, and self-esteem* (pp. 9-30). New York: Plenum.

Farnham, S. D., Greenwald, A. G., & Banaji, M. R. (1999). Implicit self-esteem. In D. Abrams, & M. A. Hogg (Eds.), *Social cognition and social identity.* London: Blackwell.

Felson, R. B. (1984). Patterns of aggressive social interaction. In A. Mummendey (Ed.). *Social psychology of aggression: From individual behavior to social interaction* (pp. 107-126). Berlin: Springer-Verlag.

Feshbach, S. (1970). Aggression. In P. H. Mussen (Ed.), *Carmichael's manual of child psychology* (Vol. 2, pp. 159-259). New York: Wiley.

Fitch, G. (1970). Effects of self-esteem, perceived performance, and choice on causal attributions. *Journal of Personality and Social Psychology, 16*, 311-315.

Gibbs, N., & Roche, T. (December 20, 1999). The Columbine Tapes. Time Magazine.

Greenier, K. G., Kernis, M. H., & Waschull, S. B. (1995). Not all high (or low) self-esteem people are the same: Theory and research on stability of self-esteem. In M. H. Kernis (Ed.), *Efficacy, agency, and self-esteem* (pp. 51-71). New York: Plenum.

Greenier, K. G., Kernis, M. H., Whisenhunt, C. R., Waschull, S. B., Berry, A. J., Herlocker, C. E., & Abend, T. (1999). Individual differences in reactivity to daily events: Examining the roles of stability and level of self-esteem. *Journal of Personality, 67*, 185-208.

Harter. S. (1981). *A scale of intrinsic versus extrinsic orientation in the classroom.* Denver: University of Denver Press.

Harter, S. (1993). Causes and consequences of low self-esteem in children and adolescents. In R. F. Baumeister (Ed.), *Self-esteem: The puzzle of low self-regard* (pp. 87-116). New York: Plenum.

Harter, S. (1999). *The construction of the self: A developmental perspective.* New York: Guilford.

Harter, S., Stocker, C., & Robinson, N. S. (1996). The perceived directionality of the link between approval and self-worth: The liabilities of a looking glass self orientation among young adolescents. *Journal of Research on Adolescence, 6*, 285-308.

Hattie, J. (1992). *Self-concept.* Hillsdale, NJ: Erlbaum.

Horney, K. (1950). *Neurosis and human growth: The struggle toward self-realization.* New York: Norton

Hoyle, R. H., Kernis, M. H., Leary, M. R., & Baldwin, M. W. (1999). *Selfhood: Identity, esteem, regulation.* Boulder, CO: Westview.

Huebner, E. S. (1991). Correlates of life satisfaction in children. *Social Psychology Quarterly, 6*, 103-111.

Jacobson, E. (1975). The regulation of self-esteem. In E. J. Anthony & T. Benedek (Eds.), *Depression and human existence* (pp. 169-182). Boston: Little, Brown.

Kernis, M. H. (1993). The roles of stability and level of self-esteem in psychological functioning. In R. F. Baumeister (Ed.), *Self-esteem: The puzzle of low self-regard* (pp. 167-182). New York: Plenum.

Kernis, M. H., Brockner, J., & Frankel, B. S. (1989). Self-esteem and reactions to failure: The mediating role of overgeneralization. *Journal of Personality and Social Psychology, 57*, 707-714.

Kernis, M. H., Brown, A. C., & Brody, G. H. (2000). Fragile self-esteem in children and its associations with perceived patterns of parent-child communication. *Journal of Personality, 68*, 225-252.

Kernis, M. H., Cornell, D. P., Sun, C. R., Berry, A. J., & Harlow, T. (1993). There's more to self-esteem than whether it is high or low: The importance of stability of self-esteem. *Journal of Personality and Social Psychology, 65*, 1190-1204.

Kernis, M. H., & Goldman, B. (1999). Self-esteem. In D. Levinson, J. Ponzetti, & P. Jorgensen (Eds.), *Encyclopedia of human emotions.* (pp. 593-600). New York: Macmillan Library Reference.

Kernis, M. H., Grannemann, B. D., & Barclay, L. C. (1989). Stability and level of self-esteem as predictors of anger arousal and hostility. *Journal of Personality and Social Psychology, 56*, 1013-1023.

Kernis, M. H., Grannemann, B. D., & Barclay, L. C. (1992). Stability of self-esteem: Assessment, correlates, and excuse making. *Journal of Personality, 60*, 621-644.

Kernis, M. H., Grannemann, B. D., & Mathis, L. C. (1991). Stability of self-esteem as a moderator of the relation between level of self-esteem and depression. *Journal of Personality and Social Psychology, 61*, 80-84.

Kernis, M. H., Greenier, K. D., Herlocker, C. E., Whisenhunt, C. W., & Abend, T. (1997). Self-perceptions of reactions to positive and negative outcomes: The roles of stability and level of self-esteem. *Personality and Individual Differences, 22*, 846-854.

Kernis, M. H., Jadrich, J., Stoner, P., & Sun, C. R. (1996). Stable and unstable components of self-evaluations: Individual differences in self-appraisal responsiveness to feedback. *Journal of Social and Clinical Psychology, 15*, 430-448.

Kernis, M. H., & Johnson, E. K. (1990). Current and typical self-appraisals: Differential responsiveness to evaluative feedback and implications for emotions. *Journal of Research in Personality, 24*, 241-257.

Kernis, M. H., & Paradise, A. W. (in press). Distinguishing between fragile and secure forms of high self-esteem. To appear in E.L. Deci & R. M. Ryan (Eds.), *Handbook of self-determination research.* Rochester, NY: University of Rochester Press.

Kernis, M. H., Paradise, A. W., & Goldman, B. (1999). Contingent self-esteem and anger: Preliminary observations. Unpublished data, University of Georgia.

Kernis, M. H., Paradise, A.W., Whitaker, D., Wheatman, S., & Goldman, B. (2000). Master of one's psychological domain? Not likely if one's self-esteem is unstable. *Personality and Social Psychology Bulletin, 26*, 1297-1305.

Kernis, M. H., Whisenhunt, C. R., Waschull, S. B., Greenier, K. D., Berry, A. J., Herlocker, C. E., & Anderson, C. A. (1998). Multiple facets of self-esteem and their relations to depressive symptoms. *Personality and Social Psychology Bulletin, 24*, 657-668.

Kernis, M. H., & Waschull, S. B. (1995). The interactive roles of stability and level of self-esteem: Research and theory. In M. P. Zanna (Ed.), *Advances in experimental social psychology* (Vol. 27, pp. 93-141). San Diego, CA: Academic Press.

Novaco, R. W. (1975). *Anger control: The development and evaluation of an experimental treatment.* Lexington, MA: D. C. Heath.

Olweus, D. (1994). Bullying at school: Long-term outcomes for the victims and an effective school-based intervention program. In R. Huesmann (Ed.), *Aggressive behavior: Current perspectives* (pp. 97-130). New York: Plenum.

Paradise, A. W., & Kernis, M. H. (1999). Fragile self-esteem and anger reactions. Manuscript in preparation.

Paradise, A. W., & Kernis, M. H. (in press). Self-esteem and psychological well-being: Implications of fragile self-esteem. *Journal of Social and Clinical Psychology.*

Pelham, B. W. (1995). Self-investment and self-esteem: Evidence for a Jamesian model of self-worth. *Journal of Personality and Social Psychology, 69*, 1141-1150.

Roberts, J. E., & Monroe, S. M. (1992). Vulnerable self-esteem and depressive symptoms: Prospective findings comparing three alternative conceptualizations. *Journal of Personality and Social Psychology, 62*, 804-812.

Rogers, C. R. (1959). A theory of therapy, personality, and interpersonal relationships, as developed in the client-centered framework. In S. Koch (Ed.), *Psychology: A study of science* (Vol. 3, pp. 184-256). New York: McGraw-Hill.

Rosenberg, M. (1965). *Society and the adolescent self-image.* Princeton, NJ: Princeton University Press.

Rosenberg, M. (1985). Self-concept and psychological well-being in adolescence. In R. L. Leahy (Ed.), *The development of the self* (pp. 205-246). Orlando, FL: Academic Press.

Rosenberg, M. (1986). Self-concept from middle childhood through adolescence. In J. Suls & A. G. Greenwald (Eds.), *Psychological perspectives on the self.* (Vol. 3, pp. 107–135). Hillsdale, NJ: Erlbaum.

Ryan, R. M. (1993). Agency and organization: Intrinsic motivation, autonomy, and the self in psychological development. In J. Jacobs (Ed.), *Nebraska
symposium on motivation: Developmental perspectives on motivation* (Vol. 40,
pp. 1-56). Lincoln, NE: University of Nebraska Press.

Ryan, R. M., & Connell, J. P. (1989). Perceived locus of causality and internalization: Examining reasons for acting in two domains. *Journal of Personality and Social Psychology, 57,* 749-761.

Ryan, R. M., Rigby, S., & King, K. (1993). Two types of religious internalization and their relations to religious orientations and mental health. *Journal
of Personality and Social Psychology, 65,* 586-596.

Ryff, C. (1989). Happiness is everything, or is it? Explorations on the meaning of psychological well-being. *Journal of Personality and Social Psychology,
57,* 1069-1081.

Savin-Williams, R. C., & Demo, D. H. (1983). Situational and transituational determinants of adolescent self-feelings. *Journal of Personality and
Social Psychology, 44,* 824-833.

Sheldon, K. M., & Kasser, T. (1995). Coherence and congruence: Two aspects of
personality integration. *Journal of Personality and Social Psychology, 68,* 531-543.

Skaalvik, E. M., & Hagtvet, K. A. (1990). Academic achievement and self-
concept: An analysis of causal predominance in a developmental perspective. *Journal of Personality and Social Psychology, 58,* 292-307.

Tangney, J. P., Hill-Barlow, D., Wagner, P. E., Marshall, D. E., Borenstein, J.
K., Sanftner, J., Mohr, T., & Gramzow, R. (1996). Assessing individual differences in constructive versus destructive responses to anger across the
lifespan. *Journal of Personality and Social Psychology, 70,* 780-796.

Tennen, H., & Affleck, G. (1993). The puzzles of self-esteem: A clinical perspective. In R.F. Baumeister (Ed.), *Self-esteem: The puzzle of low self-regard.*
New York: Plenum.

Tevendale, H. D., DuBois, D. L., Lopez, C., & Prindiville, S. L. (1997). Self-
esteem stability and early adolescent adjustment: An exploratory study.
Journal of Early Adolescence, 17, 216-237.

Wang, A. Y. (1994). Pride and prejudice in high school gang members. *Adolescence, 29,* 279-291.

Waschull, S. B., & Kernis, M. H. (1996). Level and stability of self-esteem as
predictors of children's intrinsic motivation and reasons for anger. *Personality and Social Psychology Bulletin, 22,* 4-13.

Zumpf, C. L., & Harter, S. (1989, April). *Mirror, mirror on the wall: The relationship between appearance and self-worth in adolescent males and females.*

Paper presented at the annual meeting for the Society for Research in Child Development, Kansas City, MO.

Author Note

Michael H. Kernis, Department of Psychology and Institute for Behavioral Research, University of Georgia. Preparation of this chapter and a portion of the research reported herein were supported by National Science Foundation Grant SBR-9618882. Address correspondence to Michael Kernis, Department of Psychology, University of Georgia, Athens, GA, 30602.

II

School and the Sense of Self

4

ON ACADEMIC IDENTITY FORMATION IN MIDDLE SCHOOL SETTINGS DURING EARLY ADOLESCENCE

A Motivational-Contextual Perspective

Robert W. Roeser, Ph.D. and Shun Lau

> *Simplicity is a high form of complexity.*
> —Unknown African-American Jazz Musician

The challenge confronting jazz musicians each time they perform a piece of music is the challenge of finding a creative and workable blend between the voice of their individual solos and the ongoing music of the collective members of the band. As President Clinton put it at a White House event honoring the contribution of American blues and jazz music to the world in the 20th century, jazz musicians, like citizens in a democracy, actively strive to blend *solo* (the individual voice) and *syncopation* (the collective voice). Perhaps jazz music can be appreciated from a third-person perspective in terms of (a) the contributions of the individual soloists, (b) the contributions of the collective members of the band, and (c) that which emerges out of their *mutual interaction over time*.

The challenge confronting jazz musicians is similar to the one confronting adolescents in the United States today as they begin to search for the "voice" of their identity amidst the people, institutions, and prevailing social ethos of American society. Erik Erikson (1968) described this focal life task of adolescence, the quest for a psychosocial identity, as a process not unlike jazz music—at once individual and collective, personal and communal, biographical and historical, psychological and social, practiced and improvisational.[1] For Erikson, the music of identity development emerges from (a) adolescents' adaptive strivings to meet ego needs; (b) the collective opportunities for growth afforded them in their families, at school, and in their communities; and (c) that which emerges out of the *mutual interactions over time between adolescents and the people and activities that comprise their worlds*.

The challenge facing researchers of adolescence today is that of studying the complex process of identity formation and development during adolescence in particular activity settings such as the home, the school, and afterschool settings. Such "situated studies" can advance our scientific understanding of adolescent development and inform educational and mental health policy and practice. Addressing this challenge continues to be an important priority among those interested in human development, mental health, and clinical interventions (Cicchetti & Toth, 1996; Millstein, Petersen, & Nightengale, 1994) as well as those interested in human motivation, education, and reforms in schools (see Deci & Ryan, 1985; Eccles, Wigfield, & Schiefele, 1998; Maehr & Midgley, 1996). In this paper, we focus on one particular aspect of early adolescents' identity formation, their identity as a student, in one particular social context—the middle grades school. We describe our conception of "student identities" and research on how the context of middle grades school can shape the quality and character of early adolescents' identities as students.

A Focus on Early Adolescence and Identity Formation

Early adolescence is the time when the "symmetry" of children's life experiences is slowly "fractured" by a series of biological, psychological, and social events that precipitate adolescents' quest for a psychosocial identity. One function of the identity formation process was, according to Erikson (1950), an individual's attempts to find a new "sense of continuity and sameness" amidst many developmental changes (p. 261). During early adolescence (ages 10 to 14), many adolescents experience pubertal development. Puberty heralds changes in adolescents' physical self-image and initiates a whole new range of emotional and social experiences—interest in romance, an interest in sex, and a desire to be with peers who are undergoing similar changes. During these years, significant development and refinement of cognitive faculties such as self-awareness, perspective taking, and means-end thinking also occurs. These faculties are increasingly employed by adolescents to question everything from self to society to the nature of their relationships with significant others such as parents. Finally, early adolescents experience rapid social development following the transition to middle school. Such a transition precipitates a need for adolescents to adjust to the new academic and behavioral demands of multiple teachers, to (re)establish connections with peers, and to learn how to navigate a school environment that is larger physically and socially (Eccles, Lord, & Roeser, 1996).

All of these changes, individually and collectively, contribute to the defining life task of adolescence—the question of discovering who one is, who one belongs with, what one is good at, and where one is going in the future. Erikson (1950) described identity development during adolescence as a process, in part, in which youth reworked their childhood adaptations to childhood worlds—only this time childhood adaptations were reworked in relation to the adult worlds toward which they were rapidly growing—secondary and tertiary education, work, marriage, and civic participation. The childhood adaptations that were thought to be reworked during the identity formation process according to Erikson (1950) involved issues of relationship (e.g., trust vs. mistrust), personal autonomy (e.g., autonomy and initiative vs. guilt, shame, and doubt), and competence (e.g., industry vs. inferiority in academic and social matters). Erikson (1968) hypothesized that adolescents reworked issues of interpersonal trust in terms of the kinds of role models, cultural ideals, and social institutions in which they might now have faith; they reworked issues of personal autonomy in terms of the kinds of self-images, activities, and ideologies to which they might now freely choose to commit; and they reworked earlier issues of academic and social competence in relation to desired occupational roles in which they might expect to *excel* and future peer and romantic relationships in which they might expect to share intimacy.

Unlike his psychoanalytic predecessors, Erikson (1973) described the "quest for identity" in adolescence not as an individual, but rather a communal project. He focused attention on the idea that society's elders were responsible for providing youth with opportunities to cultivate their academic and social talents and aspirations into a meaningful life path and plan. Of this interdependence between identity formation in young people and the actions of their elders he wrote:

> an intricate relation between inner (cognitive and emotional) develop-ment and a stimulating and encouraging environment exists from the beginning of life, so that no stage and no crisis could be formulated with-out a characterization of the mutual fit of the individual's capacity to relate to an ever expanding life-space of people and institutions, on the one hand, and on the other, the readiness of people and institutions to make him part of an ongoing cultural concern. (Erikson, 1970, p. 754)

In Figure 1, we have depicted Erikson's (1970) notion that identity emerges from the interactions of the individual with people and insti-tutions using the ancient Chinese symbol T'ai-chi T'u or simply, Tao— a symbol not necessarily designed to connote an idea, but rather to motivate a contemplation (Capra, 1991). Here, we use it to motivate a contemplation of Erikson's contention that both promising and prob-lematic patterns of identity development and behavior during adoles-cence emerge, in part, from the nature of the "fit" between adolescents' ego needs and characteristics of their contemporary social worlds and society (i.e., the "social ethos"). We return to this central idea of "fit" throughout the remainder of this chapter. However, we take it up in a way Erikson never did—in the context of trying to understand identity formation not as a domain-general process during adolescence, but as a domain-specific, situated process in which adolescents develop a range of identities in relation to the specific activity settings and contexts that comprise their lifespace.

Understanding "Student Identities" in Early Adolescence

Consistent with the contextual approach to adolescent develop-ment articulated by Erikson, this chapter explores a specific aspect of identity formation during adolescence, the development of early ado-lescents' identity as a student in the context of the middle grades school. The chapter has two main goals. First, drawing upon and syn-thesizing across several different perspectives on adolescents' identity development, motivation to learn, and experience of school, we pro-pose a working definition of "positive" (e.g., engaged) and "negative" (e.g., disengaged) forms of student/academic identities. We outline a

Time

Figure 1. Representation of Erikson's (1968) notion of psychosocial identity formation as the act of synthesizing ego needs with aspects of the prevailing social ethos.

view of identity as a situated phenomena reflecting how an individual constructs a sense of him or herself in relation to the people and tasks characteristic of a particular activity setting (e.g., the classroom). The second goal of this chapter is to describe how particular pedagogical and interpersonal aspects of middle school settings can affect the forms of identities students adopt in such settings. We discuss how positive or negative forms of student identities may emerge, in part, respectively, from a fit or mismatch between adolescents' needs and the nature of their middle school learning environments (Eccles & Midgley, 1989). We conclude with some thoughts on how middle school learning environments can be designed to support adolescents' construction of a positive student identity.

Toward a Working Definition of "Student Identities"

The goal of this section is to develop working definitions of "positive" (e.g., engaged) and "negative" (e.g., disengaged) forms of student identities in

middle school. Below we describe three different perspectives on adolescence, motivation, and development: (1) one that focuses on behavioral markers of developmental success or problems during adolescence, (2) one that focuses on the motivational processes underlying
behaviors in specific activity settings, and (3) one that draws attention
to certain basic psychological needs and environmental affordances
that "motivate" and regulate behavior and development. Common to
these three perspectives is an assumption that was also at the heart of
Erikson's thinking about identity formation: that human behavior and
development are best understood in terms of an organization of personal and social contextual factors (see Figure 1). These theoretical
perspectives, premised on this assumption, are significant for the purposes of this chapter because we are interested in understanding how
different kinds of student identities are associated with different kinds
of middle school learning environments. Practically, such an understanding could be used to prescribe how middle school learning environments could be designed so as to cultivate positive student identity
formation among adolescents.

A *behavioral competence perspective*. One approach to defining promising and problematic development during adolescence involves the
identification of behaviors that promote or undermine subsequent possibilities for development, and that are deemed as "competent" or "problematic" in a particular culture at a particular point in history. Masten
and Coatsworth (1998) recently described the behavioral indicators of
competence or problematic adjustment during adolescence as defined
in contemporary Western society. Competence was defined in relation
to positive academic achievement; the following of rules, positive conduct and free-time activity involvement; and relationships with prosocial peers. Problems were defined by poor achievement; behavioral
misconduct, engagement in antisocial activities during or after school;
and affiliations with antisocial peers. From this perspective, that
which emerges out of the organization of personal and social contextual factors depicted in Figure 1 are *behavioral outcomes*. Such a conceptualization offers a clear description of the behaviors associated with
positive or negative identity formation generally during adolescence.

Motivational systems theory. Another approach to defining promising
and problematic development during adolescence involves the identification of patterns of motivation and behavior that occur in specific
contexts such as the classroom, an afterschool club, the playing field,
and so on. Ford (1992) recently presented a theory of motivation

called motivational systems theory (MST) that provides a way of studying situated patterns of motivation and behavior. In Ford's (1992) view, motivation is a context-specific, future–oriented (anticipatory) and evaluative set of psychological processes that serve to direct, evaluate, and energize an individual to act to attain a particular outcome in a particular context. In MST, motivation consists of three component processes: Personal goals which denote what a person is trying to attain (or avoid) in a particular setting; personal agency (efficacy) beliefs which are evaluations of the probability that a person can attain his or her desired goal in that setting; and emotions that provide evaluative information but also serve to energize behavior in the direction of a particular goal. These processes ready the human to act (or not), and then other instrumental processes such as skills, abilities, and self-regulatory processes are invoked to carry out desired (motivated) action sequences for which the person has readied herself. Motivation is not primarily one or another of these three processes—it is the organized patterning of all three components in relation to specific contexts and behavioral ends. The question of whether the behavioral ends toward which individuals are motivated in particular contexts are healthy or not, appropriate or not, adaptive or not, and so on is dependent on cultural, historical, social, and situational frames of reference (Ford, 1992).

Over time, Ford (1992) posits that humans develop enduring patterns of motivation (goals, efficacy beliefs, emotions) in relation to repeatedly encountered social settings (e.g., the classroom) and repeatedly pursued behavioral ends (e.g., getting good grades). In essence, what emerges out of the dialectic in Figure 1 from Ford's (1992) perspective is both behavior and individuals' construction of long-term memory structures called "behavioral event schemas" (BES). BES are integrated internal representations of thoughts, feelings, perceptions, actions, and relevant context information that are derived from repeated experiences in contexts that are defined by specific activities, people, and goal pursuits. BES serve the function of energizing and guiding (anticipating) future behavior in relation to similar activity settings or goal pursuits. BES provide guidance about what one should pay attention to and how one should be prepared to think, feel, and act in a particular setting, including new ones that resemble those that have been encountered in the past.

We believe it may be fruitful to use MST as a way of conceptualizing and operationalizing adolescents' identities in the particular setting of the middle school classroom. Patterns of motivational processes (goals, efficacy beliefs, emotions) associated with poor educational outcomes might be indicative of forms of "negative" student identities; and patterns of motivational processes associated with desirable educational outcomes might be indicative of forms of "positive" student identities. MST provides one way of conceptualizing how motivational patterns in relation to school can develop over time. During elementary school, salient school experiences and events, teachers, and the individual's history of academic success and failure cohere into enduring school-related behavioral event schemas. These schemas are also comprised of school-related goals, efficacy beliefs, and emotions. For instance, an adolescent with a history of poor achievement likely has a school-related BES characterized by low academic efficacy, goals of avoiding challenge or situations where failure seems likely, and feelings of disenchantment with learning, with self as student, and perhaps with teachers. Such situated BES, developed in classroom settings, prepare students to act, react, or withdraw in new classroom settings based on their previous experiences and academic histories. As such, school-related behavioral event schemas are presumably "carried forward" with adolescents as they enter middle school in the form of anticipatory motivational patterns associated with "doing school" or "not doing school;" "being a good student" or "not being a good student;" "being a good reader" or "hating reading;" "being good at math" or "hating math;" and so on. In short, perhaps the MST conceptualization of situated motivational patterns (BES) is a starting point for defining situated identities such as forms of student identities found among different subgroups of adolescents in middle school classrooms.

Self-determination theory. A final approach to defining promising and problematic development during adolescence involves the emergent self and behavioral outcomes that result from the "fit" or "mismatch" of environmental affordances and basic psychological needs of the person (Ryan, 1992). Self-determination theory (SDT), developed by Deci and Ryan (1985), posits three implicit needs that form the foundation of the self and that represent the core energizing sources behind human behavior and development. These hypothesized needs include the need for relatedness (e.g., Bowlby, 1988), the need for autonomy (Deci, 1975), and the need for competence (White, 1959). In SDT, positive self-development, motivation, and behavior are thought to result when environments provide affordances for individuals to fulfill these basic needs; and negative self development, motivation, and behavior are thought to result when environments serve to frustrate the fulfillment of such needs (Connell & Wellborn, 1991; Ryan, Connell, & Deci, 1989).

From an SDT perspective, what emerges out of the dialectic in Figure 1 is a self-system of beliefs and feelings associated with an individual's history of relative fulfillments or frustrations of their basic needs (Connell & Wellborn, 1991; Ryan, 1992). One way to think about the self-system is in terms of behavioral event schemas (BES) described in MST (Ford, 1992) that are organized around an individual's history of need fulfillment or frustration in particular settings. For instance, children develop school-related behavioral event schemas that record their history of relative fulfillment and frustration of their needs for relatedness, autonomy, and competence in school (Erikson, 1950). School-related BES could be operationalized in terms of the relatedness, self-determination, and competence-related goals students pursue in middle school settings, as well as their efficacy beliefs, emotions, perceptions of the environment that are related to such goal pursuits. During adolescence, school-related BES are likely to be elaborated further in terms of the perceived costs and benefits to an adolescent's emerging social identity to be good at, or fail at, school; and in terms of his or her longer-term educational and occupational aspirations (Erikson, 1968).

A Working Definition of "Student Identities"

We are now in a position to synthesize these three perspectives to arrive at a working definition of "positive" and "negative" forms of students identities among early adolescents in middle school. Conceptual correspondences between each of the perspectives we have presented are presented in Table 1 in relation to our working definitions of positive student identities (PSIs) and Table 2 in relation to our working definition of negative student identities (NSIs). Both PSIs and NSIs are conceptualized as organized, anticipatory behavioral event schemas related to school that (a) are organized around need fulfillment (PSI) or need frustration (NSI) in school settings; (b) prepare adolescents for how to think, feel, and act in those settings; (c) energize and direct either competent or problematic behaviors while in school settings; and (d) are derived from adolescents' histories of experience, academic performance, and peer relationships in school during childhood (Erikson, 1950).

Table 1

Conceptual Correspondences and Constructs Used to Define "Positive Student Identities" During Early Adolescence

Organizational Properties of Self-System ("I")	Implicit Motivational Needs / Developmental Adaptations		Psychological Processes of Self-System ("Me")			Behavioral Outcomes
			Personal Goals	Emotions	Efficacy Beliefs	
Intrapersonal differentiation	Need for competence	Sense of industry	Mastery and excellence goals	Satisfaction, pleasure, pride, interest, surprise	High mastery efficacy	Positive academic achievement
Intrapersonal integration & interpersonal differentiation (Ego synthesis)	Need for autonomy	Sense of autonomy / initiative	Individuality and self-determination goals	Curiosity, interest, excitement, surprise	High self-regulatory efficacy	Self-regulation of conduct, follows rules
Interpersonal integration (Ego synthesis)	Need for relatedness	Sense of trust and intimacy	Belongingness and social responsibility goals	Love, affection, acceptance, trust, felt security	High social efficacy	Positive relationships with teachers and peers
Deci & Ryan (1985); Erikson (1968); Ryan (1992)	*Connell & Wellborn (1991); Deci & Ryan (1985)*	*Erikson (1950; 1968)*	*Bandura (1997); Deci & Ryan (1985); Ford (1992); Lazarus (1991); McClelland (1987)*			*Masten & Coatsworth (1998)*

References:

Table 2
Conceptual Correspondences and Constructs Used to Define "Negative Student Identities" During Early Adolescence

Organizational Properties of Self-System ("I")	Implicit Motivational Needs / Developmental Adaptations		Psychological Processes of Self-System ("Me")			Behavioral Outcomes
			Personal Goals	Emotions	Efficacy Beliefs	
Lack of intrapersonal differentiation (Identity foreclosure)	Need for competence	Sense of inferiority	Task avoidance and ego avoidance goals	Downheartedness, discouragement, depression	Low mastery efficacy	Poor academic achievement
Lack of intrapersonal integration and interpersonal differentiation (Identity diffusion / foreclosure)	Need for autonomy	Sense of shame, guilt, and doubt	Compliance and defiance goals	Disinterest, boredom, apathy, guilt, shame, worry	Low self-regulatory efficacy	Lack of emotional-behavioral self-regulation, rule transgressions
Lack of interpersonal integration (Identity diffusion)	Need for relatedness	Sense of mistrust and isolation	Withdrawal and dominance goals	Loneliness, grief, fear, anger, hostility	Low social efficacy	Alienation from teachers and peers, relationships with anti-social peers
References: Deci & Ryan (1985); Erikson (1968); Ryan (1992)	Connell & Wellborn (1991); Deci & Ryan (1985)	Erikson (1950; 1968)	Bandura (1997); Deci & Ryan (1985); Ford (1992); Lazarus (1991); McClelland (1987)			Masten & Coatsworth (1998)

Positive student identity. We propose that PSIs characterize adolescents who, among other things, have a favorable history of need fulfillment in elementary school, especially a history of positive academic performance and relationships with classmates. Such histories can eventuate in adolescents who have a positive conception of themselves as a student and as someone who can work productively with classmates (Dweck, 1996; Erikson, 1950; Roeser & Eccles, 2000; Wentzel, 1996). We operationalize PSIs in terms of an adolescents' orientation toward goals in which academic mastery and excellence, behavioral self-regulation, belongingness, and social responsibility are the aims (Ford, 1992). Additionally, positive emotions related to these goals such as pride in accomplishment, task interest, and felt security while learning; and high perceived efficacy in relation to the attainment of these goals are also central to our definition of a PSI. These psychological processes in turn are hypothesized to underlie (motivate) behaviors characteristic of adolescents with positive academic identities—approach of challenging academic work, positive performance, following of classroom and school rules, and respectful relationships with classmates and teachers. Subjectively, we assume adolescents with a PSI experience a sense of intellectual confidence, a commitment to learning; and a desire to pursue higher education and certain occupational directions.

Negative student identity. Table 2 presents our conceptualization and operationalization of negative student identities (NSIs). We propose that NSIs characterize adolescents who, among other things, have a history of need frustration in elementary school, especially a history of academic failure and difficulties in relationships with classmates. Such histories can eventuate in adolescents who have a sense of helplessness or angry defensiveness in the academic domain (see Dweck & Leggett, 1988; Roeser & Eccles, 2000) and a sense of isolation, incompetence, or victimization in relationships with classmates (Dweck, 1996; Erikson, 1950; Parker & Asher, 1987). We operationalize NSIs in relation to an adolescent's orientation toward goals in which refusal to complete work, withdrawal from academic activities due to a fear of appearing incompetent, a disproportionate desire to please or rebel against authority, and a desire to withdraw from or aggress against classmates or teachers are the aims. In addition, negative emotions associated with these goals such as discouragement, apathy, loneliness or anger; and poor efficacy in relation to the mastery of academic tasks, the regulation of behavior, and relating to others in the classroom are also part of our conception of NSIs (see Dweck, 1996; Roeser & Eccles, 2000; Wentzel, 1996). These psychological processes in turn are hypothesized to underlie (motivate) behaviors characteristic of adolescents with negative academic identities—poor achievement, withdrawal or misconduct in the classroom, and aloof or disrespectful relationships with teachers. Subjectively, we assume adolescents who adopt an NSI have a sense of intellectual incompetence, frustration with themselves as students and perhaps, their teachers, "loosening bonds" with the institution of school, and diminishing aspirations for educational attainments over the long term.

Summary. The development of an identity during adolescence requires the reworking of childhood themes of relatedness, autonomy, and competence in relation to the kinds of adult roles and social contexts adolescents are increasingly involved in and moving towards. We proposed that middle school is an important context within which to study one particular aspect of early adolescents' identity formation—their developing conceptions of themselves as students. We proposed that adolescents' identities as students in middle school are reflected in the kinds of goals, efficacy beliefs, and emotions that characterize them as they go about interacting with peers and teachers in and between their classes during the school day. These goals, we assumed, are organized around needs for competence, autonomy, and relatedness. We also assumed that an important aspect of early adolescents' "student identities" was their evolving aspirations concerning education (e.g., college) and certain occupations (Erikson, 1968). In addition to this psychological view of identity, we also proposed that adolescents' student identities are revealed in the kinds of behaviors they display in school—their academic performance, their participation in classroom learning activities and the life of the school more generally, their in-school conduct, and the quality of their relationships with classmates and teachers. Finally, we linked together the psychological and behavioral conceptions of a "student identity" we presented—suggesting that "student identities" are organized anticipatory patterns of how adolescents might think, feel, and act while in school. These patterns, we proposed, predict manifest patterns of behavior in school and are derived from adolescents' unique histories of school experience and academic performance in childhood (see Eccles et al., 1998).

Our conceptualization of what a "student identity" is draws historical notions of organizational properties of the self (Ryan, 1992); psychological needs and developmental tasks (Deci & Ryan, 1985; Erikson, 1950), motivational patterns (Ford, 1992), and behaviors (Masten & Coatsworth, 1998) together into a single conception of a situated identity. As we discuss in the next section, by defining the particular kinds of behaviors, motivational processes underlying those behaviors, and specific needs around which motivational processes are organized in school settings, we have a rather useful heuristic model with which to examine the question of how educators in middle grades schools can, through provisions of particular pedagogical and social opportunities that address adolescents' basic needs and goals, cultivate positive academic identity formation and behavior among the greatest number of students.

A Focus on Middle Grades Schools

Middle grades schools have been hailed as one of the most important institutions within which millions of American youth who are at risk for unproductive and unsatisfying lives can be recaptured and helped (Carnegie Council, 1989). Many youth, often because of conditions such as poverty, abuse or neglect in the home, and disorganized schools and neighborhoods, are probabilistically more likely to show declining grades, motivational problems, mental health problems, or engagement in problem behaviors during the early adolescent years (Dryfoos, 1990; Jessor, 1993; Roderick, 1994). For instance, it is estimated that approximately 25% of all 10- to 17-year-olds in the United States are behind their "modal grade" in school (see Dryfoos, 1990); up to 20% of all students are retained a grade at least once in their academic careers (see Durlak, 1995); and, depending on ethnic group, between 8% and 25% of youth will not complete high school (NCES, 1997).[2] Epidemiological studies yield estimates that between 12% and 30% of school-aged children and youth have moderate to serious emotional-behavioral difficulties that can interfere with their daily functioning in and outside of school and that can eventuate in curtailed educational attainments during adolescence (Institute of Medicine, 1994; Kessler, Foster, Saunders, & Stang, 1995). Many academic and social-emotional problems worsen during the early adolescent period, making this time in the life course what some have called a "turning point" (Carnegie Council on Adolescent Development, 1989).

Early adolescents' motivation to learn, level of achievement, and identity as a student are powerful marker variables that probabilistically forecast later life outcomes. For example, some studies show that these variables differentiate those early adolescents who are on promising pathways of development leading to college enrollment and later occupational success from those who are already on problematic pathways leading toward delayed graduation or failure to graduate from high school (Eccles, Lord, Roeser, Barber, Jozefowicz-Hernandez, 1997; Roderick, 1994); delayed entry to college (Roeser & Peck, 2000), and involvement in delinquent activity, pregnancy, and substance use/abuse in later adolescence (Dryfoos, 1990). Can educators cultivate adolescents' motivation to learn and identification with school by the ways in which they design middle school learning environments, and thereby direct more adolescents onto favorable developmental pathways?

Two Perspectives on Middle Grades Schools

The goal of this section is to describe two perspectives on how particular pedagogical and interpersonal aspects of middle school classrooms and the school as a whole can affect the forms of identities students adopt in school. First, we discuss how positive or negative forms of student identities may emerge, in part, respectively, from a fit or mismatch between adolescents' needs and the nature of their middle school learning environments (Eccles & Midgley, 1989). In this section, we describe a synthesis of motivational perspectives that, together, provide a means of theoretically linking features of school environments with what we have termed varieties of "student identities" (Figure 2). This synthesis is meant to provide a framework for capturing the organization of adolescents' identity within and subjective experience of one particular, important, developmental context: the middle grades school (Figure 1). Second, we map this "first-person perspective" onto a more "third-person perspective" on middle school environments in an effort to prescribe what middle school educators can actually do to cultivate adolescents' motivation to learn, identification with the role of student, and achievement-related behavior during these years (Figure 3).

A Motivational Perspective on Middle Grades Learning Environments and Student Identities

The research summarized in Tables 1 and 2 suggest that the most motivating learning environments are those that are structured to

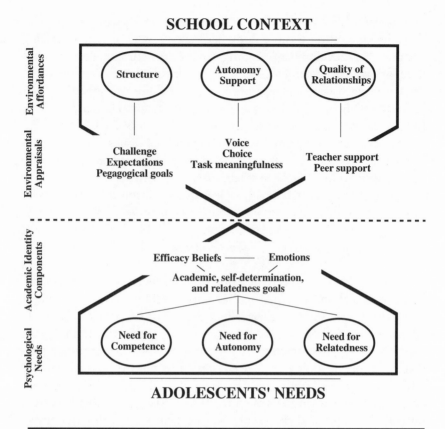

Derived from Bandura, 1997; Connell & Wellborn, 1991; Deci & Ryan, 1985; Ford, 1992

Figure 2. Motivational model linking school environmental affordances, academic identity components, and adolescents' psychological needs.

provide opportunities in which early adolescents can fulfill basic needs and attain goals associated with the development of academic competencies, the exercise of personal control over aspects of the learning environment in middle school, and participation in productive, respectful, and helpful relationships with classmates and teachers. What kinds of learning environments can assist adolescents in meeting such needs and attaining such goals?

Figure 2 presents a motivational model linking specific dimensions of learning environments, those labeled "structure," "autonomy support," and "quality of relationships" with components of adolescents' student identities, which are in turn linked to what are hypothesized to be adolescents' basic needs. This model is derived from the ideas of several motivational theorists who hypothesize that individuals attend to and make meaning of their social environments in terms of how those environments serve to frustrate or allow for the fulfillment of basic psychological needs (Deci & Ryan, 1985; Connell & Wellborn, 1991; Eccles & Midgley, 1989; Lazarus, 1991; Ryan, 1992). To the extent that clearly defined, challenging opportunities exist for adolescents to develop their academic competencies in a context of felt care and autonomy in their middle school classrooms, they should be more likely to identify positively with the role of student, espouse growth- and mastery-oriented goals, feel efficacious in relation to the demands of school, and enjoy their experiences in school (Eccles & Midgley, 1989; Midgley, 1993; Ryan et al., 1985). On the other hand, to the extent that middle school settings are characterized by a lack of clear goals, low levels of academic challenge, desultory curricula, teacher control, and a lack of positive student-teacher and student-student relationships, then adolescents should be more likely to assume a negative student identity, espouse nonacademic goals, feel inefficacious in school, and feel alienated or bored while in school (Eccles et al., 1993; Roeser, Eccles, & Sameroff, 2000). Note that the model presented in Figure 3 resembles Erikson's notion discussed earlier that promising and problematic patterns of identity development and behavior during adolescence emerge, in part at least, from the nature of the "fit" between adolescents' needs and characteristics of their contemporary social worlds (see Figure 1).

One useful way to understand the model presented in Figure 3 is by means of a thought experiment. Specifically, it is useful to imagine adolescents (implicitly) asking themselves questions about their experiences in middle school, questions linked to their quest for fulfilling basic needs and pursuing certain goals as they go about their school day. In this way, the social-contextual factors that affect different patterns of achievement behavior and forms of student identities among different adolescents may become more comprehensible.

Structure. For example, associated with the need for competence, we imagine early adolescents in middle school settings wondering: "What are the teachers' goals? I am clear on what I am expected to do and how to proceed? Does this work challenge my abilities? How am I progressing?" "What kind of feedback am I getting on how well I am doing in this class?" The term "structure" refers to features of the learning environment that can scaffold adolescents' competence development. These features can include challenging tasks, opportunities for assisted performances, and teachers who articulate clear academic and behavioral goals and expectations. Environments characterized by appropriate structure can build adolescents' sense of academic mastery efficacy through progressive mastery of challenging tasks, socialize students to adopt certain academic and behavioral goals and meet certain academic and behavioral expectations, and strengthen adolescents' feelings of pride in a job well done (Brophy, 1988; Connell & Wellborn, 1991; Deci & Ryan, 1985; McClelland, 1987).

Support of autonomy. Associated with the need for autonomy, we imagine early adolescents sometimes wonder in their classes—"Do our teachers really care about what students think?" "Can I express my opinions in this class?" "How does what I am learning relate to my own values, interests, and experiences?" Classroom features that support student autonomy include teachers' elicitation of broad patterns of student participation in classroom discussions; their provision of opportunities for students to participate in classroom decisions and make choices regarding aspects of their assignments and projects; and their teaching of curricula that speak to the developmental, cultural, and contemporary interests of early adolescents. Teachers' support of student autonomy in the middle school classroom can promote students' adoption of academic mastery and self-regulation goals, enhance students' feelings of belonging in the classroom, and nurture subject matter values and interests (Ames, 1992; Eccles et al., 1993; Goodenow, 1993).

Quality of relationships. Associated with the need for relatedness, a need that is especially intense during adolescence, we image early adolescents asking themselves at school: "Do I feel cared for and respected as a person by classmates, teachers, and administrators? Do I view my teachers as role models and do I feel that I can go to them in times of need?" "Are students respectful of one another?" "Am I given opportunities to work with students in productive ways here?" The use of small houses in which adolescents have extended contact with a small number of teachers and students throughout the day, the presence of themes of care in the curriculum, the creation of a school culture where conflict resolution skills are employed to settle disputes, the use of cooperative learning techniques, and the small things that teachers do on a daily basis (e.g., greet students at the door) are some of the relationship-linked features of middle school settings that promote adolescents' adoption of a positive student identity in middle school. Specifically, these practices are known to enhance students' affective experience of and bonding to school, classmates, and teachers (e.g., Felner et al., 1993; Hawkins,1997; Roeser, Midgley, & Urdan, 1996; Solomon, Watson, Battistich, Schaps, & Delucchi, 1992).

A Mismatch of Middle School Environments and the Needs of Youth

Unfortunately, many of the kinds of opportunities associated with structure, autonomy support, and quality relationships that would support adolescents' fulfillment of needs and attainment of related goals in middle school, and thereby promote positive academic identity formation and behavior, are often lacking. Indeed, there is evidence to suggest that the academic and social contexts of many middle grades schools in fact can promote negative academic identity formation and behavior, especially among students who transition into middle grades school with a history of academic difficulties in elementary school (Eccles, Midgley, & Adler, 1984; Eccles et al., 1993).

Eccles and Midgley (1989) developed the idea that perhaps the negative changes in various indicators of motivation, achievement, and mental health that occur around the time adolescents make the transition into junior high school happened at that particular time for a reason. Specifically, they argued that such changes might result, in part at least, from a "mismatch" between the kinds of developmental needs early adolescents had and the kinds of academic and social opportunities characteristic of the school settings into which they were transitioning. The needs Eccles and Midgley (1989) described as characteristic of early adolescents are very similar to those presented in Tables 1 and 2, except for the fact that these authors framed them in terms of "needs for specific kinds of environmental opportunities." Specifically, Eccles and Midgley (1989) suggested that early adolescents need (a) a relatively noncomparative, noncompetitive academic setting for developing their academic competencies because they are quite self-conscious during puberty and other self-related changes characteristic of early adolescence; (b) opportunities for decision making given their burgeoning intellectual capacities and desire for increased personal autonomy; (c) continuity in classmates during the school day in order to facilitate friendship formation; and (d) extended contact with teachers due to their increasing emotional autonomy from parents and concomitant need for non-parental role models.

In their review of the literature concerning changes in adolescents' adjustment and school experiences before and after the junior high school transition, Eccles and Midgley (1989) found that many of the changes in the school context that adolescents experience across this transition resulted in a "mismatch" with their developmental needs. For instance, Eccles and Midgley (1989) found evidence that junior high school teachers provided less challenging work, emphasized social comparison and competition more, provided fewer opportunities for student autonomy, and were less trusting and more controlling of students compared to the adolescents' elementary school teachers. Furthermore, they found that peer networks were disrupted during this transition due to the increased size of the junior high school and the practice of having students shift among many teachers and classmates during the school day. The conclusion of this review was that:

> the environmental changes often associated with the transition to junior high school seem especially harmful in that they emphasize competition, social comparison, and ability self-assessment at a time of heightened self-focus; they decrease decision-making and choice at a time when the desire for control is growing; they emphasize lower level cognitive strategies at a time when the ability to use higher level strategies is increasing; and they disrupt social networks at a time when adolescents are especially concerned with peer relationships and may be in special need of close adult relationships outside the home. (Eccles et al., 1993, p. 94)

The work of Eccles and Midgley (1989) provides a "menu" of things not to do if we wish to cultivate positive academic identity development and behavior among adolescents in the middle grades school settings. In addition, it has contributed important ideas in defining what "developmentally appropriate" educational settings for early adolescents look like (see Hechinger, 1993). Unfortunately, research conducted since the time of their review has suggested that many early adolescents in this country continue to transition into middle grades schools that are ill-matched with their developmental needs, although some improvements may be occurring in this regard (e.g., Felner, Favazza, Shim, Brand, & Gu, in press; Midgley & Edelin, 1998). In the next section, we return to the motivational perspectives described earlier and to our working definitions of "student identities" as a way of focusing attention on some of the specific practices middle school educators can implement in order to promote positive student identity formation, academic performance, and aspirations for college among early adolescents.

A Multilevel Descriptive Model of Middle Schools

The goal of this last section is to discuss particular classroom and school-level practices that middle school educators can implement to promote adolescents' need fulfillment in school, and thereby their identification with the role of "student" (see Figure 2). In order to translate the conceptions of "structure," "autonomy support," and "quality relationships" into a description of specific practices, at specific levels of the school context, that educators can implement, we begin this section by presenting a heuristic model of the middle school environment. Figure 3 depicts a descriptive model of middle school environments that draws attention not to the psychological affordances of the environment (see Figure 2), but rather to the actual people, pedagogical practices, and organizational processes that create such psychological affordances.

In Figure 3 we have depicted the middle grades school environment as a set of hierarchical and interdependent levels of organization. In this description of the context of middle level schools, we assume that (1) schools are systems characterized by multiple levels of organized processes (interpersonal, instructional, and organizational in nature); (2) levels of organization in school systems are more or less interdependent; (3) the processes that characterize different levels are more or less dynamic in nature, sometimes being worked out each moment between social actors (e.g., teachers teaching students); and (4) these processes "develop" or change as children move through different school levels (elementary, middle, and high school; see Eccles & Roeser, 1999, for details).

In the next section, we describe particular practices that occur at different levels of the middle school environment as depicted in Figure 3 that are known to relate to aspects of what we have called "positive student identities" (see Table 1). It is important to note at this point that none of the practices we describe below, in the absence of a change in what Sarason (1990) called the "school culture," will likely create lasting effects on students. What has become clear from decades of school reform efforts is that unless such reforms create a school culture that exists for promoting the development of students and teachers alike, a culture where both teachers and students can meet their basic needs for feeling competent, supported by others, and autonomous in relation to their work; then many of the educational practices we describe below will be like seeds falling on hard soil (e.g., Felner et al., in press; Sarason, 1990; Ryan & LaGuardia, 1999). Reforms in middle grades schools need to be schoolwide, focus on creating motivating and supportive environments for students and teachers alike, and need to address the daily practices of teaching and learning that are at the core of the school mission (Cuban, 1990; Maehr & Midgley, 1991).

Level I: Providing Challenging and Meaningful Academic Work

Academic work is at the heart of the academic endeavor and thus, changes in curriculum and the design of instruction can have immediate and enduring influences on students' goals, efficacy beliefs, task-related interests and values, skill acquisition, and knowledge development (see Eccles et al., 1998, for review). Challenging and meaningful work is essential for getting adolescents engaged in learning. Eccles and Midgley (1989) reviewed some evidence that showed the academic work assigned in the early grades of junior high school is sometimes less challenging than the work students were exposed to the year before in elementary school. Although the research is sparse in this area, a lack of challenging work may be one reason why boredom is one of the most common emotions among students in the classroom (Larson & Richards, 1991). In addition, given the press for standardized testing today (Ryan & LaGuardia, 1999), it may be that the level of academic challenge is diminished as teachers attempt to prepare students for the memorization of information often required by such tests.

Teachers' provision of not only challenging, but *meaningful* classroom work is also critical to motivating adolescents to learn. Task meaningfulness can refer to learning activities that have personal, developmental, sociocultural, or pop-cultural relevance to adolescents; to those that are characterized by cognitive aesthetics (e.g., ideas can be beautiful and therefore appealing), or to those that are justified as relevant by adults who adolescents respect and wish to please (e.g.,

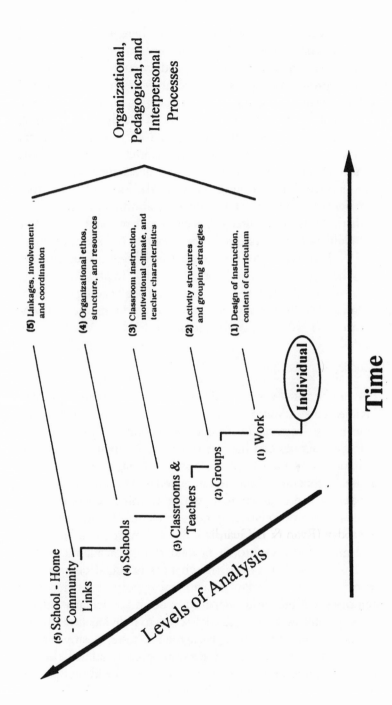

Figure 3. Descriptive model of the middle school ecology.

their parents or teachers, Blumenfeld, 1992). There is some evidence to suggest that when mathematics addresses real world problems, social studies covers material that is applied to contemporary issues, and literature representing diverse viewpoints is assigned, adolescents have more opportunities to connect their emerging identities with the academic content of their classes and value what they are learning more over time (Banks, 1993; Roeser et al., 2000). Interdisciplinary curricula that explore contemporary issues related to biotechnology, population growth and climate change, ecological destruction, interethnic contact, and the exploration of space are the kinds of topics that can help students to connect what they are learning in school in the present with the kinds of challenges, social problems, and issues they will face as adults in the future (see Jackson, Felner, Millstein, Pittman, & Selden, 1993). Fostering connections between what adolescents are learning in school with the "adult worlds" they live in and are growing toward outside of the school is the core challenge of educating early adolescents today, no less than it has been for educators during the past century (Dewey, 1902/1990; Blos, 1941; Hechinger, 1993).

Level II: Cooperative Learning

Another important aspect of middle school classrooms that can promote adolescents' adoption of positive academic identities is the use of cooperative learning techniques. Cooperative and heterogeneous grouping practices can harness the social motivation that is so prevalent among early adolescents for purposes of mastering academic competencies. Cooperative and heterogeneous grouping techniques have consistently been shown to enhance learning outcomes, self-esteem, and interethnic relations among students of different social statuses; and can diversify the dimensions upon which students form their friendships in the classroom beyond that of academic ability (Slavin & Fashola, 1998). Given the changes in social demography characteristic of America today, educational opportunities that promote interethnic contact and cooperation seem particularly important. Such opportunities can expose adolescents to individuals of diverse socioeconomic, racial, and cultural backgrounds, foster positive interethnic contact and friendships, and generally prepare adolescents for the kinds of social interactions they are likely to have in work, community, and recreational settings in the future.

Level III: Providing Effective and Motivating Academic Instructional Climates

Effective teaching practices. Equally important as *what* is taught in middle school is *how* subject matter is taught. Several decades of research have yielded a menu of teaching practices that are particularly effective in enhancing students' learning and achievement (Brophy, 1988). These practices include teachers' clear explication of the goals of their instruction and their expectations concerning appropriate classroom conduct; their choice of tasks that are at an appropriate level of challenge for a given class; their design of learning activities such that they require adolescents to employ a diverse set of cognitive operations (e.g., opinion, following routines, memory, comprehension); their structuring of lessons such that they build on each other in a systematic fashion, their explicit teaching of learning and problem-solving strategies; and their use of contingent praise and formative feedback that assist students in understanding their academic progress. These kinds of practices foster adolescents' skill and knowledge development, strengthen their academic efficacy beliefs, and promote consequent emotions such as pride in a job well done (see Bandura, 1997; Blumenfeld, 1992; Brophy, 1988; Ford, 1992; McClelland, 1987).

Provision of tutors. For students with a history of academic difficulties, challenging and meaningful work and effective instruction may not be enough to get them back on track academically. The use of tutors and other supplemental educational services in middle school is essential to helping vulnerable students overcome motivational problems and skill deficits that can lead to serious behavioral problems if not checked and remediated (Hawkins, 1997; Slavin & Fashola, 1998). Tutors that teach specific problem-solving and comprehension monitoring strategies are particularly effective with academically "at-risk" students because such students often do not spontaneously develop these strategies on their own (Brophy, 1988). Additionally, creating opportunities for both high and low achieving middle school students to tutor younger students who need academic help can enhance middle schoolers' sense of social responsibility and efficacy in helping others, as well as the tutored children's own academic skills and sense of mastery efficacy (Carnegie Council, 1989). In this way, tutoring programs in middle school can be situated within a larger school ethos in which academic mastery and helping others to learn are valued norms. Such a schoolwide ethos promotes the idea that "add-on" tutoring programs for middle schoolers are about insuring that all are learning and progressing up to their potential, rather than about isolating those who are "at risk," "behind" and so on.

Mastery-oriented classroom climate. In addition to providing challenging and engaging curriculum, using effective teaching techniques, and making supplemental educational services available to students who need them, middle school educators can also cultivate motivation, positive student identities, and learning by creating classroom climates that emphasize the "improve-ability" of adolescents' skills, knowledge, and abilities in a subject area through effort investment, persistence, use of effective learning strategies, and a commitment to progressive mastery regardless of their current level of achievement. Such classroom climates have been linked to students' adoption of academic mastery goals, positive academic efficacy beliefs and valuing of subject matters, enjoyment of learning and school more generally, and the use of deep processing learning strategies (Ames, 1992; Midgley, 1993).

The creation of mastery-oriented classroom climates rests first and foremost on a teacher's provision of challenging and meaningful tasks. In addition, teachers can create a "mastery-oriented" classroom through the kinds of things they say to students about the goals of learning, the recognition and feedback techniques they employ, and their support of student autonomy in the classroom. Mastery-oriented teachers emphasize the value of effort, persistence, and mastery; and describe the *improving* of skills and understanding rather than the *proving* of one's ability relative to other students as the "true" goals of learning in the classroom. Such teachers tell students that progressively improving their performance, investing effort, persisting after difficulty, making mistakes, seeking help, and trying alternative problem solving strategies when encountering problems are "what learning is all about" (Ames, 1992; Midgley, 1993). In terms of recognition and feedback practices, mastery-oriented teachers recognize effort and improvement over time, provide formative feedback, and allow students opportunities for revision of work to insure that content is ultimately mastered. In terms of autonomy support, mastery-oriented teachers create instruction in which students can assume some control over aspects of the learning process. Specifically, such teachers elicit student opinions in classroom discussions, provide opportunities for students to participate in classroom decision-making, and allow students to pursue projects and assignments that build on their interests and talents. By supporting autonomy in these ways, teachers communicate a sense of care to students, help them to learn how to self-regulate their learning, and promote a broad range of student relationships in the classroom as people begin to talk to and work with one another (e.g., Epstein, 1983; Roeser et al., 1996; Ryan et al., 1989). Teachers who create mastery-oriented classrooms through their pedagogy are creating learning environments that "fit" early adolescents' need for a noncomparative, noncompetitive space in which to develop their skills, knowledge, and other subject matter-specific competencies (Ames, 1992; Anderman & Maehr, 1994; Eccles et al., 1993; Maehr & Midgley, 1991; Midgley, 1993).

Level IV: An Academic-Oriented and Orderly School Culture

The fourth level of the model in Figure 3 concerns the organizational practices that define the school as a whole. The culture of the school as a whole can influence students' academic identity formation above and beyond the influences of adolescents' experiences in specific classrooms (Maehr, 1991; Rutter, 1983; Sarason, 1990). Through the principal's leadership, the use of symbolic measures and particular kinds of school-wide assemblies and recognition practices, and the creation of and enforcement of behavioral norms and rules, administrators and teachers can create a school-wide climate that assists students in clearly understanding what is expected of them both academically and behaviorally in school (see Good & Weinstein, 1986; Maehr & Midgley, 1991). Such structure is an important input to students' competence development and their identities as students more generally (see Figure 2).

One important feature of the school culture that has more or less indirect effects on student identities and performance is an explicit sense of mission. Bryk, Lee, and Holland (1993), for instance, discuss how the culture within Catholic schools is fundamentally different from the culture within most public schools. Specifically, they describe the culture of Catholic schools as promoting a clear emphasis on academics, the belief that all students can learn, and the notion that it is the business of schools to promote learning among all students. Clearly such schools try hard to get students to adopt a decidedly positive *academic* identity in school.

Another important dimension of the school culture concerns the creation and maintenance of a safe and orderly environment where rules are enforced in a fair and consistent manner. Such consistency can afford students a sense of security, surety, and safety (Rutter, 1983). Relatedly, school leaders who create an intellectually and emotionally safe school climate by having an explicit set of norms and rules that eschew sexism, racism, and any behavior predicated upon mistaken beliefs or societal biases can also positively affect students' motivation, learning, and well-being while in school (Lee, Cronninger, Linn, & Chen, 1996; Roeser et al., 2000; Tatum, 1997). Such norms provide important messages to students about responsible and respectful ways of interacting socially in school, and about issues of equity and democracy in the larger culture more generally. In sum, aspects of the whole school culture can serve to focus students on specific academic, behavioral, and social goals, promote an ethos of learning and community, and help to reduce rates of academic failure and behavioral misconduct (Hawkins, 1997; Maehr, 1991; Rutter, 1983; Solomon et al., 1992).

Level IV: Organizational Enabling Mechanisms

Many of the practices we have just described are the "wine" of effective middle school learning environments. Some types of reform efforts, however, focus on creating new "wine bottles" in middle school—those structural arrangements that provide the contexts within which pedagogical practices are delivered and social relationships cultivated. In essence, these structural arrangements "enable" other reforms to occur in the school (Midgley & Urdan, 1992), and include transition programs, schools-within-schools, advisory periods, block scheduling, and common planning time for teachers (Carnegie Council, 1989). Because the transition into middle grades school can be particularly stressful for young people occurring as it does at the same time as other biopsychosocial changes (Simmons & Blyth, 1987), and involving a move into what is often a larger, more bureaucratic, and less personal school setting (Eccles & Midgley, 1989), these types of arrangements "enable" adolescents to forge relationships with classmates and teachers more easily upon arrival in middle school; and provide opportunities for teachers to work collaboratively in creating educational environments that fit with the needs of young people.

Felner and his colleagues (1993), for instance, enacted a school transition environment project (STEP) around the junior and high school transitions. Structural reforms were initiated in the intervention schools in a manner that provided students in this condition with (a) a coherent set of classmates in a core set of team-taught classes during the year following the transition into the new school setting, (b) an advisory period/homeroom teacher with whom they could share concerns and seek guidance, and (c) a set of classes in close physical proximity to each other in the new school setting. Students in the control conditions made transitions into schools without these structural arrangements. In the evaluation of the STEP program, Felner and colleagues (1993) reported that adolescents participating in the transition programs in which smaller, less complex, and more sheltered school-within-school type environments were created were less likely to show the normative declines in academic grades, attendance, and self-concept that are usually found across these transitions (see Eccles et al., 1998). Another important finding from the STEP evaluation study was that students *not involved* in the program reported that the school environment was less stable, understandable, and supportive following the transition event. Finally, students not participating in the transition program were more likely to drop-out of school in subsequent years (Felner et al., 1993).

These findings and others recently reported by Felner and his colleagues (in press) suggest the importance of providing structural arrangements in middle schools that allow adolescents to remain with a smaller number of teachers and peers during the day. This seems to promote general "bonding" with the institution of school and helps students to feel that someone cares about them and their learning (see Hawkins, 1997). Such practices, if coupled with common planning time and team-teaching approaches for teachers, may also promote teachers' motivation. Practices such as common planning time and team-teaching may provide teachers with needed support for curriculum development, with responsibility for teaching fewer students, and relatedly, with more opportunities to share information about and to get to know their students in a personal way. In short, such practices may prove beneficial for students and teachers alike (Carnegie Council on Adolescent Development, 1995). We believe that middle school reforms involving the new wine of changes in curriculum and pedagogy, and the new wine bottles of structural rearrangements that support pedagogical and social innovations are both important and necessary.

Level V: Links Between Schools, Parents, and Community Organizations

The fifth level of the model in Figure 3 concerns the formal and informal linkages schools have with members of and agencies in the community. It is well documented that parent involvement in their child's schooling is an important factor in promoting academic success during childhood and adolescence (Eccles & Harold, 1993; Epstein, 1994). Parent involvement communicates positive educational expectations to the child, enhances his or her identification with learning and school, and contributes to a "safety net" of concerned adults (parents and teachers) who can support adolescents' academic and social-emotional development and assist them if problems arise. Unfortunately, evidence suggests that home-school connections are relatively infrequent during the elementary years and become almost nonexistent during the middle and high school years (e.g., Carnegie Council, 1995; Eccles & Harold, 1993). Building closer ties with parents through school gatherings, newsletters, programs to teach parents basic skills and ways of tutoring their children, and through other strategies that include parents in the daily life and governance of the school can be important features of highly effective schools (Good & Weinstein, 1986; Slavin & Fashola, 1998).

Closer ties between middle schools and community-based organizations (CBOs) are also very important during early adolescence, a time when youth engagement in problem behavior after school begins to rise, especially among those with nothing productive to do after school (Carnegie Corporation, 1992). School-CBO ties can help insure that middle school students have wholesome, growth-oriented, and structured afterschool activities to go to where they can interact with peers in prosocial ways, spend time with adult role models, and develop their talents and interests in a safe and supportive setting. To build such ties between school and afterschool programs, school buildings themselves can be used as afterschool activity centers (e.g., Dryfoos, 1998). In addition, educators and CBO youth workers could build bridges between their respective programs and collaborate in efforts to enhance positive youth development (see Bryce-Heath & McLaughlin, 1996).

Building a network of opportunities and adults who can support adolescents learning within and outside of the schools is the long-term goal of positive youth development efforts that take a holistic environmental perspective, and that aim to maximize the number of adolescents who stay in school, graduate, and aspire to go to college (e.g., Jessor, 1993; Larson, 2000; McLaughlin & Irby, 1994).

Summary

In sum, many of the practices that can transform middle school learning environments into developmentally supportive places are known to affect the kinds of beliefs, goals, emotions, and salient developmental needs that underlie our working definition of positive student identity discussed earlier (see Table 1). At the heart of all of these practices, if they are to be effective, are caring educators and community members who consistently reinforce the message that schools exist for the growth and development of teachers and students alike; that academics are at the center of the school's mission; that all children can learn, graduate from high school, and attend college; and that the cultivation of life-long learners is the central goal of the school in a democratic society (Sarason, 1990).

Jazz and Concluding Thoughts

The goals of this chapter were twofold. First, drawing upon and synthesizing across several different perspectives on adolescents' identity development, motivation to learn, and experience of school, we proposed a working definition of "positive" (e.g., engaged) and "negative" (e.g., disengaged) forms of student/academic identities. We defined adolescents' "student identities" as organized motivational schemas, developed in significant measure from their histories of school experience and academic performance in childhood, that are activated and serve to guide and direct their behavior in middle school learning settings and in relation to their longer-term educational and occupational goals. Second, we described how particular pedagogical and interpersonal aspects of middle school learning environments affect, in part, the forms of identities students adopt in school. We discussed how positive or negative forms of student identities emerge, in part, respectively, from a fit or mismatch between adolescents' needs and the nature of the academic and social affordances that characterize their middle school (Eccles & Midgley, 1989). Together, the two foci of this chapter were meant to illustrate how promising and problematic patterns of academic motivation and achievement behavior during early adolescence emerge, in part, as a function of (a) early adolescents' adaptive strivings to fulfill basic ego needs in the school setting; (b) the kinds of academic and social opportunities middle school educators afford adolescents in relation to their needs; and (c) that which emerges out of interactions over time between adolescents, their classroom activities, and their teachers and classmates in middle schools that provide more or less developmentally appropriate opportunities for adolescents to fulfill their developmental needs and attain their goals.

In comparing adolescents' identity formation in the particular context of school to the creation of jazz music through the dialectic of *solo* and *syncopation*, we meant to highlight the idea that adolescents, like soloists in a jazz ensemble, have a need to find their own individual voice (identity) and express it, but need to do so within the context of an ongoing collective concern that welcomes their participation and contributions. We focused on particular practices that middle school educators can use to create middle school environments in which adolescents feel safe to explore their competencies and interests, and at the same time can feel connected to others through shared activity. Specifically, we discussed pedagogical practices such as the provision of challenging and meaningful academic work, the creation of mastery-oriented classroom climates, the use of cooperative learning, and the maintenance of an academically focused, orderly, and just school culture. In this context, we also mentioned the importance of building and maintaining a school culture that exists for the development of students and teachers alike, and in which students and teachers alike can develop their competencies, take risks, try new things, and feel supported by others in the process of doing so. We also discussed structural changes such as the creation of "schools-within-schools" that can enable students to more easily establish ties with peers and teachers, especially following the transition into middle school; and that can also foster collaborative relationships among teachers in a school. Finally, we discussed the importance of creating linkages between middle schools, families, and community-based organizations. As Erikson

(1968) noted, successful adolescent development is a communal rather than single-institution or personal project.

In summary, the features of the middle school environment that we focused on in this chapter can all serve to strengthen adolescents' academic identities by (a) fulfilling their psychological needs in healthy, growth-oriented ways; (b) providing connections between what they learn in school and their larger quest for a psychosocial identity in the world that exists beyond the walls of the school; and (c) affording them opportunities to develop their skills and knowledge with teachers and peers in ways that cultivate their longer-term educational and occupational aspirations.

Although we focused in this chapter on how educators might promote positive identity development in young people, it is also important to remind ourselves that educators can also have their identities shaped by the young people in their care. Perhaps true education during adolescence requires a "growing together" of adult teachers and their adolescent students. Erikson (1973) wrote about his vision of the interdependence between successful youth and adult development in a 1973 Jefferson Lecture Series talk:

> From the point of view of development, I would say: In youth you find out what you *care to do* and who you *care to be*—even in changing roles. In young adulthood you learn whom you *care to be with*—at work and in private life, not only exchanging intimacies, but sharing intimacy. In adulthood, however, you learn to know what and whom you can *take care of* . . . what in Hinduism is called the maintenance of the world, that middle period of the life cycle when existence permits you and demands you to consider death as peripheral and to balance its certainty with the only happiness that is lasting: to increase, by whatever is yours to give, the good will and the higher order in your sector of the world. (p. 124)

Often, in writings such as these, Erikson suggested that the developmental life task of society's elders involves, in part, assisting young people in progressing along fruitful educational, social, and moral lines of development that eventuate in their full participation in an ongoing cultural concern. The concomitant developmental tasks of society's youth, Erikson suggested, involved their taking of responsibility for developing an identity and for exploring relevant opportunities to do so; their co-creating and perpetuating of society in conjunction with their elders; and sometimes, their reshaping of the future direction of society in spite of them (Erikson, 1958, 1969; Mead, 1970). In this way, Erikson repeatedly returned to the idea that promising or problematic patterns of identity development and behavior during adolescence were always a conjoint function of (a) adolescents' adaptive strivings to fulfill ego needs in relation to adult roles and institutions; (b) the opportunities afforded adolescents by the adults in their life space; and (c) that which emerged out of the mutual interactions over time between adolescents and the activities and adults that comprised their social worlds. From an intergenerational point of view, we might say that successful adolescent and adult development mutually reinforce one another. Extending this idea, we might say that the most effective and developmentally appropriate middle grades schools are those that cultivate the healthy development of adolescents and the adults that serve them *simultaneously*.

Although adolescent development today is fraught with risks that have not existed at other times in history (Carnegie Council, 1989), we believe that there exist several timeless principles that elders can follow in their attempts to cultivate successful identity development in young people both within and outside of the school setting. Furthermore, we believe that these principles have been well captured by the theories of human motivation and development we reviewed earlier. These theories set forth the idea that adolescents have basic needs and related goals that, when fulfilled and attained, support healthy self development, motivation, and behavior. These needs include a need for the development of skills, knowledge, and abilities that are linked to the "real" (adult) world; a need for caring and supportive relationships with peers and adults alike during this exciting period of exploration and growth; and a need for "structured autonomy" in which different self-images, interests, and ideologies can be "explored" and "tried on" by adolescents in safe, supervised activity settings.

By helping adolescents frame culturally meaningful academic and social goals and develop the strategies for realizing them; by providing them with challenging and meaningful activities; by giving them formative feedback on how well they are doing in relation to personally and socially valued goals; and by providing support and care as they progress towards attaining such goals, educators and other adults do a great deal to assist adolescents in developing healthy senses of themselves as students, as future members of society, and as whole individuals who can envision and attain productive and fulfilling lives.

References

Ames, C. (1992). Classrooms: Goals, structures, and student motivation. *Journal of Educational Psychology, 84*, 261-271.

Anderman, E. M., & Maehr, M. L. (1994). Motivation and schooling in the middle grades. *Review of Educational Research, 64*, 287-309.

Bandura, A. (1997). *Self-efficacy: The exercise of control.* New York: Freeman and Company.

Banks, J. A. (1993). Multicultural education: Historical development, dimensions, and practice. In L.Darling-Hammond (Ed.), *Review of research in education* (Vol. 19, pp. 3-49). Washington, DC: American Educational Research Association.

Bateson, M. C. (1990). *Composing a life.* New York: Plume.

Blos, P. (1941). *The adolescent personality: A study of individual behavior.* New York: Appleton-Century Co.

Blumenfeld, P. C. (1992). Classroom learning and motivation: Clarifying and expanding goal theory. *Journal of Educational Psychology, 84*, 272-281.

Bowlby, J. (1988). *A secure base: Parent-child attachment and healthy human development.* New York: Basic Books.

Brophy, J. (1988). Research linking teacher behavior to student achievement: Potential implications for instruction of Chapter 1 students. *Educational Psychologist, 23*, 235-286.

Bryce-Heath, S., & McLaughlin, M. W. (1996). The best of both worlds: Connecting schools and community youth organizations for all-day, all-year learning. In J.G. Cibulka & W.J. Kritek (Eds.), *Coordination among schools, families, and communities: Prospects for educational reform* (pp. 69-93). Albany: State University of New York Press.

Bryk, A. S., Lee, V. E., & Holland P. B. (1993). *Catholic schools and the common good.* Cambridge, MA: Harvard University Press.

Capra, F. (1991). *The tao of physics.* Boston: Shambhala.

Carnegie Corporation of New York (1992). *A matter of time: Risk and opportunity in the nonschool hours.* New York: Carnegie Corporation of New York.

Carnegie Council on Adolescent Development. (1989). *Turning points: Preparing American youth for the 21st century.* New York: Carnegie Corporation.

Carnegie Council on Adolescent Development. (1995). *Great transitions: Preparing adolescents for a new century.* New York: Carnegie Corporation.

Cicchetti, D., & Toth, S. L. (1996). *Rochester symposium on developmental psychopathology: Vol. 7. Adolescence: Opportunities and challenges.* Rochester, NY: University of Rochester Press.

Connell, J. P., & Wellborn, J.G. (1991). Competence, autonomy and related-ness: A motivational analysis of self-system processes. In M. Gunnar & A. Sroufe (Eds.), *Minnesota symposium on child psychology* (Vol. 23, pp. 43-77). Hillsdale, NJ: Erlbaum.

Cuban, L. (1990). Reforming again, again, and again. *Educational Researcher, 19*, 3-13.

Deci, E. (1975). *Intrinsic motivation.* New York: Plenum.

Deci, E., & Ryan, R. (1985). *Intrinsic motivation and self-determination in human behavior.* New York: Academic Press.

Dewey, J. (1902/1990). *The child and the curriculum.* Chicago: The University of Chicago Press.

Dryfoos, J. (1998). *Safe passage: Making it through adolescence in a risky society.* New York: Cambridge University Press.

Dryfoos, J. G. (1990). *Adolescents at risk: Prevalence and prevention.* New York: Oxford University Press.

Durlak, J. A. (1995). *School-based prevention programs for children and adoles-cents.* Thousand Oaks, CA: Sage.

Dweck, C. S. (1996). Social motivation: Goals and social cognitive process. A comment. In J. Juvonen & K.R. Wentzel (Eds.), *Social motivation: Under-standing children's school adjustment* (pp. 181-195). New York: Cambridge University Press.

Dweck, C. S., & Leggett, E. (1988). A social-cognitive approach to motiva-tion and personality. *Psychological Review, 95*, 256-273.

Eccles, J. S., & Harold, R. D. (1993). Parent-school involvement during the early adolescent years. *Teachers' College Record, 94*, 568-587.

Eccles, J. S., Lord, S., & Roeser, R. W. (1996). Round holes, square pegs, rocky roads, and sore feet: A discussion of stage-environment fit theory applied to families and school. In D. Cicchetti & S.L. Toth (Eds.), *Rochester sympo-sium on developmental psychopathology: Vol. 7. Adolescence: Opportunities and challenges* (pp. 47-92). Rochester, NY: University of Rochester Press.

Eccles, J. S., Lord, S., Roeser, R. W, Barber, B., & Josefowicz-Hernandez, D. (1997). The association of school transitions in early adolescence with developmental trajectories through high school. In J. Schulenberg, J. Maggs, & K. Hurrelmann (Eds.), *Health risks and developmental transitions during adolescence.* New York: Cambridge University Press.

Eccles, J. S., & Midgley, C. (1989). Stage-environment fit: Developmentally appropriate classrooms for young adolescents. In C. Ames & R. Ames (Eds.), *Research on motivation in education: Vol. 3, Goals and cognitions* (pp. 13-44). New York: Academic Press.

Eccles, J. S., Midgley, C. & Adler, T. (1984). Grade-related changes in the school environment: Effects on achievement motivation. In J. Nicholls (Ed.), *Advances in motivation and achievement* (Vol. 3, pp. 283-331). Greenwich: JAI Press Inc.

Eccles, J. S., Midgley, C., Wigfield, A., Buchanan, C. M., Reuman, D., Flanagan, C., & MacIver, D. (1993). Development during adolescence: The impact of stage-environment fit on adolescents' experiences in schools and families. *American Psychologist, 48*, 90-101.

Eccles, J. S., & Roeser, R. W. (1999). School and community influences on human development. In M. H. Boorstein & M. E. Lamb (Eds.), *Developmental psychology: An advanced textbook.* (2nd ed., pp. 503-554). Hillsdale, NJ: Erlbaum.

Eccles, J. S., Wigfield, A., & Schiefele, U. (1998). Motivation to succeed. In W. Damon (Ed.), N Eisenberg (Series Ed.), *Handbook of Child Psychology: Vol. 3. Social, emotional, and personality development* (5th ed., pp. 1017-1095). New York: Wiley.

Epstein, J. L. (1983). Selection of friends in differently organized schools and classrooms. In J. L. Epstein & N. Karweit (Eds.), *Friends in school: Patterns of selection and influence in secondary schools* (pp. 73-92). New York: Academic Press.

Epstein, J. L. (1994, November). *Perspectives and previews on research and policy for school, family, and community partnerships.* Paper presented at the Family-School Links Conference, Pennsylvania State University.

Erikson, E. H. (1950). *Childhood and society.* New York: W.W. Norton & Company.

Erikson, E. H. (1958). *Young man Luther.* New York: W.W. Norton & Company.

Erikson, E. H. (1968). *Identity, youth and crisis.* New York: W.W. Norton & Company.

Erikson, E. H. (1969). *Ghandi's truth.* New York: W.W. Norton & Company.

Erikson, E. H. (1970). Autobiographic notes on the identity crisis. *Daedalus, 99,* 730-759.

Erikson, E. H. (1973). *Dimensions of a new identity.* New York: W.W. Norton & Company.

Felner, R. D., Brand, S., Adan, A. M., Mulhall, P. F., Flowers, N., Sartain, B., & DuBois, D. L. (1993). Restructuring the ecology of the school as an approach to prevention during school transitions: Longitudinal follow-ups and extensions of the School Transitional Environment Project (STEP). In L. A. Jason, K. E. Danner, & K. S. Kurasaki (Eds.), *Prevention and school transitions* (pp. 103-136). New York: Haworth Press.

Felner, R. D., Favazza, A., Shim, M., Brand, S., & Gu, K. (in press). Whole school improvement and restructuring as prevention and promotion: Lessons from Project STEP and the Project on High Performance Learning Communities. *Journal of School Psychology.*

Ford, M. E. (1992). *Motivating humans: Goals, emotions, and personal agency beliefs.* Newbury Park, CA: Sage Publications.

Good, T. L., & Weinstein, R. S. (1986). Schools make a difference: Evidence, criticisms, and new directions. *American Psychologist, 41,* 1090-1097.

Goodenow, C. (1993). Classroom belonging among early adolescent students: Relationships to motivation and achievement. *Journal of Early Adolescence, 13,* 21-43.

Hawkins, J. D. (1997). Academic performance and school success: Sources and consequences. In R. P. Weissberg, T. P. Gullotta, R. L. Hampton, B. A. Ryan, & G. R. Adams (Eds.), *Enhancing children's wellness: Vol. 8. Issues in children's and familys' lives* (pp. 278-305). Thousand Oaks, CA: Sage.

Hechinger, J. (1993). Schools for adolescents: An historic dilemma. In R. Takanishi (Ed.), *Adolescence in the 1990s: Risk and opportunity* (pp. 64-81). New York: Teachers College Press.

Institute of Medicine (1994). *Reducing risks for mental disorders: Frontiers for preventive intervention research.* Washington, DC: National Academy Press.

Jackson, A. W., Felner, R. D., Millstein, S. G., Pittman, K. J., & Selden, R. W. (1993). Adolescent development and educational policy: Strengths and weaknesses of the knowledge base. *Journal of Adolescent Health, 14,* 172-189.

Jessor, R. (1993). Successful adolescent development among youth in high-risk settings. *American Psychologist, 48,* 117-126.

Kessler, R. C., Foster, C. L., Saunders, W. B., & Stang, P. E. (1995). Social consequences of psychiatric disorders, I: Educational attainment. *American Journal of Psychiatry, 152,* 1026-1032.

Larson, R. W., & Richards, M. H. (1991). Boredom in the middle school years: Blaming schools versus blaming students. *American Journal of Education, 99,* 418-433.

Larson, R. W. (2000). Toward a psychology of positive youth development. *American Psychologist, 55,* 1170-183

Lazarus, R. S. (1991). *Emotion and adaptation.* New York: Oxford University Press.

Lee, V. E., Croninger, R. G., Linn, E., & Chen, X. (1996). The culture of sexual harassment in secondary schools. *American Educational Research Journal, 33,* 383-417.

Maehr, M. L. (1991). The "psychological environment" of the school: A focus for school leadership. In P. Thurstone & P. Zodhiates (Eds.), *Advances in Educational Administration* (Vol. 2, pp. 51-81). Greenwich, CT: JAI.

Maehr, M. L., & Midgley, C. (1991). Enhancing student motivation: A school-wide approach. *Educational Psychologist, 26*, 399-427.

Maehr, M. L., & Midgley, C. (1996). *Transforming school cultures to enhance student motivation and learning.* Boulder, CO: Westview Press.

Masten, A. S., & Coatsworth, J. D. (1998). The development of competence in favorable and unfavorable environments: Lessons from research on successful children. *American Psychologist, 53*, 205-220.

McLaughlin, M. W., & Irby, M. A. (1994). Urban sanctuaries. Neighborhood organizations that keep hope alive. *Phi Delta Kappan, 76*, 300-306.

McClelland, D. C. (1987). *Human motivation.* Cambridge: Cambridge University Press.

Mead, M. (1970). *Culture and commitment: A study of the generation gap.* Garden City, NY: Natural History Press.

Midgley, C. (1993). Motivation and middle level schools. In M. L. Maehr & P. Pintrich (Eds.), *Advances in motivation and achievement: Vol. 8. Motivation and adolescent development* (pp. 217-274). Greenwich, CT: JAI Press.

Midgley, C., & Edelin, K. C. (1998). Middle school reform and early adolescent well-being: The good news and the bad. *Educational Psychologist, 33*, 195-206.

Midgley, C. M., & Urdan, T. (1992). The transition to middle level schools: Making it a good experience for all students. *Middle School Journal, 24*, 5-14.

Millstein, S.G., Petersen, A. C., & Nightingale, E. O. (1994), *Promoting the health of adolescents: New directions for the twenty-first century* . New York: Oxford University Press.

National Center for Educational Statistics (1997, March). *Findings from education and the economy: An indicators report.* (NCES-97-939).

Parker, J. G., & Asher, S. R. (1987). Peer relations and later personal adjustment: Are low-accepted children at risk? *Psychological Bulletin, 102*, 357-389.

Roderick, M. (1994). Grade retention and school dropout: Investigating the association. *American Educational Research Journal, 31*, 729-759.

Roeser, R. W., & Eccles, J. S. (2000). Schooling and mental health. In M. Lewis & A. J. Sameroff (Eds.), *Handbook of developmental psychopathology*, (2nd ed., pp. 135-156). New York: Plenum.

Roeser, R. W., Eccles, J. S., & Sameroff, A. J. (2000). School as a context of early adolescents' academic and social-emotional development: A summary of research findings. *Elementary School Journal, 100*, 443-471.

Roeser, R. W., Midgley, C. M., & Urdan, T. C. (1996). Perceptions of the school psychological environment and early adolescents' psychological and behavioral functioning in school: The mediating role of goals and belonging. *Journal of Educational Psychology, 88*, 408-422.

Roeser, R. W. & Peck, S. (2000, April). *On life space configurations in the prediction of adolescents' educational attainments and mental health.* Paper presented at the Biennial Meeting of the Society for Research on Adolescence, Chicago, IL.

Rutter, M. (1983). School effects on pupil progress: Research findings and policy implications. *Child Development, 54*, 1-29.

Ryan, R. M. (1992). Agency and organization: Intrinsic motivation, autonomy, and the self in psychological development. In J. E. Jacobs (Series Ed.), *Nebraska symposium on motivation: Developmental perspectives on motivation* (pp. 1-56). Lincoln, NE: University of Nebraska Press.

Ryan, R. M., Connell, J. P., & Deci, E. L. (1985). A motivational analyses of self-determination and self-regulation in education. In C. Ames & R. Ames (Eds.), *Research on motivation in education: Vol. 2. The classroom milieu* (pp. 13-51). Orlando, FL: Academic Press.

Ryan R. M., & La Guardia, J. (1999). Achievement motivation within a pressured society: Intrinsic and extrinsic motivations to learn and the politics of school reform. In T. Urdan (Ed.), *Advances in motivation and achievement: Vol. 11. The role of context* (pp. 45-85). Stamford, CT: JAI Press.

Sarason, S. B. (1990). *The predictable failure of school reform.* San Francisco: Jossey-Bass.

Simmons, R. G., & Blyth, D. A. (1987). *Moving into adolescence: The impact of pubertal change and school context.* Hawthorn, NY: Aldine de Gruyler.

Slavin, R. E., & Fashola, O. S. (1998). *Show me the evidence! Proven and promising programs for America's schools.* Thousand Oaks, CA.: Corwin Press.

Solomon, D., Watson, M., Battistich, V., Schaps, E., & Delucchi, K. (1992). Creating a caring community: Educational practices that promote children's prosocial development. In F.K. Oser, A. Dick, & J.L. Patry (Eds.), *Effective and responsible teaching: The new synthesis.* San Francisco: Jossey-Bass.

Tatum, B. D. (1997). *Why are all the Black kids sitting together in the cafeteria?* New York: Basic Books.

Wentzel, K. R. (1996). Social goals and social relationships as motivators of school adjustment. In J. Juvonen & K. R. Wentzel (Eds.), *Social motivation: Understanding children's school adjustment* (pp. 226-247). New York: Cambridge University Press.

White, R. H. (1959). Motivation reconsidered: The concept of competence. *Psychological Review, 66*, 297-333.

Endnotes

1. We were intrigued to find recently, after writing this introduction, that Mary Catherine Bateson, daughter of Gregory Bateson and Margaret Mead, in her 1989 book entitled *Composing a Life*, proposed that life could be viewed as an improvisational art; and that improvisational arts involved "recombining partly familiar material in new ways, often in ways especially sensitive to context, interaction, and response" (p. 2). She then went on to tell a story from her own adolescence when she was exposed to the improvisational arts:

> When I was teenager, I used to go to the house of my mother's sister Liza and hear her son, the jazz flutist Jeremy Steig, playing and practicing with his friends, jamming in the back room, varying and revarying familiar phrases. "Practicing improvisation" was clearly not a contradiction. Jazz exemplifies artistic activity that is at once individual and communal, performance that is both repetitive and innovative, each participant sometimes providing background support and sometimes flying free. (Bateson, 1989, pp. 2-3)

Conceptualizing identity development as "practicing improvisation" certainly seems to capture well Erikson's (1968) contention that identity formation among adolescents involved the apparently contradictory notions of "sameness and continuity" as well as a certain novelty and creativity—the latter two qualities were explored most deeply in Erikson's writings on the lives of Martin Luther (Erikson, 1958) and Mohatma Gandhi (Erikson, 1969).

2. African Americans, Latinos, Native Americans, and members of certain other immigrant groups are much more likely to withdraw early from school than their white peers, as are children who experience one or more grade retentions.

5

THE ECOLOGY OF MIDDLE GRADES SCHOOLS AND POSSIBLE SELVES

Theory, Research, and Action

Peggy Clements and Edward Seidman

How do middle grades schools affect the development of early adolescent identity? Similarly, how do contemporary reforms in middle grades schools affect early adolescent identity development? What kinds of school reform are likely to maximize early adolescent identity development? The current chapter addresses these three questions.

For the past several decades researchers and practitioners have recognized that early adolescence, with the myriad of developmental changes it encompasses, is not well served by the typical middle grades school environment. In spite of the fact that numerous recommendations have been made regarding the restructuring of schools at this level and numerous reform efforts have been undertaken, the consensus is that these efforts generally have not been successful in creating learning environments that will foster and promote early adolescents' active engagement and learning in school. As other adolescent researchers have suggested, the negative changes adolescents experience upon entering middle-level schools are due, at least in part, to the structure and social climate of these schools. Our primary objective for this chapter is to make the argument that precipitous declines in early adolescents' academic performance and interest in school during this important phase of identity development may well have a lasting impact on their self-concepts as learners and thinkers. Moreover, we postulate that these changes in young peoples' self-concepts as learners and thinkers influence their expectations for their future possible selves as well as the actual preparation needed for them to envision, achieve, and successfully fulfill their adult roles as workers and constructive members of society.

The goals of this chapter are several. First, in order to frame the special needs and circumstances of early adolescents, we briefly outline the wide range of developmental changes that take place during this period. In the second section, we describe the typical structure of middle grades schools and the research that has investigated the association between school-level characteristics and student outcomes. We are concerned with the physical structure and organization of middle grades schools (e.g., size), as well as the social regularities among teachers and students. By social regularities we are referring to the patterns of social relations that typify interactions between the members of a setting, in this case a school (Seidman, 1988; Sarason, 1971, 1982). In the third section of this chapter, we summarize the evidence regarding the typically negative adjustments students experience after moving into middle grades schools and the recommendations for restructuring these school environments. In the fourth section, we outline a framework to explain the decline in academic performance and well-being. In the final section, we review some of the recent middle grades school reform efforts that appear not only to have prevented the negative behavioral and emotional changes that often accompany early adolescents' transition into middle grades school, but may actually promote increases in their learning and academic engagement.

Developmental Changes in Early Adolescence

Early adolescence is commonly viewed as an especially sensitive period of development—not only do multiple changes take place, but the rate of development is extraordinarily rapid. During the early adolescent years (ages 10 to 14) many significant biological, cognitive, emotional, and social changes take place. Probably the most noticeable changes, at least for the observer, are the biological changes that accompany puberty. Not only is the rate of physical growth during early adolescence greater than at any other point in life other than infancy, but the development of secondary sex characteristics occurs during this time for many young people.

Simultaneous shifting social roles also impact young adolescents. Relationships with same- and opposite-sex peers become increasingly important at the same time that relationships with family members—especially parents—are changing. While the values and beliefs of adolescents and their parents may not actually differ as much as popular conceptions of the "generation gap" may suggest (Gecas & Seff, 1990), early adolescents often do have different personal tastes than their parents (regarding, for example, dress, music, and leisure activities) and feel entitled to make decisions regarding these issues. These are the kinds of issues around which adolescent-parent conflicts often develop (Smetana, 1988, 1989).

While the biological and social changes discussed above are certainly important aspects of early adolescent development, the changes among the most critical to the issue of middle grades schooling are cognitive. The cognitive developments characteristic of early adolescence include the ability to think multidimensionally and the ability to think hypothetically—to think about not only what *is* but what is *possible* (Keating, 1990). These changes are important for early adolescents in two critical ways. First, they have implications for students' intellectual development in that they make it possible for students to approach problems in a more critical, analytic, hypothetical, and in-depth way. Second, in the same way that young people can think differently about external events/situations, they can think hypothetically about themselves and their future possibilities and options. Coinciding with all of the changes that result in early adolescents appearing more mature and thinking about their futures as adults is the fact that they want to be treated in a more "grown-up" way as well and begin to desire greater autonomy and more responsibility in decision making in many areas of their life, including what goes on in school (Steinberg, 1990).

Identity development is considered the primary internal task facing adolescents (Erikson, 1968). While there is no single agreed upon definition of what exactly identity is, researchers have generally approached identity in one of three ways: (1) by examining *self-concepts*, one's ideas regarding their various traits and attributes; (2) examining *self-esteem*, how positively or negatively one feels about him- or herself; and (3) *sense of identity* or one's sense of who one is, where one comes from, and where one is going (Steinberg, 1996). Our discussion of middle grades schooling and identity development will include all three of these conceptualizations of identity. We will return to the issue of identity development—especially as it relates to the development of "possible selves"—after describing what is known about the structure of middle grades education and its relation to early adolescent development.

The Organization and Social Regularities of Middle Grades Schools

In this section, we will identify the organizational structure and social regularities of middle grades schools that distinguish them from elementary schools, and then review the research regarding the associations between these characteristics and student outcomes. Before beginning, it is important to note that while many early adolescence researchers have pointed to the larger and more complex structure of middle grades schools as being at least partly responsible for the negative adjustment of early adolescents, relatively few studies following students as they make the transition from elementary to middle grades school have directly examined the relationship between the change in school environments and student outcomes. Most researchers interested in examining the impact of the middle grades school environment on student outcomes have done so by looking for change in students' well-being over the course of the school transition, attributing any negative changes to the organization and social regularities of the new school environment. However, in spite of the fact that most studies investigating the adjustment difficulties of middle grades students have not included measurements of these social regularities in their analyses, there is a body of research (independent of the school transitions studies) that has examined the relationships between these school characteristics and student outcomes. This research demonstrates quite clearly that the organization and social regularities of middle grades schools are indeed associated with negative developmental outcomes. While some of the studies in this section focus specifically on middle grades schools, the research presented in this section is intended to review the school research more generally.

Size

Students moving from elementary to middle grades school often encounter a larger and more chaotic school environment; typically students from several elementary schools move into a single middle grades school. Compounding the social complexity of these schools is the fact that most students in middle grades schools switch rooms, teachers, and classmates multiple times a day (although in some schools students from the same homeroom move together from one class to the next). In addition, teachers in these schools are generally more departmentalized, teaching the same subject to several groups of students all day long. As a result, they may be more committed to their subject matter and department than to the school as a community.

Researchers have suggested that this type of middle grades school structure is problematic for at least two reasons. One problem is that early adolescents in the midst of a developmentally critical period in which multiple changes are taking place, including puberty and the increasing importance of peer relationships, must suddenly try to navigate a complex school social structure (Felner, Brand, Adan, Mulhall, Flowers, Sartain, & DuBois, 1993). A second complication is that school staff in typical large and impersonal middle grades schools may not have either the awareness of or the ability to help adolescents experiencing problems at school (Eccles, Flanagan, Lord, Midgley, Roeser, & Yee, 1996).

There is a sizable literature investigating the role of school size on academic achievement, academic attitudes, and school involvement suggesting that larger schools are less advantageous for children and adolescents. Miller, Ellsworth, and Howell (1986) found that among elementary schools with students from low socioeconomic backgrounds, higher reading achievement levels were associated with small school size. A study of secondary schools found that school size was negatively related to students' standardized test scores, even after controlling for socioeconomic factors (Fowler & Walberg, 1991). However, it should be noted that not all studies examining the impact of school size have found a connection to academic outcomes. For example, one study of secondary school students found no relation between school size and a number of school-related outcomes, including academic achievement (Rutter, Maughan, Mortimore, Ouston, & Smith, 1979).

Other studies, while not examining academic achievement per se, have examined other school-related outcomes such as attitudes toward school and involvement in school activities. Examining high school students, Barker and Gump (1964) found greater rates of school involvement and higher self-reported feelings of competence for students in small schools, most markedly for marginal students. A subsequent study found similar relationships between school size and students' attitudes about school at the elementary school level (Morracco, 1978).

In addition to the literature that has investigated the effects of school size on student well-being more generally, two school transition studies have systematically examined the role of school size and its relation to student adjustment following the transition from elementary to middle grades school. Simmons and Blyth (1987) found that transitioning into a larger junior high school was associated with decreases in self-esteem. In this study, all students made the transition considered to be the typical shift in school size: moving from a smaller elementary to a larger junior high school. In a second study, Australian students made the transition from primary schools (grades 1-7) to secondary schools (grades 8-12), but the transition in this study was not always from a smaller to larger school (Cotterell, 1992). As a result, Cotterell categorized study participants into groups according to the sizes of schools attended and the type of change in school size encountered. He found that the students who experienced the biggest relative shift in school size (going from a small school to a larger school) experienced the new classroom social environment as more demanding—in terms of difficulty, speed, and teacher favoritism—immediately following the transition.

Tracking

One of the most significant social regularities characteristic of almost all middle grades schools is academic ability tracking. It begins in earnest at this level of schooling, with approximately 80% of schools using some degree of ability grouping (Epstein & MacIver, 1990; Valentine, Clark, Irvin, Keefe, & Melton, 1993). The educational objective of tracking is to facilitate instruction and to increase learning by providing a structure in which teachers can tailor their instruction to the ability level of students. Advocates of ability-based grouping believe that creating classrooms in which there is a match between students' abilities and the level of instruction maximizes the efficiency and effectiveness of the teaching that takes place.

In her review of the research on tracking, Hallinan (1994) concludes that a number of rigorous empirical studies have supported some of the beliefs about tracking, but contradicted others. She identifies three primary conclusions regarding the impact of tracking on student outcomes. First, tracking provides higher tracked students with more advantageous learning environments; both the quality and the quantity of instruction increase with the level of the track. More specifically, the materials and curriculum of the higher tracks are more interesting than that of lower tracks, and less time is spent on administrative and disciplinary tasks in the higher track classrooms. (Hallinan does point out, however, that the relationship between instructional quality and track level varies across schools.) Second, the research indicates that tracking is more academically advantageous for students in higher tracks. They learn more and at a faster pace than their peers in lower tracks. Finally, it appears that tracking provides no advantage (or disadvantage) in achievement over heterogeneous grouping for students in the middle-ability ranges (Hallinan, 1994; Oakes, Gamoran, & Page, 1992; Slavin, 1987). Given that the evidence also demonstrates that minority and low-income students are more likely to be assigned to lower tracks, even after controlling for achievement level, Hallinan goes on to suggest that the disadvantages of tracking may disproportionately affect students that are from low-income or minority race/ethnic groups. Other researchers conclude that academic tracking leads to negative self-perceptions among lower ability students (Carnegie Council on Adolescent Development, 1989; Stevenson, 1992). Given that early adolescence is such an important period of identity development, these more negative self-perceptions may well result in long term damage to academic self-concepts.

Classroom Practices and Teacher-Student Relations

Several other instruction and evaluation practices become more common in middle grades schools. For example, middle grades teachers are more likely to utilize whole class instruction practices (as opposed to small-group and individualized instruction), more rigorous grading criteria, and more frequent public evaluation of class work (Eccles & Midgley, 1989). Eccles and her colleagues have pointed out that practices such as these create an environment in which students are more likely to engage in social comparisons regarding their academic abilities (Eccles, Midgley, & Adler, 1984) and suggest that for students who are less advanced academically than their peers, this comparison may well negatively impact their perceptions of their academic abilities and ultimately their motivation for and engagement in school.

Teachers' expectations of their students and relationships between teachers and students in middle grades school are markedly more negative than those in elementary schools in a number of meaningful ways. An important series of studies by Midgley, Eccles, and Feldlaufer have identified a number of these changes. First, teachers in middle grades schools emphasize control and discipline more, and provide fewer opportunities for student choice and decision-making than teachers in elementary schools (Midgley, Feldlaufer, & Eccles, 1988; Midgley & Feldlaufer, 1987). This is in spite of the fact that early adolescents are at a stage in which they desire greater autonomy and an expanded role in decision-making regarding what is going on in their lives. In fact, compared to elementary-level students, students in their first year of middle grades schools report a greater degree of incongruence between the amount of autonomy they desire and the opportunities they perceive in their classrooms (Midgley & Feldlaufer, 1987). Additionally, these researchers have also found that both students and outside observers report that junior high school math teachers are less friendly, supportive, and caring than elementary school teachers (Midgley, Feldlaufer, & Eccles, 1989). Finally, middle grades teachers report lower levels of trust for their students than teachers in the last year of elementary school (Midgley et al., 1988).

Researchers have found that these kinds of negative social regularities between teachers and students influence student academic outcomes and their perceptions of school. Weinstein and her colleagues have demonstrated that teacher expectations have a significant impact on student performance, and that when students are consciously aware of negative teacher expectations, their performance is even more significantly undermined (Alvidrez & Weinstein, 1999; McKown & Weinstein, in press; Weinstein, 1989; Weinstein & McKown, 1998). Researchers have also found that the change in perceived teacher supportiveness students experience after the transition to a middle grades school is related to changes in the extent to which students value mathematics. Specifically, students who moved from math teachers they perceived as being high in support to teachers they perceived as being low in support reported a decrease in how much they valued math, while students who experienced the opposite pattern (moving from less to more supportive teachers) reported an increase in how much they valued math (Midgley et al., 1989).

Multidimensional and Holistic Effects of Classrooms and Schools

Other researchers examining the impact of the classroom environment have taken a more holistic approach, simultaneously including a number of factors that may influence a students' classroom experience. A study of third, fourth, and fifth graders (Waxman, Huang, Anderson, & Weinstein, 1997) compared schools characterized as effective/efficient and ineffective/inefficient. For this study, efficiency was defined as how well resources such as teacher-student ratios, teacher experience, expenditure per student, student mobility and attendance were being used to improve achievement test scores. Effectiveness scores were generated by regressing the current year's achievement test scores on prior year's achievement test scores and determining to what extent student performance was outpacing what the previous year's scores would have predicted. Researchers found that students in the ineffective/inefficient schools reported more negative perceptions of their school environments, as well as lower levels of engagement compared to students in the effective/efficient schools. Specifically, they viewed their teachers as less supportive, felt less affiliation with classmates, and reported being less involved in their schools.

Roeser and Eccles' (1998) study of adolescents' perceptions of their school environment is another example of a study that assessed multiple aspects of the environment simultaneously. They found that when students had more positive perceptions of the school environment, in terms of perceiving both positive teacher regard and an emphasis on individual effort and improvement, students' academic values, self-concept, and achievement increased from the seventh to the eighth grade (Roeser & Eccles, 1998). In other research, Griffith (1995) found that teacher instruction, involvement, and support (labeled instrumental "social action" by the author) interacted with students' experience of the school's organizational structure to predict higher academic performance as measured by standardized test scores.

Midgley, Maehr, and their colleagues have focused on the policies and practices, what they refer to as the "goal structure," of middle grades schools and classrooms (Anderman & Maehr, 1994; Midgley, Anderman, & Hicks, 1995). Their research compares the use of "task" goals to the use of "performance" goals in schools and classrooms. Task goals, which research indicates are more typical of elementary school classrooms, are characterized by emphases on effort, improvement, mastery, and understanding. In contrast, performance or "achievement" goals, which Midgley, Maehr, and colleagues have found are more characteristic of middle grade schools and classrooms, emphasize the demonstration of ability along with comparing relative ability between students. A number of studies have demonstrated that the extent to which a task goal structure or an achievement goal structure is stressed is related to student motivation and attitudes toward school work. More specifically, a perceived emphasis on task mastery has been demonstrated to be associated with students' use of more effective learning strategies, more positive attitudes toward school, and higher self-concepts of ability (Ames, 1992; Ames & Archer, 1988; Midgley et al., 1995). In contrast, stress on performance goals is associated with negative achievement beliefs (Ames & Archer, 1988). Midgley and Maehr and their colleagues propose that this significant shift in goal structures from elementary to middle grades school is responsible for the decline in academic motivation that occurs in early adolescence (Anderman & Maehr, 1994; Midgley, Anderman, & Hicks, 1995).

Summary

It is clear from the research reviewed above that the organization and social regularities that characterize middle grades schools are associated with a variety of negative behavioral and psychological outcomes. Research regarding the impact of school size, while not completely consistent, offers a good deal of evidence that students in large schools generally perform less well academically than their counterparts in smaller schools, are less involved in school activities, and have less positive attitudes about school. Academic tracking, which operates in the large majority of middle grades schools, while beneficial for high achieving students, is related to negative self-perceptions among lower ability students. Furthermore, teacher, classroom, and school characteristics often encountered in middle level schools are related to lower achievement and more negative attitudes about school, lower levels of school involvement, and poorer academic self-concepts.

The Transition to Middle Grades Schools and Identity Development

Now we turn to a review of the research investigating the declines in the emotional and behavioral adjustment of early adolescents that result, at least in part, from the organization and social regularities that typify middle grades schools. As we mentioned before, the design of the bulk of these studies involves comparing student outcomes before and after the transition to a middle grades school.

Academic Achievement and Other School-related Outcomes

The picture of early adolescent academic achievement in the middle grades is generally grim. Research—regardless of whether it is conducted in rural, suburban, or urban areas—has consistently shown that students' academic performance is lower on average in middle grades school than in elementary school (Alspaugh, 1998; Crockett, Petersen, Graber, Schulenberg, & Ebata, 1989; Roderick, 1995; Seidman, Allen, Aber, Mitchell, & Feinman, 1994; Simmons & Blyth, 1987; for an exception see Chung, Elias, & Schneider, 1998; for a review see Seidman, Aber, & French, in press). Typically these studies do not find a difference in the extent of the decline for boys and girls. However, whether or not there are differences in the degree of decline in academic achievement for students of different race/ethnic groups is less clear—some studies have found comparable declines across various race/ethnic groups, while other studies have not. Seidman's study of urban, primarily poor adolescents found no differences in the amount of decrease in self-reported grade point average of black, white, and Latino students (Seidman et al., 1994). Conversely, other research also carried out in an urban area found a greater decline in GPA for African American students over the transition than for white students (Simmons, Black, & Zhou, 1991).

School transition studies have looked at other types of school-related outcomes as well. Here, too, the picture is not promising for young adolescents. After the transition to a middle grades school, students' attitudes regarding school become more negative in a myriad of ways. In a study of how students' domain specific attitudes changed upon entry into a middle grades school, Eccles and her colleagues found that students' self-concepts in both math and English became more negative after the school transition, and that students began to perceive mathematics as increasingly less important (Eccles, Wigfield, Flanagan, Miller, Reuman, & Yee, 1989). Hirsch and Rapkin (1987) found that students' perceptions of the overall quality of school life was lower in a middle grades school environment than it had been in elementary school. In this same vein, Seidman and his colleagues

(1994) found that following the transition, students perceived less social support from school staff and more daily academic hassles. This study also found that students reported being less involved in their schools and preparing less for class than they had in elementary school.

Self-esteem

Self-esteem, commonly assumed to be central to psychological health and development (Harter, 1990), is another of the developmental outcomes frequently examined in the school transition literature. Studies have generally found a decline in students' psychological adjustment in middle grades schools compared to elementary schools, but there are exceptions in the literature. Simmons and Blyth (1987) and their colleagues contrasted white, urban, socioeconomically heterogeneous students moving to a junior high school in seventh grade with students that remained in a kindergarten through eighth grade school structure. Among the students that made the school transition, self-esteem decreased for the girls, while that of students who did not make the transition, both boys and girls, remained stable. Other school transition studies examining self-esteem have found decreases in self-esteem that are robust across gender (Eccles et al., 1989) and race/ethnic group (Seidman et al., 1994). The studies that have not found overall declines in self-esteem following the transition to a middle grades school have typically been conducted in primarily white, middle-class, small or suburban communities (Fenzel & Blyth, 1986; Hirsch & Rapkin, 1987; Jones & Thornburg, 1985), which may indicate one of two things: (1) the environmental shift in the middle class or suburban schools may be less drastic and, therefore, not exact the same kind of toll on students' self-esteem that making this transition in urban schools involves, or (2) the more stressful life circumstances poor and/or urban students have may make them more vulnerable to the shift in environments involved in the school transition.

The fact that some studies found that self-esteem remained stable (or increased) across the school transition for the students as a group should not be interpreted to mean that all students in these settings fare the transition well. Hirsch, one of the researchers who did not find a negative impact overall on students' self-esteem following the school transition (Hirsch & Rapkin, 1987), conducted follow-up analyses that identified the prominent self-esteem trajectories for the early adolescents in his study (Hirsch & DuBois, 1991). Using cluster analysis, they identified four patterns of self-esteem change—consistently high (35.2% of the sample), consistently low (12.5%), small increase (31.2%), and steep decline (21.1%). Their finding indicated that the school transition negatively affected a notable number of students, even in a setting where the transition did not negatively impact the self-esteem of most students.

Long-term Implications of the Transition to Middle Grades School

While many studies examining early adolescents' experience of the school transition have followed students only into the first year of the middle grades school, there are several studies that have followed students over a longer period of time. Eccles and her colleagues examined early adolescents' patterns of self-esteem change over the school transition and then went on to investigate the long-term implications of these different patterns (Eccles, Lord, Roeser, Barber, & Jozefowicz, 1997). Using residualized change scores, Eccles and her colleagues categorized students' self-esteem as increasing, decreasing, or remaining stable across the transition. They found that in spite of the fact that the pretransition self-esteem levels were similar for adolescents in all three categories, the long term outcomes differed in important ways. By the 10th grade, students whose self-esteem decreased over the transition to a middle level school not only continued to have self-esteem lower than that of students in the other groups, but they also reported having more depressive symptoms. This group's more negative psychological adjustment persisted into the 12th grade, at which point these students began to report significantly lower grade point averages (GPAs) as well. Clearly, the negative change in self-esteem these students experienced over the transition to a middle level school was related to later negative developmental trajectories.

Simmons and Blyth, authors of one of the earlier and most seminal studies examining the impact of the school transition, followed participants in their research project through the 10th grade (Simmons & Blyth, 1987). Their initial study of this group (described above) found that the transition negatively affected the girls' self-esteem and that it had a negative impact on the GPA and level of school involvement for both girls and boys. They went on to examine how students' individual patterns of change over the transition were related to longer-term outcomes. Similar to the findings of Eccles et al. (1997), they found that adolescents whose self-esteem and GPA declined between the sixth and seventh grades were more likely to experience additional declines in these domains by the time they were in the tenth grade.

Other studies have examined long-term implications of the transition to middle grades school for multiple domains of adolescent well-being. In a study that followed students from their last year of elementary through their second year of middle grades school, Seidman, Clements, Aber, and Allen (2001) found that early adolescents' preparation for class, involvement in school activates, and perceived school social support were not only lower in the first year of the transition, but continued to decline into the second year of middle grades schooling. Furthermore, self-esteem and GPA declined as well after the transition and remained low into the second year of middle grades school; there was no "bounce back" to pretransition levels.

Summary

It goes without saying that one would hope that the structure of our young people's schooling would be such that it bolsters students' self-concepts, school-related attitudes, and academic achievement during early adolescence. Unfortunately, it appears that just the opposite holds in many, if not most, of our nation's middle grades schools. The research literature indicates that for the most part middle grades schools not only fail to support positive developments during early adolescence, but for many actually contribute to negative changes during this period that have lasting effects on their development and well-being. Furthermore, the few studies that look at individual patterns of self-esteem change over the transition demonstrate that even in settings where the impact on the overall population appears to be minimal, there are sizable groups of students that are negatively affected.

Thus far, we have described the status quo for traditional middle grades schools, reviewed the research that links characteristics typical of middle grades schools to negative student outcomes across the grade span, and identified the negative adjustments many early adolescents experience upon entering middle grades schools. In the next section, we will review a theory to explain this decline in early adolescent academic performance and well-being.

Developmental Mismatch, Academic Disengagement, and Possible Selves

Eccles and Midgley's (1989) theory of stage-environment fit proposes that negative changes in early adolescents' behaviors, values, and beliefs are due, at least in part, to the mismatch between the developmental needs of early adolescents and the structure of typical middle grades schools. Like Eccles and Midgley, we agree that many negative changes occurring during this stage are the result of systematic changes in young adolescents' social environments, particularly school, that are inappropriate and do not "fit" the developmental needs of these young people. Stage-environment fit theory focuses most specifically on classroom level organizational, instructional, and climate variables, such as the increase in ability grouping, a focus on normative (and more rigorous) grading standards, the use of competitive motivation strategies, and increased school size. While these educational conditions are not ideal for students at any stage of development, they are *"particularly* harmful at early adolescence in that they emphasize competition, social comparison, and ability self-assessment at a time of heightened self-focus; they decrease decision making and choice at a time when the desire for control is growing; they emphasize lower-level cognitive strategies at a time when the ability to use higher-level strategies is increasing; and they disrupt social networks at a time when adolescents are especially concerned with peer relationships and may be in special need of close adult friendships" (Eccles & Midgley, 1989).

The developmental mismatch that ensues upon early adolescents' entry into middle grades schools leads to a process of disengagement from the educational enterprise (Seidman & French, 1997). While we have seen that all youths are not affected equally, it is clear that a significant number experience a negative impact. We propose that the degree to which students become disengaged from school, and therefore do not have the opportunities for success in learning and other school-related activities, the extent to which they are able to construct positive possible selves, in particular their selves as thinkers and learners, may be constrained. Given that early adolescence is such a critical time for identity development, the experiences that they have during this period may greatly impact their perceptions and expectations for themselves.

Shirk and Renouf (1992), in a previous volume in this series on the self, suggest that "[i]dentity formation can only be successful if the individual is able, not only to create a cohesive *present* self, but also to integrate into the self-concept *historical* and possible *future* selves" (p. 56). "Possible selves," a term proposed by Markus and Nurius (1986), refers to aspects of one's self-concept that represent what the individual could become, would like to become, or is afraid of becoming. Early adolescence, with the onset of the ability to think abstractly and hypothetically, marks the first time young people begin to realistically consider and weigh various possible selves. The optimal outcome of this period is for adolescents to develop positive possible selves that are satisfying and that enable them to fulfill the expectations their community holds for adults. According to Markus and Nurius (1986), possible selves are an important aspect of the self-concept in that they provide the driving force as well as the direction for action, change, and development—both temporary and lasting—and without them "there would be little instrumental behavior in the direction of mastery" (p. 961).

The development of possible selves is influenced by both internal and external factors. Internal factors that possible selves are based upon include what young people know about their skills, abilities, and interests (Curry, Trew, Turner, & Hunter, 1994). Social environments affect the construction of possible selves through the social comparisons an individual makes between one's own characteristics, behaviors, and thoughts, and those of salient others (Markus & Nurius, 1986), and through experiences in which young people have the opportunity to succeed and feel competent (or the opposite) in domains relevant to the kinds of social roles they will be expected to fulfill as adults (Cantor & Kihlstrom, 1987; Greene, 1986). Thus, the social context provides the opportunity for important experiences that can significantly influence the development of adolescents' possible selves. It is in this vein that middle grades schooling plays a crucial role in influencing self and identity development during early adolescence.

Too often early adolescence is associated with major declines in academic motivation, academic achievement, and self-esteem. It is this disengagement from school and the learning process that we propose can potentially influence students' imagined future selves. Research demonstrating that the process of disengagement begins after the transition to a middle grades school has led researchers to conclude that the systematic differences in elementary and typical middle grades school environments and processes may well be responsible for the negative changes that occur in early adolescence (Eccles & Midgley, 1989).

While it is true that the negative adjustments accompanying the transition to a middle grades school do not represent marked, long-term declines in adjustment for most adolescents, for some adolescents these early decreases may represent the beginning of such long-term negative outcomes as poorer self-concepts, school failure, or leaving school altogether (Eccles et al. 1997; Seidman & French, 1997). In addition, these declines in academic adjustment are cause for concern because they often accompany other problem behaviors, for example, skipping school, delinquency, substance abuse and teen-age pregnancy (Carnegie Council on Adolescent Development, 1989). Anderman and Maehr (1994), who have written extensively on the role of middle grades schooling and its negative influence on student motivation, have said, "critical changes occurring especially during the middle grade years have enduring effects throughout life. Total alienation from school may, of course, deny the person entree to society, let alone a means of earning a living. Even seemingly slight shifts in engagement within the school setting may prove problematic. For example, developing a dislike for mathematics in the eighth grade may lead the adolescent to rule out a wide range of career interests before it is wise to do so. School investment during the middle grades may have serious and enduring effects on shaping career patterns and life choices" (p. 289).

They clearly articulate the point that what happens to youths in school can influence their interest in school as well as their self-concept regarding themselves as learners and thinkers and, consequently, their preparation and expectations for their adult roles. Eccles and Midgley (1989) point out that even though the declines in academic and emotional adjustment are not extreme for the majority of adolescents, they are significant enough that those of us interested in the well-being of adolescents should make an effort to better understand what is taking place during this period.

It is crucial that middle grades schooling provides the kinds of experiences that will foster students engagement in school and positive expectations of themselves in this domain. Without this, the chances that students will remain engaged in school, and obtain the education they need for their future success, is diminished. This is the topic we turn to in the next section.

Middle Grades School Reform and Possible Selves

Drawing on the efforts of many educators and researchers, the Carnegie Corporation has produced two of the most important reports on middle grades school reform. The first report, *Turning Points: Preparing American Youth for the 21st Century*, by the Carnegie Council on Adolescent Development (CCAD, 1989), was published the same year as Eccles and Midgley's initial article on stage-environment fit (1989). Jackson and Davis (2000), two of the principle contributors to the original report, have recently written an expanded and revised version of the original report, *Turning Points 2000: Educating Adolescents in the 21st Century*. Given the scope and depth of the reports, in particular *Turning Points 2000*, we refer any individual or group interested in a full presentation of the Turning Points model for middle grades school reform to the full reports. In the context of this chapter, it is not feasible for us to adequately cover all of the research and recommendations, nor can we do justice to the reports' clear, thoughtful, and committed voice. However, given that we advocate the recommendations made in the Turning Points reports as the most promising for creating more developmentally appropriate and academically rigorous middle grades schools, we will cover some of the recommendations we see as most promising for supporting positive self-identity development during early adolescence.

The first Turning Points report (CCAD, 1989) is one of the most widely distributed and read reports on educational reform (Jackson & Davis, 2000) and was utilized as the foundation for a number of middle grades school reform projects (for example, the Middle Grade School State Policy Initiative). While the authors of the report were careful not to stress the importance of any of its recommendations over the others, it is interesting to note what the first three (of a total of eight) recommendations were:

- *Create small communities for learning* where stable, close, mutually respectful relationships with adults and peers are considered fundamental for intellectual development and personal growth. The key elements of these communities are schools-within-schools or houses, students and teachers grouped together as teams, and small group advisories that ensure that every student is known well by at least one adult.

- *Create a core academic program* that results in students who are literate, including in the sciences, and who know how to think critically, lead a healthy life, behave ethically, and assume the responsibilities of citizenship in a pluralistic society. . . .
- *Ensure success for all students* (CCAD, 1989, p. 9)

In the time since the first report was issued, a number of respected researchers involved in school reform have agreed that the structural reforms called for in the first recommendation—changing the school structure to promote better relationships among students and teachers—have been more widely implemented than the recommendation for academic reforms, with positive results for young adolescents' socio-emotional well-being (Jackson & Davis, 2000; Lipsitz, Mizell, Jackson, & Austin, 1997; Mergendollar, 1993; Midgley & Edelin, 1998). While there is disagreement about how widespread these kind of changes have been successfully implemented throughout the country (Felner, Jackson, Kasak, Mulhall, Brand, & Flowers, 1997), it does appear that many middle grades reform efforts have thus far focused more on structural change than academic change. In spite of the disagreement regarding the extent to which structural reforms have been successfully implemented, the evidence suggests that these kinds of structural changes may be related to better socio-emotional and academic outcomes for middle grades students.

In their most extensive investigation into the effectiveness of structural reforms in middle grades education, Felner and his colleagues (Felner et al., 1997) studied 73 schools that were part of the Illinois Middle Grades Network (IMGN) in 1996. Felner and colleagues argue that for a restructuring plan to be effective, its implementation must be comprehensive, not piecemeal. The changes Felner and his group have identified as critical include:

- Teams of less than 120 students
- No fewer than four common planning times for team teachers per week
- Student/teacher ratios smaller than the "mid-20s"
- Teacher-based advisory periods for students

The goal of the restructuring is to increase the opportunities for students to have positive experiences at school by improving their sense of connectedness and belonging within the school, thereby improving students' academic, socio-emotional, and behavioral outcomes (Felner et al., 1993).

Felner and colleagues' findings regarding the impact of these types of structural changes are quite promising. Cross-sectional analyses showed an association with a variety of positive outcomes (Felner et al., 1997). Comparisons of schools at different levels of implementation demonstrated that students in the schools with the highest level of implementation had: (a) higher standardized achievement scores (mathematics, language, reading); (b) higher self-esteem; (c) less fear that they would be victimized or that something bad would happen at school; and (d) fewer behavioral problems than those in schools that had implemented little or no structural reform. It is important to note that the schools that made up each of the level-of-implementation categories were heterogeneous in terms of size, percentage of students eligible for free/reduced-price lunch, and per-pupil expenditures. In other words, the differences in academic achievement and socio-emotional adjustment between the groups cannot be attributed to systematic demographic differences in the schools at each level of implementation.

Preliminary longitudinal analyses of data from these schools are even more encouraging. Students in the most fully implemented schools averaged a gain of almost 21 points on standardized math and reading test scores (where 25 points represents one-half of a standard deviation on the tests used in these schools) (Felner et al., 1997). Conversely, the standardized test scores of students in schools where there had been no reform implementation stayed basically the same. Felner et al. conclude that the implementation of *Turning Points* recommendations not only prevents the negative adjustment among early adolescents that often accompanies entering middle-level schools, but actually leads to improvement in students' academic achievement.

Given the widespread evidence indicating intellectual underachievement among students in the United States, this increase in students' academic achievement is an extraordinarily important finding. In a Phi Delta Kappan special section on middle grades school reform, Lipsitz, Mizell, Jackson, and Austin (1997), using data from the Third International Mathematics and Science Study (TIMSS), point out that U.S. seventh- and eighth-graders ranked 28th in mathematics and 17th in science proficiency among students from 41 countries. They go on to say, "these statistics about young adolescents' academic performance suggest that many middle grades schools are failing to enable the majority of students to achieve at anywhere near adequate levels."

This concern with the relatively poor academic achievement of U.S. young adolescents assumes a more critical prominence in the recent *Turning Points 2000* report (Jackson & Davis, 2000). As was the case in the earlier report, the authors do not intend to suggest that successful middle grades educational reform can take place by applying some recommendations and not others. However, the order of the recommendations is changed somewhat, and this is not trivial. The first four recommendations presented in *Turning Points 2000* are:

- Teach a curriculum grounded in rigorous, public academic standards for what students should know and be able to do, relevant to the concerns of adolescents and based on how students learn best.
- Use instructional methods designed to prepare all students to achieve higher standards and become lifelong learners.
- Staff middle grades schools with teachers who are expert at teaching young adolescents and engage teachers in ongoing, targeted professional development opportunities.
- Organize relationships for learning to create a climate of intellectual development and a caring community of shared educational purpose. (Jackson & Davis, 2000, p. 23)

Jackson and Davis state that they "have reordered the list of recommendations . . . to reflect the centrality of teaching and learning to ensuring every student's success" (2000, p. 25). They clearly articulate that they view the primary objective of middle grades education to be promoting intellectual development—learning how to think creatively, solve problems to communicate effectively, and develop the factual knowledge and skills necessary for these "higher order" activities. While we would, again, refer interested readers to the report for more thorough coverage of the full set of recommendations, there are several points we see as particularly relevant to the development of positive academic-related possible selves. We will then point out where we fear their re-ordering of priorities in the new report may compromise the ultimate success of the reforms being recommended.

Jackson and Davis emphasize the importance of ensuring that the ultimate goal of any reform effort is the success of *every* child—and they clearly communicate that by *every* they mean *all* adolescents, not most. In fact, Jackson and Davis point that reform efforts have occurred least often where they are most needed—in high-poverty rural and urban areas, where academic underachievement is most pronounced. Even in schools where low academic achievement is not the norm, Jackson and Davis insist that educational reforms must address the intellectual development of every student. Without a doubt, ensuring the academic success of all children must certainly be a primary goal of all school reform efforts. The students who are at greatest need of receiving the interpersonal and academic support necessary to develop a positive academic self-concept and better academic skills are those whose school environments and academic skills are most compromised. Jackson and Davis (2000), citing statistics reported elsewhere (Edwards, 1989), state that two thirds or more of students in urban schools with high concentrations of poor children do not achieve minimum standards on national tests. Furthermore, between 60 and 75% of black and Hispanic eighth graders score below basic mathematics and science achievement levels. While it goes without saying that we do not intend to suggest that all black or Hispanic students are poor or urban, it is true that many of the students in poor, urban schools are black or Hispanic. These statistics demonstrate that many of these students are not receiving the educational training that will enable them to successfully complete middle grades and high school, much less to enter and compete in a technologically advanced workforce.

At the same time, however, the authors caution against utilizing academic tracking in an attempt to meet students' diverse academic needs because tracking obstructs achieving the two primary goals *Turning Points 2000* sets for middle grades education: academic equity and academic excellence. Drawing on numerous studies to support the argument against academic tracking, *Turning Points 2000* enumerates several ways in which tracking hinders achieving academic excellence for all students (Jackson & Davis, 2000, pp. 65-68). First, in spite of the supposed objectivity of criteria used to track students, minority and economically disadvantaged students are overrepresented in lower tracks. Given that the instructional quality in the lower tracked classrooms is typically of poorer quality, the consequence is that minority and economically disadvantaged students are systematically provided with poorer quality instruction. Both equity and excellence are impeded. Second, tracking assumes that intelligence is fixed and can not be changed—a view that has been proven to be incorrect. Therefore, tracking students interferes with achieving excellence in education in that it translates into setting lower expectations for students in the lower tracks. Third, teachers in lower tracked classes are often those with the least amount of experience or the least successful teaching records. Again, academic excellence and equity are being compromised. Furthermore, the simple facts that almost all middle grades students are academically tracked (Valentine et al., 1993), over 35% of all eighth grade students fail to meet basic achievement levels in mathematics or science, and over 25% do not meet basic standards in reading (National Center for Education Statistics (NCES), 1998 Reading Assessment; NCES, 1996 Mathematics Assessment; & NCES, 1996 Science Assessment; all as cited in Jackson & Davis, 2000) combine to demonstrate that tracking does not benefit their educational attainment. Many students are not receiving the education they need or deserve. Jackson and Davis acknowledge that providing instruction that meets the needs of students with divergent strengths is a very challenging task. Yet they maintain that diverse, challenging instruction is essential if all students are to be able to meet high academic standards.

In re-ordering the priority of recommendations in *Turning Points 2000* we fear that the higher priority afforded to academic reforms may occur at the expense of acknowledging that structural reforms are critical if the more challenging academic reforms are to be accomplished. While it is clear that the authors do recognize the importance of a smaller school structure for early adolescents, we are surprised that they appear to be de-emphasizing the importance of structural reform. This may be due to the fact that they (and others) are concerned that too many middle grades school reform efforts have not proceeded past the structural changes. We advocate that establishing smaller school structures constitutes the first necessary but not sufficient step in creating the environments that will best support middle grades school reform and, subsequently, the development of positive academic selves. Specifically, as was recommended in both Turning Points reports, large middle grades schools need to be reorganized into small academic "houses" or "schools-within-schools," in which a team approach to teaching and learning is utilized. Creating smaller school structures is critical to middle grades reform in at least two important ways. In order for students to see themselves as belonging in school, a number of factors must be present.

First, for students to be engaged and learning they have to perceive themselves as belonging in school. Given the importance of peer relations in adolescence, schools must be structured in such a way that young adolescents have the opportunity to form a strong and positive peer network. Furthermore, for both their emotional and academic well-being, adolescents will benefit from having close relationships with adults in their school. Teachers and other staff members can then work more effectively with young people to help them attain their academic goals and offer the guidance that all young people can benefit from. As Jackson and Davis point out, "for young adolescents, relationships with adults form the critical pathways for learning; educations 'happens' through relationships" (2000, p. 121). The closer and more meaningful relationships young adolescents form with other students and school staff will foster their involvement in the school culture and their academic engagement.

Equally important is the fact that the deeper and more difficult to accomplish goals of curricular and instructional reform are likely to be unattainable without putting the structural changes in place first. The foundation of a smaller and more manageable working group of teachers, along with adequate planning time and professional development, is critical if teachers are to have a real chance at successfully undertaking the tasks they face. The restructuring will provide the organizational foundation teachers will need to tackle the extraordinary demands of developing curricula and instructional techniques necessary for them to create learning environments in which all students are expected to—and supported in—achieving high academic standards. Once the structural changes are in place, teachers and other school staff can begin to set up the learning experiences that will support student achievement and the development of students' positive academic selves. The tasks that middle grades school reformers (and society as a whole) are presenting teachers are monumental. We must ensure that their work environment will foster their success.

Providing interesting and involving learning experiences, along with opportunities for demonstrating mastery, will facilitate the development of achievement-related self concepts and motivation. If young adolescents are to apply themselves in school to the degree necessary for them to remain actively engaged in school and achieving at high levels, schools must provide them with the circumstances that support the development of positive academic self-concepts, including possible selves. There are many ways in which school environments can foster engaged, high-level learning that will greatly benefit young adolescents in both the short and long term, and, at the same time, support the development of positive academic self-concepts. School environments must support the development of curricula and instruction that meet the needs, interests, and concerns of students. They must respect the differences in students' academic abilities while at the same time providing appropriate instruction to foster learning and opportunities to demonstrate mastery for all students. Schools need to be staffed with teachers who are prepared to meet the intellectual needs and respect the emotional needs of young adolescents. Too many middle grades classrooms rely on passive drill and practice activities rather than engaging young adolescents' developing cognitive skills with the kinds of challenging and meaningful course work they need. Drawing students into the learning process by fostering their understanding of important information will provide students with the knowledge that they are capable of making great academic strides.

Conclusion

Our primary goal in this chapter has been to demonstrate the considerable influence of middle grades schooling on early adolescents' well-being overall and, in particular, how it may influence their perceptions of themselves as learners and thinkers. Our argument is that for young adolescents to be and remain engaged in school and learning, thereby gaining the education critical to their later occupational success, middle grades schools must be restructured to better meet the developmental needs of these young people. Students who feel as if they are part of the school, whose learning is supported, and who have opportunities to demonstrate mastery in school will have the chance to know they are capable of academic achievement and will be able to see themselves as learners.

Clearly, the goals of the educational reforms articulated in *Turning Points 2000* are larger than promoting the development of positive academic possible selves. The hope is for adolescents to reap a multitude of benefits, including intellectual development, emotional health, preparation for the future, and a safe school environment. Nonetheless, our position is that the type of reforms described here also support the development of an important component in the equation for young adolescent's intellectual development and engagement in school—a positive self-concept of themselves as learners and thinkers.

As we stated earlier, possible selves are an important aspect of the self-concept—they function to motivate action and development in particular directions. One's image of their possible selves, and therefore the potential for growth, is determined by both external and internal factors. School environments that work to engage all students and support their academic endeavors and accomplishments will provide the type of social environment that will foster the development of positive academic possible selves. Simultaneously, many of these same experiences will provide young adolescents with positive learning opportunities that will affect how they view their skills, abilities, and interests—the kinds of internal factors that influence the development of adolescents' perceptions of their possible selves. Positive school experiences—including high quality learning—will promote adolescents' academic engagement and academic success, and, as a result, young adolescents will develop perceptions of themselves as learners, and as capable of continued achievement. Their self-concepts regarding where they are and where they want to go in their lives will most certainly benefit.

Many researchers identify early adolescence as a particularly tumultuous period. Even those who have worked to shift the general perception of adolescence from that of a period of extreme storm and stress to one characterized by more relative growth and stability, acknowledge that early adolescence is a stressful and disorienting period for many (Demo & Savin-Williams, 1992). Given that early adolescence is acknowledged to be a difficult time, as well as a critical period of identity development, we propose that young adolescents would benefit from attending middle grades schools organized in such a way that teaching and learning foster positive, productive learning experiences for all students. These positive learning experiences, combined with positive interactions between teachers and students, would lead to a greater level of engagement with the schooling process and more positive academic self-concepts, including the formation of positive academic possible selves. No one proposes that making the kinds of reforms recommended here would be easy. In fact, the challenges facing such fundamental and broad-based reforms are considerable. However, our economy has developed to the point that most young people entering the workforce must be able to work with complex technologies, solve complex problems, communicate and work with others, and, importantly, continue to learn throughout their careers (Marshall & Tucker, 1992). For this to take place, all young people need more than just access to knowledge. They need the kinds of educational experiences that will support their engagement in the academic process and the development of their identity as people who are capable of thinking, learning, and succeeding.

References

Alspaugh, J. W. (1998). Achievement loss associated with the transition to middle school and high school. *Journal of Educational Research, 92,* 20-25.

Alvidrez, J., & Weinstein, R. S. (1999). Early teacher perceptions and later student academic achievement. *Journal of Educational Psychology, 91,* 731-746.

Ames, C. (1992). Classrooms: Goals, structures, and student motivation. *Journal of Educational Psychology, 84,* 261-271

Ames, C., & Archer, J. (1988). Achievement goals in the classroom: Students' learning strategies and motivation processes. *Journal of Educational Psychology, 80,* 260-267.

Anderman, E. M., & Maehr, M. L. (1994). Motivation and schooling in the middle grades. *Review of Educational Research, 64,* 287-309.

Barker, R., & Gump, P. (1964). *Big school, small school: High school size and student behavior.* Stanford, CA: Stanford University Press.

Cantor, N., & Kihlstrom, K. (1987). *Personality and social intelligence.* Englewood Cliffs, NJ: Prentice Hall.

Carnegie Council on Adolescent Development (1989). *Turning points: Preparing American youth for the 21st century.* New York: Carnegie Corporation.

Chung, H., Elias, M., & Schneider, K. (1998). Patterns of individual adjustment changes during middle school transition. *Journal of School Psychology, 36,* 83-101.

Cotterell, J. L. (1992). School size as a factor in adolescents' adjustment to the transition to secondary school. *Journal of Early Adolescence, 12,* 28-45.

Crockett, L. J., Petersen, A. C., Graber, J. A., Schulenberg, J. E., & Ebata, A. (1989). School transitions and adjustment during early adolescence. *Journal of Early Adolescence, 9,* 181-210.

Curry, C., Trew, K., Turner, I., & Hunter, J. (1994). The effect of life domains on girls' possible selves. *Adolescence, 29,* 133-150.

Demo, D. H., & Savin-Williams, R. C. (1992). Self-concept stability and change during adolescence. In R. P. Lipka & T. M. Brinthaupt (Eds.), *Self-perspectives across the life span* (pp. 116-148). Albany, NY: State University of New York Press.

Eccles, J. S., Flanagan, C., Lord, S., Midgley, C., Roeser, R., & Yee, D. (1996). Schools, families, and early adolescents: What are we doing wrong and what can we do instead? *Journal of Developmental and Behavioral Pediatrics*, 17, 267-276.

Eccles, J. S., Lord, S. E., Roeser, R. W., Barber, B. L., & Jozefowicz, D. (1997). The association of school transitions in early adolescence with developmental trajectories through high school. In J. Schulenberg & J. L. Maggs (Eds.), *Health risks and developmental transitions during adolescence* (pp. 283-320). New York: Cambridge University Press.

Eccles, J. S., & Midgley, C. (1989). Stage/environment fit: Developmentally appropriate classrooms for young adolescents. In R. E. Ames & C. Ames (Eds.), *Research on motivation in education* (Vol. 3, pp. 139-186). New York: Academic Press.

Eccles, J. S., Midgley, C., & Adler, T. (1984). Grade-related changes in the school environment: Effects on achievement motivation. In J. G. Nicholls (Ed.), *The development of achievement motivation* (pp. 283-331). Greenwich, CT: JAI Press.

Eccles, J. S., Wigfield, A., Flanagan, C. A., Miller, C., Reuman, D. A., & Yee, D. (1989). Self-concepts, domain values, and self-esteem: Relations and changes at early adolescence. *Journal of Personality*, 57, 283-310.

Edwards, V. B. (Ed.). (1998, January 8). Quality Counts '98. The urban challenge: Public education in the 50 states [Special Issue]. *Education Week*, 17.

Epstein, J. L., & MacIver, D. J. (1990). *Education in the middle grades: National practices and trends*. Columbus: OH: National Middle School Association.

Erikson, E. (1968). *Identity: Youth and crisis*. New York: Norton.

Felner, R. D., Brand, S., Adan, A. M., Mulhall, P. F., Flowers, N., Sartain, B., & DuBois, D. L. (1993). Restructuring the ecology of the school as an approach to prevention during school transitions: Longitudinal follow-ups and extensions of the School Transitional Environment Project (STEP). *Prevention in Human Services*, 10, 103-136.

Felner, R. D., Jackson, A. W., Kasak, D., Mulhall, P., Brand, S., & Flowers, N. (1997). The impact of school reform for the middle years: Longitudinal study of a network engaged in Turning Points based comprehensive school transformation. *Phi Delta Kappan*, 78, 528-532, 541-550.

Fenzel, L. M., & Blyth, D. A. (1986). Individual adjustment to school transitions: An exploration of the role of supportive peer relations. *Journal of Early Adolescence, 9*, 315-329.

Fowler, W. J., & Walberg, H. J. (1991). School size, characteristics, and outcomes. *Educational Evaluation and Policy Analysis, 13*, 189-202.

Gecas, V., & Seff, M. (1998). Families and adolescents: A review of the 1980s. *Journal of Marriage and the Family, 52*, 941-958.

Greene, A. L. (1986). Future time perspective in adolescence: The present of things revisited. *Journal of Youth and Adolescence, 15*, 99-113.

Griffith, J. (1995). An empirical examination of a model of social climate in elementary schools. *Basic and Applied Social Psychology, 17*, 97-117.

Hallinan, M. T. (1994). Tracking: From theory to practice. *Sociology of Education, 67*, 79-91.

Harter, S. (1990). Processes underlying adolescent self-concept formation. In R. Montemayor, G. R. Adams, & T. P. Gullotta (Eds.), *From childhood to adolescence: A transitional period?* (pp. 205-239). Newbury Park, CA: Sage Publications.

Hirsch, B. J., & DuBois D. L. (1991). Self-esteem in early adolescence: The identification and prediction of contrasting longitudinal trajectories. *Journal of Youth and Adolescence, 20*, 53-72.

Hirsch, B. J., & Rapkin, B. D. (1987). The transition to junior high school: A longitudinal study of self-esteem, psychological symptomology, school life, and social support. *Child Development, 58*, 1235-1243.

Jackson, A. W., & Davis, G. A. (2000). *Turning points 2000: Educating adolescents in the 21st century*. New York: Teachers College Press.

Jones, R. M., & Thornburg, H. D. (1982). Social characteristics of early adolescents: Age versus grade. *Journal of Early Adolescence, 2*, 229-239.

Keating, D., (1990). Adolescent thinking. In S. Feldman and G. Elliot (Eds.), *At the threshold: The developing adolescent* (pp. 197-224). Cambridge, MA: Harvard University Press.

Lipsitz, J., Mizell, M. H., Jackson, A. W., & Austin, L. M. (1997). Speaking with one voice: A manifesto for middle-grades reform. *Phi Delta Kappan, 78*, 533-540.

Markus, H., & Nurius, P. (1986). Possible selves. *American Psychologist, 41*, 954-969.

McKown, C., & Weinstein, R. S. (in press). Modeling the role of child ethnicity and gender in children's differential response to teacher expectations. *Journal of Applied Social Psychology*.

Mergendollar, J. R. (1993). Introduction: The role of research on the reform of middle grades education. *Elementary School Journal, 93*, 443-446.

Midgley, C., Anderman, E., & Hicks, L. (1995). Differences between elementary and middle school teachers and students: A goal theory approach. *Journal of Early Adolescence, 15*, 90-113.

Midgley, C., & Edelin, K. C. (1998). Middle school reform and early adolescent well-being: The good news and the bad. *Educational Psychologist, 33*, 195-206.

Midgley, C., & Feldlaufer, H. (1987). Students' and teachers' decision-making fit before and after the transition to junior high school. *Journal of Early Adolescence, 7*, 225-241.

Midgley, C., Feldlaufer, H., & Eccles, J. S. (1988). The transition to junior high school: Beliefs of pre- and post-transition teachers. *Journal of Youth and Adolescence, 17*, 543-562.

Midgley, C., Feldlaufer, H., & Eccles, J. S. (1989). Student/teacher relations and attitudes toward mathematics before and after the transition to junior high school. *Child Development, 60*, 981-992.

Miller, J. W., Ellsworth, R., & Howell, J. (1986). Public elementary schools which deviate from the traditional SES-achievement relationship. *Educational Research Quarterly, 10*, 31-50.

Morracco, J. C. (1978). The relationship between the size of elementary schools and pupils' perceptions of their environments. *Education, 98*, 451-454.

Oakes, J., Gamoran, A., & Page, R. N. (1992). Curriculum differentiation: Opportunities, outcomes, and meanings. In P. Jackson (Ed.), *Handbook of research on curriculum*. New York: Macmillan.

Roderick, M. (1995). School transitions and school dropout. In K. Wong (Ed.), *Advances in educational policy*. Greenwich, CT: JAI.

Roeser, R. W., & Eccles, J. S. (1998). Adolescents' perceptions of middle school: Relation to longitudinal changes in academic and psychological adjustment. *Journal of Research on Adolescence, 8*, 123-158.

Rutter, M., Maughan, B., Mortimore, P., & Ouston, J. with Smith, A. (1979). *Fifteen thousand hours: Secondary schools and their effects on children*. Cambridge, MA: Harvard University Press.

Sarason, S. B. (1971). *The culture of the school and the problem of change*. Boston: Allyn & Bacon.

Sarason, S. B. (1982). *The culture of school and the problem of change* (2nd ed.). Boston: Allyn & Bacon.

Seidman, E. (1988). Back to the future, community psychology: Unfolding a theory of social intervention. *American Journal of Community Psychology, 16*, 3-24.

Seidman, E., Aber, J. L., & French, S. (in press). Restructuring the transition to middle/junior high school: A strengths-based approach to the organization of schooling. In K. Maton, C. Schellenbach, B. Leadbeater, & A. Solarz (Eds.), *Investing in children, families, and communities: Strengths-based research and policy*. Washington, DC: American Psychological Association.

Seidman, E., Allen, L., Aber, J. L., Mitchell, C., & Feinman, J. (1994). The impact of school transitions in early adolescence on the self-system and perceived social context of poor urban youth. *Child Development, 65*, 507-522.

Seidman, E., Clements, P., Aber, J. L., & Allen, L. (2000). *Do urban adolescents living in poverty bounce back from the negative impact of the transition to junior high school?* Manuscript in preparation. New York University.

Seidman, E., & French, S. E. (1997). Normative school transitions among urban adolescents: When, where, and how to intervene. In H. J. Walberg, R. P. Weissberg, & O. Reyes (Eds.), *Urban children and youth: Interdisciplinary perspectives*. Newbury Park, CA: Sage.

Shirk, S. R., & Renouf, A. G. (1992). The tasks of self-development in middle childhood and early adolescence. In R. P. Lipka & T. M. Brinthaupt (Eds.), *Self-perspectives across the life span*. Albany, NY: State University of New York Press.

Simmons, R. G., & Blyth, D. A. (1987). *Moving into adolescence: The impact of pubertal change and school context*. Hawthorn, NY: Aldine de Gruyler.

Simmons, R. G., Black, A., & Zhou, Y. (1991). African-American versus white children and the transition to junior high school. *American Journal of Education, 99*, 481-520.

Slavin, R. E. (1987). Ability grouping and student achievement in elementary schools: A best-evidence synthesis. *Review of Educational Research, 57*, 293-336.

Smetana, J. (1988). Adolescents' and parents' conceptions about actual family conflict. *Child Development, 59*, 321-335.

Smetana, J. (1989). Adolescents' and parents' reasoning about actual family conflict. *Child Development, 59*, 1052-1067.

Steinberg, L. (1990). Autonomy, conflict, and harmony in the family relationship. In S. Feldman & G. Elliott (Eds.), *At the threshold: The developing adolescent* (pp. 71-97). Cambridge, MA: Harvard University Press.

Steinberg, L. (1996). *Adolescence* (4th ed.). New York: McGraw Hill.

Stevenson, C. (1992). *Teaching ten to fourteen year olds*. New York: Longman.

Valentine, J., Clark, D. D., Irvin, J. L., Keefe, J. W., & Melton, G. (1993). *Leadership in middle level education: A national survey of middle level leaders and schools* (Vol. 1). Reston, VA: National Association of Secondary School Principals.

Waxman, H. C., Huang, S. Y. L., Anderson, L., & Weinstein, T. (1997). Classroom process differences in inner-city elementary schools. *Journal of Educational Research, 91*, 49-59.

Weinstein, R. S. (1989). Perception of classroom processes and student motivation: Children's views of self-fulfilling prophecies. In R. E. Ames & C. Ames (Eds.), *Research on motivation in education* (Vol. 3). New York: Academic Press.

Weinstein, R. S., & McKown, C. (1998). Expectancy effects in "context": Listening to the voices of students and teachers. *Advances in Research on Teaching, 7*, 215-242.

III

Peer Relationships and Behavioral Problems

6

SELF, SELF-ESTEEM, CONFLICTS, AND BEST FRIENDSHIPS IN EARLY ADOLESCENCE

Margarita Azmitia

While the exploration and evaluation of self is a lifelong project, it takes center stage at certain points in the life span, such as adolescence (Demo & Savin-Williams, 1992; Erikson, 1968; Harter, 1999). Early adolescence is a particularly important period for the self-project because in all cultural communities, adolescents experience biological, cognitive, and social changes that can lead them to revisit and potentially revise their self-systems, that is, their theories of self and their self-esteem. Although the particular experiences, the meaning attributed to them, and the opportunities for self-exploration vary between and within cultures (Hart & Edelstein, 1992; Harter, 1999), two universal developmental shifts help early adolescents rethink and rework their self-systems. First, the growth of abstract cognitive skills and perspective-taking abilities allows them to consider their self-theories in the context of how they see themselves and how others perceive them (Harter, 1999). Second, the growth of intimacy in friendships or in relationships with siblings and cousins that function as friendships (see Duff, 1996; Seginer, 1992) allows early adolescents to engage in self-exploration and evaluation in the safety and comfort of a close relationship with a relative equal (Sullivan, 1953).

As early adolescents reflect on their self-systems, they begin to write the life story or coherent autobiography that will allow for self-continuity and understanding across the life span. While the composition of this life story continues throughout adulthood, its foundation is located in adolescence (Habermas & Bluck, 2000). Research has shown late adolescents' and young adults' memories of friendship experiences during early adolescence play a significant role in the these life stories (Kate McLean, personal communication March 5, 2001), a finding that supports Sullivan's (1953) theory of the importance of friendship for self-exploration and evaluation.

Sociocultural opportunities, practices, and pressures also play a role in early adolescents' self projects and life stories. In most societies, the transition to adolescence brings about new roles and responsibilities. These new expectations can lead to disruptions and insecurities as well as to positive growth (Cole & Cole, 2001). In the United States, for example, early adolescents often transition into a new and bigger school context that requires them to manage challenging academic and social situations at the same time that they are coping with the stresses of puberty and sexual exploration. This is also a time when communities, families, peers, and early adolescents themselves start thinking about and planning for the future. Finally, early adolescents are actively engaged in renegotiating their relationships with their parents in ways that will grant them more autonomy in their time, decision making, and activities. Some early adolescents living in the United States and early adolescents in other cultures may have different sociocultural and personal experiences, but most communities mark the transition to adolescence with rites that signal new rights, roles, and obligations and prompt a reconsideration and reframing of self.

This chapter addresses the role of friendship in early adolescents' reexamination and reevaluation of the self system. I pay particular attention to the association between early adolescents' serious conflicts with best friends and their self-esteem. I focus on conflicts because these times of stress and turmoil in relationships may be particularly likely to prompt individuals to revisit their self-systems and their views about relationships (see also Surra & Bohman, 1991).

The chapter is organized as follows. First, I review literature on early adolescents' self-systems. I summarize the major theoretical perspectives, the developmental characteristics of self-exploration and self-evaluation processes, and gender variation in self-evaluation (i.e., self-esteem).

Second, I discuss early adolescents' self-system in the context of a key relationship in their lives, friendship. Third, I address the association between early adolescents' self-esteem and their conflicts with best friends. To this end, I analyze the conflict narratives of high and low self-esteem early adolescents (fifth through eighth grade) who participated in a study of early adolescents' best friendships, conflicts, and self-esteem (Azmitia, Kamprath, & Ittel, in preparation, Azmitia, Lippman, & Ittel, 1999). Although the participating sample was sufficiently large to carry out quantitative statistical analyses, in the present chapter I relied on qualitative analyses of early adolescents' conflict narratives to illustrate the potential of this methodology for illuminating the texture and dynamics of early adolescents' self-system as it develops in the context of friendships.

Early Adolescents' Self-System

Developmental theories of self and self-understanding (e.g., Damon & Hart, 1988; Harter, 1999; Rosenberg, 1990) generally take William James' (1892) ideas about self as a starting point and assume that cognitive development plays an important role in developmental changes in self-theories, self-understanding, and self-esteem. Briefly, James proposed that (1) individuals' self-concept includes their beliefs about their strengths and weakness, and (2) their self-esteem is based on the value they attribute to the different aspects of self. Individuals with positive self-esteem place more importance on their strengths than their weaknesses and the opposite is true for those with low self-esteem.

In contemporary scholars' work, James' theory is reflected in frameworks that emphasize the differentiation and integration of self over the life span. Some theories also address the processes through which individuals emphasize or discount domains of self. For example, in Harter's (1999) model, adolescents' self-concept includes their ideas about their competency in a variety of domains, such as school, peer acceptance, close friendship, and physical appearance. With development, self-theories become more differentiated, both in terms of domains of self-evaluation as well as in the relational contexts in which adolescents construct and evaluate their selves. Like James, Harter proposed that self-esteem is based on how individuals weight their perceived competencies and deficiencies (i.e., the relative importance that they place on their strengths and weaknesses). While

Damon and Hart (1988) did not incorporate James' formula for calculating self-esteem into their model, they also propose a dimensional model of self-understanding. In their framework, self-understanding involves four self-schemes, the physical self, the active self, the social self, and the psychological self. With development, different self-schemes become more or less salient.

Early adolescence is characterized by intense self-focus, introspection, and self-consciousness (Demo & Savin-Williams, 1992). Although the growth of abstract thinking allows early adolescents to revisit their self-systems, early adolescents' self-theories are still not very coherent. Thus, unlike middle and late adolescents, they are not particularly troubled by inconsistencies in their theories, for example, I am wild around my friends but circumspect around my family (Harter & Monsour, 1992). This is not to say, however, that early adolescents do not have concerns. Among other things, they often worry about whether their peers and friends approve of them, whether they will be able to coordinate and meet their families', peers', schools', and communities' tasks and expectations, and whether they will be happy with the "product" of the many biological, cognitive, and social changes they are experiencing.

Although to an extent self-exploration is a private affair, it does not occur in a sociocultural vacuum. Early adolescents draw on their interactions with family, peers, close friends, teachers, and the messages they glean from the media and other cultural artifacts or institutions to constitute and evaluate their self-theories. In his classic book, *Mind, Self, and Society from the Standpoint of a Social Behaviorist*, George Herbert Mead (1934) elaborated on Cooley's (1902) ideas about the interpersonal nature of self-knowledge and proposed the construct of *looking glass self* as a metaphor for the social construction of the self-system. In a nutshell, this metaphor refers to the view that our self-systems are constructed from our perceptions of how others see us. As Harter (1999) stated: "For Cooley, significant others constituted a social mirror into which the individual gazes in order to detect their opinions toward the self" (p. 17). Contemporary scholars (e.g., Damon & Hart, 1988; Demo & Savin-Williams, 1992; Harter, 1999; Rosenberg, 1990) have elaborated on this metaphor and demonstrated the phenomenon empirically. Their research has shown that early adolescents are especially attuned to others' feedback about their competencies because the many changes they are experiencing heighten social comparison, especially to peers who are undergoing the same changes and transitions (see also Savin-Williams & Berndt, 1990). Given the competition and anxiety that can accompany social comparison, it is not surprising that boys and girls are more likely to experience declines in self-esteem during early adolescence than in any other period of the life span (Demo, 1992; Harter, 1999).

Much attention has been paid to the causes and consequences of declines in self-esteem during early adolescence. At least in the United States, early adolescents' positive sense of self can be challenged by the increased social press to make their own decisions and live with the consequences, the move into junior high school, the reconfiguration of peer groups, puberty, and the beginning of romantic relationships (Demo & Savin-Williams, 1992; Simmons, Rosenberg, & Rosenberg, 1973). Low self-esteem can hinder positive development. It has been associated with depression (Harter, 1998; 1999), delinquency (Rosenberg, Schooler, & Schoenback, 1989), and poor academic performance (Rosenberg et al., 1989; Seidman, Allen, Aber, Mitchell, & Feinman, 1994). It is important to note, however, that the evaluative processes that lead to positive or negative self-esteem are already in motion in infancy (Erikson, 1950). Nevertheless, early adolescence may be a particularly key time to revise self-theories because the many developmental changes and tasks boys and girls experience and because their intense preoccupation with themselves coupled with the growth of reflective processes result in their devoting considerable attention to their self projects. For some young adolescents, these self-evaluative processes will lead to less positive self-concepts; for others, their positive self-views will be reaffirmed and elaborated.

Once a self-theory is created, it can be difficult to change because the key experiences that serve as its foundation are likely to be highly charged emotionally and exert their influence at a relatively unconscious level (Harter, 1999; Swann, 1996; 1997). Moreover, individuals tend to attend selectively to feedback that confirms their theory and to discount information that does not; often, the desire to confirm self-views overrides the desire to protect the self from negative self evaluations (Swann, 1997). Finally, the social context (e.g., relationships, activities) promotes stability because it creates expectations for behavior. That is, while individuals can try to change, change can be difficult because others' expectations of what they are like, how they behave, and their goals and values can make this change difficult to implement. For this reason, contemporary therapeutic and nontherapeutic approaches to self-change emphasize the need to alter *both* the individual and his/her contexts.

Invariably, discussions about sources of individual differences in early adolescents' self-exploration and evaluation turn to gender. Reviewing the large literature on gender variations in early adolescents' self systems is beyond the scope of this chapter. For the present purposes, I will only address the work on gender variation in self-esteem. Studies (e.g., Block & Robbins, 1993; Simmons & Blyth, 1987) have shown that during early adolescence, girls are more likely than boys to experience declines in self-esteem. Three explanations have been offered for this gendered pattern. First, girls are generally more unhappy with their bodies than boys, and body image is the best predictor of self-esteem (Harter, 1999). Second, in early adolescence girls are increasingly confronted with societal and school structures that favor boys and with pressure to conform to gender role prescriptions that limit their avenues for exploration (Basow & Rubin, 1999). Both of these societal conditions can lead to feelings of dissatisfaction and inadequacy. Finally, girls are more likely than boys to worry and ruminate about their problems. This tendency puts them at risk for depression, a strong correlate of self-esteem (Harter, 1999; Nolen-Hoeksema & Girgus, 1994).

Despite the availability of research showing greater declines in girls' than boys' self-esteem and the attention that girls' crisis of self has received in the media and the popular literature (e.g., Orenstein, 1994; Pipher, 1994), current research shows that the declines in girls' self-esteem may not be as great as previously assumed (Eccles, Barber, Josefowicz, Malenchuk, & Vida, 1999; Kling, Hyde, Showers, & Buswell, 1999). Moreover, the gendered patterns for self-esteem differ as a function of ethnicity. In comparisons involving early adolescents, European-descent girls are more likely than African-descent girls to experience declines in self-esteem; in fact, African-descent girls often show an increase in self-esteem during this period. Latinas, in contrast, experience a drop in self-esteem in middle adolescence, when they enter high school (Basow & Rubin, 1999). Taken together, the results of these recent studies suggest that we need to revisit the widespread assumption that early adolescence is necessarily characterized by a crisis of self.

Rather than emphasizing between ethnic or gender group differences, the time may be ripe for a within-group variability approach.

That is, it may be productive to consider *which* boys and *which* girls are at risk for experiencing declines in self-esteem during early adolescence. Harter, Waters, Whitesell, and Kastelic (1998) adopted this perspective in their study of false-self behavior (i.e., suppression of one's true self) in European-descent adolescents. As predicted, they found no overall gender differences in false-self behavior. However, girls who endorsed values, attributes, and behaviors associated with femininity and boys and girls who perceived that significant others did not value their opinions were more likely to report low levels of voice in their close relationships, that is, they refrained from expressing their true opinions. In turn, low levels of voice were predictive of low self-esteem.

Early Adolescents' Friendships as Contexts for Self-Exploration and Self-Evaluation

Peer relationships in general, and friendships in particular, become increasingly important over the course of adolescence (Hartup, 1993; Youniss & Smollar, 1985). For early adolescents, friendships can provide a sense of belonging, of having a place in the world at a time when so many potentially bewildering changes are taking place (Savin-Williams & Berndt, 1990). The safety and comfort of friendships is due, at least in part, to boys' and girls' growing understanding of reciprocity, commitment, and equality (Hartup, 1993).

Sullivan (1953) proposed that the increased intimacy and emotional support that characterize close friendships in adolescence make them ideal contexts for self-exploration, validation, and evaluation. In support of Sullivan's proposal, researchers have shown that as boys and girls move into adolescence they seek out friends who share their experiences, values, and goals and co-construct with them peer cultures and personal identities that recreate, expand, and innovate aspects of their cultural communities (Azmitia & Cooper, 2001; Eckert, 1989; Finders, 1997; Willis, 1977). Azmitia and Cooper (2001), for example, reported that academically- and college-oriented Latino youth enrolled in community organizations that promoted college ideation for minorities in large part to develop friendships with similarly-minded peers. These friendships provided safe havens from their school-friends' teasing and accusations that by succeeding academically and seeking to attend college, these minority students were "acting white" and loosing a key part of their identitites. Academics and career ideation are not the only domains of personal identity that are constructed in friendship. Finders (1997) highlighted how early ado-lescent girls constructed their gender and sexual identities in conver-sations with friends and Eckert (1989) and Willis (1977) showed how friends' dialogues and interactions contribute to the reproduction of societal prescriptions concerning social class.

It is important to point out, however, that early adolescents do not always place a premium on their friends' views about their personal qualities and worth. Harter (1990), for example, found that adoles-cents weighted feedback from peers more heavily than feedback from their friends. She suggested that early adolescents' preference for peers' over friends' feedback reflects their expectation that their friends will choose supportiveness over truthfulness. In this case, peers' feedback will be more accurate than friends' feedback. In addition, because early adolescents want to be accepted by desired peer cliques and crowds, peers' feedback about appropriate attributes, values, and behaviors is essential. Finally, adolescents may pay more attention to peers' than friends' feedback because they tend to choose friends who are similar to them, and thus, receive more information that validates their self-system than information that challenges it (Demo & Savin-Williams, 1992). Given that an important part of the self-project involves revis-iting and potentially revising the self-system, early adolescents may turn to peers to fulfill this function.

Early adolescent girls spend more time than boys with their close friends and often have smaller, more exclusive, circles of friends (Belle, 1989). In her longitudinal study of the transition between elementary to junior high school, Hardy (2000) found that girls also experience more changes in their friendship circles than boys, that is, they make and lose more friends. Regardless of the stability of their friendship cir-cle, however, both genders face the challenge of balancing the often-competing needs of being involved with and accepted by the larger peer group and being a loyal and valued member of a circle of friends. In early adolescence, the needs for peer acceptance and popularity often override loyalties to friends (Eder, 1985). Over time, however, adolescents begin to place a premium on gaining and keeping their friends' trust (Azmitia et al., 1998; Berndt, 1999; Youniss & Smollar, 1985). Indeed, by middle and late adolescence, many boys and girls would not only endorse but also try to live their lives by E. M. Forster's (1951) statement in *Two Cheers for Democracy,*

If I had to choose between betraying my country and betraying my friend, I hope I should have the guts to betray my country.

Despite the inherent tension between friendship and peer acceptance in early adolescence, it is still the case that close friendships give early adolescents opportunities for sharing and discussing their "deepest and darkest" secrets, their joys, sadnesses, problems, and fears. As they experiment with and learn about appropriate ways to engage in self-disclosure, boys and girls often fear that their friends will betray their confidences. At times, their fears are well founded when their friends reveal their secrets or use them as powerful commodities to gain the acceptance of more popular peers (Azmitia, et al., 1998; Eder & Sanford, 1986). When their friends betray them, early adolescents experience intense and prolonged negative emotions—sadness, hurt, anger, and at times, despair (Whitesell & Harter, 1996). Girls are more likely than boys to worry about potential betrayals of their trust (Eccles et al., 1999). This gender difference may occur because relative to boys' friendships, girls' friendships are more exclusive (Brown, Way, & Duff, 1999), have higher expectations of loyalty and commitment (Claes, 1992; Clark & Bittle, 1992), and are generally characterized by more self-disclosure (Camarena, Sarigiani, & Petersen, 1990; Leaper, 1994). Nevertheless, when they experience violations of their friendship expectations, boys and girls usually work equally hard to repair the relationship (Azmitia et al., 1998).

Relative to the wealth of knowledge about friendship formation, little is known about friendship deterioration and termination (Hartup, 1993). In early adolescence, friendships often end when friends fail to meet each other's expectations, develop different interests, or make new friends (Azmitia, et al., 1999; George, 1999). Situations in which their friends behave in an untrustworthy manner may be particularly damaging for self-esteem because early adolescents already feel vulnerable that their friend knows quite a bit about their private, intimate self. Also, their friends' untrustworthy behavior may lead boys and girls to question their value as a person at a time when they are already feeling insecure. After all, if a friend who supposedly accepts and values them betrays them, what might others who have less of an investment in their welfare think of them? As I will show, however, it is likely that boys' and girls' self-esteem mediates their reactions to their friends' infractions. Specifically, low self-esteem individuals may ruminate over their friends' actions, attributing the most negative meanings to them and questioning whether the relationship has a future. As they reflect on the friendship, their negative self-theories may lead them to retrieve more negative than positive memories, thus increasing their dissatisfaction with themselves and their relationships. The opposite may be the case for high self-esteem individuals, because they are better able to discount negative events and to also avoid dwelling on them (see also Swann, 1997).

Self-esteem can also influence individuals' choice of friends. Swann (1996) showed that low self-esteem adults often gravitate to relationships in which they are denigrated or abused. He argued that this pattern results from our desire to maintain a stable identity by bringing others to see us as we see ourselves, even when that requires that they view us negatively. Repeated negative experiences in relationships reinforce individuals' negative self-concept, thus making it very difficult for people to break the cycle of abuse. In a short-term longitudinal study, Nancy Kamprath and I (Azmitia & Kamprath, 1993) found that Swann's proposal may also apply to children and early adolescents. We interviewed participants about their friendships in the fall and spring of the school year. We also assessed changes in their self-esteem over the two time periods. For boys, increases or decreases in self-esteem were unrelated to positive or negative changes in their friendships.[1] For girls, decreases in self-esteem were associated with negative changes in friendships—a friendship had deteriorated or ended and the girl found herself without close friends or the girl was involved in a new friendship that she was still unsure of. As predicted by Swann, low self-esteem girls were more likely to remain in poor quality, and sometimes emotionally abusive, friendships. During their interviews, some of these low self-esteem girls made excuses for their friends' hurtful behaviors or explained that they had brought them on themselves. Cara's[2] assessment of her friend's tendency to routinely tease her in public about her weight problem illustrates this point:

> She can't really help it because its true. In a way, I feel lucky that she stays my friend because she could hang out with the more popular kids if she wanted. She says she only sticks with me because we've been friends since preschool and she feels kinda sorry for me.[3]

Taken together, the literature and our data suggest a less romantic view of friends' influence on early adolescents' self-esteem. While it is the case that friendship can provide a safe and comfortable haven for positive self-exploration and evaluation, for low self-esteem adolescents poor quality friendships can reinforce their already negative view of themselves.

Friendships, Conflicts, and Self-Esteem

Because most research to date has focused on how friendships promote self-esteem, we chose to focus our research on the "dark side" of these relationships (see also Berndt, 1999; Dishion, Eddy, Hass, Fuzhong, & Spracklen, 1997; Rawlins, 1992). Rawlins (1992) stated our position very succinctly: "friends not only help with problems, they also cause them" (p. 87). His research has shown that although friendships become less exclusive over the course of adolescence, early adolescents, and especially girls, are still grappling with their jealousy of their friends' other close friendships and relationships. Jealousy may be more of an issue for girls because their friendships are more exclusive and they have higher expectations of loyalty and commitment. Because boys typically prefer to engage in large group activities, they are more inclusive than girls and may not expect as much loyalty and commitment (Henry, 1963).

In our research (Azmitia et al., 1998; Kamprath & Azmitia, 1995), girls often stated that although they understood that their best friend had other friends and needed to devote time to those relationships, they still experienced jealousy and hurt feelings when their friend spent time with others or, when in a group activity, their friend devoted more attention to the other girls. One of Rawlins' (1992) interviewees illustrates this point in her response to the question: "What causes the most problems between friends?"

> Jealousy, and it's jealousy with other girls too. Like, if Karen's spending more time with somebody else that I don't really care for or I don't know that well, why is she spending time with *her* instead of me? (p. 87)

The boys who participated in Rawlins' study did not report as much jealousy as girls (or at least did not disclose these feelings). They believed that what causes the most trouble between friends is competition, the need to prove oneself worthy of friendship by showcasing one's competencies (see also Berndt, Hawkins, & Hoyle, 1986; Tesser & Smith, 1980). Rawlins suggested that while adolescents understand the egalitarian nature of friendships, the competitiveness of the male peer hierarchy often overrides the desire for equality. This competitiveness is illustrated by Gene's competition with Phinney in John Knowles' (1959) famous novel *A Separate Peace*:

> I was more and more certainly becoming the best student in the school; Phineas was without question the best athlete, so in that way we were even. But while he was a very poor student, I was a pretty good athlete and when everything was thrown into the scales they would in the end tilt definitely toward me. The new attacks of studying were his emergency measures to save himself. I redoubled my effort. (p. 47)

In our attempts to understand how friendships contribute to negative self-evaluations, we have been investigating early adolescents' interpretations and resolutions of events in which their friends violate a key expectation of the friendship. We focused on these episodes because we were interested in how adolescents maintain their friendships; weathering serious violations of relationship expectations is an important factor in the longevity of relationships. Of course, these infractions can also lead to the deterioration or dissolution of relationships, and we hoped that adolescents' descriptions of the unfolding of these events would provide some clues about why some infractions can be worked out and even strengthen friendships and others damage them irreparably. Finally, we wanted to map potential changes in early adolescents' conceptions of friendship and self-theories and reasoned that events that were inconsistent with their expectations of their friend and the relationship would be especially likely to lead to change (see also Surra & Bohman, 1991).

In one study (Azmitia et al., 1999; Azmitia et al., in preparation) we interviewed 217 fifth, sixth, seventh, and eighth graders about their views about the causes of negative changes in their best friendships (i.e., decreases in closeness or friendship dissolution). Based on focus groups and the literature on the obligations of adolescents' friendships (e.g., Eder & Enke, 1991; Hartup, 1993; Rawlins, 1992; Savin-Williams & Berndt, 1990; Youniss & Smollar, 1985), we created a list of 10 vignettes that represented the infractions that most often challenge adolescents' friendships (e.g., breaking a promise to keep a friend's secret, excluding friends from activities, gossiping about them behind their backs, going on a date with their boyfriend or girlfriend, teasing friends about their weight or appearance in public). Participants were first surveyed about which of the 10 infractions they had experienced recently in a best friendship. For each infraction, they rated its emotional loading and the degree to which it had disrupted the friendship. One week later, the early adolescents were asked to narrate two of these experiences. If they had indicated that they had experienced only one or none of the 10 friendship infractions, they were asked to narrate other experiences in which a friend had done something to them that had led them to question the future of the relationship.[4]

Our analyses of early adolescents' narrations showed that at times, violations of friendship expectations led to interpersonal conflicts. These conflicts typically occurred because their friends made light of the situation or failed to apologize when the injured parties confronted them about the infraction. At other times, conflicts (but not hurt feelings) were avoided because the friends acknowledged that they were at fault, apologized, and made attempts to repair the friendship and the injured parties' trust. Given that most adolescents viewed their friends' actions as very upsetting and indicated that they had disrupted the relationship, it is surprising that in 38% of the narrations, the injured party did not talk to the friend about what he or she had done and opted for either avoiding or "forgetting" the issue. In these situations, the injured parties reported high levels of *intrapersonal* conflict as they grappled with the meaning of their friend's infraction and the impact that it would have on the friendship. While boys were slightly more likely than girls to avoid confronting their friends, the difference was not statistically significant.

Although the early adolescents reported that most of the friendship infractions we studied disrupted relationships at least temporarily, at the time of the interview several boys and girls reported that their relationship had not been permanently damaged as a result of the problem. Some of the early adolescents who had engaged in interpersonal negotiation of the infraction and its meaning stated that the process of discussing the issue and revisiting the friendship and its obligations had strengthened the relationship (Azmitia et al., 1999). However, particularly for high self-esteem adolescents,[5] repeated infractions were associated with friendship deterioration or dissolution.

Berndt (1996) reported that low self-esteem adolescents have more conflicts with their friends than high self-esteem adolescents, but we (Azmitia et al., in preparation) did not replicate his finding.[6] Both studies did converge, however, in showing that low self-esteem early adolescents may have more difficulties working through their friends' infractions than high self-esteem adolescents, particularly when the issue concerns exclusion. Exclusion may be a particularly threatening issue for early adolescents because the changes in their school context and peer groups result in their being very concerned with acceptance and fitting in. Samp and Solomon (1998) have suggested that low self-esteem individuals may find their friends' violations to be especially challenging because they lead them to question their already fragile view of themselves. Our findings (Azmitia et al., 1999) lend support to their position; we found that low self-esteem adolescents viewed the same violation as more serious than high self-esteem adolescents.

Low self-esteem adolescents' avoidant strategies may have also con-tributed to their difficulties working through their friends' infractions. These adolescents were more likely than high self-esteem adolescents to state that even though they were very upset about their friends' behavior, they had not talked to him or her about it. It is interesting that low self-esteem early adolescents were more conflict-avoidant than high self-esteem adolescents because during the interviews, they often ruminated extensively about their friends' infractions. In fact, some revisited their friends' problematic behavior in their responses to ques-tions that were unrelated to this topic. This pattern was especially com-mon in girls.[7] Finally, low self-esteem adolescents also perceived their friendships as more unstable and fragile and displayed more ambiva-lence toward the friendship. The following excerpt from the interview of a low self-esteem eighth grade girl illustrates this point:

Interviewer (I): Can you tell me about what happened when your friend broke her promise to keep your secret?

Adolescent (A): Before I tell you about that, I want to say that for a while I felt like I didn't have any good friends and I was feeling really bad because I mean, I just needed people I could talk to and I don't know, it didn't feel right not to have anybody I could like depend on to talk to and have a good time with and stuff and that's . . . I guess that's why its good to have someone to depend on.

I: And how does this fit in with your friend telling your secret?

A: I just wanted to explain that she's not a bad person and she is a friend I can depend on. Well, usually, unless she does something that makes me not want to trust her, but not really, she's still my friend. Well, she isn't my best friend, just a close friend, and I actually had to tell her things 'cause I had to talk to a friend about things, and I'd tell her something and she'd just tell people and then I'd say, "Why did you tell them?" and she'd say "Well, they won't tell anyone else" but they did. It happens a lot and I guess it should make our friendship a little bit less each time it happened, but she's really nice to me most of the time and she always listens to my secrets . . . I guess it really bothers me that she tells people but she's a really good listener and I can count on her to listen to me.

I: Is there a specific time that you remember in which she told one of your secrets, a secret she promised not to tell?

A: Oh yeah just last week . . . (the early adolescent proceeds to talk about when her friend told the boy she was interested in that she [the narrator] liked him).

Lest the reader think that ambivalence was only a feature of girls' relationships, the following is an excerpt from the conflict narrations of a low self-esteem seventh grade boy who also happened to be in the group of low self-esteem early adolescents who reported a large number of serious conflicts with their friends. This conversation took place after the early adolescent had already narrated one of his friend's infractions:

I: Ok, so let's move on to the next one. We are going to talk about . . .

A: (interrupts) Let's just do them all in order. I'll just say what happened in each one.

I: Oh, um, I only need two of them and we already talked about one . . . I know, why don't you tell . . .

A: (interrupts) I mean, I'll answer 4, 5, 6 . . . (he's referring to the numbers that correspond to the conflict vignettes.)

I: How about you tell me about only two? I don't want to keep you out of class too long . . .

A: Uh, that's OK. I already finished the report. I'll give you some extras. How about two extra?

I: OK.

A: OK, we'll start with 4 (a vignette describing a situation in which the protagonist discovers his two best friends have been excluding him from activities). What happened is that I have two friends that I went, I mean I go out and did things with. And then, huh, they started going out and doing things by themselves. I'm talking about (friend's name) and (friend's name). They're also in the study, so you probably talked to them already. Well, when I found out I was kind of upset . . . well, they've been friends longer but still, I didn't know why they were doing this to me . . . they probably weren't thinking . . . don't you think that could be it? Sometimes people don't think, uh, don't think before they do something. I mean, we have always just gone out and done things . . . you know, actually (friend's name) and I have been friends longer than (friend's name) and (friend's name) and we've always had fun hanging. So it's kinda weird that they are going off by themselves. Uh, they are still my best friends but at times they do things on their own and I have to find out later. You think I should talk to them about it . . . huh . . . maybe its . . . its . . . no big deal. But last Saturday they didn't tell me they were going to a party and I had nothing to do . . . they probably tried to call me and I wasn't home . . . we're still friends. Best friends. Huh . . . let's just talk about another one. How about the gossip one?

I: OK, but before we go on, I just want to clarify . . . have you done anything about how you feel about them leaving you out of things?

A: Huh? Oh, no, its no big deal anyway. They're my best friends. When they talk about things they did together I just act like it doesn't bother me.

I: So their leaving you out of things hasn't changed your friendship?

A: Well, yeah . . . huh . . . no . . . I guess not. They're still my best friends.

It is not that high self-esteem adolescents did not experience serious violations of their friendship expectations. Rather, our analyses suggest that they had usually reached some closure about their friends' infractions either in dialogue with their friend or after working through the issue by themselves or with the help of another friend or a family member. An excerpt from an eighth grade girl's narration of how she handled a situation in which she overheard her best friend gossiping about her illustrates this point:

I: Can you tell me about what happened when your friend talked about you behind your back to be accepted by the popular girls?

A: Well, it was during a play . . . it was just a few weeks ago and I was on . . . they have like a wall between two dressing rooms to make the boys' and girls' sides and I went to the boys' side to get my costumes because they keep the costumes on that side and I was just standing there and like all of these popular girls came in and started talking about me to (friend's name). At first I didn't pay any attention to them, I didn't care what they were talking about because they just trash talk anyway, but then I heard (friend's name) calling me stuck up because I want to go to Stanford and calling me a gossip . . . that really hurt my feelings because she knows that when someone tells me stuff I don't tell, she's always saying how she trusts me with her secrets. So later when she came over after the play I said, "You know what, I was on the other side of the dressing room and I was really hurt when you said I was a gossip." She said "I didn't say anything to them," but I said, you know I don't lie, I was there. So she had to admit it and then we just talked for a long time about it. She said that she did it just because other people were doing it and they were popular, and she's going out with (names a very popular boy) and just wanted to fit in. So I felt like it was OK because I can understand wanting to fit in.

I: Did what happen change your friendship in any way?

A: Well, I think in a little way. It's harder for me to trust her now, but we are still there for each other, and of course, I know that she really can't stand up to peer pressure, and I've known that about her all my life—we've been friends forever. I'm sure that there are things I do that hurt her feelings too, like I know that it upsets her that I want to go to Stanford because she doesn't have the grades to get in and she wants us to go to college together.

I: So what do you think is going to happen to your friendship when you graduate from high school?

A: Oh, we'll still be friends. Just because I'm going to Stanford doesn't mean I'm going to ditch her. We've been through too many things to stop being friends.

This example illustrates a characteristic of many of the narrations of high self-esteem early adolescents: They were able to understand their friends' infractions and acknowledged that they were not perfect either. This more mature approach to relationships may be fostered by early adolescents' comfort with their own strengths and weaknesses and their ability to consider and put in perspective others' good points and fallibilities.

Summary and Conclusions

In this chapter, I proposed that examining situations in which friends' violate key expectations of the relationship can provide a window into early adolescents' self systems and their continuity over time. I have also shown how early adolescents' self-esteem acts as a filter for interpreting the meaning of relational episodes and evaluating friendships. Low self-esteem adolescents appear to have lower quality friendships than high self-esteem early adolescents, perhaps because they feel that these types of relationships are all they can aspire to, because they seek out friendships that will allow them to maintain their negative self-image, or because they may lack the skills to develop and maintain high quality friendships.

When their friend violates their expectations, low self-esteem adolescents often rationalize their friends' infraction or engage in self blame. When in a similar situation, high self-esteem adolescents weigh the negative episode against a wealth of positive experiences and are usually able to work through it and repair their view of their friend or their relationship.[8] Perhaps because of their positive approach, these adolescents see their friends' violation of relationship expectations as a problem to be solved and not as an event that feeds their insecurities and ambivalence about the relationship.

Low self-esteem adolescents', and especially girls' tendency to ruminate about the meaning of their friends' infractions may be indicative of depression, a high negative correlate of self-esteem. However, it may also reflect their enduring concerns about themselves and their relationship—"unfinished business." so to speak (see also Thorne, Cutting, & Skaw, 1998). Their lack of closure is compounded by their avoidant approach to their friends' infractions. Over time, as their negative feelings about these relationships accumulate and fester, their relationships and self-esteem may deteriorate further, thus providing further confirmation of their self-theories.

In contrast, high self-esteem adolescents appear to weather difficult situations by confronting their friend and working to solve the problem before it causes too much damage to the relationship. As illustrated by the excerpt from the conflict narration of the high self-esteem eighth grader, it also appears that these adolescents have a more realistic approach to friendships than low self-esteem adolescents. That is, they do not expect their friends to be perfect because they realize that they are not perfect themselves. Thus, high self-esteem adolescents appear to be able to attend to the broader picture of relational life, the good and the bad, and not get bogged down in their or their friends' failures. Although the developmental research on self-confirming bias in self-projects has largely focused on low self-esteem adolescents, it seems likely that self-confirming biases are also operating in high self-esteem adolescents' self-projects and that high self-esteem adolescents selectively remember experiences that support their view of themselves as competent and likable individuals. For example, when working through a difficult conflict with their friends, high self-esteem adolescents may focus on the way on which they effectively repaired the friendship and not on the feelings of betrayal they experienced prior to conflict resolution. High self-esteem adolescents may also interpret their friends' willingness to work through the difficult situation as evidence that their friend respects and values them. These proposals, while reasonable, need to be tested empirically.

In the future, I would like to continue exploring similarities and differences in low and high self-esteem adolescents' pursuit of their self-projects. I am especially interested in investigating the association between changes in early adolescents' friendships and their self-systems over time. I will continue to study negative relational events that potentially disrupt their relationships and self systems. However, I also want to look at the positive experiences that early adolescents have in their close friendships and how these experiences promote positive self-esteem.

Sullivan (1953) proposed that in the safety of an intimate positive friendship, adolescents can repair their negative models of relationships and of themselves. To date, there has not been much empirical support for Sullivan's position. In fact, as shown in this chapter, it appears that self theories are very resistant to change. However, it is possible that if low self-esteem early adolescents are able to form and maintain a close friendship with a high self-esteem, supportive, and socially skilled peer, over time sufficient evidence that challenges their self theory will accumulate and lead to change. The challenges for low self-esteem early adolescents participating in these relationships are twofold: First, they must establish them and second, they must override their tendency to focus on the negative aspects that characterize all close relationships and ignore the positives. It would be interesting to study low self-esteem boys and girls whose self-esteem improves significantly over the course of early adolescence to assess whether and how friendships played an important role in this change.

Longitudinal research on changes in early adolescents' self-esteem would also be useful for developing interventions that help low self-esteem adolescents revise their self systems. Early adolescence is a particularly ideal opportunity for these interventions because the self system is more malleable due to the intense and rapid change associated with this period of development. Moreover, because the mental health difficulties that are correlated with low self-esteem, and most notably depression, peak in middle adolescence, intervening in early adolescence, when boys and girls develop the cognitive resources to rethink their self-theories, may reduce the likelihood that they will be afflicted with depression and its associated consequences.

Harter (1999) has suggested that interventions that target specific social and cognitive skills may be more effective than interventions aimed at improving overall self-worth. Her suggestion is based on her extensive developmental and clinical research on the construction and evaluation of self. Her work has shown, for example, that low and high self-esteem adolescents differ in the ways in which they process their relational experiences and in the causal attributions that they make between these experiences and their self-worth. The research that I presented in this chapter suggests that early adolescents' perceptions of and management of conflicts with best friends may be a particularly promising area for focusing intervention efforts (see also Selman, 1980).

An additional important goal for the future is to consider the cultural context of the self project. To date, most research has been focused on middle class, European-descent early adolescents. As mentioned, there is some suggestion of ethnic variation in the construction and evaluation of self (see Kling et al., 1999). There are also potential cultural variations in both the self project and in the relationships that play a central role in this project in early adolescence. For example, Seginer (1992) found that for Arab Israeli adolescents, sisters rather than friends served as the key context for exploring and evaluating the self-system. As our theories expand to accommodate the cultural context of development, it will be important to revisit how self, self-esteem, and conflicts in best friendships play out during this very important period of development.

Author Note

The research reported in this chapter was funded by grants from the Spencer Foundation and from the Academic Senate's Committee on Research and the Social Sciences Division of the University of California at Santa Cruz. I am grateful to the adolescents, parents, principals, and teachers of Gault elementary school and Branciforte, Mission Hill, and San Lorenzo Valley junior high schools for their participation in this research. Address correspondence to Margarita Azmitia, Psychology Department, University of California, Santa Cruz, CA 95064. e-mail: azmitia@cats.ucsc.edu

References

Azmitia, M., & Cooper, C. R. (2001). Good or bad? Peer influences on Latino and European American adolescents' pathways through school. *Journal of Education for Students Placed at Risk, 6,* 45-71.

Azmitia, M., Kamprath, N. A., & Linnet, J. (1998). Intimacy and conflict: The dynamics of boys' and girls' friendships during middle childhood and early adolescence. In L. H. Meyer, H.-S. Park, M. Grenot-Scheyer, I. S. Schwartz, & B. Harry (Eds.). *Making friends: The influences of culture and development* (pp. 171-187). Baltimore: Brookes.

Azmitia, M. & Kamprath, N. A. (1993, March). *Gender differences in the influence of friendship on global self-worth in middle childhood: A short-term longitudinal study.* Paper presented at the biennial meetings of the Society for Research on Child Development, New Orleans, LA.

Azmitia, M., Kamprath, N.A., & Ittel, A. (in preparation). *Early adolescents' perceptions of violations of the "contract" of friendship.*

Azmitia, M., Lippman, D. N., Ittel, A. (1999). On the relation of personal experience to early adolescents' reasoning about best friendship deterioration. *Social Development, 8,* 276-291.

Basow, S. A., & Rubin, L. R. (1989). Gender influences on adolescent development. In N. G. Johnson, M. C. Roberts, & J. Worell (Eds.), *Beyond appearance: A new look at adolescent girls* (pp. 25-52). Washington, DC: APA Books.

Belle, D. (1989). *Children's social networks and social supports.* New York: Wiley.

Berndt, T. J. (1996). Exploring the effects of friendship quality on social development. In W. M. Bukowski, A. F. Newcomb, & W. W. Hartup (Eds.), *The company they keep: Friendship in childhood and adolescence* (pp. 346-365). New York: Cambridge.

Berndt, T. J. (1999, April). *The dark side of friendship: Questions about negative interactions between friends.* Paper presented at the biennial meetings of the Society for Research in Child Development, Albuquerque, NM.

Berndt, T. J., Hawkins, J. A., & Hoyle, S. G. (1986). Changes in friendship during a school year: Effects on children's and adolescents' impressions of friendship and sharing with friends. *Child Development, 57,* 1284-1297.

Block, J., & Robbins, R. W. (1993). A longitudinal study of consistency and change in self-esteem from early adolescence to early adulthood. *Child Development, 64,* 909-923.

Brown, L. M., Way, N., & Duff, J. L. (1999). The other girls in my I: Adolescent girls' friendships and peer relations. In N. G. Johnson, M. C. Roberts, & J. Worell (Eds.), *Beyond appearance: A new look at adolescent girls* (pp. 205-225). Washington, DC: APA Books.

Camarena, P. M., Sarigiani, P. A., & Petersen, A. C. (1990). Gender-specific pathways to intimacy in early adolescence. *Journal of Youth & Adolescence, 19,* 19-32.

Claes, M. E. (1992). Friendship and personal adjustment during adolescence. *Journal of Adolescence, 15,* 39-55.

Clark, M. L., & Bittle, M. L. (1992). Friendship expectations and the evaluation of present friendships in middle childhood and early adolescence. *Child Study Journal, 22,* 115-135.

Cole, M., & Cole, S. R. (2001). *The development of children* (4th ed.). New York: Worth Publishers.

Cooley, C. H. (1902). *Human nature and the social order.* New York: Charles Scribner's Sons.

Damon, W., & Hart, D. (1988). *Self-understanding in childhood and adolescence.* New York: Cambridge University Press.

Demo, D. H. (1992). The self-concept over time: Research issues and directions. *Annual Review of Sociology, 18,* 303-326.

Demo, D. H., & Savin-Williams, R. C. (1992). Self-concept stability and change during adolescence. In R. P. Lipka & T. M. Brinthaupt (Eds.), *Self-perspectives across the life span* (pp. 116-150). Albany, NY: State University of New York Press.

Dishion, T. J., Eddy, J. M., Hass, E., Fuzhong, L., & Spracklen, K. (1997). Friendships and violent behavior during adolescence. *Social Development, 6,* 208-223.

Duff, J. L. (1996). *The best of friends: Exploring the moral domain of adolescent friendships.* Unpublished doctoral dissertation, Stanford University.

Eccles, J. S., Barber, B., Josefowicz, D., Malenchuk, O., & Vida, M. (1999). Self evaluations of competence, task values, and self-esteem. In N. G.

Johnson, M. C. Roberts, & J. Worell (Eds.), *Beyond appearance: A new look at adolescent girls* (pp. 53-83). Washington, DC: APA Books.

Eckert, P. (1989). *Jocks and burnouts: Social categories and identity in the high school.* New York: Teachers' College Press.

Eder, D. (1985). The cycle of popularity: Interpersonal relations among female adolescents. *Sociology of Education, 58,* 154-165.

Eder, D., & Enke, J. (1991). The structure of gossip: Opportunities and constraints on collective expression among adolescents. *American Sociological Review, 56,* 495-508.

Eder, D., & Sanford, S. (1986). The development and maintenance of interactional norms among early adolescents. In P. Adler & P. Adler (Eds.), *Sociological studies of child development* (pp. 283-300). Greenwich, CT: JAI Press.

Erikson, E. H. (1950). *Childhood and society* (2nd ed.). New York: Norton.

Erikson, E. H. (1968). *Identity, youth, and crisis.* New York: Norton.

Finders, M. J. (1997). *Just girls: Hidden literacies and life in junior high.* New York: Teachers' College Press.

Forster, E. M. (1951). *Two cheers for democracy.* New York: Harcourt, Brace.

George, T. P. (1999). *Deterioration of early adolescents' friendships: Rates, reasons, and reactions.* Unpublished dissertation, University of Utah.

Habermas, T., & Bluck, S. (2000). Getting a life: The emergence of the life story in adolescence. *Psychological Bulletin, 125,* 748-769.

Hardy, C. L. (2000). *Friendship formation in early adolescence.* Unpublished doctoral dissertation, Concordia University, Canada.

Hart, D., & Edelstein, W. (1992). Self-understanding development in cross-cultural perspective. In T. M. Brinthaupt & R. P. Lipka (Eds.), *The self: Definitional and methodological issues* (pp. 291-322). Albany, NY: State University of New York Press.

Harter, S. (1990). Causes, correlates, and the functional role of global self-worth: A life-span perspective. In R. J. Sternberg & J. Kolligian Jr. (Eds.), *Competence considered* (pp. 67-97). New Haven, CT: Yale University Press.

Harter, S. (1998). The development of self-representations. In W. Damon (Series Ed.) & N. Eisenberg (Vol. Ed.), *Handbook of child psychology: Vol. 3. Social, emotional, and personality development* (5th ed. pp. 553-617). New York: Wiley.

Harter, S. (1999). *The construction of self: A developmental perspective.* New York: Guilford.

Harter, S., & Monsour, A. (1992). Developmental analysis of conflict caused by opposing attributes in the adolescent self-portrait. *Developmental Psychology, 28,* 251-260.

Harter, S., Waters, P.L., Whitesell, N.R., & Kastelic, D. (1998). Predictors of level of voice among high school females and males: Relational context, support, and gender orientation. *Developmental Psychology, 34,* 1-10.

Hartup, W. W. (1993). Adolescents and their friends. In B. Laursen (Ed.), *Close friendships in adolescence* (pp. 3-22). San Francisco: Jossey-Bass.

Henry, J. (1963). The teens. In *Culture against man* (pp. 147-181). New York: Random House.

James, W. (1892). *Psychology: The briefer course.* New York: Henry Holt.

Kamprath, N. A., & Azmitia, M. (1995, March). Gender differences in the temporal patterning of young adolescents' friendships. *Society for Research on Child Development,* Indianapolis, IN.

Kling, K. C., Hyde, J. S., Showers, C. J., & Buswell, B. N. (1999). Gender differences in self-esteem: A meta-analysis. *Psychological Bulletin, 125,* 470-500.

Knowles, John, (1959). *A separate peace.* New York: Bantam Books.

Leaper, C. (1994). Exploring the consequences of gender segregation on social relationships. In C. Leaper (Ed.), *Childhood gender segregation: Causes and consequences* (pp. 67-86). San Francisco: Jossey-Bass.

Mead, G. H. (1934). *Mind, self, and society from the standpoint of a social behaviorist.* Chicago: University of Chicago Press.

Nolen-Hoeksema, S., & Girgus, J. S. (1994). The emergence of gender differences in depression during adolescence. *Psychological Bulletin, 115,* 424-443.

Orenstein, P. (1994). *Schoolgirls: Young women, self-esteem, and the confidence gap.* New York: Doubleday.

Pipher, M. B. (1994). *Reviving Ophelia: Saving the selves of adolescent girls.* New York: Putnam.

Rawlins, W. K. (1992). *Friendship matters: Communication, dialectics, and the life course.* New York: Aldine de Gruyter.

Rosenberg, M. (1990). The self-concept: Social product and social force. In M. Rosenberg & R. H. Turner (Eds.), *Social psychology: Sociological perspectives* (pp. 593-624). New Brunswick, NJ: Transaction Publishers.

Rosenberg, M., Schooler, C., & Schoenbach, C. (1989). Self-esteem and adolescent problems: Modeling reciprocal effects. *American Sociological Review, 54,* 1004-1018.

Samp, J. A., & Solomon, D. H. (1998). Communicative responses to problematic events in close relationships: The variety and facets of goals. *Communication Research, 25,* 66-95.

Savin-Williams, R. C., & Berndt, T. J. (1990). Friendship and peer relations. In S. S. Feldman & G. R. Elliot (Eds.), *At the threshold: The developing adolescent* (pp. 277-307). Cambridge, MA: Harvard University Press.

Seidman, E., Allen, L., Aber, J. L., Mitchell, C., & Feinman, J. (1994).The impact of school transitions in early adolescence on the self-system and perceived social context of poor urban youth. *Child Development, 65,* 507-522.

Seginer, R. (1992). Sibling relationships in early adolescence: A study of Arab Israeli sisters. *Journal of Early Adolescence, 12,* 96-110.

Selman, R. L. (1980). *The growth of interpersonal understanding: Developmental and clinical analyses.* New York: Academic Press.

Simmons, R., & Blyth, D. A. (1987). *Moving into adolescence: The impact of pubertal change and school context.* New York: Aldine de Gruyter.

Simmons, R. G., Rosenberg, F., & Rosenberg, M. (1973). Disturbance in the self-image at adolescence. *American Sociological Review, 38,* 553-568.

Sullivan, H. S. (1953). *The interpersonal theory of psychiatry.* New York: Norton.

Swann, W. B. Jr. (1996). *Self-traps: The elusive quest for higher self-esteem.* New York: W.B. Freeman.

Swann, W. B. Jr. (1997) The trouble with change: Self-verification and allegiance to the self. *Psychological Science, 8,* 177-180.

Surra, C. A., & Bohman, T. (1991). The development of close relationships: A cognitive perspective. In G. J. O. Fletcher & F. D. Fincham (Eds.), *Cognition in close relationships* (pp. 281-305). Hillsdale, NJ: Erlbaum.

Tesser, A., & Smith, J. (1980). Some effects of task relevance and friendship on helping: You don't always help the one you like. *Journal of Experimental Social Psychology, 16,* 582-590.

Thorne, A., Cutting, L., & Skaw, D. (1998). Young adults' relationship memories and the life story: Examples of essential landmarks? *Narrative Inquiry, 8,* 1-32.

Willis, P. (1977). *Learning to labor: How working class kids get working class jobs.* New York: Columbia University Press.

Whitesell, N. R., & Harter, S. (1996). The interpersonal context of emotion: Anger with close friends and classmates. *Child Development, 67,* 1345-1359.

Youniss, J., & Smollar, J. (1985). *Adolescent relations with mothers, fathers, and friends.* Chicago: University of Chicago Press.

Endnotes

1. For boys, the link between peer relations and self-esteem was localized in peer acceptance.

2. Not her real name.

3. Her friend's peer acceptance was actually in the lower range of the average-accepted group, so it is unlikely that she would have been accepted by the more popular girls.

4. For more details about this study, see Azmitia et al., 1998; Azmitia et al., 1999.

5. We defined high self-esteem as scoring at least one standard deviation above the group mean in the global self-worth scale of Harter's Self-Perception Profile for Children (1985) or Adolescents (1987). We operationalized low self-esteem as scoring at least one standard deviation below the group mean in the same subscale. By this criterion, 34 of the 217 early adolescents (15 girls and 19 boys) were classified as high self-esteem and 36 early adolescents (19 girls and 17 boys) were classified as low self-esteem.

6. Although we found that the individuals who reported the most conflicts with their friends had low self-esteem, as a group low self-esteem early adolescents were very variable. Some reported many conflicts and some reported none. Some provided very rich and detailed narrations of their friendship difficulties, others' narrations were very cryptic. As a group, high self-esteem adolescents were less variable. Most narrated at least one serious conflict with a best friend in sufficiently rich detail to allow for in-depth coding and analysis.

7. It is possible that the tendency to ruminate is indicative of depression, a condition that affects more adolescent girls than boys. Because we did not gather measures of depression, we cannot say whether these adolescents' ruminations were more indicative of depression than of low self-esteem. However, Harter (1999) has repeatedly obtained very high correlations between low self-esteem and depression and suggested that it may be impossible to separate these two constructs.

8. This is not to say that they did not report that their friends' infraction had ended the friendship. While rare, the infraction that most often ended friendships involved a best friend going on a date with their boyfriend or girlfriend.

7

STABILITY AND CHANGE IN GLOBAL SELF-ESTEEM AND SELF-RELATED AFFECT

Françoise D. Alsaker and Dan Olweus

Self-esteem is interesting from a developmental perspective because of its likely centrality to an individual's general adjustment. Given that all self-evaluations may be active in forming our perceptions and decisions (Markus & Wurf, 1987), self-esteem is assumed to play a crucial role in the extent to which adolescents will engage in different activities, relationships, and so on, and thus shape their future development. This central role of self-esteem may be positive for the individual's development but also detrimental for adolescents engaging in self-derogation, leading very often to vicious circles that are difficult to stop (Alsaker & Kroger, in press).

Self-esteem is built over the years and likely to change during the entire life course. Nevertheless, as part of the general theory we construct about ourselves (Epstein, 1973), self-evaluations are expected to have a certain degree of stability helping us to organize our experiences in a meaningful way.

Adolescence is a time of change and transitions all happening at a time when formal operational thought emerges. This cognitive stage brings with it an ability to think about self in an abstract way, to go beyond the self and to conceptualize others' thoughts as well (Ellis & Davis, 1982). As a consequence this period is also characterized by an increase in self-awareness (Rosenberg, 1979). These numerous changes make great demands on the young adolescent's ability to adjust her/his self-evaluations to incoming new information about her/himself. As a consequence, it is natural to assume, as does Rosenberg (1986), that adolescence may be a difficult time for the self-concept, which does not mean that it is a period of turmoil. Given that transitions generally mean new orientations, they imply some danger of disorientation (Alsaker & Kroger, in press). In addition, the rapidly growing cognitive abilities may sometimes result in overgeneralizations about others and the self, because the ability of abstraction is not yet completely under the adolescent's control (Harter, 1983). How influential such overgeneralizations and possibly biased self-evaluations will be for the general development of the adolescent depends to a great extent on their stability over time.

The present chapter discusses three separate but closely inter-related empirical studies on the stability and change in global self-esteem and self-related affect. Study I gives an overview of the stability or longitudinal consistency of individual differences in global negative self-evaluations over time periods up to two and a half years. It is based on a large-scale, cohort longitudinal study of some 2,400 preadolescents and adolescents who were measured at several time points, yielding a total of 42 stability coefficients.

Studies II and III are concerned with experiences that are likely to affect negatively an individual's self-esteem both in the short and the long term, namely victimization or bullying by peers. In Study II, the statistical technique of Hierarchical Linear Modeling (HLM) is used to analyze how individuals' developmental pathways over a 2-year period may be influenced by the degree of victimization the individuals are exposed to. In this approach, it is possible to analyze effects of factors that determine not only the individuals' *levels* of self-esteem at a particular point in time but also the *rates* at which they change over time. The analyses make use of the same data set as in Study I.

In the third study, the possible long term sequelae of victimization by peers in school are examined in a group of young adults, at age 23. The data strongly suggest that early victimization has causal long-term effects on the individuals' self-esteem and propensity to experience depression or depressive tendencies. The participants of this study are a subsample of the second author's longitudinal project from Greater

Stockholm, Sweden, comprising in all some 900 boys/young men who have been followed up to age 23 so far (Olweus, 1978, 1991).

The overall aim of the chapter is to contribute to a better understanding of what may affect stability and change over time in global self-evaluations and related affects. Due to the overview nature of the chapter, descriptions of methodology will be kept relatively short. (For more details, see references to the various publications given for each study.)

Study I: Stability of Global Self-Evaluations

Some Terminological Distinctions

Before presenting the results from our empirical analyses a few terminological distinctions are in order. First, it is useful to distinguish between absolute and relative consistency. *Absolute consistency* indicates the extent to which an individual's behavior or "absolute" level on a certain dimension remains the same across various situations or periods of time. *Relative consistency*, on the other hand, concerns the extent to which individuals in a group retain their relative positions on a dimension across situations or measurement occasions (i.e., relative to the average value of the group studied). The degree of relative consistency for a group is usually indexed by some measure of association such as the product-moment correlation.

In the person-situation or "consistency" debate (e.g., Block, 1977; Epstein, 1977; Magnusson & Endler, 1977; Mischel, 1968, 1969; Olweus, 1979, 1980), it was also common to make a distinction between cross-situational and longitudinal consistency (Olweus, 1974, 1980). *Cross-situational (relative) consistency* concerns the extent to which individuals in a group retain their relative positions on a certain dimension across various situations at approximately the same point in time. On the other hand, *longitudinal (relative) consistency*, more often referred to as the *stability* of individual differences over time, indicates the extent to which individuals in a group retain their relative positions at different periods of time.

In our first study, which is based on a previously published article (Alsaker & Olweus, 1992), we will focus on the issue of *longitudinal relative consistency or stability in the area of global self-esteem*. Despite a wealth of studies of self-esteem, only a few have addressed the stability of this aspect of personality as a central issue.

Briefly about Methodology (Study I)

Data were collected on four large samples or cohorts of school children from Bergen, Norway. The children, who were originally in grades four through seven, came from 112 classes drawn from 28 primary schools and 14 junior high schools. A basically random procedure was used in allocating classes to the samples. Consequently, the samples can be expected to be largely equivalent in all respects (with the exception of age and age-related factors). The students were followed for a period of two and a half years. The first measurement point was May 1983, when the children's modal ages were 11 (fourth grade), 12, 13 and 14 (seventh grade) years, respectively. Data were also collected in May 1984, May 1985, and October 1985. The present study forms part of a large-scale project on bully/victim problems in school directed by the second author (see e.g. Olweus, 1991, 1993a).

The design of the study provided us with stability coefficients for "test-retest" intervals ranging from 5 months through 2 years and 5 months, but due to the nature of the design not all age groups could be represented at all test-retest intervals.

The Global Negative Self-Evaluation Scale (GSE) was developed by the authors for use with students from approximately 10 years of age through adulthood. A detailed description of the measure is given in an earlier paper (Alsaker & Olweus, 1986). GSE is a six-item six-point Likert scale, with four of the items taken from Rosenberg's (1965) Self-Esteem scale (RSE). The scale is made up of items such as: "At times I think I am no good at all" and "I would like to change many things about myself." The response alternatives ranged from "does not apply at all" (1) to "applies exactly" (6). Thus, a high score on the GSE-scale indicates a high level of *negative* self-evaluations.

As seen from the content of the items, the scale refers to global (negative) self-evaluation. It can be considered basically comparable to other scales for this domain, such as Rosenberg's RSE or the general subscale of Harter's Perceived Competence Scale (Harter, 1982). As previously documented (Alsaker & Olweus, 1986), the GSE scale has displayed good internal consistency and validity.

Results and Discussion

As expected, the stability of self-evaluations decreased as the interval between measurement points increased. For example, for an interval of 6 months the average correlation was .70 and decreased smoothly to around .60 for one year and one year and a half until it reached its lowest level for intervals of 2 years or more (r around .43). The analyses also indicated a somewhat stronger decrease of the stability coefficients with time interval for girls than for boys; this was especially true for longer time intervals.

As we were also interested in the possible effect of age on stability of self-evaluations, averages of the stability coefficients for each age level and time interval were computed. In boys, stability coefficients generally increased with age. That is, irrespective of the time interval between the measurements, boys who were older at the first time of measurement yielded higher stability coefficients than younger boys. Girls showed a slightly different pattern. Even if the same overall trend was found, girls who were 13 at the first measurement time showed clearly less stability than others. Since this particular time interval included a transition from elementary school to junior high (sixth to seventh grade) for these girls, it is tempting to speculate whether the lower stability coefficients may partly be a consequence of changes in these young adolescents' social and academic environment (cf. Simmons & Blyth, 1987). To visualize these age trends, results for the one year interval for girls and boys are plotted in Figure 1.

The most adequate comparison of our data with previous studies involves intervals up to and including one year (see Alsaker & Olweus, 1992). For these time intervals, considerable similarity of results was found. Because our study was much more homogeneous than previous studies in terms of ages, time intervals, and sample composition, it was likely to yield more consistent and dependable results. On the other hand, it may be argued that all of the stability coefficients were obtained in the same context and under roughly the same general conditions, a fact that may limit the generalizability of findings from our study. From this perspective, it is reassuring to note that for those time intervals of the reviewed studies that could be compared directly with our study, there was, for the most part, a striking similarity of findings. This result makes it reasonable to assume that the more detailed and extended findings from our study have considerable generality.

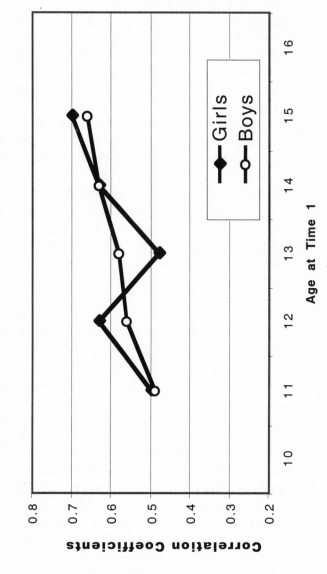

One Year Stability Coefficients

Figure 1. One-year stability coefficients (Pearson correlations) for Global negative Self-Evaluations, for different age groups and for females and males separately. Each data point represents an average coefficient for a given age group. The age groups are based on the students' modal ages at Time 1 for each interval.

On the basis of these results, we conclude that *the expected stability of global self-esteem is high for relatively short time intervals (up to one year or so) but that it declines fairly rapidly* and is considerably reduced at intervals of approximately 3 years.

In the person-situation debate, it was argued by Mischel in particular (1968, 1969) that self-perceptions show considerable stability over time, whereas most noncognitive psychological dimensions display little or no continuity. It is therefore interesting to compare our results on stability of global self-evaluation with results from other domains. Unfortunately, there are very few noncognitive dimensions that have been carefully reviewed and that would permit meaningful comparison with the data in this paper. The stability of aggression, however, has been reviewed in some detail and was also specifically mentioned by Mischel in his critique (Olweus, 1979, 1980, 1984). Accordingly, it is interesting to relate our findings on global self-esteem to those from the area of aggression.

The results presented by Olweus (1979) on the stability of aggression (based on other data sources than self-reports) for time intervals of 1 and 3 years (for males only) showed values of .77 and .73, respectively. For relatively short time intervals, there was thus a fairly small difference between expected stability coefficients for the areas of aggression and global self-esteem (e.g., .77 vs. .71 for a one-year interval). The difference in expected stability increased rapidly, however, with longer time intervals, and was fairly substantial at an interval of 3 years (.71 vs. .47).

We may thus conclude that self-perceptions in adolescence as expressed in global negative self-evaluations tend to be less stable over time than aggressive behavior. Besides being interesting in their own right, these findings are of direct relevance to one of the key issues in the heated person-situation controversy. As noted, it was argued (Mischel, 1968, 1969) that self-perceptions show considerable stability/continuity (consistency) over time while most noncognitive psychological dimensions, including aggression, evidence no or very little continuity. The latter part of this assertion had already been clearly refuted (e.g., Olweus, 1979, 1980; Block, 1977; Epstein, 1979). The present analysis, however, goes further in showing that *global self-perceptions may in fact be considerably less stable than social behavior*, in particular for somewhat longer time intervals.

Stability of Self-Esteem and Age. Age was found to be positively related to degree of stability. By and large, the stability coefficients for adjacent years of measurement showed a fairly regular pattern of slight increase with age. In summary, these results indicate that, *for a given time interval, the size of the stability coefficient for global self-esteem tends to increase with age*, within the ranges represented in the data. There is also some indication that the relationship may be somewhat stronger for boys than for girls.

The implication of these results is that adolescents' global negative self-evaluations are likely to become relatively more fixed or crystallized with increasing age. The empirical results are thus in agreement with *a gradual consolidation hypothesis* implying a generally decreasing impact of later experiences under ordinary conditions. However, periods characterized by large changes that may challenge the individuals' perceptions of themselves may result in lower stability. Accordingly, it is possible that there is a decrease in stability, for example accompanying pubertal development, during transition to college, or in periods involving changes in intimate relationships. The lower coefficients found in 13-year old girls could have been due to school transition or pubertal development. However, as discussed by the authors in their earlier paper (Alsaker & Olweus, 1992), the pattern was not independent of the time interval between the measurements. Therefore, it is difficult to offer a clear-cut interpretation of this specific drop in stability and we conclude that an overall gradual consolidation effect seems to occur in both genders. It is likely that certain changes occurring in early adolescence may have negative or positive effects on an individual's self-evaluations. However, these changes may occur at different ages in different individuals or in different cultures. They may also occur simultaneously with other changes and thus interact with them. For example, the transition from elementary to junior high school might be destabilizing for girls' self-esteem especially in Norway, or it may be destabilizing for most girls because of the co-occurrence of school transition and pubertal development (Petersen, Sarigiani, & Kennedy, 1991).

The slow gradual increase in stability coefficients with age, combined with our finding in a previous article (Alsaker & Olweus, 1993) that normative (average) changes in *level* of self-esteem across early adolescence are quite small, certainly contradicts a stressful period hypothesis or discontinuity view of self-esteem development in this period. Taken together our data support the view that *changes in self-esteem across early adolescence are very gradual and small*. This conclusion has clear implications. As Petersen (1988) has pointed out, beliefs in normative turmoil during adolescence have led to a relative neglect of psychological difficulties when they occur in this period of life. As negative self-evaluations tend to become more and more stable with age, we cannot really expect a spontaneous "recovery" other than for a relatively small number of individuals. In consequence, adolescents and early adolescents showing strong tendencies toward self-deprecation, or other self-related problems, should be taken seriously and offered suitable treatment. To explain away their difficulties with some general stressful-period theory is no longer defensible.

In sum, it is worth emphasizing that size of stability coefficient could be predicted from time interval, age, and sex with considerable accuracy, with an R^2 of approximately .70 both in reviewed studies and in our findings reported above (see Alsaker & Olweus, 1992). At the same time, it should be stressed that variables such as time interval and age, in and of themselves, do not carry much psychological meaning and that there is so far relatively little understanding of which factors and events are "hidden" behind these gross categories. It is an important task to try and increase our knowledge in these respects. An essential step in this direction would be to delineate consistent intraindividual patterns of consistency or change (individuals with varying degrees of absolute or relative consistency, or intraindividual time paths) and to try to identify some of the determinants of such patterns (Rogosa, Brandt, Zinowski, 1982; Olweus & Alsaker, 1991). This is a key task in the following study.

Study II: Self-Esteem and Concurrent Level of Victimization

The results presented in the first section of the chapter form the starting point of the second study. The absence of normative changes in global self-esteem with age (Alsaker & Olweus, 1993) and the general pattern of decreasing stability coefficients with length of interval between measurements suggest that there were intraindividual changes in self-evaluations over time, obviously occurring in both positive and negative directions. In Study II, which is based on an earlier symposium contribution (Alsaker & Olweus, 1991), we highlight some factors that may account both for an individual's *level of self-esteem* at a particular point in time and for his or her *change in self-esteem over time*.

In previous research, Olweus (1978, 1993a) has found that victimization or bullying by peers is clearly related to poor self-esteem. It is very reasonable to assume that repeated experiences with this form of peer interaction will affect an individual's self-evaluations in a negative way.

More specifically, it is expected that victimization by peers will influence both an individual's level of self-esteem at a particular point in time and his or her change in self-esteem over time. With regard to changes, we expect students who experience a decrease in victimization over time to report gradually less negative self-evaluations, and those who experience increases in victimization to report more negative self-attitudes.

Moreover, we examine the relationship between perceived general level of bully/victim problems in the student's own classroom (which may be considered one aspect of the classroom climate) and his or her self-evaluations, both as regards level of self-esteem and changes over time. We expect, generally, that a perceived high level of victimization in the classroom may have negative effects on an individual's self-esteem over and above those deriving from 'individual' victimization (victimization directed specifically at the individual himself or herself).

In the present project, a school-based intervention program against bully/victim problems was introduced approximately 4 months after the first time of data collection (Time 1). In separate analyses (see e.g., Olweus, 1991, 1992, 1993a; Olweus & Alsaker, 1991), it has been well established that the intervention program was quite effective in reducing both individual victimization by peers and perceived level of victimization in the classroom. The intervention program against bullying consisted of a student questionnaire for the anonymous measurement of various aspects of bully/victim problems, a small teacher handbook, a parent folder, and a video that showed episodes of bullying from the lives of two bullied children.[1] In general, the program aimed to increase awareness of and involvement in bully/victim problems on the part of school personnel in particular, but also among parents and students. More specifically, teachers were encouraged to have regular class meetings to discuss bullying in class, to introduce a set of classroom rules against bullying, and to improve supervision during break times, for example (see Olweus, 1993a; Olweus & Limber, 1999). The program is based on a limited set of principles derived chiefly from research on the development and modification of the implicated problem behaviors, in particular aggressive behavior. The principles have been translated into a number of specific measures to be used at the *school*, *class*, and *individual levels.* A central goal of the program is to achieve a *"restructuring of the social environment."* This is done in a number of ways including changes of the "opportunity structures" and "reward structures" for bullying behavior, resulting in fewer opportunities and rewards for bullying behavior. An overview of the program is presented in Table 1. More details are given in the book *Bullying at School: What We Know and What We Can Do* (Olweus, 1993a) and in a new teacher manual *Olweus' Core Program Against Bullying and Antisocial Behavior: A Teacher Handbook* (Olweus, 1999).

It is known that many students in the project experienced a change for the better over time as regards victimization. At the same time, it is obvious that even an effective intervention program is not likely to improve the situation for all victimized students in a school; for some students there will be no change or even an increase in victimization. For the latter group of students, one would thus expect an increase in negative self-evaluations over time, as mentioned above. It should also be noted that a considerable proportion of the students in a school are minimally or not at all involved in victimization problems and for these students, possible changes in self-esteem over time are likely to be related to other factors than victimization.

Briefly about Methodology (Study II)

In this study we use data from three of the original four cohorts. The reason for not including the students from the fourth cohort (the Grade 4 cohort) is that some of the variables to be used in the following analyses were not measured as completely for these students. The students of the three cohorts used, who were originally in grades five through seven, came from 84 classes drawn from 14 primary schools and 14 junior high schools. The number of students for whom sufficient data were available was 518 girls and 593 boys.

Global Negative Self-Evaluations (GSE). This scale, which was briefly described in the first section of the chapter, was the key dependent variable in Study II.

Victimization by Peers (VICT). The victimization scale included five items tapping what has been called direct and indirect victimization by peers, respectively (Olweus, 1991, 1993a). The children were given a "definition" of what should be considered direct victimization episodes

Table 1
Overview of Olweus' Core Program

General Prerequisites

++ Awareness and involvement on the part of adults

Measures at the School Level

++ Questionnaire survey
++ School conference day
++ Effective supervision during recess and lunch time
++ Formation of coordinating group
+ Meetings among staff and parents

Measures at the Class Level

++ Class rules against bullying
++ Regular class meetings with students
+ Meetings with parents of a class

Measures at the Individual Level

++ Serious talks with bullies and victims
++ Serious talks with parents of involved students
+ Teacher and parent use of imagination

(++ core component; + highly desirable component)

and asked to indicate how often they had experienced such things during a certain "reference period." The definition included episodes such as being hit, kicked, threatened, locked inside a room. Being the target of other students' nasty or unpleasant comments (repeated mean teasing) was also presented as examples of victimization. It was further emphasized that victimization is characterized by an asymmetric power relationship: The victim has difficulties defending himself/herself and is somewhat helpless against the students who harass him/her.

In addition, the children were asked about episodes of social exclusion or isolation from the peer group (indirect victimization). A key question was:

How often does it happen that other students don't want to spend recess with you and you end up being alone?

The five items (three on direct and two on indirect victimization) showed satisfactory reliability (Cronbach's alpha), typically around .72, at the three times of data collection.

Perceived Level of Victimization in the Class (PLVICT). Three questions were aimed at tapping the general level of victimization or bully/victim problems in the students' own classrooms, yielding reliability coefficients around .70. A representative item was:

> About how many students in your class have been engaged in bullying (victimizing) other students this term, do you think?

In the following analyses, each individual's score on this self-report index is used.

The two variables VICT and PLVICT were entered as independent variables. Additionally, to relate *changes* in these two variables to changes in self-esteem over time, difference scores were computed for Victimization by Peers (DVICT) and Perceived Level of Victimization in the Class (PLVICT). These scores were calculated as the difference between the average value of each variable for Time 2 and Time 3, on one hand, and the value for Time 1, on the other $[(T2 + T3)/2 - T1]$. The main reason for averaging Time 2 and Time 3 was that no further systematic changes in victimization were expected to occur at Time 3 over and above those changes that had already taken place at Time 2 (due to the intervention program against bully/victim problems).

These two difference variables were treated as independent variables. It should be noted that a negative difference score for these variables indicates a reduction in victimization over time, and vice versa. Frequency distributions of these variables showed that approximately 75% of the students had negative or zero difference scores.

Finally, the grade to which a student belonged at the first time of measurement was entered in the analyses. Since the main reason for including this variable was the need to control for possible age related effects, it is of little substantive interest in the following analyses and will not be discussed any further.

Statistical Analyses

For the following analyses, we have used the newly developed statistical technique of Hierarchical Linear Modeling (HLM). The statistical aspects of the analyses are presented very briefly in this context and for an exposition of the theory and the methods of estimation used in HLM, the reader is referred to other sources (Bryk & Raudenbush, 1987, 1992; see also Alsaker, 1992, and Alsaker & Olweus, 1991).

The analyses were conducted on a PC version of the HLM program developed by Bryk and Raudenbush (Bryk, Raudenbush, Seltzer, & Congdon, 1988).

The first aim of the analyses is to estimate each individual's growth "curve" or developmental trajectory. In the present study with three measurement points, only a straight line or linear growth model could be used. In such a model, two parameters or coefficients, the intercept (status or level at some arbitrary time point, in the present study at the first time of measurement) and the slope (rate of change) coefficients, are used to describe the individual's developmental trajectory (the within-subjects model). In this way, we focus our research on *interindividual differences in intraindividual growth or change*.

In a second stage, the individual linear growth coefficients are used as dependent variables in two new sets of analyses to study factors that are correlated with individual growth or change (the between-subjects model). Such factors can be characteristics of the individuals and/or of the environment. For illustrative purposes, Figure 2 shows fictional individual growth curves for five subjects and the average growth curve for the group as a whole.

Results and Discussion

The results from the estimation of the individual growth coefficients are not reported in detail in the present context. Suffice it to mention that the results indicated that the students differed clearly among themselves with regard to initial levels of self-esteem (or "status") as well as rate of change over time (see Alsaker & Olweus, 1991, for further details) .The next step was to examine whether the selected independent variables were systematically related to the individual growth coefficients.

As expected, degree of victimization at Time 1 (VICT1) was strongly related to the estimated level of negative self-evaluations (GSE) at the same point in time, for both girls and boys. Students who were victimized by peers had thus much more negative self-evaluations than those who were not exposed to such "treatment".

In addition, perceived level of victimization in the class (PLVICT1) was related to negative global self-evaluation, although only the coefficient for boys reached significance. The effect of this variable, however,

Fictional Growth Curves

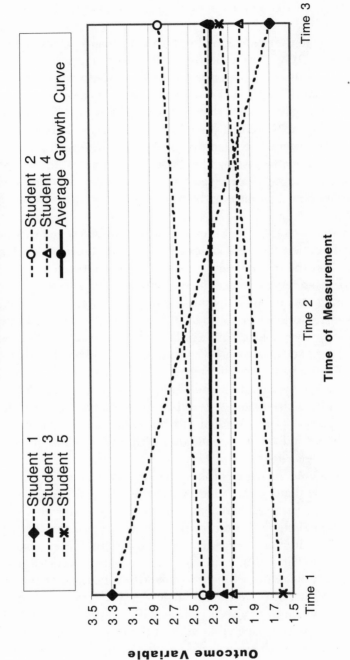

Figure 2. Fictional growth curves for five individuals. The bold curve represents the growth curve for the group as a whole.

was clearly weaker, also for boys, than for level of individual victimization (VICT1).

Turning to the prediction of growth rate, changes in individual victimization (DVICT) were clearly associated with changes in self-esteem (GSE) for girls as well as for boys. That is, students who were exposed to an increase in victimization over time tended to have positive growth coefficients, which means that they increased in negative self-evaluations over time. Conversely, students who experienced a decrease in victimization tended to improve in self-esteem. And the greater the changes in victimization, the larger the changes in self-esteem. Similarly, changes in perceived level of victimization in the student's classroom were associated with changes in the growth rate coefficient of GSE.

These results show that there are strong links between experiences of victimization by peers, on one hand, and self-evaluations or self-esteem, on the other. The students' levels of self-esteem at the first time of measurement were quite substantially predicted by the variable measuring concurrent individual victimization (VICT). In addition, the general volume of victimization in the class (PLVICT) as perceived by the student him/herself predicted level of self-esteem at Time 1 over and above what was predicted by individual victimization.

Similarly, changes in self-esteem could be predicted both by changes in individual victimization and changes in perceived level of victimization in the classroom. As could be expected, the independent predictive power of the classroom variable was generally somewhat lower than that of individual victimization with regard to both level of and change in self-esteem.

Considering the nature of the variables studied, it is very reasonable to conclude that victimization by peers and changes in victimization are *causally related* to the students' self-evaluations. Students who experience verbal/physical attacks and intentional isolation from peers, are likely to interpret these events as indications of their own worthlessness. Similarly, *changes* in such aversive experiences are likely to lead to parallel changes in the students' evaluations of themselves. Although poor self-esteem and anxiety may contribute to a student becoming victimized by peers (Olweus, 1978, 1993a), conceptual considerations make it likely that most of the causal influence goes from victimization to self-esteem, and not the other way around (see also Study III).

At the same time, it should be emphasized that an individual's self-esteem is multiply determined and that a considerable proportion of individuals in a school are not at all or only indirectly involved in victimization problems (in bystander roles, for example). Accordingly, changes in self-esteem, in both positive and negative directions, will occur for other reasons than changes in victimization by peers, and this is particulary true of individuals who are not directly involved in bully/victim problems. These facts may explain why no time-related changes in self-esteem occurred on a group level, whereas victimization problems were dramatically reduced in the same period as a consequence of the antibullying intervention program (see above).

It is also worth mentioning very briefly that the statistical method of Hierarchical Linear Modeling (and related techniques such as that of Goldstein, 1987) presents an elegant and convenient approach to the study of change and other related issues that were very difficult to handle adequately before. In our view, the usefulness of this growth approach, in particular when there are three or more points of measurement, has been amply demonstrated in our study.

It may be considered a limitation of this study that the data on both self-esteem and victimization were collected via self-reports. Presumably, no one would argue that use of a self-report instrument is inadequate for the measurement of self-evaluations. Victimization, however, could have been assessed from other sources of data. To have other measures of victimization in addition to self-reports would certainly have been an attractive feature of the study, even though it has been suggested that, for many purposes, self-reports are probably the best single source of data for the assessment of victimization (Olweus, 1991, p. 439). In light of such considerations, it is encouraging to find that the pattern of results from analyses to be presented in the next part of the chapter were highly similar, whether victimization was measured with self-reports, with peer ratings, or a combination of peer ratings and teacher nominations (such high degree of convergence of findings should not be expected as a rule, however).

Study III: Long-Term Outcomes of Victimization by Peers in School

To be regularly harassed and victimized by peers in school is no doubt a very unpleasant experience that may have considerable negative effects on the victim's self-evaluations and emotional well-being in the short term as shown in the previous study. But will the negative effects remain even several years after the bullying has ended?

Almost nothing is known about the long-term development of children who have been victimized during a sizable period of their school life. Will the reaction patterns associated with their victim status in school be found again if we study them several years later, for example, in young adulthood? Are these individuals still socially withdrawn and isolated, maybe even harassed by their working colleagues or student companions? Or, have they recovered in most respects after they have escaped the straitjacket of companionship forced upon them in comprehensive school, and they can choose more freely their own social environments? Or, does the painful experience of being victimized over long periods of time leave certain scars on their adult personality even if they seem to function well in most respects? These and related issues are explored herein drawing from a follow-up study of young men at age 23 some of whom had been victims of bullying and harassment by peers for a period of at least three years, from Grade 6 through Grade 9 (this section is based on a previous publication by Olweus, 1993b) .

Briefly About Methodology

The participants of this study were 87 men who were approximately 23 years at follow-up in the winter of 1982/83. All of them had participated in an assessment in Grade 9 when they were 16, and for the overwhelming majority, data were also available from Grade 6.

The 87 participants of the follow-up sample consisted of the following three groups:

1. A largely representative sample of 64 young men which included six former victims and five former bullies (see Olweus, Mattsson, Schalling, & Low, 1980, 1988; and Olweus, 1980, for additional information);
2. A selection of 11 additional former victims. The total number of former victims in the study was thus 17. These boys can be considered to be among the most severely victimized boys in the representative cohort of 276 boys to which they belonged;
3. A selection of 12 additional former bullies. Accordingly, the total number of former bullies was also 17. These boys were among the

most pronounced bullies in the cohort (representing about 6% of the total N of 276).

For the purposes of the present analyses only the following two groups were used: The group of 17 former victims and the representative sample of 58 young men (64 minus the six former victims). Due to missing data on some of the variables, the actual number of participants in the present analyses were 15 and 56, respectively.

To be defined as a victim in Grade 6 or 9, a student had to fulfil the following two criteria:

1. He had to have been nominated by at least one of the main class (homeroom) teachers as a victim (according to a specified definition); and

2. He had to have received an average score of one standard deviation or more above the mean of the total distribution (for approximately 275 boys) on at least one of two peer rating variables, Aggression target and Degree of unpopularity. (The average of these two variables defined the peer rating variable Degree of Victimization by Peers to be used in subsequent analyses.)

The stability of victimization status over time was quite high. In actual fact, 16 of the total group of 17 victims in the present study qualified as victims in both Grade 6 and Grade 9. Assuming continuity over the interval covered, they had thus been exposed to fairly severe bullying and harassment for a very long period of time. In addition to having the typical characteristics described elsewhere (Olweus, 1978, 1991, 1993a), the habitual victims were also found to have elevated levels of the stress hormone adrenaline at age 16 in comparison with the control boys.

At follow-up, the participants of this study completed a number of questionnaires designed to tap various dimensions of assumed relevance: Scales for being directly harassed (e.g., "Others are fairly often mean and nasty to me"), for being indirectly harassed (social isolation, loneliness), for social anxiety (shyness, social-evaluative concerns), emotionality-worrying in achievement-related situations, involvement in antisocial activities, several dimensions of aggression/assertiveness and aggression inhibition, frustration tolerance, neuroticism and extraversion (slightly abbreviated versions of the Eysenck scales; Eysenck & Eysenck, 1968), global self-esteem (7 items from Rosenberg's scale; Rosenberg, 1979), and depression (9 items from Beck's scale; Beck, Ward, Mendelson, Mock, & Erbaugh, 1961). The reliabilities of the scales were generally quite satisfactory, in most cases lying in the .80-.95 range (Cronbach's alpha).

In one of the questionnaires, the participants were asked to look back to the year they were in Grade 9 and to assess (retrospectively), among other things, the degree to which they had been exposed to direct and indirect bullying and harassment by peers. The five items covering these domains were combined into one scale.

Several samples of blood and urine were also collected from the participants at two different points in time separated by an interval of about 8 weeks. These samples were used for the assessment of several hormones including adrenaline, noradrenaline, testosterone, and cortisol.

It was considered appropriate to focus the present analyses not only on significance testing but also on effect sizes. The standardized mean difference measure d was used. It is defined as the difference between the means of the two groups divided by the standard deviation of the nonvictim or "control" group (Cohen, 1977). One reason for this strategy is that we are here mainly concerned with exploring possible causal relationships and mechanisms, and from this perspective effect size measures give better information about the relationships of interest than tests of significance. Correlation (Pearson) and regression analyses were also used.

Results and Discussion of Study III

Lack of Continuity in Victimization. The first important result to report is an absence of relationship between indicators of victimization in school and data on both direct and indirect harassment in young adulthood. The fact that a boy had been regularly victimized by his peers in school for a long period of time was thus basically unrelated to (self-reported) later harassment and social isolation. Obviously, the experience of victimization in school did not seem to increase the boy's probability of being victimized in young adulthood.

Considering this finding, one might wonder if the experience of being bullied and victimized in school had been so painful to many former victims that they had simply come to deny or repress any indications that they were being victimized as young adults. This hypothesis, however, could be safely ruled out by means of the retrospective data. Here we found substantial correlations between the retrospective estimates of degree of direct/indirect harassment in Grade 9 and Victim/Non-Victim Status ($r = .42$) as well as degree of victimization in

Grade 9 as measured by the peer ratings ($r = .58$). These findings show that a considerable proportion of the participants had a fairly realistic view of their peer relationships in school 7 years earlier. A *"denial/repression hypothesis"* was thus not a viable explanation of the lack of association between degree of harassment in school and in young adulthood.

One might also wonder if the lack of association was a consequence of the fact that different methods of assessment were used at the two time points: The categorization of the students as victims and nonvictims in school was based on a combination of teacher nominations and peer ratings, whereas the adult measure of harassment was derived from self-reports. Accordingly, one could argue that use of "noncongruent" assessment techniques, which sample partly different aspects of the phenomena under consideration, might lead to a substantial underestimate of the "true relationship."

Fortunately, this possibility could be checked within the present study since self-report data on degree of victimization/harassment in school were also available. Four items (such as "Other boys are nasty to me," and "I feel lonely and abandoned at school") which were part of the assessment battery in both Grade 6 and Grade 9, were combined into a composite averaged across grades (alpha = .84). This composite correlated .42 with concurrent Victim/Nonvictim Status and .61 with the peer rating variable Degree of Victimization by Peers (the correlation within the victim group was even higher, .73). Accordingly, the composite must be considered a valid and meaningful self-report indicator of victimization/harassment in school. When this scale of self-reported victimization in school was correlated with the adult measures of harassment, the results were very much the same as those obtained with the "other-based" measure of victimization in school.

Long-Term Effects of Victimization by Peers. In spite of the fact that the former victims were no more harassed or socially isolated than the control boys as young adults, they had clearly higher levels of depression and a more negative view of themselves (poorer self-esteem) at age 23. On the somewhat abbreviated, but highly reliable Beck scale of depression (alpha = .87), the difference between the victim and nonvictim groups was significant and the effect size d was substantial .87 (a "large" effect size according to Cohen, 1977). For the equally reliable Rosenberg scale of global self-esteem the value of d was .70.

To get a better understanding of how to interpret these results, a more elaborate analysis of the data is required. The key variables and relationships in terms of correlation coefficients are shown in Figure 3

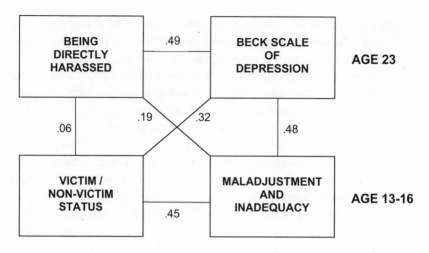

Figure 3. Overview of relations (Pearson correlations) among key variables at age 13-16 and age 23 (*n* = 71).

with the Beck scale of depression as the "ultimate" dependent variable. In Grades 6 and 9, a composite variable was used that reflected feelings of maladjustment, anxiety and personal inadequacy (Olweus, 1978). The reliability of the scale can be estimated at .92. The reaction patterns covered by this dimension can be assumed to be precursors of later depressive tendencies and this assumption was supported by the fairly substantial correlation of .48 between this scale and the Beck scale 7-10 years later.

The pattern of relations found thus far is certainly consistent with an assumption of an indirect causal effect of victimization in school on later depressive tendencies. Before drawing conclusions along these lines, however, one should also consider the possibility of a causal relationship in the opposite direction, from feelings of maladjustment and depression to victimization/harassment. Although there are some indications that early psychological characteristics of a boy (in addition to physical weakness and childrearing variables) affect his probability of being victimized (see Olweus, 1978, 1993b), the present data did not seem to support the idea of a causal relationship in this direction.

In contrast, the substantial continuity of the depression-related variables can be partly accounted for by an "indirect-effect" mechanism, if we assume that victimization/harassment exerts a causal influence on the depression-related variables. It should be added that part of the continuity of the depression-related variables is probably explained by the continuing influence of other factors not included in the model.

All in all, the above results support the view that *the major causal influence is from victimization to depression-related variables, and not the other way around.* This interpretation is strengthened by a consideration of the nature of the peer relationships concerned. As mentioned, the victims tend to be physically weaker than their peers and are typically nonaggressive and nonprovocative. Accordingly, it is very reasonable to assume that they simply fall prey to harassment and dominance on the part of other, more aggressive students (bullies, in particular). And naturally, the humiliating and hostile treatment they are exposed to is likely to affect their self-evaluations (also see Study II) and levels of anxiety/depression.

Taken together, all of this evidence indicates a pattern of causal relation among the variables as portrayed in Figure 4. Victimization in school (victim status) leads concurrently to heightened depression-related tendencies that continue to be elevated 7-10 years later, even though the former victims are no more harassed than their controls at that point in time. Depressive tendencies at age 23 are also affected by concurrent (adult) harassment but the degree of such harassment is not related to earlier victim status.

Nondeviant Development on Several Dimensions. On several adult dimensions on which it would be natural to expect differences between former victims and nonvictims, considering their situation and characteristics in Grades 6-9, there were basically no differences. These dimensions included social anxiety (shyness, social-evaluative concerns), emotionality-worrying, different forms of aggression/assertiveness and aggression inhibition, and neuroticism. In contrast to the findings from Grade 9, the victims also did not have elevated levels of the stress hormone adrenaline, nor were they more introverted than the controls at 23. In agreement with expectations, however, the former victims had been somewhat less involved in criminal activities, both according to self-reports and official records.

Major Implications of Study III

Methodological Adequacy. Before pointing out major implications, it should be emphasized that the results were based on a relatively limited number of participants. This fact should make us regard the conclusions

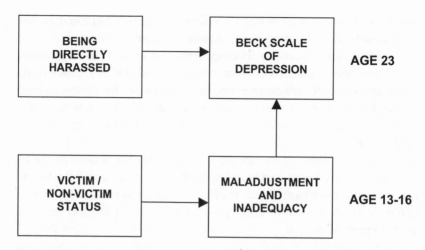

Figure 4. Presumed major causal relations among key variables at age 13-16 and age 23.

to be drawn as somewhat tentative and in need of replication. At the same time, it should be underscored that the findings obtained presented a conceptually very meaningful and coherent pattern, in addition to being quite consistent across two distinct but theoretically and empirically related "ultimate" dependent variables, depressive tendencies and global self-esteem. Also, the victim group was well delineated and its members had undoubtedly been exposed to fairly severe bullying and harassment for several years. Finally, the quality of the data was quite good according to standard psychometric criteria. These aspects of the study should lead to an increased confidence in the conclusions arrived at.

Lack of Continuity in Victimization. In all probability, this lack of continuity is an indication that the participants, after having left school, had considerably greater freedom to choose their own social and physical environments. In this way, the former victims had succeeded in escaping later harassment and victimization to approximately the same degree as their peers. This finding is, of course, encouraging though our reactions should be mitigated by the lasting negative effects of earlier victimization, to be discussed below.

It should be added that the lack of continuity with victimization as measured at age 23 does not preclude the possibility that a former school victim could have an increased probability of being victimized under more circumscribed conditions, for example, in a marital relationship.

A number of implications relating to this set of findings have been pointed out and elaborated elsewhere (see Olweus, 1993b). Since they are not directly relevant to the particular theme of this chapter, they will not be discussed in this context. The focus of the following comments is on the long-term effects of victimization on self-esteem and depressed affect.

The Negative Long Term Effects. Even though the former victims seemed to function well in a number of respects as young adults, there were two dimensions on which they clearly differed from their peers, depressive tendencies and poor self-esteem. The elevated levels on these dimensions can be interpreted as a consequence of earlier persistent victimization that had marked effects on the self-system or personality of some proportion of the young victims. In all probability, they had gradually come to *take over the social environment's* (the dominant peers') *negative evaluations* of themselves as worthless and inadequate individuals (cf. Olweus, 1991, p. 423; also see Bohrnstedt & Fisher, 1986). These negative self-perceptions, which also imply an *increased vulnerability to depressive reactions*, tended to become internalized and "cemented" within the individuals. From a different perspective, one can say that these perceptions and reaction tendencies had gradually become "functionally autonomous" (Allport, 1937), "living a life of their own" independent of their original, immediate causes.

We do not have data available to assess accurately how serious the depression-related problems of the victim group were from a clinical point of view. It is reasonable to believe, however, that they were serious enough to deprive some proportion of the victims of considerable joy and satisfaction with their lives and generally, to worsen the quality of their existence. In addition, it is quite possible that the full consequences of the increased vulnerability of the victims will become evident only at a somewhat higher age. These results make it urgent for school authorities and parents to intervene against bully/victim problems not only to stop current suffering of the victims (Olweus, 1991, 1992, 1993a) but also because of the long-term sequelae for these individuals.

It can be added that victimization/harassment by peers in school appears to be a factor whose causal role in the development of depressive reaction patterns in adolescents and young adults has been much neglected. Since it is known that a considerable proportion of young people who actually commit or attempt to commit suicide are depressed and have low self-esteem (e.g., Sudak, Ford, & Rushforth, 1984), it is by extension likely that victimization/harassment may also be an important factor in suicidal behavior.

Concluding Words

The results presented in this chapter show clearly that a (pre)adolescent's self-evaluation, though relatively (interindividually) stable over shorter periods of time, may at the same time undergo fairly marked (intraindividual) changes, to a considerable degree depending on the kind of experiences and events he or she is exposed to. In particular, painful relationships with peers in the form of persistent victimization are likely to have both short-term and long-term negative effects on the individual's self-esteem and related affects. The assumption that an individual's self-representations are permeable to new information, and expected to change in either positive or negative directions with changes in relationships, got support in Study II, in which changes in self-esteem corresponded in changes in victimization.

The slow gradual increase in stability coefficients with age combined with the clear impact of victimization experiences on adolescents' self-esteem has some important implications. First, it is reasonable to expect that positive as well as negative changes in self-esteem tend to become more and more stable during the adolescent years. This, in turn, means that positive and negative experiences may have an even greater impact on the psychosocial development of the adolescent than we could expect in childhood. Second, given that repeated negative experiences with peers in themselves may result in an *overconsolidation* of negative expectations to social situations and of negative self-evaluations, this effect may be extremely strong during adolescence. Therefore, we cannot expect any spontaneous "recovery" from a damaged self-esteem in adolescents who are exposed to victimization by peers. Third, even in the face of clear factual changes in the reactions from the environment, for example, when victimization stops, the negative self-evaluations will not necessarily change easily in a positive direction. This may be particularly true when the interactions on which the negative self-perceptions are based have elicited intense emotional experiences, including feelings of helplessness, worthlessness, mental pain, or shame. This is actually what our Study III has shown. In spite of the fact that the painful victimization experiences did not continue into adulthood, some important self-perceptions (including poor self-esteem and depressive tendencies) were to a considerable extent maintained unchanged.

These findings, combined with the positive results from the school based intervention project, indicate that the experiences children make in schools and similar institutions often have important consequences for their future development. In our view, it is essential that such knowledge becomes thoroughly incorporated in the daily operation of institutions such as schools and preschools so that they can become the safe and healthy learning environments they are meant to be.

References

Allport, G. W. (1937). The functional autonomy of motives. *American Journal of Psychology, 50*, 141-156.

Alsaker, F. D. (1992). Modelling quantitative developmental change. In J. B. Asendorpf, & J. Valsiner (Eds.), *Framing stability and change: An investigation into methodological reasoning* (pp. 88-109). Newbury Park, CA: Sage.

Alsaker, F. D., & Kroger, J. (in press). Self and identity. In L. Goosens, & S. Jackson (Eds.) *Handbook of adolescent development: European perspectives.* Hove, UK: Psychology Press.

Alsaker, F. D., & Olweus, D. (1986). Assessment of global negative self-evaluations and perceived stability of self in Norwegian preadolescents and adolescents. *Journal of Early Adolescence, 6*, 269-278.

Alsaker, F. D., & Olweus, D. (1991). *Self-derogation as a consequence of victimization.* Paper presented at ISSBD symposium, Minneapolis, July 2-6.

Alsaker, F. D., & Olweus, D. (1992). Stability of self-esteem in early adolescence: A cohort longitudinal study. *Journal of Research on Adolescence, 2*, 123-145.

Alsaker, F. D., & Olweus, D. (1993). Global self-evaluations and perceived instability of self in early adolescence: A cohort longitudinal study. *Scandinavian Journal of Psychology, 34*, 47-63.

Beck, A. T., Ward, C. H., Mendelson, M., Mock, J., & Erbaugh, J. (1961). An inventory for measuring depression. *Archives of General Psychiatry, 4*, 561-571.

Block, J. (1977). Advancing the psychology of personality: Paradigmatic shift or improving the quality of research? In D. Magnusson, & N. S. Endler

(Eds.), *Personality at the cross-roads: Current issues in interactional psychology* (pp. 37-63). Hillsdale, N.J: Lawrence Erlbaum.

Bohrnstedt, G. W., & Fisher, G. A. (1986). The effects of recalled childhood and adolescent relationships compared to current role performances on young adults' affective functioning. *Social Psychology Quaterly, 49*, 19-32.

Bryk, A. S., & Raudenbush, S. W. (1987). Application of hierarchical linear models to assessing change. *Psychological Bulletin, 101*, 147-158.

Bryk, A. S., & Raudenbush, S. W. (1992). *Hierarchical linear models: Applications and data analysis methods.* Newbury Park, CA: Sage.

Bryk, A. S., Raudenbush, S. W., Seltzer, M., & Congdon, R. T. (1988). *An introduction to HLM: Computer program and user's guide.* (Mimeo)

Cohen, J. (1977). *Statistical power analysis for the behavioral sciences.* New York: Academic Press.

Epstein, S. (1973). The self-concept revisited, or a theory of a theory. *American Psychologist, 28*, 404-416.

Epstein, S. (1977). Traits are alive and well. In D. Magnusson, & N. S. Endler (Eds.), *Personality at the cross-roads: Current issues in interactional psychology* (pp. 83-98). Hillsdale, NJ: Lawrence Erlbaum.

Epstein, S. (1979). The stability of behavior: I. On predicting most of the people much of the time. *Journal of Personality and Social Psychology, 37*, 1097-1126.

Eysenck, H. J., & Eysenck, S. B. G. (1968). *The manual to the Eysenck personality inventory.* San Diego, CA: Educational and Industrial Testing Service.

Goldstein, H. (1987). *Multilevel models in educational and social research.* London: Charles Friffin & Co.

Harter, S. (1982). The perceived competence scale for children. *Child Development, 53*, 87-97.

Harter, S. (1983). Developmental perspectives on the self-system. In P. H. Mussen (Ed.), *Handbook of child psychology: Vol. 4. Socialization, personality and social development* (pp. 275-385). New York: John Wiley & Sons.

Magnusson, D., & Endler, N. S. (Eds.) (1977). *Personality at the cross-roads: Current issues in interactional psychology.* Hillsdale, NJ: Lawrence Erlbaum.

Markus, H. R., & Wurf, E. (1987). The dynamic self-concept: A social psychological perspective. *Annual Review of Psychology, 38*, 299-337.

Mischel, W. (1968). *Personality and assessment.* New York: Wiley.

Mischel, W. (1969). Continuity and change in personality. *American Psychologist, 24*, 1012-1018.

Olweus, D. (1974). Personality factors and aggression: With special reference to violence within the peer group. In J. de Wit, & W. W. Hartup (Eds.),

Determinants and origins of aggressive behavior (pp. 535-565). The Hague: Mouton Press.

Olweus, D. (1978). *Aggression in the schools: Bullies and whipping boys.* Washington, DC: Hemisphere (Wiley).

Olweus, D. (1979). Stability of aggressive reaction patterns in males: A review. *Psychological Bulletin, 86,* 852-875.

Olweus, D. (1980). The consistency issue in personality psychology revisted—with special reference to aggression. *British Journal of Social & Clinical Psychology, 19,* 377-390.

Olweus, D. (1984). Stability in aggressive and withdrawn, inhibited behavior patterns. In R, M. Kaplan, V. J. Konecni, & R. W. Novaco (Eds.), *Aggression in children and youth* (pp. 104-137). The Hague, The Netherlands: Nijhoff.

Olweus, D. (1991). Bully/victim problems among school children: Basic facts and effects of a school based intervention program. In K. Rubin, & D. Pepler (Eds.), *The development and treatment of childhood aggression* (pp. 411-448). Hillsdale, NJ: Erlbaum.

Olweus, D. (1992). Bullying among schoolchildren: Intervention and prevention. In R. D. Peters, R. J. McMahon, & V. L. Quincy, (Eds.), *Aggression and violence throughout the life span* (pp. 100-125). Newbury Park, CA: Sage.

Olweus, D. (1993a). *Bullying at school. What we know and what we can do.* Oxford: Blackwell.

Olweus, D. (1993b). Victimization by peers: Antecedents and long-term outcomes. In K. H. Rubin, & J. B. Asendorpf (Eds.), *Social withdrawal, inhibition, and shyness in childhood* (pp. 315-342). Hillsdale, NJ: Erlbaum.

Olweus, D. (1999). *Olweus' core program against bullying and antisocial behavior: A teacher handbook.* Manuscript. Bergen, Norway: Research Center for Health Promotion (HEMIL), University of Bergen, N-5015 Bergen, Norway.

Olweus, D., & Alsaker, F. D. (1991) Assessing change in a cohort-longitudinal study with hierarchical data. In D. Magnusson, L. Bergman, G. Rudinger, & B. Trestad (Eds.), *Problems and methods in longitudinal research* (pp. 107-132). New York: Cambridge University Press.

Olweus, D., & Limber, S. (1999). The Bullying Prevention Program. In D. S. Elliott (Series Ed.), *Blueprints for Violence Prevention.* Boulder, CO: Center for the Study and Prevention of Violence, Institute of Behavioral Science, University of Colorado.

Olweus, D., Mattsson, A., Schalling, D., & Low, H. (1980). Testosterone, aggression, physical, and personality dimensions in normal adolescent males. *Psychosomatic Medicine, 42,* 253-269.

Olweus, D., Mattsson, A., Schalling, D., & Low, H. (1988). Circulating testosterone levels and aggression in adolescent males: A causal analysis. *Psychosomatic Medicine, 50,* 261-272.

Patterson, C. J., Kupersmidt, J. B., & Griesler, P. C. (1990). Children's perceptions of self and of relationships with others as a function of sociometric status. *Child Development, 61,* 1335-1349.

Petersen, A. C. (1988). Adolescent development. *Annual Review of Psychology, 39,* 583-607.

Petersen, A. C., Sarigiani, P. A., & Kennedy, R. E. (1991). Adolescent depression: Why more girls? *Journal of Youth and Adolescence, 20,* 247-271.

Rogosa, D., Brandt, D., & Zinowski, M. (1982). A growth curve approach to the measurement of change. *Psychological Bulletin, 92,* 726-748.

Rosenberg, M. (1965). *Society and the adolescent self-image.* Princeton: Princeton University Press.

Rosenberg, M. (1979). *Conceiving the self.* New York: Basic Books.

Rosenberg, M. (1986). Self-concept from middle childhood through adolescence. In J. Suls, & A. G. Greenwald (Eds.), *Psychological perspectives on the self* (pp. 107-135). Hillsdale, NJ: Erlbaum.

Simmons, R. G., & Blyth, D. A. (1987). *Moving into adolescence: The impact of pubertal change and school context.* New York: Aldine de Gruyter.

Sudak, H. S., Ford, A. B., & Rushforth, N. B. (1984). *Suicide in the young.* Boston: John Wright.

Author Note

Writing of this chapter and parts of the research reported herein were greatly facilitated through grants to Dan Olweus from the Norwegian Ministry of Children and Family Affairs (BFD), the National Association of Mental Health (Nasjonalforeningen), and from the Johann Jacobs Foundation and by a grant to Françoise D. Alsaker from the Norwegian Research Council.

Endnote

1. The intervention program against bully/victim problems consists of the Olweus Bullying Questionnaire for the anonymous measurement of bully/victim problems in school; a copy of a small book manuscript *Bullying at School: What We Know and What We Can Do,* which describes in detail and in simple language the program and its implementation (Olweus, 1992b); and a 20-

minute video cassette (with English subtitles; for European 220v or North American 110v). These materials are copyrighted, which implies certain restrictions on their use. For more details, please write to Dan Olweus, University of Bergen, Oysteinsgate 3, N-5007 Bergen, Norway.

8

INFLUENCE OF COMPETENCE AND ALCOHOL USE ON SELF-ESTEEM

Latent Growth Curve Models Using Longitudinal Data

Lawrence M. Scheier and Gilbert J. Botvin

Developmental studies indicate that competence plays a formative role in the construction of self-esteem (e.g., Nottelmann, 1987; Harter, 1985; 1990). Although competence has both broad and narrow definitions, it is regarded generally as a personal reflection of mastery and is described in terms of *"effective adaptation"* and *"behavioral effectiveness in the tasks of living"* (Masten, Coatsworth, Neemann, et al., 1995; White, 1963). Developmental psychologists interested in resilience have focused on the role of competence as a psychological resource to help children offset stress and counter adverse living conditions that influence development (e.g., Garmezy & Masten, 1991; Garmezy, Masten, & Tellegen, 1984). Operationally, the primary criteria for competence circumscribe a host of social and cognitive tasks associated with school, peer relations, family adjustment, and identity formation (e.g., Pellegrini, Masten, Garmezy, & Ferrarese, 1987). Accordingly, competent children are characterized as individuals with successful peer relations, and high academic performance, who adapt to changing environments, follow rules in school and at home, and are motivated toward success (Blechman, Tinsley, Carella, & McEnroe, 1985; Masten & Coatsworth, 1998). Conversely, maladaptation or poor competence is associated with mental health problems, deviance, peer rejection, psychopathology, and social isolation (Achenbach & Edelbrock, 1981; Blechman et al., 1985; Foster & Ritchey, 1979; Lewinsohn, Mischel, Chaplin, & Barton, 1980; Parker & Asher, 1987).

Because school occupies such a central role from childhood through adolescence, definitions of competence have become tied inextricably to academic concerns and school-related performance (i.e., grades). Harter's (1982) conceptualization of perceived competence as a sense of internalized control over academic outcomes has become a guiding focus for current assessments and has led many researchers to theorize self-regulation as a principal source of competence (e.g., Connell, 1985). Competent students are self-directed, convey autonomy with regard to achievement related behaviors and develop, according to Connell (1985), a controlled understanding of how they achieve success in school (e.g., Connell & Wellborn, 1991).

In recent years, there has been a growing interest in relations between competence, self-efficacy, and self-esteem (e.g., Mone, Baker, & Jeffries, 1995; Wigfield & Eccles, 1994). Self-efficacy is defined traditionally as a belief that one can execute the required skills to complete a task. According to a social learning formulation (Bandura, 1977), efficacy expectations (i.e., beliefs regarding mastery) serve as cognitive motivations that either dissuade or encourage task persistence. When individuals feel competent and well-equipped to take on a specific challenge, their expectation of personal effectiveness encourages them to persist even in the face of difficulty. Low feelings of efficacy, on the other hand, can dissuade or discourage participation resulting in negative devaluation of the self. Oftentimes, the perception of personal control by individuals with high self-efficacy increases their chances to obtain a goal, whereas individuals with low efficacy often blame external forces for their failure (i.e., "the test was too hard" as opposed to "I didn't study enough"). Numerous empirical studies attest to the causal role of effort and control in the formulation of self-efficacy (e.g., Bandura, 1977; 1988).

In contrast to a focus on individual skills as a building block for self-efficacy, self-esteem is less task specific and instead accentuates an individual's evaluation of self-worth (e.g., Beane & Lipka, 1986; Brinthaupt & Erwin, 1992; Coopersmith, 1967; Harter, 1990). In other words, rather than focusing on a single skill or set of skills that foster a belief that one should engage a specific task, self-esteem regards an overall evaluation of whether one's total set of skills makes them fit as a person.

Because an individual's assessment of their skill appropriateness fuels their personal evaluation, competence, or perceived self-efficacy, provides a psychological foundation for the development of self-esteem. When competence is high, and the self is regarded in a positive light, self-esteem also should be high.

As much as researchers have highlighted the pivotal role of competence in generating a positive self-esteem (e.g., DuBois & Tevendale, 1999), studies also have focused on the pitfalls of low self-esteem. An accumulation of research evidence shows that low self-esteem produces a broad constellation of maladaptive outcomes. For example, low self-esteem has been implicated as a determinant of alcohol (DeSimone, Murray, & Lester, 1994; Mitic, 1980; Kaplan, Martin, & Robbins, 1982; 1984) and drug use (Abernathy, Massad, & Romano-Dwyer, 1995; Dielman, Campanelli, Shope, & Butchart, 1987; Olmstead, Guy, O'Malley, & Bentler, 1991; Scheier, Botvin, Griffin, & Diaz, 2000; Vega, Apospori, Gil, Zimmerman, & Warheit, 1996; Wills, 1994), delinquency (Baumeister, Smart, & Boden, 1996), poor peer relations (East, Hess, & Lerner, 1987), and mental health problems (DeSimone et al., 1994; Kernis, Whisenhunt, Waschull, et al., 1998; Ohannessian, Lerner, Lerner, & von Eye, 1994; Tennen & Affleck, 1993), to name just a few of many possible adverse outcomes. Despite evidence that competence and esteem may be linked developmentally (and both may causally relate to alcohol use), the two literatures have developed somewhat independently creating certain gaps in our basic understanding of these developmental processes. Few studies have attempted to bridge conceptually these important psychological mechanisms with each other (e.g., Stanley & Murphy, 1997) and extend this framework to include an etiological connection to early-stage alcohol use. Studies that have addressed empirically the potential for overlap have at most considered linkages between competence and alcohol use (e.g., Scheier & Botvin, 1998; Wills, 1994) or, conversely, alcohol use and self-esteem (Kaplan et al., 1984; Scheier et al., 2000; Schroeder, Laflin, & Weiss, 1993). The absence of a distinct literature linking all three may be unfortunate particularly because competence may provide an essential developmental bridge linking early alcohol use and later self-esteem.

In this chapter, we propose a unique approach to understanding the proposed dynamic relations between competence, alcohol use, and self-esteem. By dynamic relations, we emphasize the developmental processes underlying growth and change in competence and alcohol use. Understanding developmental processes that involve change renders it essential to cast relations between psychological mechanisms (i.e., competence and alcohol use) in terms of temporal order and as a function of time. In the present study, we examine relations between alcohol and competence (and self-esteem) over a 4-year period from the 7th to 10th grades. There are several advantages to scrutinizing these developmental relations over an extended time period. With longitudinal data, we can satisfy certain requirements for establishing causality by casting relations in terms of temporal precedence (i.e., does event A precede event B?) and test hypotheses regarding long-term influences (i.e., does event A contribute to change in event B?). Moreover, as explained below in greater detail, when data are gathered in a sequential time-ordered fashion (each follow-up assessment adheres to a specified sequence), and with a minimum of three follow-up assessments, we can estimate the magnitude of change over time in terms of developmental growth functions.

Our focus on elements of change over time as central to understanding the relations between competence, alcohol, and self-esteem is fueled primarily by two concerns. First, epidemiological data highlight adolescence as a period of risk for initiation to alcohol use (Kandel, 1980; Newcomb & Bentler, 1986). Many youth begin a lifelong trajectory of continued alcohol use in adolescence (e.g., Kandel & Logan, 1984) and substantial research evidence shows that alcohol is an important gateway substance to later and more involved substance use (e.g., Donovan & Jessor, 1983). Most youth begin drinking sometime in middle school and prevalence rates for lifetime, annual, and past 30-day alcohol use increase precipitously between the 8th and 10th grades (Johnston, O'Malley, & Bachman, 1999). From all indications, the early portion of adolescence is characterized by rapid flux and developmental transitions, not only with regard to skills but also with respect to behaviors such as alcohol use.

Second, and no less important, competence also undergoes rapid development in adolescence and is tied inextricably to the major developmental tasks of this period. As Masten et al. (1995) point out, "competence outcomes are part of ongoing processes and therefore are inherently dynamic rather than static in nature" (p. 1636). During adolescence, most youth experience to varying degrees physical (i.e., pubertal growth and menarche for girls), emotional (e.g., striving for autonomy from parents), social (e.g., increased influence and size of peer group), and cognitive change (e.g., transition to formal operations and increased capacity of memory; for a complete review of the major developmental tasks during adolescence, see for example Feldman & Elliott, 1990). As adolescents gain proficiency in their social and cognitive worlds, they are likely to experience changes in perceived competence that parallel maturational events and incorporate the benefits of accumulated experience and behavioral consolidation. In fact, a hallmark of adolescent development is the rapid change in self-perception, the manifestation of this change in terms of identity maturation, and the effects these changes have on the developing self-system (including self-esteem: Erikson, 1968; Wigfield, Eccles, MacIver, Reuman, & Midgley, 1991). To more fully appreciate the course of alcohol involvement and to understand the dynamic forces that link change in competence with change in alcohol use requires a methodological approach that facilitates obtaining quantitative estimates of the magnitude of change as a function of time.

In addition to those substantive concerns outlined above, the methodological focus of this chapter relies on latent growth curve modeling (LGM). Recent advances in the use of random coefficient regression models provide new statistical tools to more adequately model growth (McArdle & Epstein, 1987). In particular, LGM, a type of random coefficient model, represents a powerful and innovative analytic approach to understand better developmental processes that undergo change over time. Readers interested in acquiring a more detailed understanding of the technical requirements for modeling change are referred to articles by McArdle (1988), Meredith and Tisak (1990), and Rogosa, Brandt, and Zimowski (1982). More extensive discussion regarding the utility of growth curve modeling as a means of conceptualizing developmental processes is contained in Burchinal and Appelbaum (1991) and Francis, Fletcher, Stuebing, Davidson, and Thompson (1991). Direct application of growth curve modeling techniques to understanding the etiology of alcohol and drug use are found in Curran, Stice, and Chassin (1997), Duncan, Alpert, Duncan, and Hops (1997), Scheier et al. (2000), Scheier, Botvin, Griffin, and Diaz (1999), and Wills and Cleary (1999).

Briefly, there are a number of ways in which LGM advances our ability to model growth. Conventional regression approaches (i.e., ANCOVA or linear regression), for instance, do not fully appreciate how change in one period in development influences change at some later point in time. Standard regression approaches, which residualize change between any two time-ordered assessment points (e.g., Time 1 and Time 2), cannot model the cumulative nature of growth, nor adequately capture dynamic processes as they unfold in a given portion of the life span. To illustrate this point with a three-wave design, a standard linear regression model predicting alcohol use at Time 3 from prior assessments of alcohol use at Time 2 and Time 1 does not consider how change between Time 1 and Time 2 could potentially influence levels of alcohol use at Time 3. In fact, using standard modeling practices any change in levels of alcohol use between Time 1 and Time 2 and likewise between Time 2 and Time 3 is residualized as error. Thus each component in the time-ordered sequence between assessments (i.e., Time 1–Time 2, Time 2–Time 3, and Time 1–Time 3) represents only a partial (and much dissected) view of how early alcohol use influences later alcohol use.

Taking this example one step further, a reliance on conventional regression methods to estimate change in alcohol use between three (or more) successive time points provides information describing a series of static relations extended over time. However, this same approach does prohibit obtaining a more detailed view of the changing nature of alcohol use across time (e.g., Stoolmiller, 1995). For instance, estimation of the optimal regression coefficients from a fixed-effect autoregressive model (i.e., Time 1 alcohol use influences Time 2 alcohol use and this equation can be extended to include prediction of Time 3 alcohol use) captures effects associated with discrete packets of influence. In the event that follow-up data collections are staged with sufficient intervening time spans, the estimated regression effect captures influences that span a considerably longer period of time (i.e., Time 1 effects on Time 3) but does not consider the cumulative nature of change nor express this dynamic set of processes in a quantitative fashion.

Even if we extend this basic model to include estimating whether change in a second developmental function (i.e., competence) has any influence on change in alcohol use, we are still left with a static model. Normally, with repeated measures, a researcher will construct a cross-lagged panel design (CLPD) to estimate cross-domain effects with two or more developmental constructs. Again, using methods familiar to CLPD, a regression path from early competence (i.e., Time 1) to later alcohol use (i.e., Time 2) addresses directly whether Time 1 levels of competence influence later (Time 2) alcohol use controlling for early levels of alcohol use (Time 1). The obtained regression coefficients do not account for the possibility that incremental changes in alcohol use during the intervening time period are responsible for overall change in competence. Once we begin to expand our model to include additional follow-up assessments (i.e., Time 3), and continue to rely on standard regression approaches, we are left without a means of estimating quantitatively the continuum of change underlying the focal developmental processes.

In contrast to the use of conventional regression methods, a growth curve approach provides a unique means to parameterize behavior as a function of time. Thus, if alcohol use increases at a steady clip during the early stages of adolescence, growth curve analyses can provide estimates of how rapidly alcohol use increases (or decreases). One way to understand this estimation process is to think about whether the rate of growth over the successive time points is relatively slow or fast (i.e., a flattened curve or one that depicts rapid acceleration). Plotting the means for all of the students in a study at the different time points provides some indication of how the group is behaving, but then plotting how each individual deviates from the group profile is entirely more complex (and unwieldly if you think about plotting 100 or even more deviation curves). A second important consideration is whether the rate of growth is positive (upward) reflecting acceleration or downward, reflecting negative or declining growth. The parameters obtained through growth curve modeling detail the direction and magnitude of growth for each developmental function independently. In a more complex model with more than a single developmental construct under study, it is possible to estimate growth parameters simultaneously (i.e., effects in a combined two-factor growth model are considered conditioned).

Given the ability to model growth trajectories for multiple domains of interest in a single model, LGM represents a more flexible approach to understand the precise influence of one developmental construct on another (i.e., the influence of alcohol on competence). With LGM, a researcher utilizes a repeated measures design to model change in the observed means of the measures over time (i.e., as alcohol or competence changes from year to year in the early portions of adolescence). Through a series of planned estimation steps, a growth trajectory is plotted (estimated) for the group and then this information is used to estimate further the magnitude of individual differences (i.e., how much each individual deviates from the group trajectory). This latter step is essential because not every individual's score will fall exactly on the line best fitting the group trajectory. This very brief discussion of the main parameters of interest in a growth modeling framework is meant only to familiarize readers with the basic concepts and to facilitate further reading of the empirical findings associated with the present study. Readers who are interested in more technical descriptions of growth estimation procedures are referred to Francis et al. (1991), McArdle and Epstein (1987: also McArdle [1988] for elemental statistics), and Willett and Sayer (1994).

Our primary interest in testing growth curve models for alcohol and competence rests with the assumption that there may be unspecified linkages between the two developmental functions. In the present study, we systematically explored these relations in a stepwise manner. First, we constructed growth models for alcohol and separately for competence. Subsequently, we examined whether the relative forms of growth are mutually influential or represent independent events (i.e., growth in alcohol has no influence on growth in competence). A further concern relates to whether initial levels of one construct influence growth in the other construct. In growth curve modeling, the mean term for the intercept growth function details the group average prior to estimation of growth. One possible scenario suggests that initial levels of competence influence how fast youth become involved with alcohol. That is, youth reporting low levels of perceived competence may grow much faster in their reported levels of alcohol use compared to youth reporting relatively higher initial levels of perceived competence (the latter of which is construed as protective).

Subsequent to establishing the relative rates of growth for both competence and alcohol use and their conditioned influence (i.e., how growth in one construct influences the other), we examined whether growth in either construct influences later self-esteem. Self-esteem was modeled also as a latent factor, thus improving the model by attenuating measurement error. By adding self-esteem as a criterion construct, we are able to estimate whether effects of changing levels of competence and alcohol use and their dynamic interplay influence perceived self-worth. This stepwise and systematic form of testing growth curve models was arranged specifically in order to test three basic hypotheses. First, we hypothesize that early levels of competence and alcohol use are informative with respect to later self-esteem. This portion of the model maps conceptually to a static influence approach and suggests that deficits in competence and the effects of precocious alcohol use carry forward in time and influence later self-evaluations. Even though this is not a primary focus of the growth modeling process, it remains an invaluable part of the model testing procedure. Reflecting on the competence portion of the model, the first hypothesis suggests that youth with low reported levels of problem-solving efficacy, low levels of perceived personal control (in academic situations), and poorly established self-reward systems (i.e., self-reinforcement) are likely to report low self-esteem. Using the same longitudinal framework, but relying on a somewhat different argument, we also hypothesize that precocious alcohol use influences adversely the self-system and promotes negative self-esteem. This portion of the growth model suggests that early alcohol use interferes with learning mechanisms that are particularly important in the academic environment and fosters negative evaluations of the self. Poor school performance coupled with low grades, feelings of peer rejection, and disenfranchisement from primary socializing agents such as school and family will undoubtably influence feelings toward the self.

A second hypothesis concerns the influence of developmental trajectories (and not static influences) on self-esteem. As levels of competence change over time, internalization of positive experiences regarding growth (i.e., self-efficacy) fosters positive feelings regarding the self. The collective set of effects from improvements in perceived mastery is protective and likely to offset motivations to use alcohol. Conversely, increases in alcohol use can potentiate a breakdown of self-regulation and diminish conventional behavior. With a loss of regulatory control, youth may move away from conventional standards and become attracted to deviant support mechanisms. Kaplan and colleagues (Kaplan & Lin, 2000; Kaplan, Martin, & Robbins, 1982; 1984) provide a theoretically detailed accounting of the relations between alcohol, self-esteem, and self-derogation. Based on their explanatory framework, we would expect dissimilar growth trajectories for competence and alcohol use and opposite patterns of influence for these two processes on later self-esteem. High competence should yield high self-esteem and high alcohol use should promote low self-esteem.

A third hypothesis concerns the influence of early competence on the rate of growth in alcohol use and respectively, the effect of early alcohol involvement on growth in competence. Our original set of hypotheses is constructed around a theme that suggests low competence generates alcohol use through either self-medication or reliance on ineffective (palliative) coping strategies. Troubled and challenged by the viccissitudes of adolescent development, many youth rely on affective-based coping mechanisms as a means of offsetting negative self-evaluations that accompany feelings of failure and disenfranchisement (from school or family). Feelings of poor perceived mastery in social (i.e., interpersonal) and nonsocial (i.e., academic) arenas catalyze movement away from conventional groups (i.e., school) and set in motion a pattern of deviant peer bonding. Self-derogation theory suggests that despite their deficient status, deviant peer groups represent an important source of self-acceptance (e.g., Kaplan, 1980). Deviant peer groups provide new behavioral standards that sanction alcohol use and thus are likely to foster increased rates of alcohol use among poorly competent youth.

Consistent with the notion that early levels of one construct can influence growth in the other, we also hypothesize that early levels of alcohol influence (retard) growth in competence. Hypotheses related to this longitudinal relation are not detailed explicitly in the literature but prevail on the assumption that alcohol abstention has protective effects, whereas precocious alcohol use is risk engendering. Using problem-behavior theory as a guide (Jessor & Jessor, 1977), the motivations for abstaining from early-stage alcohol use likely stem from self-regulation and cognitive controls against deviance, a high regard for academic performance, and reinforcement from primary socializing agents (i.e., family) for conventional behavior. Collectively, these conditions are likely to engender competence and set into motion the development of a positive sense of self.

Overview of Study Design and Sample Characteristics

Participants in this study were part of a prospective, randomized, drug abuse prevention trial conducted between 1987 and 1991 in the northeastern United States. To avoid any confounding associated with treatment effects, only nontreatment (no-contact) participants are used for the current analyses. Extensive documentation regarding sample selection methods, survey administration, experimental design, and research protocols are available elswhere (G. Botvin, Baker, Dusenbury, Tortu, & E. Botvin, 1990; Botvin, Baker, Dusenbury, Botvin, &

Diaz, 1995). The parent study included 56 schools surveyed in the fall and 44 schools surveyed in the spring. The study included a three-form design for questionnaire administration to maximize the number of risk and protective factors surveyed while diminishing response burden. The present analyses rely on a single form containing all of the focal measures of interest with data used from both fall and spring cohorts. Briefly, a pretest assessment was conducted in the fall (or spring) of 7th grade (T1: n = 1181) and follow-up assessments were conducted annually through the 10th grade (T3 = 8th: n = 974, T4= 9th: n = 900, and T5=10th grades: n = 822; T2 represented an immediate 3-month posttest and data for this period is not included in the current study). The final panel sample consisted of 740 students present at the pretest who provided data at all three follow-up assessments.

Survey content assessed substance use behaviors (alcohol, cigarettes, and marijuana) as well as hypothesized psychosocial correlates and causes of early-stage drug use. The sample was 90% White and (based on zipcode information) 82% lived in suburban areas, 7% in urban areas, and 11% in rural areas. Seventy-two percent of the participants reported living with both biological parents, 26.5% reported living with one parent (mother or father), and 2% with family other than their parents. A single item tapping parental education indicated that 30% of the participant's fathers had finished high school and 39% of their mothers had a minimum of a high school education.

In addition to examining self-reported levels of alcohol and drug use, students also responded to a wide range of items assessing hypothesized correlates and predictors of early-stage alcohol and drug use. Major domains of risk assessed included normative beliefs (perceived peer drug use), social (interpersonal) skills, perceived competence (efficacy), knowledge regarding the near and short-term effects of drug use, and personality (i.e., risk-taking). Detailed descriptions regarding individual measures, information pertaining to their psychometric properties, and published sources are available elsewhere (Botvin et al., 1990; Botvin et al., 1995; Scheier & Botvin, 1998; Scheier, Botvin, Diaz, & Griffin, 1999). Briefly, measures of alcohol use were available at all four assessment points (7th to 10th grades) and included items assessing frequency ("How often [if ever] do you drink alcoholic beverages?"), intensity ("How much [if at all] do you usually drink each time you drink?"), and drunkenness ("How often [if ever] do you get drunk?"). Anchored response categories for these items ranged from never tried alcohol to high frequent (i.e., daily) or intense use (i.e., more than six drinks per occasion) and high levels of drunkenness (i.e., daily). The three alcohol items were used to reflect a latent construct of Alcohol Involvement (higher scores indicated more frequent, intense, and problematic drinking) and this specification was repeated at each of the four assessment points.

Multi-item scales assessing perceived competence included measures of self-reinforcement (Heiby, 1983: "I find I feel better and do better when I silently praise myself for even small achievements"), personal efficacy (perceived control: Paulhus, 1983: "When I get good grades in school, it is always because of my own ability and hard work"), and problem-solving confidence (Heppner & Petersen, 1982: "With enough time, I think I can solve most problems that come up"). Reliabilities for the multi-item scales ranged from a low of .73 for personal efficacy and control to a high of .77 for self-reinforcement. Five-point anchored response categories were used for all of the items (strongly disagree to strongly agree). The three composite indicators (self-reinforcement, personal control, and problem-solving confidence) were used to reflect a latent construct of Competence and this specification was repeated at each assessment point.

Six items tapping negative features of self-rejection (e.g., "I feel I do not have much to be proud of") and four items tapping positive feelings of self-worth (e.g., "I take a positive attitude toward myself") were used to reflect a latent construct of global self-esteem in the 10th grade (Rosenberg, 1965). The negative self-esteem items were reverse coded and averaged along with the positive items (α = .83). Three random parcel indicators were then constructed from the pool of 10 items and these three indicators used to reflect a latent construct of Self-Esteem.

Alcohol prevalence rates for this sample are consistent with current published reports for secondary students (Johnston, O'Malley, & Bachman, 1999). Scheier et al. (2000) reported, based on the present sample, that less than one quarter of the seventh grade students reported experimental alcohol use (21.3%). Alcohol use increased precipitously as evidenced by the larger proportion of youth reporting experimental use in each grade (8th: 38%; 9th: 53%; and 10th: 64%). The pattern of increasing alcohol involvement also was reinforced by the sheer number of youth with each passing year that reported intense (i.e., quantity) and problematic drinking, the latter defined by a minimum of two or more drinks per occasion (7th: 10%; 8th: 27%; 9th: 43%;

and 10th: 56%). Comparatively fewer students reported being drunk on a regular basis, although prevalence rates indicated increased rates of problematic drinking with each passing year (3%, 7%, 12%, and 19% of the sample reported being drunk at least two or three times a month in each of the four years, respectively). In addition, gender differences noted in the present sample were consistent with national trends that indicate higher rates of alcohol use by males. Although females reported comparatively lower rates of alcohol use, an increasing number of female students became involved with alcohol over time (i.e., 7th:14%; 8th: 34.9%; 9th: 49.8%; and 10th: 63.2%).

Levels of perceived competence (based on reported mean levels for the multi-item scales) declined progressively over time. For instance, levels of self-reinforcement went from a mean of 31.60 in the 7th grade to 31.15 in the 10th grade. Personal efficacy declined from a mean of 19.69 in the 7th grade to a mean of 19.26 in the 10th grade. The one exception was problem-solving confidence, which increased from a mean of 24.89 in the 7th grade to 25.09 in the 10th grade.

Extensive attrition analyses for this sample have been reported elsewhere (Scheier et al., 2000). Overall, these analyses indicate there was some loss of high-end alcohol users, a disproportionate loss of male students, and a greater representation of two-parent households in the panel sample. In addition to the observed demographic differences between dropout and panel youth, a regression model predicting retention indicated that panel students reported higher levels of social concern, greater self-esteem, and higher grades. Across all 4 years of the study a little more than one third of the sample (38%) was lost to follow-up.

Prior to examining the growth portion of the analyses, we assessed the psychometric adequacy of the hypothesized latent constructs. This stage in the analysis represents an important step because statistically reliable constructs are needed to estimate growth without the undue influence of measurement error. Table 1 contains the factor intercorrelations from a confirmatory factor analysis (CFA: measurement model) using the repeated measures available at each wave as manifest indicators of latent constructs. Latent constructs of alcohol use and competence were specified in each of the four grades and a single construct reflecting self-esteem was posited in the 10th grade. Findings from the CFA model provide a means to examine the psychometric properties of the latent constructs (i.e., are the latent constructs statistically

Table 1
Factor Intercorrelations from the Confirmatory Measurement Model

	1	2	3	4	5	6	7	8	9
1. Alcohol Use (7th)	—								
2. Alcohol Use (8th)	.69	—							
3. Alcohol Use (9th)	.37	.65	—						
4. Alcohol Use (10th)	.28	.49	.68	—					
5. Competence (7th)	-.46	-.31	-.14**	-.15**	—				
6. Competence (8th)	-.21	-.28	-.20	-.16**	.56	—			
7. Competence (9th)	-.20	-.23	-.29	-.21	.54	.67	—		
8. Competence (10th)	-.16	-.26	-.18	-.23	.38	.54	.67	—	
9. Self-Esteem (10th)	-.09*	-.09*	-.10*	-.07m	.27	.39	.41	.62	—

Note. $n = 740$ (panel sample participants)
Unless otherwise indicated, all p's < .001.
*p<.05, **p<.01, mp<.07

reliable based on the pattern of observed indicators). Furthermore, the CFA model provides information regarding the magnitude of cross-sectional and longitudinal associations both within the same (i.e., alcohol to alcohol) and across different constructs (i.e., alcohol to competence or alcohol to self-esteem). There were a number of interesting patterns that emerged from the CFA model. First, intercorrelations among all of the latent factors were in the expected direction. Alcohol related negatively both with competence and self-esteem and this pattern held across cross-sectional and longitudinal associations. Competence and self-esteem were related positively. Second, there was evidence of temporal erosion across time. A careful inspection of the correlation patterns showed that associations within time were relatively larger in magnitude than associations across time. Using competence and self-esteem as an example, the association between 7th grade competence and 10th grade self-esteem was much smaller in magnitude ($r = .27$, $p \leq .001$), than the association between 10th grade competence and self-esteem ($r = .62$, $p \leq .001$).

There also was evidence of shrinkage in the associations between alcohol and competence across time. In effect, relations between alcohol and competence were of a relatively larger magnitude when the measures of alcohol use and competence were within the same time period (i.e., 7th grade alcohol and 7th grade competence) as opposed to across time periods (i.e., 7th grade alcohol and 10th grade competence). Interestingly, the magnitude of association between alcohol use and self-esteem remained relatively stable across time (correlations ranging from .09 to .10).

Results of the Growth Curve Modeling Analyses

The format of the unspecified two-factor growth model for alcohol is depicted in Figure 1a. The repeated measure indicators depicted as F (frequency), Q (quantity or intensity), and D (Drunkenness) represent observed self-report measures. The first set of large circles directly below these measured indicators represents the latent constructs (i.e., statistical dimensions) reflecting level of alcohol involvement. These latent constructs are not "observed," but rather implied (hypothesized); high scores for alcohol involvement represent frequent, intense, and problematic drinking at an early age. A single latent construct is hypothesized corresponding to each time period from the 7th through 10th grades. The second tier of large circles (Intercept and Slope Factors) represents the growth curve portion and helps to specify this particular model as a curve of factors model. That is, growth is being estimated based on the changing means in the latent constructs across time, rather than based on changes in the observed mean structure corresponding to the indicators (i.e., based on F, Q, or D). Turning to the alcohol intercept factor, basis loadings of "1" are included at each time point, which essentially establishes seventh grade as a reference (beginning) point from which to estimate growth (i.e., all the individual curves begin at this inflection point). The alcohol slope growth factor, which captures the rate of growth across time, posits basis loadings of 0, 1, 2, and 3 to designate a linear form of growth over time.

For ease of presentation, only summary statistics concerning growth are presented. More detailed fit indices and precise statistical information corresponding to each of the model testing steps can be obtained from the first author. A model positing linear growth for alcohol fit well and accounted for 85% of the variation in the sample variances and covariances. A significant positive slope mean indicated that, on average, the group level of reported alcohol use increased about one half of a measurement unit each year. A significant variance term for the slope factor indicated substantial variability (i.e., individual differences) existed about the estimated rate of growth. The initial reference point, captured in the mean term for the intercept growth factor also was significant and established the height of the reference curve prior to growth. If we rescale this estimate back to the observed variable metric, the mean levels of alcohol involvement reflected very low levels of experimental alcohol use falling just above abstention. There also was significant variability in this intial reference point, indicating a wide range in the patterns of initial alcohol involvement for these youth.

Although not shown in Figure 1a, there also was an estimated correlation between the intercept and slope growth factors. This association determines whether knowledge of initial levels of alcohol involvement in the seventh grade provides information regarding rate of growth in alcohol involvement over time. This association was positive and significant indicating that youth reporting higher levels of initial alcohol use grew at a faster rate in their alcohol involvement over time compared to youth reporting initially lower levels of alcohol use (who also may have grown in their reported levels of alcohol use but at a much smaller pace). A negative correlation between the intercept and slope

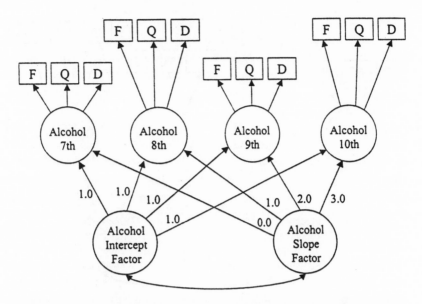

Figure 1A. Two-factor unconditional growth model depicting developmental trajectory for alcohol use. Equal interval basis loadings for slope factor indicates linear growth form (0, 1, 2, 3). Curved line with two-headed arrows represents association between initial status (intercept) and rate of growth (slope).

factors indicates that lower levels of alcohol use in the seventh grade are associated with more rapid acceleration over time.

Figure 1b shows a two-factor unspecified growth model positing linear growth over time for competence. This model fit somewhat better than the model for alcohol involvement and captured 96% of the sample variances and covariances. However, unlike the positive mean growth estimated in the alcohol model, mean levels of competence decreased in a negative (albeit slow) trajectory over time. A significant variance term for the slope growth factor suggests there was variability in this pattern of decline and perhaps indicated that not all of the students reported this precise downward trajectory. The mean of the intercept growth factor, indicating the average starting point for the group prior to estimation of growth, also was significant and there was significant variability in this initial reference point for the group as a whole. There was a marginally significant and positive association between the intercept and slope growth factors ($r = .20$, $p \geq .10$), indicating that youth with relatively higher levels of competence showed relatively

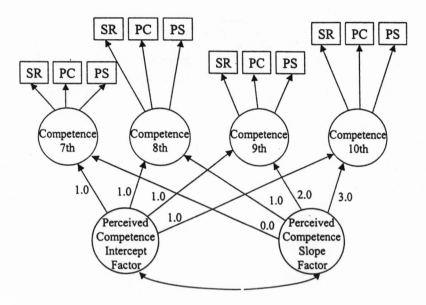

Figure 1B. Two-factor unconditional growth model for competence.

smaller decreases in competence over time compared to youth with lower initial reported levels of competence.

The next step in the model testing procedure combined the two individual growth models into a single growth framework. The combined two-level model is quite informative with regard to whether the respective growth processes influence each other. In other words, the combined model provides an opportunity to determine specifically whether initial levels of alcohol use influence growth in competence, and conversely, whether initial levels of competence influence growth in alcohol use. Figure 2 shows the results of the combined growth model. This model fit adequately accounting for 88% of the sample variances and covariances (a bit less than the benchmark of .90, but acceptable at this point). With the addition of the bidirectional influences (regression adjustments) there was some slight change in the magnitude of the mean and variance terms for the intercept and slope growth factors; however, all of the terms remained significantly different from zero. Initial reported levels of competence were inversely related to alcohol involvement ($r = -.44$, $p \leq .001$), indicating that higher reported alcohol use was associated with lower reported levels of competence. The two slope factors also were related inversely ($r = -.38$, $p \leq .001$), indicating that the two growth trajectories were mov-

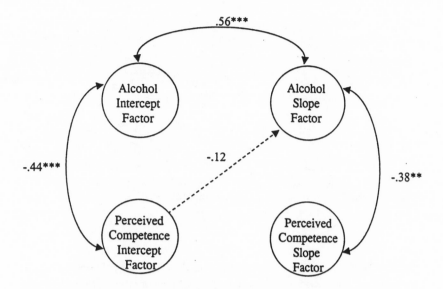

Figure 2. Combined two-factor growth models depicting developmental trajectories for alcohol use and competence from 7th to 10th grades.

ing in opposite directions over time. Consistent with the findings from the unspecified two-factor alcohol growth model, initial level of alcohol involvement was positively and significantly associated with rate of change in alcohol involvement. In addition to the associations among the growth factors, there was a marginal trend ($\beta = -.12$, $p \leq .06$) for a longitudinal association between initial levels of competence and rate of change in alcohol involvement. Because the mean for the alcohol slope growth factor is positive, the inverse relation suggests that youth with relatively lower levels of early competence grew in their reported levels of alcohol involvement at a much faster pace than youth with higher levels of reported competence.

A final step in the growth modeling procedure included examining the effects of growth both in alcohol involvement and competence on subsequent self-esteem. The conditional, two-factor growth model tested previously (i.e., alcohol and competence) was respecified to include a latent construct reflecting self-esteem assessed in the 10th grade. Figure 3 shows the results of the final growth model with an outcome construct of self-esteem. The results of this model are depicted in Figure 3 (trimmed with respect to nonsignificant paths and nonsignificant associations). The associations among the intercept and slope factors within and across constructs remained intact and are consistent with

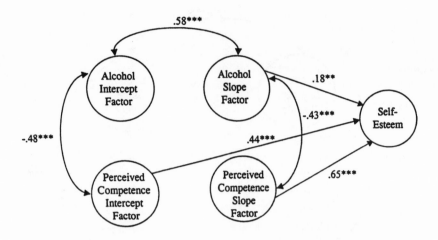

Figure 3. Final latent growth curve model depicting growth trajectories for competence and alcohol and their respective influence on later self-esteem. Model is trimmed with respect to nonsignificant paths.

findings from the conditional, two-factor growth model (see Figure 2). With the addition of self-esteem in the model, the marginally significant path capturing an effect of early levels of competence on growth in alcohol use was not significant. Among the predictors of self-esteem, initial levels of competence predicted significantly later self-esteem ($\beta = .44$, $p \leq .001$). In addition to the long-term relation from initial levels of competence to self-esteem, both slope growth factors predicted significantly later self-esteem (competence slope: $\beta = .65$, $p \leq .001$ and alcohol slope: $\beta = .18$, $p \leq .01$). It is essential to interpret these predictive relations in light of the slopes for each developmental construct. Growth in competence was characterized by a negative developmental trajectory. One interpretation of the positive effect of the competence slope growth factor on later self-esteem is that a larger decrease in competence over time was associated with lower self-esteem in the 10th grade. Alcohol involvement, on the other hand, was characterized by a positive growth trajectory. In this respect, as youth increased their reported levels of alcohol use more rapidly they reported higher levels of self-esteem.

One means of clarifying these complex developmental relations involves plotting the respective trajectories (i.e., high vs. low) against the levels of another construct. The upper portion of Figure 4a shows

change in reported level of competence as a function of three indicated levels of alcohol use. The three levels correspond to tertiles in
the distribution of alcohol use (e.g., 33%, 66% and > 66%). As this
figure shows, youth reporting the lowest levels of alcohol use reported
the highest initial levels of competence but also declined steadily in
their reported levels of competence over time. In contrast, youth
reporting the highest levels of alcohol use (initial levels in the seventh
grade) reported considerably lower initial levels of competence and
actually showed a slight upswing in competence between the 9th and
10th grades. Youth reporting intermediate levels of alcohol use in the
7th grade increased in their reported levels of competence and then
showed a dramatic downturn between the 9th and 10th grades (i.e.,
piecemeal growth).

Figure 4b shows the same type of plot based on the three tertiles of
competence. In all three cases, alcohol involvement increased in a linear fashion. Despite the overall trend for increasing levels of alcohol
involvement in this sample, competence exerted a protective effect.
Students most vulnerable and scoring in the lowest levels of competence (i.e., highest risk for poor self-efficacy) reported the highest initial levels of alcohol use and accelerated their alcohol involvement at
the steepest rate. Students reporting the highest levels of competence
in the 7th grade also show a steep increase in their reported levels of
alcohol involvement. However, in the period from the 8th to 10th grades,
the slope of their trajectory slackened and crossed under the trajectory
for the intermediate (medium) competence group.

Figure 4c shows growth in alcohol use as a function of later levels of
self-esteem. As depicted, the slopes of all three "risk" groups are relatively parallel in form although the reference intercept value for each
trajectory varies slightly. The highest levels of self-esteem are protective and this is depicted by the line closest to the lower values of alcohol use (line connected by small boxes). Despite the diminution of
alcohol use among youth reporting relatively higher levels of self-
esteem, the overall relation between self-esteem and alcohol use is positive. Importantly, these figures do not paint the complete picture of
the developmental relations between competence, alcohol, and self-
esteem. That is because each picture is somewhat isolated from the full
context and reflects growth in two constructs (i.e., a bivariate relation).
In reality, the effect of growth in alcohol use, for instance, on later self-
esteem is conditioned by the effects of growth in competence. What is

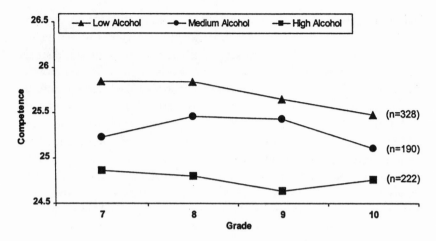

Figure 4A.

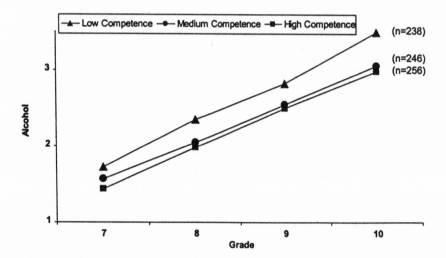

Figure 4B.

Figure 4. Plots of (a) competence by alcohol risk status; (b) alcohol use by competence risk status; (c) alcohol use as a function of self-esteem risk status; and (d) competence as a function of self-esteem risk status.

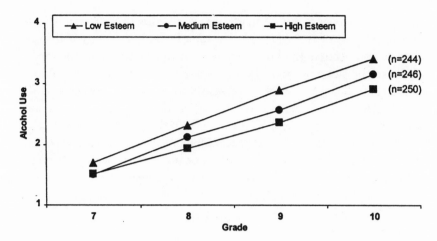

Figure 4C.

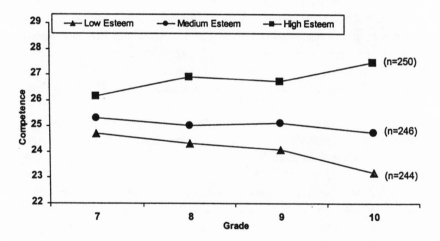

Figure 4D.

necessary to establish a veridical picture of these relations is a three dimensional space that captures the full effect of growth in alcohol use, growth in competence, and initial levels of competence (which significantly influenced later self-esteem) on self-esteem.

Figure 4d depicts growth in competence as a function of later levels of self-esteem. This figure provides some clarity to the overall positive association between the competence slope growth factor and self-esteem. Not all of the youth in this sample declined in their overall levels of competence (and this perhaps contributes to the smaller magnitude of the slope mean). The highest self-esteem group (designated by the small boxes) showed increases in competence between the 7th and 8th grades, a decline between the 8th and 9th grades and a second upturn between the 9th and 10th grades. Both the medium and low self-esteem groups indicated negative developmental trajectories in reported levels of competence. However, the most precipitous decline in competence was observed for the low self-esteem group.

Discussion

We began this study addressing several important concerns regarding the relative role of competence and alcohol use as potential determinants of later self-esteem. An important component to the current study is that we conceptualized these relations as a function of time and not as static, fixed-effect influences. In this regard, we used latent growth curve modeling to verify empirically developmental trajectories for competence and alcohol use between the 7th and 10th grades and linked these trajectories with an assessment of self-esteem conducted in the 10th grade. This conceptualization represents an important departure from the existing literature and may help to uncover the true relations between early-stage alcohol use and cognitive/evaluative components of the developing self-system. Findings from the present study fall into three broad areas of interest. First, tests of the independent growth trajectories indicated that levels of reported alcohol use increased in a linear fashion over the 4-year period. Prevalence rates for alcohol involvement increased precipitously with each passing year, and increased numbers of youth reported frequent and intense alcohol use. As an indication of their intensity, with each passing year, more and more youth reported problem drinking, defined by frequent drunkenness and intense levels of alcohol use.

The two-factor unconditional growth model for competence, on the other hand, revealed that levels of reported competence decreased progressively over time. This finding comports with other investigations that have reported declines in competence that may parallel the unsettling time period surrounding the transition from elementary to middle school (e.g., Wigfield & Eccles, 1994). Mastery beliefs may decline during this time period because of seemingly insurmountable levels of stress or because many youth do not feel adequately prepared to deal with the full range of developmental tasks that unfold during early adolescence (e.g., Larson & Ham, 1993).

A second area of concern regards the relative influence of the two-growth processes. Once the two individual growth models were coalesced into a single framework a more complex picture emerged. Associations between the intercept growth factors indicated that, in the early portions of adolescence, higher competence was associated with lower alcohol use. This finding comports with previous empirical evidence highlighting a protective effect for competence (e.g., Scheier & Botvin, 1998). However, just as we reported in the earlier study, early competence did not influence significantly later alcohol use. In the earlier study, we examined these relations using latent variable structural equation modeling and reported that competence was associated cross-sectionally with less alcohol use in the 7th and 9th grades. However, the present study offers a more realistic conceptualization of the transitions experienced during adolescence and suggests that underlying transformations in competence influence changes in alcohol involvement as much as change in alcohol use influences self-efficacy. Despite the greater precision afforded by the latent growth curve approach, we found that early levels of competence had a marginally significant effect in reducing the rate of growth in alcohol use.

Despite not exerting a powerful and direct protective effect on growth in alcohol use, several pieces of information attest to an indirect role of competence in reducing growth in alcohol use. For instance, a more careful examination of the full set of relations among growth functions indicates that early levels of alcohol use are informative with regard to the rate of growth in alcohol use. Youth reporting relatively higher levels of alcohol use in the seventh grade accelerated in their reported levels of alcohol use more rapidly over time. This dynamic relation is captured in the positive association between the alcohol intercept and slope growth factors. Furthermore, the inverse relation between the competence and alcohol intercept growth factors indicates that relatively higher levels of initial competence are associated with lower levels of alcohol use. In effect, the protective role of competence affects growth in alcohol by lowering initial levels of alcohol use and thereby influencing indirectly the rate of growth in alcohol use.

Related to this second area of concern is the relative influence of the two respective growth processes. The significant and inverse relation between the two slope growth factors highlights the dissimilar growth trajectories for alcohol and competence. As youth increased their rate of alcohol involvement they also decreased their reported levels of competence. This finding presents a somewhat unique picture of the developmental relations that was not evident in our earlier work (e.g., Scheier & Botvin, 1998) and underscores the utility of modeling relations between behavior and skills as a function of time (i.e., dynamic growth processes).

A third concern relates to the role of growth in alcohol involvement and competence on later self-esteem. Once we established the conditional effects on growth for alcohol and competence, we added the final piece of the puzzle and included a measure of later self-esteem in the final growth model. Two important findings emerged from this portion of the analyses. First, initial levels of alcohol did not influence significantly later self-esteem. This finding is consistent with a number of empirical studies that also have reported weak or null associations between alcohol and self-esteem (Brook, Whiteman, Nomura, Gordon, & Cohen, 1986; Kaplan et al., 1984; Scheier et al., 2000; Schroeder et al., 1993; Wills, 1994).

One explanation for the absence of any influence of early alcohol on later self-esteem concerns our use of a global, rather than a domain-specific, assessment of self-esteem (e.g., Dolcini & Adler, 1994). It may be prudent, for instance, to conceptualize self-esteem in terms of specific areas of development that are likely to be susceptible to the early influence of alcohol use. Two aspects of self-esteem likely to be associated with risky behaviors include peer-related and academic esteem. According to self-derogation theory, low peer esteem is likely to foster feelings of peer rejection, elevate feelings of disenfranchisement, and pave the way for deviant associations. These deviant associations, in turn, contribute to perceptions that alcohol is socially acceptable and personally functional (i.e., drinking will help me to gain friends). Equally likely, poor academic esteem can instill feelings of rejection through social comparison processes. Negative or downward comparisons engender feelings of rejection and self-derogation that fuel alcohol use as a form of emotion-focused coping (e.g., Labouvie, Pandina, White, & Johnson, 1990). In either case, the use of a global assessment, rather than a domain-specific assessment of esteem is likely to mask the true underlying relations between alcohol and esteem.

A second finding related to the growth processes concerns the relatively smaller positive effect of alcohol growth on later self-esteem. The positive nature of this relation indicates that as youth accelerated in their alcohol involvement they also reported higher self-esteem. A number of other studies also have implicated alcohol, specifically, and deviance in general, in the development of positive self-esteem (e.g., Bynner, O'Malley, & Bachman, 1981; Jang & Thornberry, 1998). These and related studies accentuate the role of disenfranchisement and delinquent peer associations in providing a social context for early alcohol use (e.g., Brendgen, Vitaro, & Bukowski, 1998; Kaplan et al., 1984). Several additional studies also show that social skills are associated positively with alcohol use (e.g., Scheier & Botvin, 1998; Wills, Baker & Botvin, 1989). The role of social skills, peer associations, alcohol use, and self-esteem may not be quite straightforward and future studies may want to widen the scope of inquiry and consider the motivational significance of alcohol to the self-system (i.e., perceived functions and benefits of alcohol use).

Consistent with theoretical arguments outlining a pivotal role of competence in self-esteem formation (e.g., Harter, 1982), the present study indicates that early competence and growth in competence over time both contributed to later self-esteem. Perceptions of mastery are likely to reinforce engagement across a broad spectrum of tasks including both social and nonsocial events. According to self-efficacy formulations (Bandura, 1977), associations between mastery beliefs and behavior generate reinforcement contingencies (i.e., outcome expectancies) that promote future task engagement. What is not clearly articulated in any developmental theories is whether these reinforcement contingencies facilitate positive self-evaluations that form a cornerstone in the development of self-esteem (e.g., Harter, 1993). In effect, what is missing from current theorizing is a clear understanding of precisely which factors provide a cognitive framework for the development of self-esteem.

Toward this goal, we identified three components of perceived mastery and competence that actively contribute to self-esteem. The latent construct of competence reflected personal efficacy, self-reinforcement, and problem-solving confidence. Personal efficacy essentially taps perception of an internal locus of control for problem solving. Youth reporting high levels of personal efficacy consider ability and hard work as necessary ingredients to solve difficult tasks. Self-reinforcement taps frequency of internal reward systems (e.g., positive self-statements). High self-reinforcing youth accrue positive rewards for small accomplishments and this cognitive reinforcement process contributes to an overall positive self-evaluation. Problem-solving confidence reflects a perception of mastery for difficult and challenging problems. Youth reporting high levels of problem-solving confidence believe they possess the requisite personal resources to master difficult challenges. Together, these three facets of mastery beliefs represent a self-regulatory mechanism that relates integrally to positive self-worth.

There also were methodological considerations stemming from the present study. For instance, despite the observation that competence declined for the sample as a whole, not every individual's growth trajectory adhered to this functional form of growth. The significant variance term for the slope growth factor indicated substantial departures from the group growth trajectory. Moreover, plots of competence developmental trajectories based on levels of alcohol risk and separately for levels of self-esteem (low, medium, and high) indicated diverse patterns of growth over time. In fact, these plots clarified that, for some youth, competence increased rather than decreased. The increases in competence were associated with declines in alcohol use and relatively higher levels of reported self-esteem. Attempts to model piecemeal and non-linear growth patterns for competence were unsuccessful and the basic linear (but negative) growth trajectory provided the best model fit.

There are several limitations associated with the present study that are worth noting. The data collection methods relied solely on self-report assessment, only an abbreviated set of risk factors were modeled, assessments focused primarily on global self-esteem and a broad range of competence skills tapping academic concerns and perceived efficacy. Empirical studies reinforce that self-report methods provide accurate estimates of behavior (e.g., Stacy, Widaman, Hays, & DiMatteo, 1985) and the present study relied on psychometrically sound measures of self-esteem and competence. Notwithstanding, reliance on a single method of data collection can introduce some method variance and ultimately bias model estimation (i.e., the method variance can contribute to stability variance and bias correlations). Reliance on self-report for assessing self-esteem also may restrict our focus to include only reported experience of self-esteem (e.g., DuBois & Tevendale, 1999) and neglect a more complete and multidimensional elaboration of self-esteem that could be observed in applied situations (e.g., DuBois, Felner, Brand, Phillips, & Lease, 1996). Using multiple agent data (i.e., observational measures) to corroborate self-report skills and experiences would clarify and strengthen measurement validity and improve the generalizability of these findings.

Research also shows that gender socialization factors into the developmental processes that foster alcohol use (Windle & Barnes, 1988), and influences the development of competence and self-esteem (Kling, Hyde, Showers, & Buswell, 1999; Josephs, Markus, & Tafarodi, 1992). Perhaps the most significant finding from previous research is that girls may face a different landscape of emotional considerations that influences their self-esteem (Blyth, Simmons, & Carlton-Ford, 1983; Brown, McMahon, Biro, et al., 1998). The combined pool of knowledge from these studies is that boys report more intense and more frequent alcohol use and girls report lower levels of self-esteem in the early portion of adolescence. Additional studies show that relations between self-esteem and other developmental processes (i.e., competence, well-being, and social anxiety) differ based on gender (Scheier & Botvin, 1997). To correctly model developmental processes and avoid misspecification, future studies need to consider gender socialization as it influences both alcohol etiology, competence, and self-esteem.

The influence from subject attrition is also worth noting. In particular, attrition analyses for the present sample indicated that dropouts were more likely to report alcohol use at baseline and to have lower grades, lower self-esteem, and report less social and personal efficacy. These differences could have altered the relations between self-esteem and alcohol use, given that more high-risk, alcohol-abusing youth were lost to follow-up. Finally, despite the use of four waves of data to model longitudinal growth, it is possible that our modeling efforts did not elaborate fully the precise sequencing of growth that ties together alcohol, competence, and self-esteem. In particular, it was possible only to model contemporaneous growth mechanisms based on four waves of data. Added to this methodological concern, the measures of self-esteem also were contemporaneous with the 10th grade follow-up assessment. It is important that future studies consider alternative mechanisms of growth that involve more extensive time frames. For instance, it would be informative to examine whether the observed negative declines in competence precede growth in alcohol use and that change in both mechanisms contribute temporally to self-esteem. Use of more extended time frames accompanied with specific hypotheses regarding the sequencing of these mechanisms can only help to elucidate further the major cornerstones of adolescent development.

Despite reservations and cautions based on design, assessment, and conceptual criteria, there are a number of implications for prevention stemming from this study. The present findings reinforce that alcohol etiology is a complex multifactorial process and that competence plays an integral role in the development and continuation of early-stage alcohol use. Two different pieces of analytic information highlight the protective function of competence, including findings from the growth model showing that competence was associated with lower reported levels of alcohol use and that increased levels of competence retarded growth in alcohol use. Additionally, the bivariate plots accentuate that trajectories of alcohol use were relatively lower for students reporting high competence and likewise the same basic pattern was observed for self-esteem; relatively higher levels of self-esteem were observed in youth reporting higher competence.

Recent research findings accentuate the success of school-based interventions designed to enhance social and personal competence in reducing alcohol and other drug use (e.g., Botvin et al., 1990; 1995; Ellickson & Bell, 1990; Pentz, Dwyer, MacKinnon et al., 1989). Programs that emphasize cognitive-behavioral skills and strategies to improve self-efficacy have been shown to provide an effective antidote to a wide range of behavioral problems (e.g., Botvin, 1995; Botvin & Dusenbury, 1987; Lochman, 1992). These and related findings have prompted several researchers to offer a general paradigm for primary prevention suggesting that many behavioral problems could potentially be avoided with a "dual focus on promoting competent young people and creating competence-enhancing environments" (Weissberg, Caplan, & Harwood, 1991, p. 830). The unique possibilities offered through a systems-based approach that relies on existing school resources to promote competence and enhance self-esteem is especially attractive given its efficient use of community resources to promote successful living. Schools provide natural conduits for prevention activities and much of the focus of social and personal competence enhancement programs can successfully utilize school-related tasks as a format for delivering didactic instruction (i.e., improving study habits).

Skills training in these types of programs include participation in interactive skits with peers to rehearse newly acquired skills, developing appropriate cognitive schemas to offset negative social influences (e.g., refusing active drug offers), behavioral rehearsal in the form of home-work assignments to stimulate family interaction, and didactic discussions that open channels to test, modify, and augment age-appropriate skills. Youth are taught specific strategies to reward themselves for small accomplishments, anxiety reduction and self-management skills to help offset pressures that crop up during adolescence, a full range of interpersonal skills to help them initiate conversations, approach adult authority, strengthen assertiveness behavior (e.g., teaching students methods to express countervailing opinions and return defective merchandise, to name just a few), and behavioral coping skills that buttress specifically perceived mastery and build confidence in applied problem-solving situations (Botvin, 1995).

Collectively, these skills are hypothesized to reduce vulnerability to early-stage alcohol and drug use by offsetting intraindividual motivations (including personality factors such as risk-taking and low self-esteem) for problem behaviors. Once interventions of this nature are fully integrated with the fabric of school life, they can be expanded to include family-based interventions that draw on the full social ecology influencing adolescents (e.g., Kumpfer & Turner, 1990). Corollary issues that may fall under the umbrella of broad-based programs such as those outlined above include reducing school dropout, mitigating academic underachievement, improving health-protective behaviors, and offsetting adverse effects associated with exposure to high-risk environments that have been implicated as antecedents of childhood disorders and mental health problems (e.g., Brooks-Gunn, Duncan, & Aber, 1997). Overall, the attractiveness of school-based competence promotion programs rests with their cost-effectiveness, program accessibility, wide application, and ease of implementation. A challenge for primary prevention programs of this scope is to determine whether effective forms of generic life skills training generalize beyond a small set of problems to a wider arena of maladaptive disorders (e.g., Weissberg et al., 1991).

Finally, it is worth noting that although the present study was not concerned with evaluating individual components associated with an intervention (but is based, in part, on a theoretically rich intervention that targets reduced alcohol and drug use through competence enhancement), the findings do lend support for including strategies that target competence as an essential means of reducing alcohol use and improving self-esteem. In this regard, important advances can be made from this type of prospective empirical inquiry; on the one hand articulating the specific features of risk that promote alcohol use and simultaneously learning about the emergence and dynamic interplay of prominent and malleable developmental factors that fuel the formation of a self-system.

References

Abernathy, T. J., Massad, L., & Romano-Dwyer, L. (1995). The relationship between smoking and self-esteem. *Adolescence, 30*, 899-907.

Achenbach, T. M., & Edelbrock, C. S. (1981). Behavior problems and competencies reported by parents of normal and disturbed children aged 4 through 16. *Monographs of the Society for Research in Child Development, 46* (Whole No. 188).

Bandura, A. (1988). Self-regulation of motivation and action through goal systems. In V. Hamilton et al. (Eds.), *Cognitive perspectives on emotion and motivation* (pp. 37-61). Norwell, MA: Kluwer Academic Publishers.

Bandura, A. (1977). Self-efficacy: Toward a unifying theory of behavior change. *Psychological Review, 84*, 191-215.

Baumeister, R. F., Smart, L., & Boden, J. M. (1996). Relation of threatened egotism to violence and aggression: The dark side of high self-esteem. *Psychological Review, 103*, 5-33.

Beane, J. A., & Lipka, R. P. (1986). *Self-concept, self-esteem, and the curriculum*. New York: Teachers College Press.

Bentler, P. M. (1990). Comparative fit indexes in structural models. *Psychological Bulletin, 107*, 238-246.

Bentler, P. M. (1995). *EQS structural equations program manual*. Encino, CA: Multivariate, Inc.

Bentler, P. M., & Bonett, D. G. (1980). Significance tests and goodness of fit in the analysis of covariance structures. *Psychological Bulletin, 88*, 588-606.

Blechman, E. A., Tinsley, B., Carella, E. T., & McEnroe, M. J. (1985). Childhood competence and behavior problems. *Journal of Abnormal Psychology, 94*, 70-77.

Blyth, D. A., Simmons, R. G., & Carlton-Ford. S. (1983). The adjustment of early adolescents to school transitions. *Journal of Early Adolescence, 3*, 105-120.

Botvin, G. J. (1995). Principles of prevention. In R. H. Coombs & D. M. Ziedonis (Eds.), *Handbook on drug abuse prevention: A comprehensive strategy to prevent the abuse of alcohol and other drugs* (pp. 19-44). Boston, MA: Allyn & Bacon.

Botvin, G. J., Baker, E., Dusenbury, L., Botvin, E., & Diaz, T. (1995). Long-term follow-up of a randomized drug abuse prevention trial in a white middle-class population. *Journal of the American Medical Association, 273,* 1106-1112.

Botvin, G. J., Baker, E., Dusenbury, L., Tortu, S., Botvin, E. M. (1990). Preventing adolescent drug abuse through a multimodal cognitive-behavioral approach: Results of a three-year study. *Journal of Consulting and Clinical Psychology, 58,* 437-446.

Botvin, G. J., & Dusenbury, L. (1987). Life Skills Training: A psychoeducational approach to substance abuse prevention. In C. A. Maher & J. E. Zins (Eds.), *Psycoheducational interventions in schools: Methods and procedures for enhancing student competence* (pp. 46-65). New York: Pergamon Press.

Brendgen, M., Vitaro, F., & Bukowski. W. M. (1998). Affiliation with delinquent friends: Contributions of parents, self-esteem, delinquent behavior, and rejection by peers. *Journal of Early Adolescence, 18,* 244-265.

Brinthaupt, T. M., & Erwin, L. J. (1992). Reporting about the self: Issues and implications. In T. M. Brinthaupt & R. P. Lipka (Eds.), *The self: Definitional and methodological issues* (pp. 137-171). Albany, NY: State University of New York Press.

Brook, J. S., Whiteman, M., Nomura, C., Gordon, A. S., & Cohen, P. (1986). Dynamics of childhood and adolescent personality traits and adolescent drug use. *Developmental Psychology, 22,* 403-414.

Brooks-Gunn, J., Duncan, G., & Aber, J. L. (Eds.). (1997). *Neighborhood poverty: Context and consequences for children* (Volume 1). *Policy implications in studying neighborhoods* (Volume 2). New York: Russell Sage Foundation Press.

Brown, K. M., McMahon, R. P., Biro, F. M., Crawford, P., Schreiber, G. B., Similo, S. L., Waclawiw, M., & Striegel-Moore, R. (1998). Changes in self-esteem in black and white girls between the ages of 9 and 14 years. *Journal of Adolescent Health, 23,* 7-19.

Burchinal, M., & Appelbaum, M. I. (1991). Estimating individual developmental functions: Methods and their assumptions. *Child Development, 62,* 23-43.

Bynner, J. M., O'Malley, P. M., & Bachman, J. G. (1981). Self-esteem and delinquency revisited. *Journal of Youth and Adolescence, 10,* 407-441.

Connell, J. P. (1985). A new multidimensional measure of children's perception of control. *Child Development, 56*, 1018-1041.

Connell, J. P., & Wellborn, J. G. (1991). Competence, autonomy, and relatedness: A motivational analysis of self-system processes. In M. R. Gunnar & L. A. Sroufe (Eds.), *The Minnesota symposia on child psychology: Vol. 23. Self processes and development* (pp. 43-77). Hillsdale, NJ: Lawrence Erlbaum.

Coopersmith, S. (1967). *The antecedents of self-esteem.* San Francisco, CA: Freeman.

Curran, P. J., Stice, E., & Chassin, L. (1997). The relation between adolescent alcohol use and peer alcohol use: A longitudinal random coefficients model. *Journal of Consulting and Clinical Psychology, 65*, 130-140.

DeSimone, A., Murray, P., & Lester, D. (1994). Alcohol use, self-esteem, depression and suicidality in high school students. *Adolescence, 29*, 939-942.

Dielman, T. E., Campanelli, P. C., Shope, J. T., & Butchart, A. T. (1987). Susceptibility to peer pressure, self-esteem, and health locus of control as correlates of adolescent substance abuse. *Health Education Quarterly, 14*, 207-221.

Dolcini, M. M., & Adler, N. E. (1994). Perceived competencies, peer group affiliation, and risk behavior among early adolescents. *Health Psychology, 13*, 496-506.

Donovan, J. E., & Jessor, R. (1983). Problem drinking and the dimension of involvement with drugs: A Guttman scalogram analysis of adolescent drug use. *American Journal of Public Health, 73*, 543-552.

DuBois, D. L., Felner, R. D., Brand, S., Phillips, R. S. C., & Lease, A. M. (1996). Early adolescent self-esteem: A developmental-ecological framework and assessment strategy. *Journal of Research on Adolescence, 6*, 543-579.

DuBois, D. L., & Tevendale, H. D. (1999). Self-esteem in childhood and adolescence: Vaccine or epiphenomenon? *Applied and Preventive Psychology, 8*, 103-117.

Duncan, S. C., & Duncan, T. E. (1996). A multivariate latent growth curve analysis of adolescent substance use. *Structural Equation Modeling, 3*, 323-347.

Duncan, S. C., Alpert, A., Duncan, T. E., & Hops, H. (1997). Adolescent alcohol use development and young adult outcomes. *Drug and Alcohol Dependence, 49*, 39-48.

East, P. L., Hess, L. E., & Lerner, R. M. (1987). Peer social support and adjustment of early adolescent peer groups. *Journal of Early Adolescence, 7*, 153-163.

Ellickson, P. L., & Bell, R. M. (1990). Drug prevention in junior high: A multi-site, longitudinal test. *Science, 247*, 1299-1305.

Erikson, E. H. (1968). *Identity, youth, and crisis.* New York: Norton.

Feldman, S. S., & Elliott, G. R. (Eds.) (1990). *At the threshold: The developing adolescent.* Cambridge, MA: Harvard University Press.

Foster, S. L., & Ritchey, W. L. (1979). Issues in the assessment of social competence in children. *Journal of Applied Behavior Analysis, 12,* 625-638.

Francis, D. J., Fletcher, J. M., Stuebing, K. K., Davidson, K. C., & Thompson, N. M. (1991). Analysis of change: Modeling individual growth. *Journal of Consulting and Clinical Psychology, 59,* 27-37.

Garmezy, N., & Masten, A. S. (1991). The protective role of competence indicators in children at risk. In E. M. Cummings, A. L. Greene, & K. H. Karraker (Eds.), *Life-span developmental psychology: Perspectives on stress and coping* (pp. 151-174). Hillsdale, NJ: Lawrence Erlbaum.

Garmezy, N., Masten, A. S., & Tellegen, A. (1984). The study of stress and competence in children: A building block for developmental psychopathology. *Child Development, 55,* 97-111.

Harter, S. (1982). The perceived competence scale for children. *Child Development, 53,* 87-97.

Harter, S. (1985). Competence as a dimension of self-evaluation: Toward a comprehensive model of self-worth. In R. L. Leahy (Ed.), *The development of the self* (pp. 55-121). Orlando, FL: Academic Press.

Harter, S. (1990). Causes, correlates and the functional role of self-worth: A life-span perspective. In R. J. Sternberg & J. Kolligian (Eds.), *Competence considered* (pp. 67-97). New Haven, CT: Yale University Press.

Harter, S. (1993). Causes and consequences of low self-esteem in children and adolescents. In R. Baumeister (Ed.), *Self-esteem: The puzzle of low self-regard* (pp. 87-111). New York: Plenum Press.

Heiby, E. (1983). Assessment of frequency of self-reinforcement. *Journal of Personality and Social Psychology, 44,* 1304-1307.

Heppner, P. P., & Petersen, C. H. (1982). The development and implications of a personal problem-solving inventory. *Journal of Counseling Psychology, 29,* 66-75.

Jang, S. J., & Thornberry, T. P. (1998). Self-esteem, delinquent peers, and delinquency: A test of the self-enhancement thesis. *American Sociological Review, 63,* 586-598.

Jessor, R., & Jessor, S. L. (1977). *Problem behavior and psychosocial development: A longitudinal study of youth.* New York: Academic Press.

Johnston, L. D., O'Malley, P. M., & Bachman, J. G. (1999). *National survey results on drug use from the Monitoring the Future Study, 1975-1995: Vol. I. Secondary school students.* National Institute on Drug Abuse (NIH Pub. No. 99-4139). Washington, DC: Government Printing Office.

Josephs, R., Markus, H., & Tafarodi, R. (1992). Gender and self-esteem. *Journal of Personality and Social Psychology, 63*, 391-402.

Kandel, D. B. (1980). Drug and drinking behavior among youth. *Annual Review of Sociology, 6*, 235-285.

Kandel, D. B., & Logan, J. A. (1984). Patterns of drug use from adolescence to young adulthood: I. Periods of risk for initiation, continued use, and discontinuation. *American Journal of Public Health, 74*, 660-666.

Kaplan, H. B. (1980). *Deviant behavior in defense of self.* New York: Academic Press.

Kaplan, H. B., & Lin, C-H. (2000). Deviant identity as a moderator of the relation between negative self-feelings and deviant behavior. *Journal of Early Adolescence, 20*, 150-177.

Kaplan, H. B., Martin, S. S., & Robbins, C. (1984). Pathways to adolescent drug use: Self-derogation, peer influence, weakening of social controls, and early substance use. *Journal of Health and Social Behavior, 25*, 270-289.

Kaplan, H. B., Martin, S. S., & Robbins, C. (1982). Application of a general theory of deviant behavior: Self-derogation and adolescent drug use. *Journal of Health and Social Behavior, 23*, 274-294.

Kernis, M. H., Whisenhunt, C. R., Waschull, S. B., Greenier, K. D., Berry, A. J., Herlocker, C. E., & Anderson, C. A. (1998). Multiple facets of self-esteem and their relations to depressive symptoms. *Personality and Social Psychology Bulletin, 24*, 657-668.

Kling, K. C., Hyde, J. S., Showers, C. J., & Buswell, B. N. (1999). Gender differences in self-esteem: A meta-analysis. *Psychological Bulletin, 125*, 470-500.

Kumpfer, K. L., & Turner, C. W. (1990). The social ecology model of adolescent substance abuse: Implications for prevention. *International Journal of the Addictions, 25*, 435-463.

Labouvie, E. W., Pandina, R. J., White, H. R., & Johnson, V. (1990). Risk factors of adolescence drug use: An affect-based interpretation. *Journal of Substance Abuse, 2*, 265-285.

Larson, R., & Ham, M. (1993). Stress and "storm and stress" in early adolescence: The relationship of negative events with dysphoric affect. *Developmental Psychology, 29*, 130-140.

Lewinsohn, P. M., Mischel, W., Chaplin, W., & Barton, R. (1980). Social competence and depression: The role of illusory self-perceptions. *Journal of Abnormal Psychology, 89*, 203-212.

Lochman, J. E. (1992). Cognitive-behavioral intervention with aggressive boys: Three-year follow-up and preventive effects. *Journal of Consulting and Clinical Psychology, 60*, 426-432.

Masten, A. S., & Coatsworth, J. D. (1998). The development of competence in favorable and unfavorable environments. *American Psychologist, 53*, 205-220.

Masten, A. S., Coatsworth, J. D., Neemann, J., Gest, S. D., Tellegen, A., & Garmezy, N. (1995). The structure and coherence of competence from childhood through adolescence. *Child Development, 66*, 1635-1659.

McArdle J. J. (1988). Dynamic but structural equation modeling of repeated measures data. In J. R. Nesselroade & R. B. Cattell (Eds.), *Handbook of multivariate experimental psychology* (2nd ed.). (pp. 561-614). New York: Plenum.

McArdle J. J., & Epstein, D. (1987). Latent growth curves within developmental structural equation models. *Child Development, 58*, 110-133.

Meredith, W., & Tisak, J. (1990). Latent curve analysis. *Psychometrika, 55*, 107-122.

Mitic, W. R. (1980). Alcohol use and self-esteem of adolescents. *Journal of Drug Education, 10*, 197-208.

Mone, M. A., Baker, D. D., & Jeffries, F. (1995). Predictive validity and time dependency of self-efficacy, self-esteem, personal goals, and academic performance. *Educational and Psychological Measurement, 55*, 716-727.

Newcomb, M. D. (1992). Understanding the multidimensional nature of drug use and abuse: The role of consumption, risk factors, and protective factors. In M. Glantz & R. Pickens (Eds.), *Vulnerability to drug abuse* (pp. 288-297). Washington, DC: American Psychological Association.

Newcomb, M. D., & Bentler, P. M. (1986). Frequency and sequence of drug use: A longitudinal study from early adolescence to young adulthood. *Journal of Drug Education, 16*, 101-120.

Nottlemann, E. D. (1987). Competence and self-esteem during transition from childhood to adolescence. *Developmental Psychology, 23*, 441-450.

Ohannessian, C. M., Lerner, R. M., Lerner, J. V., & von Eye, A. (1994). A longitudinal study of perceived family adjustment and emotional adjustment in early adolescence. *Journal of Early Adolescence, 14*, 371-390.

Olmstead, R. E., Guy, S. M., O'Malley, P. M., & Bentler, P. M. (1991). Longitudinal assessment of the relationship between self-esteem, fatalism, loneliness, and substance use. *Journal of Social Behavior and Personality, 6*, 749-770.

Parker, J., & Asher, S. R. (1987). Peer acceptance and later personal adjustment: Are low-accepted children at risk? *Psychological Bulletin, 102*, 357-389.

Paulhus, D. L. (1983). Sphere-specific measures of perceived control. *Journal of Personality and Social Psychology, 44*, 1253-1265.

Pellegrini, D. S., Masten, A. S., Garmezy, N., & Ferrarese, M. M. (1987). Correlates of social and academic competence in middle childhood. *Journal of Child Psychology and Psychiatry, 28*, 699-714.

Pentz, M. A., Dwyer, J. H., MacKinnon, D. P., Flay, B. R., Hansen, W. B., Wang, E. Y., & Johnson, C. A. (1989). A multicommunity trial for primary prevention of adolescent drug abuse: Effects on drug use prevalence. *Journal of the American Medical Association, 261,* 3259-3267.

Rogosa, D., Brandt, D., & Zimowski, M. (1982). A growth curve approach to the measurement of change. *Psychological Bulletin, 92,* 726-748.

Rosenberg, M. (1965). *Society and the adolescent self-image.* Princeton, NJ: Princeton University Press.

Scheier, L. M., & Botvin, G. J. (1998). Relations of social skills, personal competence, and adolescent alcohol use: A developmental exploratory study. *Journal of Early Adolescence, 18,* 77-114.

Scheier, L. M., & Botvin, G. J. (1997). Psychosocial correlates of affective distress: Latent-variable models of male and female adolescents in a community sample. *Journal of Youth and Adolescence, 26,* 89-115.

Scheier, L. M., Botvin, G. J., Griffin, K.W., & Diaz, T. (2000). Dynamic growth models of self-esteem and adolescent alcohol use. *Journal of Early Adolescence, 20,* 178-209.

Scheier, L. M., Botvin, G. J., Griffin, K.W., & Diaz, T. (1999). Latent growth models of drug refusal skills and adolescent alcohol use. *Journal of Alcohol and Drug Education, 44,* 21-48.

Scheier, L. M., Botvin, G. J., Diaz, T., & Griffin, K.W. (1999). Social skills, competence, and drug refusal efficacy as predictors of adolescent alcohol use. *Journal of Drug Education, 29,* 251-278.

Schroeder, D. S., Laflin, M. T., & Weis, D. L. (1993). Is there a relationship between self-esteem and drug use? Methodological and statistical limitations of the research. *The Journal of Drug Issues, 23,* 645-665.

Stacy, A. W. Widaman, K. F., Hays, R., & DiMatteo, M. R. (1985). Validity of self-reports of alcohol and other drug use: A multitrait-multimethod assessment. *Journal of Personality and Social Psychology, 49,* 219-232.

Stanley, K. D., & Murphy, M. R. (1997). A comparison of general self-efficacy with self-esteem. *Genetic, Social and General Psychology Monographs, 123,* 79-99.

Steiger, J. H., & Lind, J. M. (1980, May). Statistically based tests for the number of common factors. Paper presented at the annual meeting of the Psychometric Society, Iowa City, IA.

Stoolmiller, M. (1995). Orderly change in a stable world: The antisocial trait as a chimera. In J. M. Gottman (Ed.), *The analysis of change* (pp. 85-138). Mahwah, NJ: Lawrence Erlbaum.

Tennen, H., & Affleck, G. (1993). The puzzles of self-esteem: A clinical perspective. In R. Baumeister (Ed.), *Self-esteem: The puzzle of low self-regard* (pp. 241-262). New York: Plenum.

Vega, W. A., Apospori, E., Gil, A. G., Zimmerman, R. S., & Warheit, G. J. (1996). A replication and elaboration of the esteem-enhancement model. *Psychiatry, 59*, 128-144.

White, R. W. (1963). *Ego and reality in psychoanalytic theory.* New York: International Universities Press.

Weissberg, R. P., Caplan, M., & Harwood, R. L. (1991). Promoting competent young people in competence-enhancing environments: A systems-based perspective on primary prevention. *Journal of Consulting and Clinical Psychology, 59*, 830-841.

Wigfield, A., & Eccles, J. S. (1994). Children's competence beliefs, achievement values, and general self-esteem: Change across elementary and middle school. *Journal of Early Adolescence, 14*, 107-138.

Wigfield, A., & Eccles, J. S., Mac Iver, D., Reuman, D. A., & Midgley, C. (1991). Transitions during early adolescence: Changes in children's domain-specific self-perceptions and general self-esteem across the transition to junior high school. *Developmental Psychology, 27*, 552-565.

Willett, J. B., & Sayer, A. G. (1994). Using covariance structure analysis to detect correlates and predictors of individual change over time. *Psychological Bulletin, 116*, 363-381.

Wills, T. A. (1994). Self-esteem and perceived control in adolescent substance use: Comparative tests in concurrent and prospective analyses. *Psychology of Addictive Behaviors, 8*, 223-234.

Wills, T. A., Baker, E., & Botvin, G. J. (1989). Dimensions of assertiveness: Differential relationships to substance use in early adolescence. *Journal of Consulting and Clinical Psychology, 57*, 473-478.

Wills, T. A., & Cleary, S. D. (1999). Peer and adolescent substance use among 6th-9th graders: Latent growth analyses of influence versus selection mechanisms. *Health Psychology, 18*, 453-463.

Windle, M., & Barnes, G. (1988). Similarities and differences in correlates of alcohol consumption and problem behaviors among male and female adolescents. *International Journal of the Addictions, 23*, 707-728.

Author Note

Preparation of this article was partially supported by a research grant to Gilbert J. Botvin (P50DA-7656-07) from the National Institute on Drug Abuse.

Correspondence concerning this chapter should be addressed to Lawrence M. Scheier, Department of Public Health, Institute for Prevention Research, Weill Medical College of Cornell University, 411 East 69th Street, Kips Bay 201, New York, NY 10021, (212) 746-1270. Electronic mail may be sent via Internet to lmscheie@med.cornell.edu.

IV

EARLY ADOLESCENT INTERVENTIONS

9

IDENTITY IN EARLY ADOLESCENCE VIA SOCIAL CHANGE ACTIVITIES

Experience of the Adolescent Social Action Program

Lily Dow Velarde, Randall G. Starling, and Nina B. Wallerstein

Introduction

Early adolescence is filled with many challenges, but the quest for identity is most glaringly apparent when young people involved in the primary prevention program known as the Adolescent Social Action Program (ASAP) question who they are, as individuals and as members of their peer group. Adolescence is a transitional period whose onset, for most purposes, can be arbitrarily defined as concurrent with puberty but with an end point that is vague, sequencing into what the culture defines as adulthood (Blos, 1976). The vagueness of adolescence defined, is experienced as nebulously by youths undergoing this transitory period. Rapid changes in every area of life—physical, cognitive, affective, and social—are manifested and characterize this period of life. Schmiedect (1979) described adolescence as a phase of intense conflict, of insecurity and of idiosyncratic self-environments. Adolescent participants in the ASAP Program express the conflict and insecurity when they query their purpose in life, explore values, investigate beliefs and attitudes, and test an array of behaviors, all as part of their search for identity.

While in ASAP and in their group discussions, the youth question their identity, including issues of gender, ethnicity, and self (Dow y Garcia Velarde, 1999; Heaven, 1996; Phinney, 1997). As one Hispanic youth painfully declared, "I don't know if I'm Spanish, Hispanic, Latino, Chicano, or Mexican American!" Identity issues are once again confronted when the youth wrestle with peer pressure to engage in risky health behaviors. The internal struggle of weighing the youths' fundamental values; consequences that may result from participating in risky behaviors; and the desire to identify with their peers may lend itself to eminent inner conflict. The ASAP participants most encounter the question of identity when they are asked to take on roles and responsibilities required of them during the social action component of the program. In their young lives (and for many reasons), adults have spared or sheltered youth from participating in many social roles or responsibilities.

As a program, ASAP attempts to engage the adolescents, as they are undergoing maturation and identity formation along with their society, which is also in a constant state of change. According to Juhasz (1982), adolescents are developmentally programmed: to seek separate and unique identities; to try and make a difference both in the here and now and from a wider social perspective in the future; and to search for something to be faithful to, such as an idea, task, or ideal. The adolescent identity, including their values, emerge from the context of familial and the social milieu. Society's moral nature provides the content in which adolescents interact and against which they react.

According to Jessor (1982), experimentation and problem behavior is primal among this age group. Within the last decade, the implications of Jessor's theory have been recognized in the rates of alcohol use. Consumption of alcohol in young adolescents has grown, with experimentation starting at earlier ages. As age of onset of alcohol use has declined, experimentation and use among middle school youth, in particular, has been increasing (Kann, Warren, Harris, Collins, Douglas, Collins, et al., 1995; Kann, Kinchen, Williams, Ross, Lowry, Hill, et al., 1998). Hispanic and Native American youth are most at risk, with rates of alcohol use higher than the white and black populations (Ramirez, Gallion, Espinoza, McAlister, & Chalela, 1997). Thus, social pressures appear to have increased for younger and younger age groups.

In the early 1990s, ASAP examined the alcohol youth behavior data in New Mexico and found there was a doubling between 7th and 9th grade of alcohol use, from 23.7% to 52.8%; and of experimentation, from 27.6% to 58.5% (Research & Polling, Inc., 1994). To maintain its prevention emphasis, therefore, ASAP decided to focus exclusively on the seventh grade. ASAP staff acknowledge the fifth stage of Erik Erikson's Eight Stages of Development, Identity vs. Role Confusion (Butler, 1997), when developing social action activities for the ASAP participants. During this stage young adolescents view themselves in the eyes of others while bridging the skills, experiences, and roles of the past with the future. Butler refers to the bridge of past and future as the occupational paradigm (p. 107). The ASAP social action activities provide an assortment of experiences designed to include peer group tasks, responsibilities, and roles. The hands-on activities also support individual skill development and knowledge. The combined efforts of group activity and hands-on experiences nourish youth to sample a taste of the occupation paradigm. To support a positive future orientation, ASAP encourages youth to interact with role models such as university students and health and social welfare professionals, along with subsequent social action activities in which adolescents may elect to participate.

The final session of the curriculum is designed to involve the participants in a social action project of their choosing, in which adolescents practice and put into place their acquired decision-making, communication, and leadership skills. The school personnel, facilitators, or parents work with the adolescents in a supportive role to assist the adolescents to achieve their social action project. The adolescent participants assume various responsibilities, duties, and roles designed to motivate and prepare them to become leaders, co-teachers, facilitators, and advocates in their projects. Many of the adolescents' projects involve going before peers, school personnel, parents, community leaders, and corporate personnel to secure resources such as money or materials; permission to use public and private properties; and to promote or inform the public about their health projects. The roles and responsibilities inherent in social interaction and project development serve to inoculate or reduce the conflict and insecurity encountered by adolescents unaccustomed to such experiences. Interactive and action-oriented programs such as ASAP offer support to youth identity formation by: (1) including adult role models that help shape young

peoples' identity; (2) providing opportunities for young people to practice "adult" experiences in a safe and nurturing environment; (3) bridging the adolescents' past real-life experiences to create solutions to
future problems; and (4) creating a sense of belonging and purpose
through school and community-based projects.

The Adolescent Social Action Program is an experiential, primary
prevention program, for volunteer middle school students from predominantly minority, high-risk environments in New Mexico. ASAP's
goals are to reduce the mortality and morbidity of alcohol and drug use
among adolescents, and to empower adolescents as social change agents
in their school and community. The program staff implement a 6-week
structured curriculum, bringing the students out of their school environments and into the larger community. The students meet at the
local university hospital and county detention center to interview pre-
selected patients and jail residents about the social, medical, and legal
consequences of drug and alcohol abuse. After the interviews the students attend a debriefing session to discuss the patients' and detention
residents' stories, and to participate in dialogue about the students'
own health-related choices.

Upon completion of the structured sessions, the student participants return to their schools and communities to plan and subsequently engage in social action projects that address the health, legal,
and social issues they encountered while in the larger community. The
social action projects are intended to encourage the students to
actively assume proactive health promotion roles in society along with
the guidance and support of trained adult facilitators.

This chapter will present an overview of the ASAP's core curriculum, the theoretical foundation, and the program outcomes, and will
focus on the social actions implemented by the adolescents, with conclusions and recommendations for social action prevention programming with adolescents.

The Adolescent Social Action Program:
A Program for Early Adolescents

The Adolescent Social Action Program was originally developed in
1983 to address the devastating impact of alcohol problems in New
Mexico. Alcoholism is over three times the national average, and New
Mexican's per capita crash fatality rate leads the nation with 60% of

these crashes involving alcohol. Among adolescents and young adults ages 15-24 in the United States, the mortality rate due to accidents is 38.5/100,000 with 76.6% of these deaths the result of motor vehicle accidents.

When examining gender, the New Mexico mortality and morbidity statistics by accidents among youth ages 15-24 again outpace the national average. Among males, the national average for mortality by all accidents is 56.2/100,000 with 73.6% of these deaths the result of motor vehicle accidents. For New Mexico, the rate is 87.2/100,000 with 75.8% of the mortality due to motor vehicle accidents. The mortality rate in New Mexico for Caucasian males from all accidents is 66.8/100,00 (72.9% by motor vehicle), Hispanic males 85.4/100,000 (74.8% due to motor vehicles), 77.2/100,000 for African-American males (87.5% by motor vehicle) and 181.6/100,000 for Native American males with 80.3% of the deaths due to motor vehicle accidents (New Mexico Selected Health Statistics, 1996).

Based out of the University of New Mexico (UNM) School of Medicine and the UNM Center for Substance Abuse and Addictions, ASAP has partnered with schools, parents, community centers, agencies, and organizations and the University Hospital and Bernalillo County Detention Center to create a long-standing prevention collaboration. The goals of ASAP are to reduce the mortality and morbidity of alcohol and drug use among adolescents, and to empower adolescents as social change agents in their school and community.

The nature of ASAP is to encourage the students to guide their participation in the program based on the values and ideals of their ethnic and youth culture, while also maintaining a structured ASAP curriculum. More of this concept will be discussed in the section on, "Background Theories and Framework." In ASAP's 15 years, the program has operated throughout New Mexico's vast southwestern terrain. ASAP's primary prevention service has been implemented in over 30 communities of diverse geographical and cultural boundaries. For example, ASAP serves predominantly Hispanic, Native American, and low-income Anglo (white non-Hispanic) populations who live in rural, urban, and reservation lands.

The ASAP staff contact the various middle school administrators to discuss possible implementation of the ASAP program in the school. The discussions outline the procedures for operation and coordination of the various components of ASAP within and outside the school.

An example of some procedural matters include parental consent, student recruitment, transportation, school/teacher sponsors, and social action activities. Thereafter, ASAP staff coordinate the visits to the hospital and detention center as well as recruit, select, and train adult facilitators who will accompany and guide the student participants.

The teacher/sponsor or ASAP staff solicit student interest about the program through presentations given in health or life science classes. Health and life science classes are ideal settings from which to recruit student volunteers to the program. The previously mentioned classes have the potential for supplementing information about health and supporting potential social action venues. Lastly, the real-life experiences of the ASAP student participants may augment the regular school curriculum used in the health and life science classes.

After contacting school administrators, designating a teacher or school sponsor, recruiting students, and securing consent among the volunteer students and their parents (or legal guardians) is complete, then it is time to begin the students' experience in ASAP. The students interested in participating in ASAP receive a letter inviting the parent/s or legal guardian to attend an orientation. The orientation is designed to bring the students, parents, teacher/sponsor, ASAP facilitators, and staff together in one setting. A video about the ASAP program is shown to all in attendance and questions about the goals, expectations, and procedures for participation are discussed.

Small groups of the five to seven students participate in the 6-plus week community-based ASAP program. The supervised student participants (two adults/seven students) meet at the University Hospital to interview patients, their families, and hospital personnel about the potentially harmful and multifaceted consequences of using alcohol, drugs, inhalants, and tobacco. Patients and their families are screened by the facilitators and hospital staff prior to the youth interviews. Initial screening serves two purposes to: (1) determine the suitability of the patient(s) for the group interview and (2) assure the patient(s) that the information shared will remain confidential. The young participants also interview detention center residents who are incarcerated because of drug-related offenses. Once again, the objective of the screening process is similar to that of the patients with the exception that the detention center coordinator assumes the screening responsibility.

Trained university students act as facilitators to guide the youth through structured dialogue using the Hospital/Detention Center Curriculum (H/DC) (Buntz, Aragon, Wallerstein, & Dow, 1994; Sanchez & Wallerstein, 1988). The patients and detention center residents respond to the youths' impromptu (sometimes prepared) questions regarding their experiences with drugs and the social, medical, legal, emotional, and financial cost associated with drug use. The curriculum experientially involves the adolescents in several skill building sessions such as communication, media literacy, critical thinking, refusal skills, decision making, and group development. The information or knowledge base is derived from the real-life experiences of the patients, detention center residents, hospital and detention center personnel, the adolescent participants, and the college facilitators.

The Hospital/Detention Center Curriculum (H/DC)

The H/DC curriculum is composed of six sessions (each session building on the previous session) to develop the participants' affective, cognitive, psychosocial, and behavior domains. Knowledge about the physical, mental, social, legal, and financial cost of alcohol and drug use is acquired throughout each session. Prior to the six sessions, a parent orientation is conducted at the participants' school. The intent of the orientation is to inform the parents and students of the program goals and objectives; to acquaint the participants with the adult facilitators; acquaint the parents with the adult facilitators; discuss the policies and procedures of the program; and to secure parent consent and involvement.

The first session is a team building/group trust meeting held at the participants' school. The school is familiar territory to the participants, generally close to home, and more readily accessible to the parents. A predesignated class or meeting room is made available to the young people as they come together for the first time to meet their peers and the two ASAP facilitators. Several activities are implemented to acquaint and foster trust among the participants and the adult facilitators during session one. This session sets the stage for the youth to identify with other students that might have an interest in substance abuse prevention and for the participants to get to know each other.

The second session focuses on communication held in the local hospital. Session two primes the youth on how to ask open-ended questions, prepares them for patient interviews through discussions of confidentiality and respect, and engages the youth in patient interviews, followed by group debriefing. Through structured dialogue led by trained facilitators, the youth discuss the patients' life stories, their own lives, and their options for helping themselves and their communities. Through dialogue, the youth become subjects of their own learning, in which they identify their problems and engage in critical thinking to analyze the cultural and societal context for these problems. The goal of dialogue is praxis, or the ongoing interaction between reflection and the actions youth can take to improve their lives.

Session three (also held at the hospital) is used to reinforce the skills and knowledge acquired in sessions one and two. Refusal and decision-making skills are interlaced in the H/DC Curriculum along with continued patient interviews and debriefing discussions. Session four is held at the local detention center. This session offers the participants an opportunity to interview a small panel of four (mixed female and male) detention center residents about the legal consequences and social ramifications associated with the use of alcohol and drugs. Session five is the last hospital session and it emphasizes community involvement, media literacy, and the initiation of the planning process for social action activities. Facilitators and adolescents come together for the sixth and last session and potluck at the participants' school. The adolescent participants, friends, and family members are brought together to explore and discuss possible group or social action activities in which the youth and adults may engage. Certificates, T-shirts, and food are included in the culminating celebration of the students' participation in ASAP's H/DC curriculum. It is this point were the students social action projects or activities are formalized and initiated.

Background Theories and Frameworks

In the last 2 decades, prevention efforts have been increasingly targeted at students, grades six through eight, primarily in school-based settings. While some interventions have shown poor evaluation results (e.g., Project Dare, Ennett, Rosenbaum, Flewelling, Bieler, Ringwalt, & Bailey, 1994) or no sustained effects at long-term follow-up (Bell, Ellickson, & Harrison, 1993), others based in cognitive-behavioral, normative, and social skills approaches, have shown some effectiveness in tobacco, alcohol, or marijuana knowledge and use (Botvin, Baker, Dusenbury, Tortu, & Botvin, 1990; Graham, Johnson, Hansen, Flay, & Gee 1990; Hansen, 1992; Hansen, Johnson, Flay, Graham, & Sobel, 1988; Perry,

Williams, Veblen-Mortenson, Toomey, Komro, Anstine, et al., 1996; Shope, Copeland, Kamp, & Lang, 1998).

To be effective, there is an increasing recognition of the importance of multifaceted prevention approaches that target both the individual and social environment (Dryfoos, 1993; Pentz, Dwyer, MacKinnon, Flay, Hansen, Wang, et al., 1989; Perry, Williams, Forster, Wolfson, Wagenaar, Finnegan, et al., 1993; Wechsler & Weitzman, 1996). This comprehensive approach is intended to change the individual's beliefs and attitudes concerning alcohol and other drugs and to effect changes in social environmental conditions that may act as risk factors for alcohol and substance abuse (MacNeil, Kaufman, Dressler, & LeCroy, 1999; Wolfgang, 1997). The most effective interventions act simultaneously on the multiple levels. Some cognitive-behavioral approaches have shown promise for minority youth (Botvin, 1988; Botvin, Batson, Witts-Vitale, Bess, Baker Dusenbury, 1989; Botvin, Dusenbury, Baker, James-Ortiz, & Kerner, 1989; Harris, Davis, Ford, & Tso, 1988), especially if they are sensitive to cultural competencies (Orlandi, 1986; Ramirez et al., 1997).

As a theory-driven primary prevention intervention, ASAP is centered on the psychosocial dialogue approach of Brazilian educator Paulo Freire (Freire, 1970, Wallerstein & Sanchez-Merki, 1994). A Freirian approach is based in psychological theories of critical consciousness change; culturally based experiential learning; and community change theories, supporting the participants to adopt both individual and social responsibility.

Unlike scared-straight programs that have been proven to be ineffective (Job, 1988; Rogers & Mewborn, 1976), ASAP also incorporates protection-motivation theory of threat and coping appraisals directed at attitude and behavior change (Rippetoe & Rogers, 1987; Rogers, 1984; Rogers, Deckner, & Mewborn, 1978; Stainback & Rogers, 1983). The patient and jail resident interviews arouse the student's threat appraisal of their own susceptibility and of the potential severity of the problem, such as the likely consequences of drinking and driving. The structured dialogue and other curriculum exercises increase their coping appraisal in their abilities to engage in self-protective and socially responsible behaviors. An increase in self-efficacy, the belief that one has the ability to successfully complete a task, and in response efficacy, the belief that one's actions will make the desired difference, improve the likelihood of protective behavior.

To implement the Freirian structured dialogue model, which integrates threat and coping appraisals, a listening-dialogue-action methodology is used. The ASAP program starts from the participants listening to the stories of patients and jail residents. The youths' emotional responses to these stories trigger both threat appraisal and empathy with people who are suffering. After leaving the patients' room, students engage in dialogue that creates an increased cognitive awareness of the precursors and consequences to alcohol and other drug problems.

The dialogue coupled with social skills training and other elements of successful prevention programs, leads to increased coping appraisal, or youth self-efficacies to protect themselves. The ASAP curriculum has sought to incorporate those understandings from successful prevention models, such as developmentally appropriate information about the short-term and negative effects of drugs (Shope, Copeland, Marcoux, & Kamp, 1996); social resistance skills training (Raynal & Chen, 1997; Shope, Copeland, Kamp, & Lang, 1998) normative re-education (Dusenbury & Falco, 1995; Simons-Morton, Greene, & Gottlieb, 1995; Steffian, 1999); personal and social competence training in decision-making skills, critical thinking, and social skills (Harrington & Donohew, 1997; Kim, Crutchfield, Williams, & Hepler, 1998); interactive teaching techniques, such as role-plays (Patterson, Bethann, Bechtel, & Rose-Colley, 1997); and cultural sensitivity and relevance (Freimuth, Plotnick, Ryan, & Schiller, 1997; Harrington & Donohew, 1997; Lalonde, Rabinowitz, Shofsky, & Washienko, 1997; Ramirez et al., 1997).

Finally, through empathy and an analysis of societal forces in a safe group context, the bridge is created between one-dimensional behavioral change and group efforts for social change. In the last hospital session and in activities in their schools, youth engage in planning, and implementation of social action activities, which further develop their self and collective efficacies for socially responsible behaviors.

In sum, this three-part process is a participatory orientation to learning rather than a passive mode of receiving information. ASAP participants enter the program at the listening stage and, upon completion of the curriculum, leave in a social action mode. Freirian action emphasizes that youth become advocates with each other for community change, rather than as lone actors, particularly for programs serving minority youth.

Social Action Activities

Adolescent Social Action Program participants experience occasions to work in the community to develop social action projects. ASAP's definition of a social action project is any project designed to actively involve youth to improve the health conditions of the youths' school or community. The adolescent participants are encouraged to play active roles in the initial research, design, planning, implementation, and (in some cases) the evaluation of their self-selected projects. Several social action projects have been developed throughout the years beginning in 1984. The young people utilize ideas, skills, knowledge and concepts they acquire via their participation in ASAP to plan and implement their projects.

Social action includes exploring advertising and marketing strategies that relate to alcohol, tobacco, and other drug use, and changing health norms in their communities. Social action endeavors may include the production of materials for information dissemination or to create awareness about certain health issues among people in the community.

The projects, although developed by the adolescents, include the assistance of adults. Adult facilitators foster the adolescents' development by acting as role models, offering guidance, support, and some of the necessary resources needed to accomplish the project. The adults volunteer their efforts to work with the adolescents after school and on the weekends. Adults interested in participating in the program are reminded that the project's ownership belongs to the adolescents. Such a reminder serves to inform the adults about the adolescents' primary role in the project.

Over the years, the scope and the range of social action projects have varied; they have been designed to have impacts on either the individual, school, community, the state or multiple facets of society. Individual projects developed by lone participants have included speaking to family members or friends about the experiences they had at the hospital or detention center and the consequences of drug use to the patients, their families, and detention center residents. In situations where the young participants lived in similar circumstances to that of the patients and detention center residents, the students asked questions and relayed information that were relevant to the youths' personal experiences. The students could identify themselves with the patients' and detention center residents' family members or significant others.

Social action projects designed to impact the youths' school have included chartering and creating ASAP clubs at their schools; initiating and implementing health promotion clubs such as Students Against Driving Drunk (SADD); creating drug awareness activities for school assemblies; and assisting with their school's "October Fiesta" fund-raiser and gaming booth. Long-term projects experienced by the youth included planning, designing, and painting murals that depict the health issues faced by the youths. Lastly, the youths have given presentations in the feeder elementary schools about the social, medical, and legal circumstances of drug use.

In the community, social action projects have included youth participation in panel discussions at the ASAP Summer Institutes and facilitator trainings; presiding at health fair information booths such as "Music and Talent Festivals," and in Albuquerque's Civic Plaza's, "A Day Without Colors"; participating on advisory panels; conducting various community service projects; production of videotapes, community murals, and fotonovelas (photo novels); and participating as advisory committee and task force members of the Albuquerque South East Community Gang Task Force and the "Street Reach" gang prevention project, sharing the health information and coping strategies they have learned through ASAP. Other project examples include the youths' design of T-shirts, health messages for billboards, and the development of television public service announcements targeted at teens.

In Albuquerque's Civic Plaza, youth participated in an antigang rally, "A Day Without Colors," by directing activities and running the ASAP booth. In 1994, ASAP youth helped plan "A Day Without Alcohol Is Fair for the New Mexico State Fair." ASAP youth have been involved in a local television station's youth-produced program on teenagers. They have helped cook and serve Thanksgiving dinner at a local community center. The youth have brought their issues concerning alcohol and drug use via Centers for Substance Abuse Prevention and the Albuquerque Partnership Press Conference.

Outside of Albuquerque, ASAP youth have participated in many projects implemented throughout New Mexico. They have contributed written articles to the *Peace Maker*, the New Mexico Department of Health's statewide violence prevention newsletter. The youth

have joined in the Red Ribbon campaigns to assist with ribbon distribution among peers and youth and to rally against using drugs. They
have presented at state conferences, such as the New Mexico Public
Health Association, the El Puente Hispano/Latino Youth Institute,
and the New Mexico Peer Leadership Conference, which examined
existing tobacco legislation. One year, ASAP teens assisted in training
peers to resist alcohol, tobacco, and drugs for the Santa Fe Mountain
Center (Youth Training), in Santa Fe, New Mexico. The ASAP participants produced an agenda for policy change and presented their
legislative ideas to the governor. ASAP adolescents have participated
in Youth Link, a statewide effort that engages young people in policy
development.

Several social action groups have had the opportunity to produce
videos, fotonovelas or photo novels, and print materials. The youth
conceptualized, wrote and produced several ASAP videos, *Wild Side*
and *South Valley Pride*. A reception and premier was held in the participants' communities. Parents, relatives, friends, and neighbors were
invited to attend the premier, thus spotlighting the hard and creative
work of the ASAP participants.

Social Action "Fotonovelas"

The Fotonovela Project extensively involved the ASAP youth participants in social action media production. The spanish word "fotonovela" is also termed photo novels (Rudd et al., 1994), sequential art
(Clark, 1994), and photo stories (AIM, 1974). Fotonovelas are a graphic
form of communication, similar to comics. ASAP participants communicated high-risk behaviors and the consequences of the behaviors
through the medium of fotonovelas.

Three ASAP participant groups from two different middle schools
developed fotonovelas or photo novels, which were distributed throughout their schools and public health agencies. The ASAP participants
selected health issues considered pertinent to their lives such as alco-
hol/drugs and teen pregnancy and violence prevention. Adult facilitators demonstrated the technical skills needed to format and assemble a
fotonovela. Once the technical skills were acquired, the ASAP Fotonovela Project participants researched the selected health issues with
the goal of educating their peers and the community. The ASAP staff
and youth participants distributed copies of the fotonovelas, "What's

Love Got To Do With It?"; "Where Do I Go From Here?"; and "Two Sides of Life: The Story of Gangs and Their Consequences," to the local schools and community centers. The fotonovelas are used as aids along with other educational and organizing endeavors to promote youth problem-posing, resource identification, and community competence. In addition to being an educational product, the fotonovelas reflect the faces, voices, ethnic, and youth culture of the local youth.

Qualitative research examined the "meaning" of participation in the Fotonovela Project for the ASAP participants. The research produced several themes, Participation, Skills Building, Impact, and Informal Learning. The findings indicate that the youth learned how to work together, gain new skills, problem-solve, make decisions, communicate with each other, express their culture (age and ethnicity), and feel a sense of pride and accomplishment about a quality product and completed task (Dow y Garcia Velarde, 1999, pp. 90-140).

Many participants defined or structured their individual and social identity among their peers or within society by setting parameters for themselves. For example, one youth stated, "I thought it would be good for me to get involved so then it would keep me out of trouble and stuff like that" (Dow y Garcia Velarde, p. 94). In this case the participant indicates their identity by attempting to identify with peers who avoid potentially trouble-producing situations. Another teen involved in the Fotonovela Project indirectly spoke about social identity through the health advocacy role she assumed while working on the project. She states, "I like doing things for my community and getting to know people better" (Dow y Garcia Velarde, p. 95). Her identity is realized among the larger society as she sees herself as not only a part of the community, but also doing something for her community. Lastly, the issue of social skills such as communication that resulted from the youths' participation (not common in traditional classroom settings) allude to their sense of identity because the skills they acquired, "were useful in enhancing the youths' ability to reduce friction, ease shyness, and interact with each other in a positive and or productive manner" (Dow y Garcia Velarde, p. 156). The Fotonovela Project was a testimonial to the youths' attempt to establish identity not only as individuals using print media, but as a social group advocating for youth voice and an organizational group establishing roles, responsibilities, and boundaries.

Each of the above projects requires the adolescents' total participation, that is, there is a role and a purpose for all who are involved. In the end, the adolescents have a contribution and perhaps a product to give society.

Program Effectiveness

Over the years, there have been various evaluations and opportunities to research the ASAP program. In the 1980s, the results of a pilot experimental investigation with middle school ASAP adolescents revealed that ASAP participants demonstrated an increased awareness of the riskiness of drinking and driving (Bernstein & Woodall, 1987). This increased awareness countered the normal developmental trend of decreased perception of riskiness as students age (Finn & Brown, 1981).

A qualitative research study in the late 1980s, involving two low-income sites (a Native American reservation and an Hispanic, semirural barrio within Albuquerque), uncovered new variables and hypotheses of ASAP program effects (Wallerstein, 1989; Wallerstein & Bernstein, 1988; Wallerstein & Sanchez-Merki, 1994). Variables from this study were subsequently included in the ASAP research instrument for the next series of studies and included: self-efficacy, empathy, social responsibility, and communication with others to influence behaviors.

A quantitative research study was conducted for middle school youth completed in the early 1990s. Two extended versions of the ASAP curriculum (a social action curriculum and a peer education curriculum) were contrasted with a control group, which received the core hospital/detention center intervention at a later date. The peer education groups were charged with implementing a series of well-defined presentations at feeder elementary schools. The social action groups were to develop their own strategies at the local level after the hospital/detention center curriculum.

For this study, 375 participants were randomly assigned to one of the three program conditions, with the randomization occurring at the individual level within school sites. The three randomly assigned program groups were assessed on program-related measures at pretest, posttest, and at an 8-month follow-up posttest, constituting a three (social action, peer education, and control group) x three (pretest, posttest, 8-month follow-up posttest) mixed factorial design (see Table 1).

Table 1
Research Design for Demonstration Study

	Social Action Curriculum	Peer Education Curriculum	Control Group
Pretest	Yes	Yes	Yes
H/DC Curriculum	Yes	Yes	No
Posttest	Yes	Yes	Yes
Follow-up curriculum	Yes	Yes	No
8 month posttest	Yes	Yes	Yes

Statistical analysis, using analysis of variance for repeated measures, of the self-efficacy variables revealed participants in both curriculum groups were found to increase their self-efficacy for protecting others over time, whereas control group participants' self-efficacy for protecting others decreased over time.

Drinking effects for boys and girls were also analyzed. Similar to the previous analysis, a 3 x 3 analysis of variance for repeated measures revealed a statistically significant group X time interaction for male participants for the number of days reported drinking variable. The interaction mean from the three groups showed that for the control group, the average number of days drinking by male participants decreased from pretest (mean = 25.28) to posttest (mean = 19.28) and remained about the same at the 8-month follow-up posttest (mean = 20.78). The peer education curriculum group reported zero drinking days at pretest and at posttest but strongly rebounded to the highest level of the three groups for reported drinking days for male participants (mean = 32.92). For the social action curriculum group, the number of days reported drinking by male participants at pretest was initially lower than the delayed participation group (mean = 8.94) and decreased at post-test (mean = 5.69), and then rebounded at the 8-month follow-up posttest (mean = 12.44). This resulted in the lowest level of days reported drinking by males of the three design groups. The pattern of these means suggests that the social action curriculum had the most effective program impact overall in terms of decreasing alcohol use among male participants.

A separate 3 x 3 analysis of variance for repeated measures was performed on alcohol use measures for female participants. Results revealed a statistically significant group X time interaction for the average number of drinks consumed per occasion variable for female participants. The pattern of interaction means for this variable showed that for the delayed participation group the average number of drinks reported by female participants increased from pretest (mean = 2.81) to posttest (mean = 3.37) and then declined at the 8-month follow-up posttest to pretest levels (mean = 2.81). For the peer education group the average number of drinks reported by female participants decreased from pretest (mean = 3.40) to posttest (mean = 1.70) and then slightly increased at the 8-month follow-up posttest (mean = 2.55). The average number of drinks reported by female participants in the social action group decreased sharply from pretest (mean = 5.58) to posttest (mean = 1.16) and then increased slightly at the 8-month follow-up posttest (mean = 2.05).

The pattern of interaction means suggests that the social action curriculum had the most effective impact for female participants in decreasing alcohol consumption per occasion, but that the peer education curriculum results also reflect modest effects. Unlike the results for male participants, both curricula were superior to the control group on this variable for the female participants.

Overall, these results do suggest program effects for alcohol-related behaviors. It is not clear why significant program effects were obtained for males and females on different alcohol related variables, but the program appears to have had an impact on both male and female participants in terms of alcohol-related behavior. When interpreting these data, it is important to consider that these effects were obtained from a design that was weakened by cross-group contamination, since the level of randomization occurred at the individual level within school sites, and that the results were obtained with a relatively small subsample of participants in the study who were active drinkers in the study. Given these limiting design factors, the impact of the program on alcohol outcomes may be larger than what these effects suggest.

Another quantitative study conducted in the early 1990s represented the ASAP program's first attempt to include tobacco in the curriculum, in addition to alcohol and other drugs. In this study, a research design was implemented that minimized cross-group contamination. Instead of randomization occurring at the individual level within school sites, randomization occurred at the school sites, so that schools were randomized into one of two groups: a control group or a participant group. Both groups were assessed on program-related measures at pretest, posttest, and at a 6-month follow-up posttest.

An analysis of variance for repeated measures statistical test revealed significant outcomes for participants in the active group when compared to the control group. These outcomes included higher perceived severity of problems due to alcohol, drugs, and tobacco; increased self-efficacy for communicating about alcohol, drug and tobacco issues; and higher self-efficacy to influence their friends to not drink, smoke, or take drugs.

Similar to the above analyses, an analysis of variance for repeated measures revealed significant group X time program effects for two alcohol behavior variables: number of days drinking alcohol during the past 6-months, and number of days drinking alcohol in the past 6-weeks. Over time, for the active participation group, the number of days drinking decreased while increasing slightly for the control group.

Salivary cotinene was measured in this investigation at pretest and at the 6-month follow-up posttest for determining the presence of nicotine in the participants. An analysis of the cotinene data did not reveal statistically significant differences across time or between groups in participant smoking behavior.

The reader should note that the ASAP program is currently engaged in evaluation of a 5-year NIAAA-funded prevention project that focuses on alcohol prevention for adolescents. The research design for the current investigation includes randomization at the school site level into either participant or control group and assessment of program-related measures at pretest, posttest, at a 6-month follow-up posttest and at a 15-month follow-up posttest. Data from this study are currently undergoing analysis.

In summary, some ASAP investigations have provided evidence of program effects in terms of various cognitive variables, such as perceptions of riskiness, self-efficacy to protect others and a variety of other self efficacy and cognitive variables, and provided initial evidence of program effects in behavioral outcomes. It may be that increased coping appraisal processes (such as self-efficacy, critical appraisal of maladaptive coping, critical appraisal of industry targeting) are important variables for minority youth in making healthier choices to protect themselves and others.

Limitations and Concerns

Ideally, the philosophy of ASAP is to engage adolescents as change agents in promoting well-being (drug and violence prevention) in society. The voice and experiences of adolescents are valued by the program staff because they reflect a youth culture that is seldom acknowledged by adult society in a positive manner. The reality encountered by program participants is met with many barriers. Issues of adultism, the prejudice, discrimination, and oppression (Dow y Garcia Velarde, 1999; Flasher, 1978; Males, 1996; and Westman, 1991) of youth are but one barrier confronted by adolescents involved in social action projects. The young people also experience competition for resources (Stoneman & Bell, 1988), "fear and loathing" (Males, 1996, p. 294), and legitimized power over them (Flasher, 1978) by adults. The pervasiveness of adultism hold the youths captive in their efforts to give voice to their projects, thus limiting their identity as contributors to society.

Although ASAP attempts to combat the adultism faced by adolescents, youth cannot work in a vacuum. Adult support is needed for many activities or projects to come to fruition. Issues of liability, parental consent, and confidentiality contribute to some of the limitations youth face while attempting the role of social agents.

Other limitations and concerns that exist among the program participants include the lack of: transportation, political clout, experience, financial or material resources, and confidence. Additionally we must ask ourselves, "How much responsibility can young adolescents assume as social change agents?" We do not want to set up the hopes of young people only to have them fail in their endeavors because of prominent barriers. The intention of the program staff is to help young people develop to the fullest of their ability. Another intention is to help young people identify or secure a place for themselves in society.

Conclusion

The entire hospital/detention center curriculum, plus the social action projects experienced by ASAP participants, provide a foundation to foster young peoples' social and individual identity. Since ASAP's inception 19 years ago, adolescents and adults have joined forces to aid in the mutual growth and development of all people, but especially the young people. Middle and high school educators and personnel could help the youth realize their potential and identity in the larger society in several ways: by incorporating the students' social action activities with the classroom curriculum; encouraging students to engage in learning activities that promote social action within the school and among the youths' communities; and by supporting and promoting school and community partnerships that seek to extend the students' learning experiences beyond the classroom. Incentives such as extra credit or public recognition for community service might encourage students to participate in programs such as ASAP.

Schools and youth serving agencies that incorporate social action projects may experience a positive public relations opportunity, greater investment by youth in learning, a contribution to schools and communities, and ownership in the institutions that foster learning and development. The multitude of social action projects in which the youth participated have helped them to develop their skills, knowledge, roles and responsibilities in life. Many of these roles and responsibilities introduce young people to their potential identity as working adults in society. The skills and knowledge help prepare the youth to become more confident in tasks and assignments they may someday assume. The real-life interactions and situations encountered by the ASAP participants, plus the guiding hands of caring and nurturing adults, help the youth to realize their potential and identity.

References

Apperception-Interaction Method (AIM). (1974). A creative approach to teaching adults. *World Education*. New York: Author.

Bell, R. M., Ellickson, P. L., & Harrison, E.R. (1993). Do drug prevention effects persist into high school? How Project ALERT did with ninth graders. *Preventive Medicine, 22*, 463-483.

Bernstein, E., & Woodall, G. (1987). Changing perceptions of riskiness in drinking, drugs, and driving: An emergency department based alcohol and substance abuse prevention program. *Annals of Emergency Medicine, 16*, 1350-1354.

Blos, P. (1976). When and how does adolescence end? *Adolescent Psychiatry, 5*, 5-17.

Botvin, G.J. (1988). "Defining success" in drug abuse prevention. *NIDA Research Monograph. 90*, 203-12.

Botvin, G. J., Batson, H. W., Witts-Vitale, S., Bess, V., Baker, E., & Dusenbury, L. (1989). A psychosocial approach to smoking prevention for urban black youth. *Public Health Reports, 104*, 573-582.

Botvin, G. J., Dusenbury, L., Baker, E., James-Ortiz, S., & Kerner, J. (1989). A skills training approach to smoking prevention among hispanic youth. *Journal of Behavioral Medicine, 12,* 279-290.

Botvin, G. J., Baker, E., Dusenbury, L., Tortu, S., & Botvin, E. M. (1990). Preventing adolescent drug abuse through a multimodal cognitive-behavioral approach: Results of a 3-year study. *Journal of Consulting and Clinical Psychology, 58,* 437-446.

Buntz, J., Aragon, L.C., Wallerstein, N. B., & Dow, L. A. (1989). *What we can do curriculum: In-class curriculum.* Unpublished.

Butler, J. T. (1994). *Principles of health education & health promotion.* (2nd ed.) Englewood, CO: Morton Publishing Co.

Clark, L. (1994). Comics and fotonovelas for health promotion. *Learning for Health, 5,* 3-6.

Dow y Garcia Velarde, L.A. (1999). Privileging the voice of youth: Youth produced fotonovelas. *UMI Dissertation Services* (UMI Microform #9926831).

Dryfoos, J. G. (1993). Preventing substance use; Rethinking strategies. *American Journal of Public Health, 83,* 793-795.

Dusenbury, L., & Falco, M. (1995). Eleven components of effective drug abuse prevention curricula. *Journal of School Health, 65,* 420-25.

Ennett, S. T., Rosenbaum, D. P., Flewelling, R. L., Bieler, G. S., Ringwalt, C. L., & Bailey, S. L. (1994). Long-term evaluation of drug abuse resistance education. *Addictive Behaviors, 19,* 113-125.

Finn, P. & Brown, J. (1981). Risks entailed in teenage intoxication as perceived by junior and senior high school students. *Journal of Youth and Adolescence, 10,* 61-76.

Flasher, J. (1978). Adultism. *Adolescence, 13,* 517-524.

Freimuth, V. S., Plotnick, C. A., Ryan, C. E., & Schiller, S. (1997). Right turns only: an evaluation of a video-based multicultural drug education series for seventh graders. *Health Education and Behavior, 24,* 555-567.

Freire, P. (1970). *Pedagogy of the oppressed.* New York: Seabury Press.

Graham, J. W., Johnson, C. A., Hansen, W. B., Flay, B. R., & Gee, M. (1990). Drug use prevention programs, gender, and ethnicity: Evaluation of three seventh-grade Project SMART cohorts. *Preventive Medicine, 19,* 305-313.

Hansen, W. B., Johnson, C., Flay, B., Graham, J., & Sobel, J. (1988). Affective and social influences approaches to the prevention of multiple substance abuse among seventh grade students: Results from Project SMART. *Preventive Medicine, 17,* 135-154.

Hansen, W. B. (1992). School-based substance abuse prevention: A review of the state of the art in curriculum, 1980-1990. *Health Education Research*, 7, 403-430.

Harrington, N. G., & Donohew, L. (1997). Jump Start: A targeted substance abuse prevention program. *Health Education & Behavior*, 24, 568-586.

Harris, M. B., Davis, S. M., Ford, V. L., & Tso, H. (1988). The checkerboard cardiovascular curriculum: A culturally oriented program. *Journal of School Health*, 58, 104-107.

Heaven, P. C. L. (1996). *Adolescent health: The role of individual differences.* London: Routlege.

Job, R. F. S. (1988). Effective and ineffective use of fear in health promotion campaigns. *American Journal of Public Health*, 78, 163-167.

Kann, L., Warren, C. W., Harris, W. A., Collins, J. L., Douglas, K. A., Collins, M. E., Williams, B. I, Ross, J. G., & Kolbe, L. J. (1995). *Youth risk behavior surveillance—United States, 1993.* Division of Adolescent and School Health, National Center for Chronic Disease Prevention and Health Promotion, CDC, Rockville, Maryland.

Kann, L., Kinchen, S. A., Williams, B. I., Ross, J. G., Lowry, R., Hill, C. V., Grunbaum, J. A., Blumson, P. S., Collins, J. L, & Kolbe, L. J. (1998). *Youth risk behavior surveillance—United States, 1997.* Division of Adolescent and School Health, National Center for Chronic Disease Prevention and Health Promotion, CDC, Rockville, Maryland.

Kim, S., Crutchfield, C., Williams, C., & Hepler, N. (1998). Toward a new paradigm in substance abuse and other problem behavior prevention for youth: Youth development and empowerment approach. *Journal of Drug Education*, 28, 1-17.

Jessor, R. (1982). Problem behavior and developmental transition in adolescence. *The Journal of School Health*, May, 295-300.

Lalonde, B., Rabinowitz, P., Shofsky, M. L., & Washienko, K. (1997). La esperanza del valle: Alcohol prevention novelas for Hispanic youth and their families. *Health Education and Behavior*, 24, 587-602.

MacNeil, G., Kaufman, A. V., Dressler, W. W., & LeCroy, C. W. (1999). Psychosocial moderators of substance use among middle school-aged adolescents. *Journal of Drug Education*, 29, 25-39.

Males, M. A. (1996). *The scapegoat generation: America's war on adolescents.* Monroe, ME: Common Courage.

New Mexico Selected Health Statistics Annual Report (1996). Dept. of Health/Public Health Division. Office of Information management. New Mexico Vital Records & Health Statistics. Published Nov. 1998.

Orlandi, M. A. (1986). Community-based substance abuse prevention: A multicultural perspective. *Journal of School Health, 56,* 394-409.

Patterson, S., Bethann, C., Bechtel, L. J., & Rose-Colley, M. (1997). Instructional strategies for introducing outcome based education in professional preparation programs. *Journal of Health Education, 28,* 378-380.

Pentz, M. A., Dwyer, J. H., MacKinnon, D. P., Flay, B. R., Hansen, W. B., Wang, E. Y., & Johnson, C. A. (1989). A multicommunity trial for primary prevention of adolescent drug abuse. *Journal of the American Medical Association, 261,* 3259-3273.

Perry, C. L., Williams, C. L., Forster, J. L., Wolfson, M., Wagenaar, A. C., Finnegan, J. R., McGovern, P. G., Veblen-Mortenson, S., Komro, K. A., & Anstine, P. S. (1993). Background, conceptualization and design of a community-wide research program on adolescent alcohol use: Project Northland. *Health Education Research, 8,* 125-136.

Perry, C. L., Williams, C. L., Veblen-Mortenson, S., Toomey, T. L., Komro, K. A., Anstine, P. S., McGovern, P. G., Finnegan, J. R., Forster, J. L., Wagenaar, A. C., & Wolfson, M. (1996). Project Northland: Outcomes of a communitywide alcohol use prevention program during early adolescence. *American Journal of Public Health, 86,* 956-971.

Phinney, J. S. (1997). Ethnic and American identity as predictors of self-esteem among African American, Latino, and white adolescents. *Journal of Youth and Adolescence, 26,* 165-185.

Ramirez, A. G., Gallion, K. J., Espinoza, R., McAlister, A., & Chalela, P. (1997). Developing a media- and school-based program for substance abuse prevention among Hispanic youth: A case study of *Mirame!*/Look at me! *Health Education & Behavior, 24,* 603-612.

Raynal, M. E., & Chen, W. W. (1996). Evaluation of a drug prevention program for young high risk students. *International Quarterly of Community Health Education, 16,* 187-195.

Research & Polling, Inc. (1994). Drug Free Schools and Communities Program. Children, Youth and Families Department, Albuquerque Public Schools Summary. Tobacco, Alcohol and Drug Survey.

Rippetoe, P. A., & Rogers, R. W. (1987). Effects of components of protection-motivation theory on adaptive and maladaptive coping with a health threat. *Journal of Personality and Social Psychology, 52,* 596-604.

Rogers, R. W. (1984). Changing health-related attitudes and behavior: The role of preventive health psychology. In R. McGlynn, Maddox, C. Stoltenbery, & Harvey (Eds.), *Interfaces in Psychology.* Lubbock, TX: Texas Tech University Press.

Rogers, R. W., Deckner, C. W., & Mewborn, C. R. (1978). An expectancy-value theory approach to the long-term modification of smoking behavior. *Journal of Clinical Psychology, 34,* 562-566.

Rogers, R. W., & Mewborn, C. R. (1976). Fear appeals and attitude change: Effects of a threat's noxiousness, probability of occurrence, and the efficacy of coping responses. *Journal of Personality and Social Psychology, 34,* 54-61.

Rudd, R. E., Comfort, L. R., Mongillo, J. M. & Zani, L. (1994). Student-produced health education materials. In A.C. Matiella (Ed.), *The multicultural challenge in health education* (pp. 177-207). Santa Cruz, CA: ETR Associates.

Sanchez, V., & Wallerstein, N. B. (1988). *Alcohol substance abuse prevention: Teacher implementation manual.* Unpublished.

Schmiedeck, R. A. (1979). Adolescent identity formation and the organizational structure of high schools. *Adolescence, 53,* 191-196.

Shope, J. T., Copeland, L. A., Maharg, R., Dielman, T. E., & Butchart, A. T. (1993). Assessment of adolescent refusal skills in an alcohol misuse prevention study. *Health Education Quarterly, 20,* 373-390.

Shope, J. T., Copeland, L. A., Marcoux, B. C., & Kamp, M. E. (1996). Effectiveness of a school-based substance abuse prevention program. *Journal of Drug Education, 26,* 323-337.

Shope, J. T., Copeland, L. A., Kamp, M. E., & Lang, S. W. (1998). Twelfth grade follow-up of the effectiveness of a middle school-based substance abuse prevention program. *Journal of Drug Education, 28,* 185-197.

Simons-Morton, B. G., Donohew, L, & Crump, A. D. (1997) Health communication in the prevention of alcohol, tobacco, and drug use. *Health Education & Behavior, 24,* 544-554.

Stainback, P. D., & Rogers, R. W. (1983). Identifying effective components of alcohol abuse prevention programs: Effects of fear appeals, message style, and source experts. *International Journal of the Addictions, 18,* 393-405.

Steffian, G. (1999). Correction of normative misperceptions: An alcohol abuse prevention program. *Journal of Drug Education, 29,* 115-138.

Stoneman, D., & Bell, J. (1988). *Leadership development.* New York: Youth Action Program.

Wallerstein, N. B. (1988). Empowerment education: Freire's theories applied to health: A case study of alcohol prevention for Indian and Latino youth. Ann Arbor, MI: UMI Dissertation Information Service.

Wallerstein, N. B., & Bernstein, E. (1988). Empowerment education: Freire's ideas adapted to health education. *Health Education Quarterly, 15,* 379-394.

Wallerstein, N., & Sanchez-Merki, V. (1994). Freirian praxis in health education: Research results from an adolescent prevention program. *Health Education Research, 9,* 105-118.

Wechsler, H., & Weitzman, E. R. (1996). Editorial: Community solutions to community problems—preventing adolescent alcohol use. *American Journal of Public Health, 86,* 923-925.

Westman, J. C. (1991). Juvenile ageism: Unrecognized prejudice and discrimination against the young. *Child Psychiatry and Human Development, 21:* 237-256.

Wolfgang, L.A. (1997). Alcohol may impair problem-solving ability through effects on the frontal lobe. *Alcohol, Health, and Research World, 21,* 283-285.

Author Note

We would like to acknowledge Gill Woodall, Ph.D. Associate Professor in Communications and Journalism, University of New Mexico, for his assistance with the data analysis.

10

A PLACE TO CALL HOME

Youth Organizations in the Lives of Inner City Adolescents

Nancy L. Deutsch and Barton J. Hirsch

> *Oh! That feeling of safety, of arrival, of homecoming. . . . We can make homeplace that space where we return for renewal and self-recovery, where we can heal our wounds and become whole.*
> —bell hooks (1990)

When we consider the social environments of urban adolescents, we often focus on the risks they pose rather than the supports they provide (Leadbeater & Way, 1996; McLanahan & Sandefur, 1994; Musick, 1993; National Research Council, 1993; Spencer & Dornbusch, 1990). Youth development organizations can offer valuable resources to urban and poor youth (Hirsch, Roffman, Deutsch, Flynn, Loder, & Pagano, 2000; McLaughlin, Irby, & Langman, 1994; Pittman & Wright, 1991; Roth, Brooks-Gunn, Murray, & Foster, 1998; Tierney, Grossman, & Resch, 1995). Yet research on these settings is sparse. In examining youth organizations, it is tempting to focus on the programs they offer. As we have spent time in them, however, we have increasingly come to emphasize the setting's broader social climate as key to attracting youth and promoting positive developmental change.

Qualities of a social setting, such as emotional support, involvement, independence, organization and control, and physical comfort

294 UNDERSTANDING EARLY ADOLESCENT SELF AND IDENTITY

have been noted to impact people's functioning and development (Moos, 1976). Settings that do not provide opportunities that fit adolescents' developmental needs can lead to negative psychological changes (Eccles, Midgley, Wigfield, Buchanan, Reuman, Flanagan, & Mac Ivar, 1993). Indeed, urban youth may be attracted to gangs because they meet specific needs that are not being met by the youth's larger environment, such as a sense of belonging, companionship, safety, status, a loyal support system, and self-worth (Branch, 1999; Clark, 1992; Flannery, Huff & Manos, 1998). The social climate of youth organizations, similarly, may be important to their ability to attract adolescents and support their development.

The goal of this chapter is to explore this type of social ecological approach to understanding youth development organizations. Our approach integrates theories of development, identity, and self-esteem into how we view the overall setting. We are especially interested in how youth organizations can serve as "home-places" for inner city youth. A home-place is not limited to one's familial or residential home, but is any place a youth chooses to call home. Calling a place a home implies a substantial emotional attachment. We may have many places that we consider important or in which we spend a lot of time, but far fewer places that we would call a home. Such home-places may share common qualities that have developmental significance for adolescents. We will consider how youth currently use such nonfamilial home-places based on research conducted at six inner-city Boys & Girls Clubs. The qualities that adolescents ascribe to the club when describing it as a home will be identified. Case studies will be provided of how particular youth use the club-as-home to support and develop the self. Practical implications for how the club-as-home construct may be used to guide organizational and program development with urban youth will then be explored.

Overview of Research

This chapter emerges from a study to evaluate a gender equity initiative undertaken by a large, metropolitan affiliate of the Boys & Girls Clubs of America. The Boys & Girls Clubs of America, which has been one of the leading youth organizations in the 20th century, serves nearly 3 million boys and girls at more than 2,000 facilities nationwide. Approximately 70% of the youth they serve live in urban areas and 56% are from minority families. The clubs officially went co-ed on a national level in 1990, although many had begun to incorporate girls in the 1980s. The current membership is approximately 60% boys and 40% girls. Despite this, there have not been many programs developed specifically for girls and the clubs have had trouble attracting and retaining adolescent female members. A gender equity initiative was proposed by this regional affiliate to address these issues. The initiative includes multiple strategies and levels of action, including the development of new programs, staff training in gender equity issues, liaison with women's community groups and social service agencies, and gender equitable personnel policies. We were retained to evaluate these programmatic efforts and to examine psychosocial processes that can in turn inform program design (Hirsch et al., 2000).

In the first year of the study, from which the majority of results reported here are taken, four inner city clubs were examined. The clubs serve primarily African American and Hispanic youth. All four clubs rank in the poorest 35% of the city's communities. Methods included ethnographic participant-observation, survey research, and structured interviews of club members and staff. Three hundred boys and girls ages 10 and up completed surveys, and 112 were interviewed. Researchers spent at least one afternoon and evening per week at each club over the course of an academic year.

The Club-as-Home Model

The club-as-home model sprung from the voices of the children and adolescents that were observed and interviewed during the initial phase of the research project. We were struck by the large percentage of children at the clubs who spontaneously referred to the clubs as their "second-home" or "home-away-from-home" during informal conversations. In fact, 74% of members interviewed reported thinking of the club as a home. In choosing the word home to describe the club, youth are insinuating a particular attachment to it. The word home carries with it the baggage of cultural expectations of what a home should be. For the poet Robert Frost (1914), it is the place where "when you have to go there they have to take you in." To writer Ntozake Shange (1982), home is where you return to when you need to "find the rest of yourself." Youth workers, too, often describe their organizations as families to the youth they serve. Much of the literature on youth programs, especially those serving urban youth, use the language of home and family to describe their organizations (McLaughlin et al., 1994). Yet little is known about youth's particular attachment to non-familial homes, how such bonds can help foster adolescents' development and self-esteem, and what qualities of a place facilitate a youth's feeling at home in it.

When we say that a place is home, are we referring to its physical qualities? Do we respond to a warm kitchen, a comfortable chair, a safe and pleasantly decorated room in which to engage in our favorite activities? Or are we referring to specific psychosocial qualities of the space? Is it the supportive presence of other people, feelings of being safe, nurtured, and cared for, and the ability to choose our own actions and express our own opinions that make us feel at home? Is calling a place a home in part a function of the amount of time we spend there? These are important questions to ask if we are to describe youth organizations as homes for youth and expect such home-places to positively impact the lives of the youth that they serve.

Ascribing the language of home to a place implies an attachment that may both reflect and affect the way in which the place impacts the development of the individual. It can be argued that the Boys & Girls Clubs serve as an important place for all the youth who use them. Our survey data indicate that 68% of the children come to the club 4 or 5 days a week and 70% stay for 2 or more hours each day. The sheer amount of time children spend at the clubs arguably make the clubs important places for them. But for some youth, this bond with the clubs is strong enough to warrant their using the word home to describe it. The qualities that transform the clubs from a place to a home and their possible role in youth's development will be addressed in the sections that follow.

Impact of Environment on Identity and Self-Esteem

The notion that places play a role in the development of an individual's identity and self-esteem has been increasingly accepted over the past 20 years. Research on the ways in which humans develop within an environmental context, including the personal meanings of those spaces, has been growing. Individuals' bonds with environments have been studied as entities in their own right, and there has even been suggestion of a separate place-identity that contributes to one's overall sense of self (Proshansky et al., 1983; Rubinstein & Parmelee,

1992). In addition, the personalities of places have been examined in an attempt to better understand how the social climate of an environment may impact human behavior and development (Moos, 1976).

Place attachment is an integrating concept to which affect and emotions are central (Low & Altman, 1992). An individual forms an emotional bond with a particular space as a result of experiences that occur in that space over time. The physical space is then transformed into a place through personal significance and a sense of belonging (Rubinstein & Parmelee, 1992; Sime, 1986). A place, therefore, is a physical space that has special meaning for an individual. It may be assumed that the clubs are such places for their members.

The process of place attachment has been posited to serve a number of functions, including providing a sense of ongoing security and stimulation, social linkages, symbolic bonds to other people, links to social institutions and culture, fostering individual, group and cultural self-esteem and self-worth, as well as maintenance of identity over time (Chawla, 1992; Cotterell, 1991, 1993; Korpela, 1989, 1992; Korpela & Hartig, 1996; Low & Altman, 1992; Marcus, 1992; Rubinstein & Parmelee, 1992). Place attachment has also been suggested to serve as a form of environmental self-regulation in dealing with threats to an individual's sense of balance, unity, or self-esteem (Korpela, 1989, 1992; Korpela & Hartig, 1996). The majority of place attachment studies have focused on either private spaces such as natural settings or bedrooms, or on large, shared public spaces (Chawla, 1992; Cotterell, 1991, 1993; Korpela, 1989, 1992; Korpela & Hartig, 1996; Marcus, 1992). As a result, little is known about the process of place attachment in contexts such as schools and youth organizations.

Childhood places have been reported to support the development of self-identity by providing settings in which children can try out predefined social roles or by offering unprogrammed space. While families form the center of place attachment for young children, in middle childhood friendships that develop within a space appear to play an integral role in facilitating attachment (Chawla, 1992). Childhood place attachments also provide a basis for strengthening identity over time, and integrating the past into present self-concepts, by providing links between an individual's history and contemporary events (Chawla, 1992; Marcus, 1992; Rubinstein & Parmelee, 1992).

Place attachment in adolescence is tied to the youth's emerging sense of self during this period (Marcus, 1992). Favorite places are used to gain a feeling of control, autonomy and overall sense of self and to integrate adolescents' past and future selves (Korpela, 1989, 1992; Korpela & Hartig, 1996; Marcus, 1992). Favorite places also are used to regain a sense of balance when experiencing threats to self-esteem (Korpela, 1989, 1992; Korpela & Hartig, 1996). Adolescents may transform spaces into places as an expression of self-identity (Marcus, 1992) or as an idealized alternative to inadequate actual circumstances (Chawla, 1992).

Studies of adolescent favorite places have generally focused on the physical space itself rather than on the social experiences that take place within the space (e.g. Korpela, 1989, 1992; Korpela & Hartig, 1996). Many researchers have concentrated on private spaces in an attempt to examine the individual psychological processes that occur in favorite places. Those studies that investigate adolescents' use of public spaces tend to look at use of broad spaces, such as areas within a World's Fair, to explore the physical qualities of spaces that attract adolescents (Cotterell, 1991, 1993). Studies of favorite places have provided insight into how place attachment may function as a self-esteem or identity building tool for adolescents and what types of environmental settings attract groups of adolescents. They do not, however, allow for systematic study of the processes through which a particular space becomes, over time, a place to which an individual is attached, or the qualities that promote attachment above and beyond initial attraction. In addition, many of the spaces studied may not be available to urban youth, who may be more bound by their environment and, therefore, in need of alternate spaces, such as schools or youth organizations, to which they may attach.

Some have suggested that attachment to "home" is a particularly important form of place attachment and that appropriation of a home-place is a universal and vital process that is essential to psychological well-being and a foundation of our identities as individuals (Feldman & Stall, 1994; Relph, 1976). A home can provide continuity for an individual over time through patterns of repetition and recurring activities. It may represent important relationships in the person's life and reflect cultural values to which the individual ascribes (Werner, Altman, & Oxley, 1985). The home may also be a nurturing place of political resistance and self-empowerment (Feldman & Stall, 1994; hooks, 1990).

It has been suggested that an imposed environment is unlikely to become a home unless it is congruent with the individual's culture, values, preferences and needs (Rapoport, 1985). The notion of choice, when applied to a Boys & Girls Club, as well as to schools and other youth programs, provides an interesting means for exploring how the use of such settings changes as the children grow older. For many young children, coming to the club is not a choice but is imposed by parents. As they reach adolescence, club members can choose whether or not to continue coming to the club. This choice may be informed by whether or not they have transformed the club from a space in which they are required to spend time to a home-place, which supports their own identity in a variety of ways. This transformation may in turn be determined by whether or not the organization reflects the youth's own values and needs.

Because adolescence is the time when youth separate from their families and begin to explore their own independence and identities outside their familial homes (Eccles et al., 1993; Steinberg, 1990), the desire for new, supportive, spaces may be particularly strong during these years. Adolescents, as they begin to explore the larger environment outside their families, may feel a need for places that still reflect the values of their families and provide similar support, but that allow them to develop an identity separate from their family. Attachment to a home-place, therefore, may fill a need for alternate environments that adolescents can seek out as augmentations to the families from which they are separating.

Individuation from family is but one part of identity development, the primary developmental task of adolescence. During early adolescence, formal operational thinking evolves (Elkind, 1970; Miller, 1993) and allows for the consideration of identity. The formation and consolidation of identity during adolescence involves both integration and differentiation. Adolescents integrate their own self-descriptions into a generalized concept of self (Erikson, 1959; Harter, 1990) and attempt to balance that self-concept with other people's views of them and their place in the world at large (Kroger, 1989; Lavoie, 1994). Although the resulting identity structure is primarily self-constructed, it exists within a psychosocial system and is developed within social relationships (Adams & Marshall, 1996; Erikson, 1959; Harter, 1990; James, 1890; Kroger, 1989; Lavoie, 1994; Lykes, 1985; Miller, 1993).

The role of social context in identity development has been increasingly emphasized, especially by researchers studying identity development in ethnic minorities and women (Burton, Allison, & Obeidallah, 1995; Gilligan, 1982; Heath & McLaughlin, 1993a&b; Lavoie,

1994; Lykes, 1985; Markstrom-Adams & Spencer, 1994; Phinney, 1989; Phinney & Tarver, 1988). Because identity development comes to the forefront during adolescence, when youth's social worlds are expanding, the consideration of the impact of social context on identity development is particularly important. As youth expand the number and types of social environments in which they move, they may find themselves occupying different social roles in different contexts. A variety of social roles across environments can be a positive, motivating force for youth and provide examples of possible selves that youth may explore and to which they may aspire. If the various roles are conflicting, however, and the youth cannot integrate the roles into a harmonious self-concept, differing roles may prove disturbing and even damaging (Markus & Nurius, 1986; Harter, 1990; Harter, Bresnick, Bouchey, & Whitesell, 1997). For some minority and economically disadvantaged groups, the social context of adolescence is characterized by ambiguous and often conflicting social roles (e.g., being expected to act as adults at home by caretaking for younger siblings or working to financially assist the family, but being treated as children in school). This results in a conflict between societal and familial expectations and self-attributes (Burton, et al., 1995; Harter, 1990; Harter et al., 1997; McLaughlin, 1993).

Social supports are important in helping adolescents bridge these potentially conflicting roles (Harter, 1990; Harter et al., 1997; Heath & McLaughlin, 1993; McLaughlin, 1993). Most social contexts in which adolescents move tend to bring one role or identity domain to the forefront (e.g., academic/student role in school, caretaker at home, confidant or buddy with friends). Youth development organizations can act as sites for the integration of social roles. They provide a setting in which youth can simultaneously enact multiple social roles (e.g., acting childlike and athletic by playing sports but also being a responsible worker or caretaker by helping out with the younger kids). Staff members, in turn, can actively support adolescent's multiple and changing social roles through their responses to youth across these varied activities. Receiving support from an adult for these varied roles can provide a crucial support for identity integration (see Hirsch & Jolly, 1984, for an extended discussion of how social networks can support multiple roles). A home-place that embeds multiple social roles and supports may provide youth with the space they need to address the developmental concerns associated with identity formation.

Although there is little research on place attachment and identity development in urban youth specifically, Pastor, McCormick, and Fine (1996) have studied the specific role of home-places in the lives of urban girls. They describe a home-place as a place of synthesis where urban girls can bring together and make sense of a variety of personal traits and societal norms. A home can be a geographic, concrete structure; it is also an emotional space inside the self (Pastor et al., 1996). It is in the coming together of these two conceptualizations of home that urban girls create their own home-places. Pastor and her colleagues discuss the variety of ways that a home-place works for urban girls: as a comforting and safe environment as opposed to the constricting environment they may feel in their familial homes; a space for resistance against social and political norms; a place to develop in relationship with others, both adults and peers; and, a space for cultural connectedness where girls can "knit bridges" across boundaries that exist in other spaces in their lives (generational, cultural, etc.) (Pastor et al., 1996). The home is a space where girls can be connected to each other and to their inner selves—a place for exploration and resistance that the authors do not see as existing elsewhere for girls, especially urban and minority girls, in society at large.

A home-place, then, is not necessarily one's familial home or place of residence. It is a place that is specified by the individual. A home-place provides a means for self-regulation and identity maintenance as well as community and self-empowerment. Appropriation of such a home, one that is linked to both the individual self and the community, may have special significance for urban youth living in poverty.

What Makes a Club a Home?

Analyzing the clubs not just as a place, but as a home-place, provides the tools necessary to hone place attachment theory to the specific situation of the Boys & Girls Clubs that we studied and, perhaps, to urban youth organizations in general. A home is more than a place. If a space is transformed into a place through personal meaning, then a place is further transformed into a home through characteristics that imbue it with deeper personal significance. Through connections with the physical neighborhood in which the clubs are located, relations with staff and other children, activities that promote self-expression, and memories of childhood years at the clubs, the adolescents may develop an attachment to the clubs that helps to support and maintain their identities and self-esteem.

Studying the qualities that adolescents ascribe to places they call home will help us clarify the processes by which a home-place can foster adolescents' identities and esteem and how we may better create such places for youth. Data from our interviews with adolescents at the clubs provide an opportunity for such understanding.

Members of the research team interviewed a total of 112 adolescents across the four clubs. As part of the interview, youth were told that "some children have described the club as a second home to them. Others do not seem to think of the club as a home," and were asked whether they would describe the club as a home to them. Eighty-three (74%) of the youth interviewed responded "yes." They were then asked "what makes it feel like a home to you?" The responses were coded into two major categories: psychosocial and physical. Psychosocial responses were those that referred to an emotional or affective state or to relationships with others. Physical responses were those that referred to a specific physical characteristic of the club, such as furnishings, or to the club as a physical boundary from the outside world. All responses could be further coded into four subcategories: relationships, time, safety, and activities. The subcategories could fall under the umbrella of any of the two major categories with the exception of relationships, which could only be coded under psychosocial. A response that received no major code could still receive one or more subcodes.[1] A response could be coded for any number of major categories and subcategories.[2]

Seventy-three percent of the youth reported at least one psychosocial reason for why the club felt like a home to them. Table 1 provides a list of sample psychosocial responses. The vast majority of these, 91%, referred to youths' interactions with other club members or staff. Feeling cared about by staff and seeing the adults as resources to them appeared to be of particular importance. An ability to come to the staff for help with problems on everything from homework to family issues was noted as key by a number of respondents. The emotional state associated with being at the club (e.g., happy, loved, relaxed) also played a role in youths' describing the club as a home. Many of these emotional qualities are related to the youth's relationships with or views of the staff. Responses such as "people at the club make you feel welcome," and "people care about me, [I] feel safe here and comfortable here" demonstrate how relationships affect the youths' emotional

TABLE 1
Sample Psychosocial Reasons for Why Club Feels Like Home

Everyone sticks together and tries to love each other

The workers are nice, try to treat you like family

The people care about you . . . come here and just hang loose, relax

They care about me, they're concerned about my school and all that

When I come here everybody treats me the same as other people

It feels safe, you don't have to worry about nothing

Because all the people are interested in what I do and how I feel

Because most of the people here I grew up with

People here always listen to you and help you if you have problems, just like your
parents, tell you what to do and what not to do so you won't get into trouble

state of mind in the clubs. It is clear that staff play a key role in transforming a place to a home-place for a majority of these urban adolescents (Hirsch et al., 2000).

Only 13% of youth reported a physical reason for why the club was a home and half of those included an aspect of safety in their answer. Sample responses coded as physical are listed in Table 2. Few respondents listed only physical reasons for why the club is a home but many of those who did referred to the club as an alternative to the streets. The club as a physical boundary from the outside world is implied in their references to the club keeping them out of trouble and away from gangs. Whereas this is an important aspect to consider in how the club may function as a home to youth, it is apparently much less significant in youths' descriptions of the club as a home than the psychosocial aspects, especially relationships. It may be that while the safety of the club initially draws children to it and perhaps even keeps them involved as adolescents, it does not have the same impact on their transformation of the club from an important place to a home-place as the psychosocial aspects of the club.

The subcategories also provide some insight into the qualities that transform a place into a home for these youth. Table 3 provides percentages of responses that were coded into each of the subcategories, regardless of the major category code. Relationships with peers and staff at the club are by far the most important aspect for a majority of the youth who see the club as a home. Forty-two percent of the youth whose responses were coded for relationships directly mentioned or

TABLE 2

Sample Physical Reasons for Why Club Feels Like Home

It's better than being out on the streets

When I'm indoors in my house nothing happens but sometimes shooting, but I'm safe here

You stay off the street, away from trouble

You get to sit down in certain areas, seats are comfortable

Because it's clean

implied staff. Of those, 45% referred to feelings of being cared for by staff and 59% highlighted the support or advice they get from staff, including academic help. Approximately one quarter of the responses that were coded for relationships discussed the role of friends and other children at the club.

The activities that youth engage in at the club also play a role in their thinking of the club as a home.[3] Homework was the most frequently referred to specific activity. General activities such as playing and helping with the children were also popular answers. No specific club programs or structured activities were mentioned as a reason the club feels like a home and, in a separate section of the interview, only 5% mentioned organized programs as among their favorite activities at the clubs. Although these findings suggest that structured programming, including psychosocial programs, does not contribute to youths' attachment to a place as a home, such programming may provide a venue for youth to form the relationships with staff and other youth that they cite as important. Through discussions with peers and adults during structured programs, youth may develop an openness that extends to their overall interactions with the staff and youth at the club. For example, one program for early adolescent girls covers such topics as sexuality and self-esteem. The open and honest atmosphere of such conversations within group meetings may help foster lasting ties between the adult who runs the group and the girls who participate in it. In addition, activities such as homework or sports that provide time for youth to interact with staff one-on-one or in small groups can help create and sustain adult-youth bonds. Our research indicates that, when planning structured activities, it is important to consider the opportunities that they provide for social interaction and relationship building between youth and adults as well as youth and their peers.

TABLE 3
Responses by Subcategory [a]

Relationships with staff or peers at the club	66%
Activities at the club	31%
Amount of time spent at the club	18%
Safety	16%

[a] Because each response can be coded for more than one subcategory, or no subcategories, the percentages do not add up to 100.

The amount of time spent at the club (i.e., "I come here every day" or "I've grown up here") was only mentioned explicitly by 18% of respondents. We do know, however, that many youth have been coming to the clubs for a number of years by the time they reach adolescence and that most spend a large amount of time there. Eighty percent of the children had been attending the club for more than one year, with half attending since they were 8 years old or younger. In addition, as mentioned previously, the majority attends the club at least 4 days a week and remains there for the maximum number of hours. The fact that the youth do not directly mention this as an influencing factor, while suggesting that it is not salient to them as a reason the club is a home, does not necessarily mean that it is not important. In fact, it has been reported that attachment to places, especially home-places, grows over time, with the resulting sense of endurance helping to reinforce the meaning of the home-place (Relph, 1976).

Case Studies

Let us now turn to two case studies to explore how the club functions as a home for specific youth. Both Sammy and La La[4] are African American teens who are members at the same club. The club is located in a multi-ethnic neighborhood of a large city. The neighborhood has one of the largest Asian communities in the city, although the club is comprised primarily of African American youth and staff. The club is located on a busy, commercial street but has a backyard that is fenced off from the sidewalk. The majority of club members live in the immediate neighborhood, which includes a number of high rise apartment buildings, some of which are public housing. The neighborhood is situated only a few blocks from a body of water along which lie a number of parks and recreational areas. Although some of the adolescents can remember playing in the parks as children, they say that they generally stay out of the parks now, especially at night, due to the level of gang activity. Many of the members know each other not only from the club but also from school and the neighborhood.

Case Study #1: Sammy

Sammy is a 16-year-old African American male with a dark complexion and a lean frame. He stands approximately 5'10" with closely cropped hair and thin metal-framed glasses. Sammy usually wears khaki pants and a T-shirt or a casual button-down shirt tucked into his pants. His appearance is always neat and he carries himself tall and makes eye contact when he speaks to you. Although his expression is often serious, he is quick to break into a smile and to laugh and talk with staff members, other children, and volunteers. Sammy has been coming to the club for almost 7 years. Most nights he can be found in the computer room working on homework or scholarship and college applications, or talking with other adolescents and staff.

When asked during the interview what his favorite activities are at the club, Sammy lists all physical activities, such as weight lifting and swimming, despite the fact that Sammy is almost always observed in academic or service activities. Access to the wide assortment of activities at the club allows him to explore a variety of possible selves (Markus & Nurius, 1986). Whereas the academics may be important to Sammy, he may also enjoy the opportunity to try different roles through different activities. The club may also serve as a setting where he can receive academic support without the stigma that may be attached to such tutoring programs amongst his peer group. Academic success is sometimes equated with "acting white" for African American youth, for whom school achievement may carry with it an association with acceptance and assimilation into white culture (Fordham, 1996). The club, therefore, may provide Sammy and other youth who are academically oriented an opportunity to focus on academics while still being able to participate in activities that their peers value as traditionally associated with African American males.

Sammy is at the club nearly every night and often arrives prior to the official opening time for the adolescents (6:45). The club closes from 6:00-6:45 for staff lunch break, with the children (5-12) leaving by 6 and the adolescents (13-18) arriving at 6:45. Sammy and another teen boy are usually in the club during this break. Many nights Sammy and his friend watch one 6-year-old girl until her mother comes to pick her up. For this, the mother pays a nominal fee to a service club to which Sammy and his friend belong. During this time, Sammy and his friend often informally chat and joke with staff members.

Sammy lives with his mother and father and has three sisters. A staff member to whom Sammy is close reports that Sammy's family is tight-knit and has a lot of family values and tradition, including going to church together on Sundays. He also notes that Sammy has a lot of respect for his father and worries a lot about helping his family financially. According to the staff member Sammy is very smart, listens well, and is good at working with his hands.

One night, while Sammy is sitting in the Game Room of the club, he asks one of the researchers for help on an essay he has to write for a Boys & Girls Club Youth of the Year application. The topic of the essay is what the club means to him. Sammy takes a notebook out of his bag and opens it to an outline he has begun to write for the essay. His outline begins with the statement "the club is a second home to me." Underneath the heading he has written such topics as "quiet space to do work, place to bond with friends, place to get away from peer/family pressure, place to confide in adults, safe space to get off the streets." Sammy begins the essay with the sentence "[S]ome people do not have any home. I have been granted the gift of having two homes: my home and the _____ Boys and Girls Club."

When Sammy writes about his bonds with adults at the club he carefully considers how to word his feelings. He initially refers to these bonds simply as bonds with adults, but then voices a fear that such wording will cause people to think that he is disrespecting his own family. The researcher suggests that it is possible to take pleasure in confiding in adults who are not family members while still appreciating and confiding in your own family. Sammy agrees with this and settles his internal conflict by adding the word "nonfamilial" to the sentence. Sammy then writes that the club "allows me to express myself mentally, verbally, physically and artistically." In discussing how the club does this he mentions the various activities he is involved with at the club and the opportunities they provide him to participate in such disparate pastimes as art, basketball, weight lifting, school work, and service organizations. For Sammy, the club is a place where he can experiment with different selves through a multitude of activities and integrate his identity by expressing the various aspects that are a part of his own self-conception (Markus & Nurius, 1986).

In describing what the club means to him, Sammy spontaneously uses the framework of home to discuss the role that the club plays in his life. He was not asked whether the club is a home to him but to describe what the club means to him. In discussing why the club is a home to him he combines the physical with the psychosocial, mentioning factors ranging from the provision of a quiet place to work to the support of nonfamilial adults. His reasons include relationships, activities, and safety. He also talks about how the club provides him with a place to express himself and "put [his] self-image in perspective." When Sammy is asked during a structured interview a few months later what makes the club feel like a home Sammy responds: "It's like where I'm at. One third of my life is spent here." This time Sammy does not discuss specific psychosocial or physical aspects of the club but the amount of time he spends there.

The club appears to provide Sammy with a mixture of external and internal support, allowing for development within a social context yet with an introspective aspect. He appreciates both the quiet space to do school work and the bonds he has developed with peers and staff. In addition, the amount of time that he spends at the club contributes to its feeling like a home-place for him.

It is important to note the conflicting attitude that Sammy voices regarding his bonds with adults at the club. These bonds are clearly of great importance to him. Anyone observing Sammy's interactions with staff members will note the closeness, affection, and concern that characterizes Sammy's relationships with staff as well as other members. He is well liked by everyone and easily shifts from serious discussions of club events or concerns to joking stories and conversations about what people are wearing, what girl likes what boy at school, or the latest song by a popular group. Yet when writing about the importance of the staff to him, he is very careful not to imply that they are a replacement to his family, but an augmentation to it. This desire not to disrespect his own home and family may be important for youth workers to consider when thinking about how the club can serve as a home to youth. If Sammy's response reflects a common sentiment among adolescents who use the clubs, then it would be important for staff to ensure that they are not presenting themselves and the organization as attempting to replace the youth's own home and family, but as an addition to them. Creating ties between the clubs and youths' familial homes may be a useful tool for encouraging a view of the club as a home that integrates, rather than competes with, various parts of the youths' lives.

Case Study #2: La La

La La is a 15-year-old African American female who is a fixture at the club in the evenings. Although her full name is Yolanda everyone at the club calls her La La. La La has been coming to the club everyday for 10 years. Her brother, who is a year and a half older than her, is a close friend of Sammy's and helps him baby-sit the 6-year-old girl while the club is closed. Both La La and her brother have "grown up in the club," according to one staff member. La La has one other sibling besides her brother and lives in a single-parent home. Her brother has many health problems and during the year that we were at the club he is in and out of the hospital. La La does not mention this, even when specifically asked during her interview if anyone in her family has been seriously ill.

La La is a friendly and sociable girl, who smiles a lot and talks with people easily. She has dark skin and short chin-length hair that she generally wears straightened and pulled back with colorful barrettes. La La is nearly always smiling and laughing and appears full of energy. She can often be found in the computer room or the game room with her best friend, Sally, who is also an active club member. The two girls frequently dance to a CD or the radio and chat with each other, staff, or other male and female adolescents who hang out at the club.

La La lists groups such as an academic achievement club and recreational programs such as dancing and basketball as among her favorite activities at the club. Her biggest complaint about the club is that she sometimes finds it boring, a common criticism among the adolescent girls to whom we spoke at all four clubs. In addition, she notes that there often aren't enough people there at night. In fact, she and Sally are often the only adolescent girls at the club in the evenings, although there are about a half dozen or so other girls their age who attend periodically and a few who come for specific academic programs.

When asked if she would describe the club as a home, La La says that she would. "Everyone treats each other the same and it seems like they try to show a sense of comfort and love here. Everyone sticks together and tries to love each other." Her stated reason for feeling that the club is a home is purely psychosocial, based on the emotional atmosphere of the club created by the staff and members at the club. This is not surprising, given the strong social attachment she appears to have to the club. Despite the fact that she says it is sometimes boring, she comes every night, often simply hanging around with whatever other adolescents happen to be there or the staff, especially one female staff member to whom many girls in the club are quite close. The activities that take place at the club, therefore, do not seem to be the draw for La La but, instead, the relationships that she has developed and sustains at the club. She strongly identifies with other club members. Written on her backpack in large letters is "La La and Sally Friends 4-Ever." She states that she does not get into as many arguments at the club as she does with her siblings at home, despite the fact that her brother is always at the club with her, often in the same room.

Based on observations of La La, it appears that the club supports a positive identity for her. Much of this support seems to be in the form of relationships with staff and peers. Given the relational theory of female development, which posits that girls develop more in relation to other people than boys do (Gilligan, 1982; Jordan, 1997; Lykes, 1985; Miller, 1990), it may be that the club provides a context for La La to build and sustain such identity supporting relationships, in line with her developmental needs.

The cases of Sammy and La La demonstrate ways in which the Boys & Girls Club works for urban adolescents. In both cases, the club has successfully provided an environment that is meeting the developmental needs of these youth. Be it through relationships with nonfamilial adults and peers, a safe space to spend time without the pressures of home, or activities that provide opportunities for self-expression in a variety of mediums, the clubs are helping these two youth navigate the waters of their adolescent years. These youth clearly feel attached to the club and have built various facets of their participation in the club into their identities, whether it be via identification with friends who are club members or through their own membership in groups or activities at the club. Both identify the club not only as an important place but as a home, a place where there is "love, caring" and where they can "express themselves."

Implications for Working with Youth

It is sometimes assumed that the best way to address self-esteem and iden-tity issues in adolescents is through specific interventions designed to address these topics. There are psychosocial development programs in place at several of the Boys & Girls Clubs. One in particular, which is aimed at early adolescent females, has elements directed at self-esteem enhancement directly. Although this program and a few others enjoy popular support and participation at some of the clubs, they were never mentioned as a reason that the club felt like a home. In addition, such groups were almost always missing from members' lists of favorite activ-ities, even among those girls who are known to be active members of such groups and who speak highly of them.

This suggests that whereas targeted interventions may have a place in youth organizations and may be a means of fostering identity and esteem among adolescents, they may not be the most effective way to initiate or maintain the participation of older adolescents. The envi-ronment of the clubs themselves may not only play a role in involving adolescents in programs and activities but may also impact the youth's development directly. Studies of school settings have indicated that envi-ronmental factors may indeed affect youth outcomes (Lipsitz, 1984; Rut-ter, Maughan, Mortimore, Ouston, & Smith, 1979). Evidence suggests that, although the physical and administrative aspects of a school do not appear to impact student outcomes, the processes that make up the social climate of the school do play such a role. Although there may not be a particular set of processes that produce positive outcomes, characteristics of schools including teacher expectations, value and belief systems of teachers and students, academic goals, time spent on instruction and homework, and the nature of teacher-student relation-ships do impact youth (e.g., Anderson, 1982; Phillips, 1997; Rutter et al., 1979). The quality of the environment itself, therefore, may have a more dramatic effect on youth than previously thought.

The idea of creating an environment that is a home-place for youth is inviting. Although it is tempting to address this issue through the vehicle of the physical atmosphere, by adding couches, televisions, or special rooms for adolescents, it should be noted that these qualities were not prominent in the youth's own descriptions of what makes the club a home. The psychosocial aspects of the space may be more diffi-cult to address. However, our research indicates that it is these aspects that have the most impact on the youth. In particular, the relationships that are formed within the walls of the clubs appear to play a large role in determining the youth's attachment to the club. Feelings of being cared for or loved by the staff and other club members were reported as particularly important to the youth. In addition, the support and advice that children received at the club, with both academic and personal problems, were referred to specifically by nearly a third of the children whose responses received a code for relationships. The combination of feeling cared for and feeling that they can come to the club when they need help or advice may play an important part in the youth's process of attachment to the club. It may be that this attachment is what then keeps the youth involved in the club, providing the opportunity for it to have a continuing influence on the adolescent's development.

The initial results of our research suggest that special emphasis should be placed on the role of staff in youth programming. More than a quarter of all the youth who said that the club was a home referred to the staff as a reason for this feeling, underscoring the important role that the adults at the club play. This poses a challenge to youth organizations, as staff turnover rates tend to be high. It may be in the best interest of the organizations to pay closer attention to the staff. This means not only hiring staff who are likely to be able to form strong bonds with members but also doing more to sustain the staff's motivation to continue their work at the clubs. Youth workers are often underpaid and overworked, due to budget constraints and high turnover rates. Perhaps more attention should be given to supporting staff in their jobs and providing them with opportunities to grow within their positions. Listening to the ideas and suggestions of staff and allowing them to implement programs in which they have a strong interest may help decrease turnover, thereby sustaining and increasing bonds with youth. In encouraging staff to implement new programs, however, organizations must be careful to balance additional expectations with current responsibilities, so as not to further overload already busy staff.

In addition, ensuring that children have access to adults outside of structured activity time may help foster relationships. One staff member said that what many adolescent girls really want is the social interaction with her and the particular activity is not important: "I could tell them we're going to stand here and throw a rock back and forth for hours and they'd say 'cool.'" Although she has started a number of successful programs for adolescent girls, she is flexible about their content. There are times when she will simply sit and chat informally with a group of girls and she sees this as just as important as having a structured group meeting. Whereas it is often assumed that staff are not truly working if they are hanging out with youth without any structured activity, these informal moments may allow a unique opportunity for youth to develop close relationships with adults. Providing staff with periods of time, besides their breaks, when they are free from other administrative and program duties may give youth greater and more relaxed availability to the adults without adding time pressure to the staff. It should be recognized that such interactions do take time and energy on the part of the staff and that these bonds may be a key factor in transforming the organizations into a home and maintaining youths' participation, which tends to decline in adolescence (Cotterell, 1996). Similar interventions could be used in environments such as schools, where teachers, counselors, and other staff can be encouraged, through the provision of additional time, to develop supportive bonds with the youth.

The role of peer relationships must also be considered in program and organizational development. At one club, a psychosocial program failed in part because of a conflict between two peer groups (Hirsch et al., 2000). Additionally, as noted previously, a number of children mentioned simply being with friends as an important aspect of the club and 69% prefer to hang out with children who go to the club as opposed to those peers who are not club members. The case study of La La also indicates the importance of peer relationships in maintaining youth participation. Recruiting groups of youth from schools and neighborhoods may help encourage positive peer ties and social groups within organizations. Special activities, such as dances and sleepovers, that invite members' outside friends into the clubs may also serve to encourage and foster friendships within the walls of the organization. Similarly, schools and other institutions that have a predetermined population of children should be aware of peer ties when developing new programs and scheduling classes (Lipsitz, 1984). The presence of supportive or conflicting peer groups may help determine the level of participation as well as youth outcomes.

Although the warm atmosphere implied by the home model is appealing, it should be recognized that adolescence is a time of separation and individuation (Eccles, et al., 1993; Freud, 1958; Hauser, 1991; Steinberg, 1990). Developmentally, adolescents are differentiating themselves from their families and distinguishing themselves as unique individuals. If the club is viewed as a home, therefore, as members approach adolescence, they may want to separate from the clubs, seeing them as a place for children, associated with their childhood. For some adolescents this association works in the club's favor; many youth talk about having grown up there as a positive aspect that creates continuity for them. The stability and support provided by the atmosphere of the home-place enhance certain youths' ties to it, while for others it may push them away. Without activities or relationships that recognize their developing selves, adolescents may associate their attachment to the club with childhood and discard it in search of more contemporary attachments.

By providing adolescents with new opportunities as they grow older, organizations can acknowledge and integrate youths' changing identities and needs. Opportunities to work as junior staff, administrative workers, or tutors to younger children can give adolescents new roles that recognize their age and the contributions they can make to the organization. This may allow adolescents to maintain their relationship with the organization, engaging and supporting their growing needs for autonomy and control without feeling trapped by the club's association to their childhood. Encouraging youth to view an organization as a home necessitates giving them a voice within that home and recognizing that this voice will change as they mature. Youth's own ideas for programs and activities should be listened to and implemented when possible. While the metamorphosis of adolescent-adult relationships in such a way may prove challenging, respect for the adolescents' developmental stage and needs may be a key to their continued attachment to and participation in the organization.

Nevertheless, no intervention works for all youth. Some adolescents may need and respond positively to a home-place, whereas such an atmosphere may eventually smother other youth. Individual characteristics of the youth as well as qualities of the place may play a role in determining both who sees the club as a home and who continues to use the clubs. More research is needed in this area.

The club-as-home approach allows us to think about youth organizations in a manner that emotionally resonates with our own cultural images of important places. Although it is easy to say that a place is a home, it is more difficult to say why. Yet it is those often undefined qualities that motivate youth to attach themselves to particular places and that are key, therefore, to understanding how such places support and sustain their development. If we are to successfully address the developmental needs of adolescents, especially those living in urban areas and in poverty, we must explore the unique meanings that adolescents themselves ascribe to places they call home and how these meanings impact their lives. By creating spaces that youth transform to home-places we may be providing them with much needed support for their own developmental needs and processes. By focusing on specific qualities of the environment, we are broadening our view of the types of programs that benefit adolescents and allowing for the possibility that home-places may provide adolescents with unique and diffuse supports for their developing sense of self.

References

Adams, G. R., & Marshall, S. K. (1996). A developmental social psychology of identity: Understanding the person-in-context. *Journal of Adolescence, 19,* 429-442.

Anderson, C. S. (1982). The search for school climate: A review of the research. *Review of Educational Research, 52,* 368-420.

Branch, C. W. (1999). Pathologizing normality or normalizing pathology? In C. W. Branch (Ed.), *Adolescent gangs: Old issues, new approaches* (pp. 197-211). Philadelphia: Brunner/Mazel.

Burton, L. M., Allison, K. W., & Obeidallah, D. (1995). Social context and adolescence: Perspectives on development among inner-city African-American teens. In L. J. Crockett & A. C. Crouter (Eds.), et al. *Pathways through adolescence: Individual development in relation to social contexts. The Penn State series on child and adolescent development* (pp. 119-138). Mahwah, NJ: Lawrence Erlbaum.

Chawla, L. (1992). Childhood place attachments. In I. Altman & S. M. Low (Eds.), *Human Behavior and Environment: Advances in Theory and Research: Vol. 12. Place attachment* (pp. 63-86). New York: Plenum Press.

Clark, C. M. (1992). Deviant adolescent subcultures: Assessment strategies and clinical interventions. *Adolescence, 27,* 283-293.

Cotterell, J. L. (1991). The emergence of adolescent territories in a large urban leisure environment. *Journal of Environmental Psychology, 11,* 25-41.

Cotterell, J. L. (1993). Do macro-level changes in the leisure environment alter leisure constraints on adolescent girls? *Journal of Environmental Psychology, 13,* 125-136.

Cotterell, J. (1996). *Social networks and social influences in adolescence.* New York: Routledge.

Eccles, J., Midgley, C., Wigfield, A., Buchanan, C., Reuman, D., Flanagan, C., & Mac Ivar, D. (1993). Development during adolescence: The impact of stage-environment fit on young adolescents' experiences in schools and in families. *American Psychologist, 48,* 90-101.

Elkind, D. (1981). *Children and adolescents: Interpretive essays on Jean Piaget.* New York: Oxford University Press.

Erikson, E. (1959). *Identity and the life cycle.* New York: Norton.

Feldman, R., & Stall, S. (1994). The politics of space appropriation: A case study of women's struggles for homeplace in Chicago public housing. In I. Altman & A. Churchman (Eds.), *Human Behavior and Environment: Advances in Theory and Research: Vol. 13. Women and the environment* (pp. 167-199). New York: Plenum Press.

Flannery, D. J., Huff, C. R., & Manos, M. (1998). Youth gangs: A developmental prospective. In T. P. Gullotta, G. R. Adams, et al. (Eds.), *Advances in adolescent development: An annual book series: Vol. 9. Delinquent violent youth: Theory and interventions* (pp. 175-204). Thousand Oaks, CA: Sage.

Fordham, S. (1996). *Blacked out.* Chicago: The University of Chicago Press.

Freud, A. (1958). Adolescence. *Psychoanalytic Study of the Child, 13,* 255-278.

Frost, R. (1914). The Death of the Hired Man. In A. Allison, H. Barrows, C. Blake, A. Carr, A. Eastman, & H. English, Jr. (Eds.) (1983). *The Norton Anthology of Poetry* (3rd ed., pp. 909-912). New York: W.W. Norton & Company.

Gilligan, C. (1982). *In a different voice.* Cambridge, MA: Harvard University Press.

Harter, S. (1990). Self and identity development. In S. Feldman & G. Elliott (Eds.), *At the threshold: The developing adolescent* (pp. 352-387). Cambridge, MA: Harvard University Press.

Harter, S., Bresnick, S., Bouchey, H. A., & Whitesell, N. R. (1997). The development of multiple role-related selves during adolescence. *Development and Psychopathology, 9,* 835-853.

Hauser, S. with Powers, S., & Noam, G. (1991). *Adolescents and their families: Paths of ego development.* New York: Free Press.

Heath, S. B., & McLaughlin, M. W. (1993b). Ethnicity and gender in theory and practice: The youth perspective. In S. B. Heath & M. W. McLaughlin (Eds.), *Identity and inner-city youth: Beyond ethnicity and gender* (pp. 13-35). New York: Teachers College Press.

Hirsch, B., & Jolly, E. A. (1984). Role transitions and social networks: Social support for multiple roles. In V. L. Allen & E. van de Vliert (Eds.), *Role transitions: Explorations and explanations* (pp. 39-51). New York: Plenum.

Hirsch, B., Roffman, J., Deutsch, N., Flynn, C., Loder, T., & Pagano, M. (2000). Inner city youth development organizations: Strengthening programs for adolescent girls. *Journal of Early Adolescence, 20,* 210-230.

hooks, b. (1990). *Yearning: Race, gender, & cultural politics.* Boston: South End Press.

James, W. (1890). The consciousness of self. Reprinted from *The Principles of Psychology.* New York: Holt.

Jordan, J. (Ed.) (1997). *Women's growth in diversity.* New York: Guilford.

Korpela, K. M. (1989). Place-identity as a product of environmental self-regulation. *Journal of Environmental Psychology, 9,* 241-256.

Korpela, K. M. (1992). Adolescents' favourite places and environmental self-regulation. *Journal of Environmental Psychology, 12,* 249-258.

Korpela, K. M., & Hartig, T. (1996). Restorative qualities of favorite places. *Journal of Environmental Psychology, 16,* 221-233.

Kroger, J. (1989). *Identity in adolescence: The balance between self and other.* New York: Routledge.

Lavoie, J. C. (1994). Identity in adolescence: Issues of theory, structure and transition. *Journal of Adolescence, 17,* 17-28.

Leadbeater, B., & Way, N. (Eds.) (1996). *Urban girls: Resisting stereotypes, creating identities.* New York: New York University Press.

Lipsitz, J. (1984). *Successful schools for young adolescents.* New Brunswick, NJ: Transaction Books.

Low, S. M., & Altman, I. (1992). Place attachment: A conceptual inquiry. In I. Altman & S. M. Low (Eds.), *Human Behavior and Environment: Advances in Theory and Research: Vol. 12. Place attachment.* (pp. 1-12). New York: Plenum Press.

Lykes, M. B. (1985). Gender and individualistic vs. collectivist bases for notions about the self. *Journal of Personality, 53,* 356-383.

Marcus, C. C. (1992). Environmental memories. In I. Altman & S. M. Low (Eds.), *Human Behavior and Environment: Advances in Theory and Research: Vol. 12. Place attachment* (pp. 87-112). New York: Plenum Press.

Markus, H., & Nurius, P. (1986). Possible selves. *American Psychologist, 41,* 954-969.

Markstrom-Adams, C., & Spencer, M. B. (1994). A model for identity interventions with minority adolescents. In S. L. Archer (Ed.), *Interventions for adolescent identity development* (pp. 84-102). Thousand Oaks, CA: Sage.

McLanahan, S., & Sandefur, G. (1994). *Growing up with a single parent: What helps, what hurts.* Cambridge, MA: Harvard University Press.

McLaughlin, M. W. (1993). Embedded identities: Enabling balance in urban contexts. In S. B. Heath & M. W. McLaughlin (Eds.), *Identity and inner-city youth: Beyond ethnicity and gender* (pp. 36-67). New York: Teachers College Press.

McLaughlin, M., Irby, M., & Langman, J. (1994). *Urban sanctuaries: Neighborhood organizations in the lives and futures of inner city youth.* San Francisco: Jossey-Bass.

Miller, J. (1990). The development of women's sense of self. In C. Sanardi (Ed.), *Essential papers on the psychology of women* (pp. 437-454). New York: New York University Press.

Miller, P. H. (1993). *Theories of developmental psychology.* W.H. Freeman & Co.

Moos, R. (1976). *The human context: Environmental determinants of behavior.* New York: John Wiley & Sons.

Musick, J. (1993). *Young, poor, and pregnant: The psychology of teenage motherhood.* New Haven, CT: Yale University Press.

National Research Council, Panel on High Risk Youth (1993). *Losing generations: Adolescents in high-risk settings.* Washington, DC: National Academy Press.

Pastor, J., McCormick, J., & Fine, M. (1996). Makin' homes: An urban girl thing. In B. Leadbeater & N. Way (Eds.), *Urban girls: Resisting stereotypes, creating identities* (pp. 15-34). New York: New York University Press.

Phillips, M. (1997). What makes schools effective? A comparison of the relationships of communitarian climate and academic climate to mathematics achievement and attendance during middle school. *American Educational Research Journal, 34,* 633-662.

Phinney, J. S. (1989). Stages of ethnic identity development in minority group adolescents. *Journal of Early Adolescence, 9,* 34-49.

Phinney, J. S., & Tarver, S. (1988). Ethnic identity search and commitment in black and white eighth graders. *Journal of Early Adolescence, 8,* 265-277.

Pittman, K., & Wright, M. (1991). *Bridging the gap: A rationale for enhancing the role of community organizations in promoting youth development.* Washington, DC: Carnegie Council on Adolescent Development.

Proshansky, H. M., Fabian, A. K., & Kaminoff, R. D. (1983). Place identity: Physical world socialization of the self. *Journal of Environmental Psychology, 3,* 57-83.

Rapoport, A. (1985). Thinking about home environments: A conceptual framework. In I. Altman & S. M. Low (Eds.), *Human Behavior and Environment: Advances in Theory and Research: Vol. 8. Home environments* (pp. 255-86). New York: Plenum Press.

Relph, E. (1976). *Place and placelessness.* London: Pion Limited.

Roth, J., Brooks-Gunn, J., Murray, L., & Foster, W. (1998). Promoting healthy adolescents: Synthesis of youth development program evaluations. *Journal of Research on Adolescence, 8,* 423-459.

Rubinstein, R. L., & Parmelee, P. A. (1992). Attachment to place and the representation of the life course by the elderly. In I. Altman & S. M. Low (Eds.), *Human Behavior and Environment: Advances in Theory and Research: Vol. 12. Place attachment* (pp. 139-163). New York: Plenum Press.

Rutter, M., Maughan, B., Mortimore, P., & Ouston, J., with Smith, A. (1979). *Fifteen thousand hours: Secondary schools and their effects on children.* Cambridge, MA: Harvard University Press.

Shange, N. (1982). *Sassafrass, cypress & indigo.* New York: St. Martin's Press.

Sime, J. (1986). Creating places or designing spaces? *Journal of Environmental Psychology, 6,* 49-63.

Spencer, M., & Dornbusch, S. (1990). Challenges in studying minority youth. In S. Feldman & G. Elliott (Eds.), *At the threshold: The developing adolescent* (pp. 123-146). Cambridge, MA: Harvard University Press.

Steinberg, L. (1990). Autonomy, conflict, and harmony in the family relationship. In S. Feldman & G. Elliott (Eds.), *At the threshold: The developing adolescent* (pp. 255-276). Cambridge, MA: Harvard University Press.

Tierney, J., Grossman, J., & Resch, N. (1995). *Making a difference: An impact study of Big Brothers/Big Sisters.* Philadelphia: Public/Private Ventures.

Werner, C., Altman, I., & Oxley, D. (1985). Temporal aspects of home: A transactional perspective. In I. Altman & S. M. Low (Eds.), *Human Behavior and Environment: Advances in Theory and Research: Vol. 8. Home environments* (pp. 1-32). New York: Plenum Press.

Author Note

We are grateful to Cecilia Bocanegra, Nithya Chandra, Cathy Flynn, Amy Geary, Tyrone Gooch, Erin Higgins, Susan Israel, Diana Kalter, Miriam Landau, Tondra Loder, Maria Pagano, Jennifer Roffman, Sarah Watson, and Kathryn Young for their help in conducting this research. Funding was provided in part via awards from a (anonymous) regional affiliate of the Boys & Girls Clubs of America and the Northwestern University/University of Chicago Joint Center for Poverty Research.

Endnotes

1. A total of 17 responses (21%) received no major code.
2. All codes had satisfactory inter-rater reliability (Kappa ranged from .89 to 1.0)
3. Responses that referred only to the youth's being able to choose what they do at the club, without reference to a specific activity, were *not* coded as

"activity." Such responses were seen as focusing on the autonomy of the child, rather than on the activity itself (e.g., "I can do what I want here"). Responses such as "they do what I like to do" *were* coded as "activity," however, as they were seen as referring to more specific preferred behaviors, even though the particular activity was not named.

4. All names have been changed.

11

Esteem-Enhancement Interventions During Early Adolescence

David L. DuBois, Carol Burk-Braxton, and Heather D. Tevendale

Beginning with the Affective Education movement of the late 1960s, the past several decades have witnessed a remarkable proliferation of programs for youth that have as one of their primary aims the enhancement of self-esteem. This has involved, perhaps most notably, the widespread adoption of packaged curricular programs for enhancing self-esteem by elementary and secondary schools. One of these programs alone, Power of Positive Students (POPS), has reached over 5,000 schools (Dryfoos, 1998). Esteem-enhancement activities have received further emphasis in numerous other educational and social innovations (e.g., advisory programs in middle schools) as well as the programming of prominent youth development organizations (e.g., Boys & Girls Clubs of America). Even when not a specific focus of program activities, benefits pertaining to self-esteem often are seen as a key ingredient in the success of many of the most popular preventive interventions for youth in today's society (e.g., mentoring).

In many ways, the value of helping youth to feel good about themselves seems intuitive and thus hardly a controversial idea. Yet in recent years programs that have this focus have come under increasingly intense scrutiny and criticism. Several noted scholars (Damon, 1995; Kohn, 1994), including a past president of the American Psychological

Association (Seligman, 1993), for example, have seriously questioned the effectiveness of such programs and even gone so far as to suggest that they be abandoned altogether in favor of other types of interventions that seem more promising. Outside academia, equally strong opposition has been encountered from those who perceive esteem-enhancement activities to constitute a significant threat to important personal or religious values. Affective education programs are seen by these critics as sending the dangerous message to youth that they should be concerned with feeling good about themselves above all else. Young people participating in such programs thus may be encouraged to adopt a "means justifies the ends" mentality in which there is little concern with the morality or appropriateness of behaviors that are engaged in to bolster self-esteem (e.g., "What Caused Columbine?," 1999). In sum, to many observers, the emphasis that continues to be placed on esteem-enhancement as an intervention strategy in working with youth misses the mark at best and, at worst, runs the risk of serving to exacerbate some of the very problems that such programs seek to address.

In the midst of this mounting scientific and public skepticism, it is an opportune time to give careful consideration both to the rationale that currently exists for involving youth in esteem-enhancement programs and to directions for improvement that could make them more effective and acceptable to others in the future. Four fundamental questions are important to address in this regard. First, to what extent is there a need for esteem-enhancement interventions? That is, are there significant numbers of youth who either currently exhibit low self-esteem or, relatedly, are likely to do so in the future without the benefit of intervention? Are there particular stages of development when such trends are most apparent? How strong is the evidence that low self-esteem, in turn, directly increases the susceptibility of youth to serious adjustment difficulties such as depression, delinquency, and academic failure? And, to complicate matters further, are there additional youth who, despite perhaps reporting an overall favorable sense of self-regard, nonetheless have liabilities or deficits in one or more specific facets of their self-esteem such as how they see themselves in certain areas of their lives (e.g., body-image)? Do still others exhibit positive feelings of self-worth that are supported in large part by maladaptive tendencies in their behavior, thinking, or value systems? Do these types of underlying patterns in self-esteem, apart from whether it is simply high or low, constitute significant threats to healthy youth adjustment?

Second, independent of the existence of any need that can be established, the issue of whether self-esteem *can* be enhanced is an entirely separate and important question. That is, can self-esteem be increased (or otherwise strengthened) through systematic intervention and, relatedly, can predictable declines in self-esteem be prevented? If so, what procedures are most effective for achieving these goals (i.e., "best practices")? Can gains in self-esteem be established that are lasting as opposed to temporary? And, to what extent do the answers to these questions depend on the backgrounds and characteristics of the youth involved, such as their preexisting levels of self-esteem?

Third, even if lasting enhancements in self-esteem can be achieved, it is important also to consider whether such improvements are likely to translate into desired consequences for the overall adjustment of youth. That is, are gains in self-esteem produced through programs beneficial for emotional and behavioral functioning, academic achievement, and physical health? Are positive effects more likely for some indicators of adjustment and well-being than for others?

Finally, should esteem-enhancement interventions be supported and disseminated? This is an important and separate question for several reasons. Consider, for example, that even if found to be effective, it can be asked whether the benefits expected to result from the implementation of such programs compare favorably to those demonstrated for competing types of intervention strategies and, relatedly, whether the expenditure of resources involved are justified relative to the anticipated payoff. If a basis does exist to support dissemination of programs, how can this goal be accomplished most successfully and in a manner most likely to be found acceptable to targeted "consumers" (i.e., youth, parents, teachers, etc.)? Furthermore, what is the role of values in the process of self-esteem enhancement?

In the present chapter, we review theory and research relating to each of the preceding four areas of concern. Guided by this overview, we then propose an integrative conceptual model to guide self-esteem enhancement activities. We maintain a focus throughout on implications for esteem-enhancement during early adolescence specifically. As will become evident, the basic elements of a rationale for esteem-enhancement intervention are readily apparent for this age group. Furthermore, consideration of applications to a specific age group will serve to highlight the importance of taking developmental issues into account within esteem-enhancement interventions more generally.

The Self During Early Adolescence

Prior to beginning our review of the rationale for esteem-enhancement intervention during early adolescence, it will be useful to briefly consider the important role of the self during this stage of development. The transition to adolescence brings with it profound change in nearly all aspects of the youth's life (Hamburg, 1974). Because of the high cumulative levels of stress that often are produced by these changes, early adolescence may be a particularly important period of development during which to have a strong sense of self-worth available as a resource to aid in coping efforts (Simmons & Blyth, 1987). Emerging capacities for complexity and abstraction in the thought processes of young adolescents, in conjunction with tendencies toward increased egocentrism and self-consciousness, also bring the task of forming a coherent and favorable personal identity to the forefront of the developmental concerns for this age group (Adams, 1992). This type of introspection presents important new opportunities for self-growth. Recent research indicates, for example, that during early adolescence many youth may first become able to make productive use of time spent alone for self-reflection in ways that enhance psychological well-being (Larson, 1997). These same processes, however, also may increase the susceptibility of young adolescents to negative views and feelings about the self and their adverse consequences. Concerns about particular areas of development (e.g., pubertal changes), for example, may for some youth interact with heightened self-preoccupation at this age to detract significantly from feelings of self-adequacy.

It is important to keep in mind, furthermore, that the preceding types of self processes are unfolding in the dynamic and changing social contexts of the lives of young adolescents. Thus, as relationships with peers change and efforts to negotiate greater autonomy from parents increase, corresponding facets of social identity and their positive integration may take on special significance as influences on feelings of self-worth at this age (Adams, 1992). With increased independency and sense of agency, efforts of youth to actively develop and secure positive feelings of self-worth for themselves may become more prominent as well (Harter, 1986). As will be discussed, whether such esteem-enhancement efforts represent a good "fit" with the norms and expectations of significant others in the lives of young adolescents such as parents and teachers may be an issue of particular concern.

Is There a Need for Esteem-Enhancement Interventions?

With this consideration of the role of self during early adolescence as background, we now turn to the first of our four guiding questions: to what extent is there a demonstrated need for esteem-enhancement interventions. Relatedly, does this need appear to be any greater during early adolescence than at other points in development?

Prevalence of Low Self-Esteem

Typically, self-esteem is measured using questionnaires in which youth are asked to indicate the extent to which various statements describe their views or feelings about themselves as persons (e.g., "On the whole, I am satisfied with myself"). A consistent finding in this research is that youth, on average, report levels of self-esteem that are positive rather than negative or even neutral (Wylie, 1989). That is, when asked whether they generally have favorable views or feelings about themselves, youth tend to agree rather than disagree or indicate that they are undecided; in a corresponding manner, they typically disavow that they feel inferior to others or that they perceive themselves as lacking in desirable qualities as a person. It is reassuring to know that most youth seemingly are not plagued by pervasive feelings of insecurity or self-doubt. This also implies, however, that interventions designed to enhance self-esteem are likely to be of most effect in raising self-esteem that is already positive to an even higher level. This prospect is not ideal from the practical standpoint of program evaluation. This is because if most youth already score high on an outcome measure such as self-esteem, it generally becomes more difficult to demonstrate that even higher scores on the measure resulted from an intervention (this phenomenon is referred to commonly as a "ceiling effect"). It also is not clear based on recent research (to be described later in this chapter) that raising levels of self-esteem to unusually high levels is necessarily a desirable goal. Nor does it seem likely even if it were that this objective would serve as an effective rallying point for gaining the support of key stakeholders in the implementation and dissemination of esteem-enhancement programs such as parents, teachers, school administrators, and community leaders.

These overall trends, however, may mask the presence of significant minorities of youth who do develop overall negative feelings about themselves (i.e., low self-esteem; Hirsch & DuBois, 1991). This could be the case especially during stages of development when youth experience heightened vulnerability to low self-esteem. Because of the inherently challenging and varied changes that characterize the transition from childhood to adolescence, many theorists have viewed early adolescence as a time of increased risk for the emergence of negative feelings about the self (Arnett, 1999). Research findings do indeed indicate an overall decline in self-esteem at this age. The magnitude of this decrease, on average, is relatively small and offset by subsequent gains in self-esteem during the remainder of adolescence (Cairn, 1996).

Research employing more refined analyses, however, has revealed that an important subgroup of approximately one in five young adolescents experience more marked and lasting declines in self-esteem (Hirsch & DuBois, 1991; Zimmerman, Copeland, Shope, & Dielman, 1997). In one of the studies (Hirsch & DuBois, 1991), these youth went from reporting positive feelings of self-worth in late childhood (i.e., sixth grade) to a strong dislike of themselves only two years later; in the other investigation (Zimmerman et al., 1997), a corresponding group of youth reported a similar declining trajectory of self-esteem over a 4-year period that extended into middle adolescence (i.e., 10th grade). Notably, results of these studies also indicate that a further subgroup comprising as many as 15% of youth enter early adolescence already experiencing negative self-esteem and then continue to exhibit low levels of self-regard throughout this period (and potentially beyond this time as well).

Early adolescence thus presents a promising opportunity for esteem-enhancement interventions to be used not only to prevent sharp declines in self-esteem for youth who enter this stage of development feeling relatively good about themselves, but also to curtail the prolongation of preexisting low levels of self-esteem for significant numbers of additional youth. Further strengthening this argument is the finding that young adolescents demonstrating unfavorable self-esteem trajectories also exhibit significant impairment in a wide range of other areas of functioning including, for example, poor school performance, heightened levels of psychiatric symptomatology, and involvement in substance use (Hirsch & DuBois, 1991; Zimmerman et al., 1997). This important issue of the linkage between self-esteem and youth adjustment now will be considered in greater depth.

Consequences for Youth Adjustment

It has been assumed widely that high levels of self-esteem make a significant contribution to healthy overall adjustment and positive functioning during development (Meggert, 1996). Considerable research support exists for this view, as indicated in the following summary from a recent review of the literature (DuBois & Tevendale, 1999, p. 104):

> High levels of self-esteem among youth have been linked to a variety of favorable outcomes, including positive mood and happiness (Rosenberg, 1985), life satisfaction (Huebner, 1991), physical fitness and desirable health practices (Doan & Scherman, 1987; Yarcheski & Mahon, 1989), adaptive classroom behavior (Lerner et al., 1991), and academic achievement (Hattie, 1992). Conversely, children and adolescents lacking in self-esteem have been indicated to be more prone to symptoms of depression and anxiety (Ohannessian, Lerner, Lerner, & von Eye, 1994; Rosenberg, 1985; Towbes, Cohen, & Glyshaw, 1989), interpersonal difficulties such as loneliness (Ammerman, Kazdin, & Van Hasselt, 1993) and rejection by peers (East, Hess, & Lerner, 1987), conduct problems/ delinquent behavior (Cole, Chan, & Lytton, 1989; Hinde, Tamplin, & Barrett, 1993; Rosenberg & Rosenberg, 1978), and a wide range of health-risk behaviors and outcomes, including substance use (Schroeder, Laflin, & Weis, 1993), gang membership (Wang, 1994), teen pregnancy (Crockenberg & Soby, 1989), obesity (Jarvie, Lahey, Graziano, & Framer, 1983), eating disorder symptomatology (Brooks-Gunn, Rock, & Warren, 1989), and suicidal tendencies (Lewinsohn, Rohde, & Seeley, 1993).

In longitudinal studies, levels of self-esteem at one point in development also have been demonstrated to predict future trends in other areas of adjustment over follow-up periods lasting up to several years (DuBois & Tevendale, 1999). These latter findings provide a particularly strong basis for concluding that higher levels of self-esteem contribute to the healthy development of youth. Nonetheless, not all studies have been successful in finding support for this conclusion nor is it always clear that the associations found, even when "statistically significant," are large enough to be of practical importance (DuBois & Tevendale, 1999). If only inconsistent or relatively small benefits can be expected in other important outcomes when levels of self-esteem are increased in interventions, this clearly serves to detract from at least part of the rationale for investing time and resources in the implementation and dissemination of esteem-enhancement programs.

Weaknesses in Other Facets of Self-Esteem

Thus far, however, consideration has been limited to a view of self-esteem as unidimensional and undifferentiated. This perspective is at odds with recent research indicating that the structure of self-esteem is actually multifaceted and quite complex (Bracken, 1996; DuBois & Hirsch, 2000; Harter, 1999). The extent to which youth exhibit weaknesses in distinct facets of self-esteem is therefore an additional important concern, as are the implications of such weaknesses for differing aspects of their adjustment.

Multidimensional views of self. Even among youth who report relatively high overall or general self-esteem, it is not uncommon for views of the self to be negative for one or more specific areas (Harter, 1993). In research with young adolescents, DuBois, Felner, Brand, and George (1999) found that a profile of consistently high evaluations of the self across each of five areas (i.e., peers, school, family, body image, sports/athletics) was characteristic of only a minority of youth. By contrast, the majority of the remaining profiles included significant deficits in views of the self for one or more specific areas (e.g., school). Notably, a pattern of pervasive self-derogation across all areas was evident for as many as 15% of the youth studied (DuBois et al., 1999).

Domain-specific views of the self, in turn, also have the potential to influence youth adjustment. This may be especially true with regard to aspects of functioning that are conceptually related to the areas of self-esteem involved. A favorable academic self-concept seems to facilitate better school performance (e.g., Marsh & Yeung, 1997), for example, whereas girls who report a negative body image are at greater risk for developing symptoms of eating disorders (e.g., Attie & Brooks-Gunn, 1989). In further research, overall profiles of self-esteem have been demonstrated to be useful predictors of the adjustment of young adolescents. A pervasive pattern of negative self-esteem across multiple areas at this age, for example, appears to take a heavy toll on emotional well-being in the form of both clinically significant levels of depressive symptomatology (DuBois et al., 1999) and suicidal ideation

(Harter, Marold, & Whitesell, 1992). Profiles reflecting an emphasis on peer-oriented sources of self-esteem to the relative exclusion of adult-oriented sources such as school and family are of additional note (Harter, 1999). Even though affording relatively high overall feelings of self-worth, this latter type of self-esteem profile has been found to be associated with increased risk for both behavioral problems (e.g., delinquency) and poorer school performance during early adolescence (DuBois, Bull, Sherman, & Roberts, 1998; DuBois et al., 1999).

Self-esteem stability. Most theorists and researchers have emphasized a trait-oriented conceptualization of self-esteem. This perspective focuses on an individual's characteristic level of self esteem as it is reflected across time and situations. There is growing interest, however, in also examining fluctuations or volatility in feelings of self-worth (see Kernis, this volume). A substantial minority of youth do indeed appear to experience considerable flux in their feelings about themselves (Rosenberg, 1985; Savin-Williams & Demo, 1983b; Verkuyten, 1995). Rosenberg (1985), for example, found that between 19 and 32% of a large sample of children and adolescents (ages 8-18) reported a high degree of instability in their self-esteem. Notably, there also was evidence of increased instability during the initial years of adolescence (Rosenberg, 1985). Lack of stability in self-esteem may be associated with fragile or vulnerable feelings of self-worth and thus heightened susceptibility of adjustment problems such as depression and aggressive behavior (Kernis, 1993). Adverse consequences of this type for unstable self-esteem are evident in the findings of several recent studies of youth (DuBois & Tevendale, 1999), including research conducted specifically with young adolescents (Tevendale, DuBois, Lopez, & Prindiville, 1997).

Presented self-esteem. Building on the writings of the early psychologist William James (1890/1950), several contemporary theorists (Combs, Soper, & Courson, 1963; Demo, 1985; Harter, 1990, 1999; Savin-Williams & Demo, 1983a) have made a further distinction between aspects of self-esteem that pertain to the experienced self and presented self, respectively. The presented self corresponds to "that dimension which an individual verbally and non-verbally reveals to the social world" (Savin-Williams & Demo, 1983a, p. 123), whereas the experienced self represents "the self as evaluated by the individual" (p. 124). Based on their findings in a series of studies that included young adolescents, Savin-Williams and Demo (Demo, 1985; Savin-Williams & Demo,

1983a, 1984; Savin-Williams & Jaquish, 1981) concluded that presented and experienced dimensions of self-esteem could be reliably distinguished. This raises several interesting issues relevant to assessing the need for esteem-enhancement interventions. One is the possibility of bias in existing estimates of the frequency with which low levels of self-esteem occur among youth. Consider, for example, that even if less than optimal feelings of self-regard are not apparent for a given youth on the basis of his or her own report (i.e., experienced self-esteem) that such feelings might nonetheless be fairly readily apparent to others who are in a good position to observe the youth's behavior on a regular basis (i.e., presented self-esteem). Few studies have addressed this concern. Coopersmith (1967), however, did report that scores on a subjective, self-report measure of self-esteem and a measure of behavioral manifestations of self-esteem administered to teachers exhibited significant divergence for a portion of the youth he studied. Of further note is that not all types of discrepancies were equally likely. Those that were most common involved divergence in the direction of youth self-report ratings of self-esteem exceeding those obtained from their teachers.

This latter finding is especially noteworthy because of its direct implications for estimating the numbers of youth who legitimately can be regarded as demonstrating manifestations of low self-esteem. Theoretically, it has been noted that individuals who assert high levels of self-esteem despite contrary assessments from others may attempt to maintain their sense of positive self-worth through defensive or maladaptive tendencies that end up having a significant negative effect on their mental health (Colvin & Block, 1994). Indeed, based on available research findings, those youth for whom this type of "defensive" self-esteem is evident appear notably similar in their overall adjustment to those youth who *do* actually report low self-esteem. Coopersmith (1967), for example, reported that such youth were characterized by limited acceptance by peers, relatively poor academic performance, and greater susceptibility to pressure for conformity in social situations. Findings of more recent studies of youth of varying ages point to a similar pattern of problematic adjustment when acknowledgment of low self-esteem is limited primarily to the observations and impressions of others (Connell & Ilardi, 1987; Colvin, Block, & Funder, 1995; Hughes, Cavell, & Grossman, 1997; Strain et al., 1983).

Liabilities in esteem formation and maintenance processes. Even for those youth who can be agreed to exhibit high self-esteem, the possibility remains that positive feelings of self-worth do not have a healthy underlying foundation. In normal development, self-esteem is derived from both a sense of personal competence or efficacy and a perception that one is accepted and valued by others (Coopersmith, 1967; Hales, 1979; Harter, 1986, 1987, 1990, 1993; White, 1960). For many youth, feelings of self-worth thus may stem from experiences of mastery or success in school and various extracurricular activities as well as from patterns of appropriate conduct that generate positive validation from parents, peers, and other important persons in their lives (e.g., teachers). In addition to these relatively objective and straightforward sources of self-esteem, however, youth have at their further disposal a potentially wide array of self-protective or self-enhancing strategies that can be used to facilitate their efforts to form and maintain a sense of self-worth. As described by Kaplan (1986),

> Self-protective—self-enhancing responses . . . are oriented toward the goal of (1) forestalling the experience of self-devaluing judgements and consequent distressful self-feelings (self-protective patterns) and (2) increasing the occasions for positive self-evaluations and self-accepting feelings (self-enhancing patterns). (p. 174)

Kaplan (1986) further distinguished three general forms of self-protective–self-enhancing responses relating to self-referent cognition, personal need-value systems, and personal behaviors that increase the likelihood of approximating self-values. The use of self-protective–self-enhancing strategies is quite commonplace among both adults (Blaine & Crocker, 1993) and youth (see Harter, 1986, Kaplan, 1986, and Rosenberg, 1979, for reviews). Illustratively, youth have been found to demonstrate a tendency to selectively view as more credible the opinions of persons who they perceive to have more favorable perceptions of them and to regard as correspondingly less believable feedback emanating from those with whom they associate a more critical perspective (Rosenberg, 1979). Children and adolescents also demonstrate an inclination to attach greater value or importance to those aspects of their self-concepts which are most favorable and, by contrast, to discount the significance of those areas in which they see themselves as having only limited success (Harter, 1986). From a behavioral standpoint, youth also may actively seek out greater association with those persons whom they regard as most likely to hold positive views of them (Faunce, 1984; Kaplan, 1986; Rosenberg, 1979). In many respects, these tendencies are not surprising. It is the rare youth, after all, who can be expected to achieve success in all endeavors, unfailingly accept in stride the criticisms of others, and universally be liked and well regarded. Some degree of reliance on self-protective or self-enhancing strategies thus seems an inevitable and functional necessity for maintaining a robust sense of self-worth during development (Harter, 1987).

The possibility exists, however, for self-protective and self-enhancing strategies to become a significant source of concern. This could occur, for example, if such strategies are relied on to such an extent that they begin to function as a substitute for more fundamental sources of self-esteem or if the strategies pursued themselves are maladaptive. It is clear, for example, that some youth enhance their perceptions of themselves to the point of having notably unrealistic or inflated self-concepts and that when this occurs the implications for adjustment are most likely to be negative rather than positive (Colvin et al., 1995; Connell & Ilardi, 1987; DuBois et al., 1998; Harter, 1986; Hughes et al., 1997). It is equally apparent that some youth seek out affiliation with deviant peer groups as a means of attempting to enhance their feelings of self-worth and that doing so heightens their risk for becoming involved in delinquent behavior (Kaplan, 1986). Within the academic realm, many of the most prominent counterproductive behaviors engaged in by students (e.g., procrastination) similarly often appear to stem from their desire to avoid ability-based (and hence esteem-threatening) attributions for possible poor school performance (Covington, 1989). Substantial numbers of additional youth restrict their opportunities for achievement even further by devaluing the importance of school altogether in an effort to maintain feelings of self-worth (Whaley, 1993).

Much of the preceding research has been conducted with young adolescents. As noted previously, self-protective and self-enhancing strategies may assume increased importance during this stage of development (Harter, 1999). This may occur in part because cognitive abilities become notably more complex and sophisticated at this age and hence more capable of being used to construct a positive sense of self-worth from available information. The transition to adolescence also brings with it intensified striving for autonomy and differentiation from parents and other symbols of adult authority, thereby increasing the range of potential avenues that are available to youth in seeking to fulfill needs for self-esteem. Intervention strategies directed toward establishing healthy esteem formation and maintenance processes thus might be especially beneficial for the early adolescent age group.

Summary

The most commonly understood rationale for esteem-enhancement programs is to raise the self-esteem of youth to more desirable levels. The goal in doing so has been to promote healthy development and thus prevent negative outcomes such as serious emotional disturbance, delinquent behavior, and academic failure. There is less strong evidence than might be expected, however, to support the often perceived need for this type of intervention. This is both because a majority of youth already have some degree of positive feelings of self-worth and because available research has not always revealed a strong connection between higher overall self-esteem and improvements in youth adjustment. These points offer some support for the arguments of those in recent years (e.g., Kohn, 1994) who have cautioned against the further proliferation of esteem-enhancement programs in the absence of appropriate critical scrutiny.

Nevertheless, it is precisely this closer and more refined type of examination that yields the most compelling evidence of a need for interventions and policies that address the role of self-esteem in the lives of youth. One significant area of concern is heightened vulnerability of youth to low levels of self-esteem at key points of transition in their development. Early adolescence, in particular, is a time of substantial risk for steep declines in self-esteem from earlier higher levels as well as the chronic persistence of already existing low levels of self-esteem. These trends are noteworthy too for the manner in which they are tied to a progressive worsening of overall socioemotional and academic adjustment at this stage of development.

Equally apparent is a need for enhancement of numerous aspects of self-esteem other than simply general (i.e., undifferentiated) feelings of self-worth. These include the feelings youth have about themselves relating to specific areas or domains of their lives, the extent to which their self-esteem demonstrates stability from one situation or day to the next, and whether or not feelings of self-worth are communicated to others through their behavior. Deficits or weaknesses in self-esteem relating to each of these concerns seem to be exhibited by noteworthy numbers of youth and are predictive of significant problems in adjustment. Of further note are the processes of thought, values, and behavior that may be relied on to enhance and maintain a high level of self-esteem. In the quest for a sense of self-worth it appears that many youth engage in self-enhancing or self-protective strategies that unfortunately can be expected to do more to hinder than to promote their overall development.

Can the Self-Esteem of Youth Be Enhanced?

If the preceding arguments are taken as evidence of a need for esteem-enhancement activities directed toward youth, it then becomes important to consider whether this goal is indeed attainable. That is, can the self-esteem of youth be raised or otherwise strengthened through the use of systematic strategies of intervention? This is in many respects essentially a practical question. Nevertheless, it should be kept in mind that efforts to answer it have the potential to offer insight into important theoretical issues, such as the causes and consequences of varying levels and patterns of self-esteem among youth. The capacity for applied intervention research to enhance basic knowledge of real-world phenomena was captured succinctly by Bronfenbrenner (1977) in what he referred to as Dearborn's Dictum (in recognition of the mentor to whom its origin was attributed): "If you want to understand something, try to change it" (p. 517).

Overall Trends in Program Effectiveness

Several literature reviews have considered the effectiveness of esteem-enhancement programs for youth (Gurney, 1987; Haney & Durlak, 1998; Hattie, 1992; Marsh, 1990; Offord, 1987; Strein, 1988). Two of these are of particular note because of their use of meta-analytic procedures to review the results of relevant studies (Haney & Durlak, 1998; Hattie, 1992). Meta-analysis provides an objective method of quantitatively assessing the overall magnitude of the effect produced by any given type of intervention on one or more outcome measures (e.g., self-esteem). More specifically, estimates of "effect size" are derived from findings reported in the research literature for all identified evaluations of a selected treatment or intervention. This common metric then is used as a basis for aggregating estimates to produce an averaged effect size across all studies (Cooper, 1998). A powerful feature of meta-analytic procedures is that they can be used to investigate differences in effect size along any dimension of interest that varies across studies included in the review such as participant characteristics, program features, and type of evaluation methodology (Cooper, 1998).

In the meta-analyses of esteem-enhancement programs, Hattie (1992) reported an average effect size of .37 across 89 studies. This finding indicates that positive change on self-concept or self-esteem was evident for 65% of participants in the typical intervention.[1] Haney and Durlak (1998) similarly found an average effect size of .27 on measures of self-concept/self-esteem across the 120 evaluations included in their more recent review. Overall, these results indicate that programs typically have been successful in increasing the scores of youth on measures of self-concept and self-esteem. The size of the effects reported are in the small to medium range when compared to other, related types of psychological, educational, and behavioral interventions (Lipsey & Wilson, 1993) and are indicative of gains in self-esteem that are moderate rather than large in magnitude.

Several important qualifications to these estimates should be kept in mind. First, the potential always exists for the findings of meta-analyses to be biased by a failure to locate and include all relevant studies. Of particular concern is the possible omission of evaluations of esteem-enhancement programs that were never published because they produced nonsignificant or even unexpectedly negative results (Cooper, 1998). Second, a simple comparison of the number of programs known to have been evaluated relative to the several hundred if not thousands of interventions with a significant esteem-enhancement component that have been implemented to date (e.g., California Department of Education, 1990) leads to the seemingly inevitable conclusion that only a small minority of such initiatives have been subjected to any type of formal outcome-based assessment. Indeed, it may well be the case that it is the most well-designed and thus likely effective interventions that have received the greatest degree of attention from researchers. Despite the promising findings reported, there thus clearly is a need for considerable caution to be exercised in attempting to use them to derive any general or "universal" conclusions about the effectiveness of esteem-enhancement programs.

There also is little information available concerning the potential for programs to enhance any of the multiple, distinct facets of self-esteem described previously. In the most noteworthy exception to this trend, some consideration has been given to whether interventions can influence views or feelings about the self relating to specific content areas or domains. The meta-analysis conducted by Hattie (1992) found evidence of positive effects of programs on several differing facets of self-perception, including those relating to academic, family, and physical domains. Assessment of effects of programs on these types of outcomes typically has been limited to dimensions of self-concept or self-esteem that have direct relevance to aims of the program, such as those relating to academics in educational interventions and those relating to physical abilities or appearance in programs emphasizing exercise and fitness activities. Comparable research is lacking with regard to the potential for interventions to be successful in strengthening other important aspects of self-esteem, such as its day-to-day stability or presented feelings of self-worth.

A further significant concern is whether programs are able to have a desirable influence on the processes that youth rely on to support a high level of self-esteem. This might conceivably entail reductions in excessive reliance on maladaptive self-protective/self-enhancing strategies (e.g., biased positive views of the self, associations with deviant peer groups) as well as increases in the extent to which efforts are made to derive self-esteem from more normative sources (i.e., skill development and positive relationships with others). These types of benefits possibilities have not received attention as they relate specifically to esteem-enhancement programs. Other types of interventions have been demonstrated to affect outcomes relevant to concerns in this area, however, such as, for example, patterns of association with delinquent peers (Henggeler, Schoenwald, Borduin, Rowland, & Cunningham, 1998) and levels of motivation to succeed in school (Weinstein et al., 1991).

Factors Influencing Program Effectiveness

Both meta-analyses (Haney & Durlak, 1998; Hattie, 1992) investigated different types of factors that could influence program effectiveness. The factors examined relate to (a) characteristics and backgrounds of youth participating in programs; (b) features of the programs themselves; and (c) methodological issues pertaining to research design and measurement of program outcomes.

Youth characteristics. Haney and Durlak (1998) reported a nonsignificant association between mean age of participants and effect size in their review, which included only evaluations of programs for children and adolescents. Hattie (1992), however, found average effect sizes to be higher for programs geared toward adults (.52) and children (.31) in comparison to those in which participants were preadolescents (.20) or adolescents (.23). Participants in the age ranges most proximal to early adolescence thus demonstrated the least responsiveness to programs. This is a noteworthy finding given the status of early adolescence as a period of development during which there appears to be an especially salient need for effective esteem-enhancement interventions.

Adequate data apparently were not available in either review to assess the gender or race/ethnicity of participants as an influence on program effectiveness. Hattie (1992) did, however, find evidence of larger effects for programs targeting youth from low socioeconomic backgrounds. This is a noteworthy trend, given that such youth are likely to be experiencing heightened levels of environmental stress. Relatedly, substantially larger positive effects on self-esteem were evident in both reviews when considering programs directed toward youth with preexisting problems (Haney & Durlak, 1998; Hattie, 1992). The types of problems involved include low self-esteem specifically as well as various other indicators of difficulties in emotional, behavioral, and academic functioning. Factors that could contribute to greater program benefits for youth with preexisting problems include greater malleability of low or negative self-views as well as ceiling effects on measures of self-esteem or self-concept for those exhibiting normal functioning (Haney & Durlak, 1998; Hattie, 1992).

Program features. Hattie (1992) found effect sizes to be similar for programs regardless of whether they sought to increase self-esteem directly (e.g., curriculum) or by indirect methods (e.g., enhancing academic achievement). Haney and Durlak (1998) made a distinction between interventions that had a primary goal of changing self-concept or self-esteem (i.e., referred to by the authors as "SE/SC interventions") and those that did not have this specific aim but nonetheless did assess change in self-concept or self-esteem as a program outcome (i.e., "non-SE/SC interventions"). Less than half of the studies included in their review were evaluations of SE/SC interventions. The average effect size for these programs (.57) was found to be substantially higher than that of non-SE/SC interventions (.10). Based on this finding, Haney and Durlak (1998) concluded that "significant improvements [in self-concept/self-esteem] are unlikely unless interventions specifically focus on SE/SC"

(p. 429). In other words, it should not be assumed that gains in self-esteem are likely to occur unless this is a specific goal of the program. Taken together, the preceding results suggest that it is important for interventions to have a specific aim of enhancing self-esteem (Haney & Durlak, 1998), but that indirect approaches to achieving this goal can work at least as well as those that are more direct in their orientation (Hattie, 1992).

A related and perhaps even more fundamentally important characteristic of programs could be the extent to which the specific change strategies used have a basis in relevant theory or empirical research. Consistent with this view, Haney and Durlak (1998) found that programs with either a theoretically or empirically based rationale produced substantially larger gains in self-esteem or self-concept than those without such a rationale; this factor alone predicted nearly one third of the overall variation in program outcomes. Both theory and research, it will be recalled, indicate that normative sources of self-esteem during development consist of a sense of competence and a perception of being valued and accepted by others. It is noteworthy, therefore, that favorable results have been reported for several interventions oriented toward enhancing these sources of self-esteem. Hattie (1992), for example, reported particularly large positive effects on self-esteem/self-concept for a subgrouping of physically oriented programs that emphasized learning and interpersonal skill development in outdoor settings (e.g., Outward Bound). Interventions with related aims reporting significant positive effects on self-esteem include school restructuring and reform initiatives at both the elementary and secondary school levels (Cauce, Comer, & Schwartz, 1987; Felner et al., 1993) as well as community-based programs involving mentoring (Turner & Scherman, 1996) and volunteer service (Moore & Allen, 1996). There is also research suggesting enhanced effectiveness for esteem-enhancement programs that incorporate components designed specifically to improve teacher-child and parent-child relationships (Gurney, 1987). Relationships with others that youth establish through their involvement in programs may be a further important source of esteem-enhancement. In an investigation of participation in inner-city Boys & Girls Clubs (Hirsch, Roffman, Pagano, & Deutsch, 2000), relationships that youth formed with club staff were found be a positive predictor of both self-esteem and other measures of psychosocial functioning.

A common theme in the preceding types of interventions is a focus on seeking to produce change in relevant aspects of the actual, day-to-day or "real world" experiences and behaviors of youth, thus enhancing their ability to demonstrate competence in important areas of their lives and form rewarding relationships with significant others. It is noteworthy therefore that approximately two thirds of the programs categorized as SE/SC interventions by Haney and Durlak (1998) were commercially available "prepackaged" curricula. The intervention strategies noted for other programs in this category similarly reflect a mostly didactic and individual orientation toward enhancing self-esteem (e.g., affective education). Combined with findings noted previously, this trend suggests that one factor limiting program effectiveness has been an underutilization of environmentally oriented approaches to esteem-enhancement. Without a comprehensive psychosocial approach in which there is attention to both "inner" and "outer" forces affecting views of the self, it may be difficult for programs to achieve optimal results (Hamachek, 1994). The need to recognize and seek to address the negative impact that broader societal factors such as poverty, racism, and social injustice can have on the self-perceptions of youth is a further important concern in this regard with the potential to influence program effectiveness (Beane, 1994).

A further significant consideration is the intensity and duration of programs. The typical (i.e., average) program included in the review conducted by Haney and Durlak (1998) included a total of 16 sessions occurring over a period of 20 weeks. Despite considerable range on these indicators, neither apparently was found to be a significant predictor of program outcomes (Haney & Durlak, 1998). Hattie (1992) similarly reported a nonsignificant relationship between total time in programs and effect size. One possible explanation for this result is that esteem-enhancement interventions are not necessarily presently structured to take optimal advantage of extended periods of program participation. The curricular format that seems to characterize most programs, for example, may not provide the context needed for youth to utilize longer periods of involvement to pursue skill development or stronger relationships with others as ongoing normative sources of self-esteem in naturalistic settings. This interpretation is consistent with the results of more environmentally oriented programs noted previously in which youth have in fact been indicated to experience significant gains in self-esteem in conjunction with more extended periods of exposure to interventions. With direct relevance to these considerations, one study recently compared the extent to which young adolescents benefitted in terms of changes in self-esteem from relationships lasting varying lengths of time with mentors in Big Brothers/Big Sisters programs (Grossman & Rhodes, in press). Youth whose relationships lasted a year or longer were found to report significant positive change both in overall feelings of self-worth and social and scholastic areas of self-concept (as well as several others indicators of positive adjustment). By contrast, these types of gains were not evident for youth whose relationships lasted shorter periods of time; in fact, for those whose relationships ended after less than three months, significant *declines* in self-esteem and other indicators of functioning were apparent (Grossman & Rhodes, in press). These results call attention to the manner in which environmentally oriented approaches to intervention focused on naturalistic or real-world settings may present not only important opportunities for effective promotion of self-esteem, but also special challenges for program design and implementation that merit careful consideration as well.

Research methodology. With regard to the methodological quality of studies of esteem-enhancement programs, Hattie (1992) noted the following:

> Approximately 650 studies were located and only 89 contained sufficient data that could be analyzed via the meta-analysis procedures. That so many studies had to be rejected is a reflection of the quality of research conducted in the area of self-concept change. Too often programs to enhance self-concept are discussed but no evaluations of the programs are conducted. (p. 227)

This conclusion reinforces concerns noted previously regarding the possible lack of representativeness of the self-esteem interventions that have been subjected to adequate evaluation.

A further issue meriting note is that gains on outcome measures of self-concept and self-esteem also have been evident for youth in control groups (i.e., those who did not receive the intervention; Hattie, 1992). These types of gains are most apparent when such youth have received at least some type of minimal attention from researchers in an effort to control for the influence of nonspecific factors on outcomes for those in the intervention group (Haney & Durlak, 1998). It appears therefore that some of the benefits resulting from participation in esteem-enhancement programs are attributable to factors other than those intended to be most influential. Viewed from a somewhat different perspective, it seems that it is perhaps easier than might be anticipated to enhance the self-esteem of youth to at least some limited extent. But are the gains observed in programs substantial enough to be of lasting significance? It is this issue that is considered next.

Follow-Up Effects

The extent to which interventions can produce lasting increases in self-esteem that remain evident for significant periods of time after participation has ended is an important issue. It is possible, for example, that some of the positive effects observed are attributable to "euphoria" or good feelings at the end of programs and that these effects dissipate relatively quickly thereafter (Marsh, Richards, & Barnes, 1986). It is thus unfortunate that follow-up effects have been assessed for only a small proportion of programs that have been evaluated (i.e., only 4 of the 89 studies in the Hattie, 1992, meta-analysis, and 24 of the 120 programs in the Haney & Durlak, 1998, meta-analysis). Moreover, the intervals separating follow-up assessments from the end of active participation in programs have been relatively brief, ranging on average from 1 month (Hattie, 1992) to 16 weeks (Haney & Durlak, 1998). Haney and Durlak (1998) reported evidence of sustained effects at follow-up, whereas Hattie (1992) found decreased, but still positive effects on self-esteem. Both cautioned, however, that too few studies were involved to use their results as a basis for conclusions regarding program durability.

This caveat notwithstanding, available findings do indicate success in producing more than only very short-lived increases in the self-esteem of program participants. As noted, in most instances follow-up intervals have been relatively brief. Yet there are a few exceptions in which the durability of effects of measures of self-concept and self-esteem have been assessed over longer periods of time following participation in programs with encouraging results. Cauce et al. (1987), for example, found that positive effects of a systems-oriented school reform intervention experienced during elementary school on the multidimensional self-perceptions of youth continued to be evident even after they had made the transition to junior high school. Even more impressive perhaps are the results of a recent meta-analysis of evaluations of Outward Bound and Adventure Education programs (Hattie,

Marsh, Neill, & Richards, 1997). In this research, the immediate gains that programs produced in both general and domain-specific aspects of self-concept (e.g., physical ability) were found to *increase* substantially in size over periods of follow-up assessment that averaged nearly 6 months (Hattie et al., 1997). This finding suggests that some programs have a capacity to set in motion processes for enhancing self-esteem that then continue to be influential even after formal program involvement has ended. Of further note is that both of the preceding interventions also were demonstrated to be successful in promoting competence in areas such as academic achievement and physical fitness (Cauce et al., 1987; Hattie et al., 1997). This finding is consistent with the benefits cited previously for environmentally oriented approaches to intervention that seek to increase opportunities for youth to derive self-esteem from sources important to normative development.

Summary

Overall, available research indicates that it is indeed possible to significantly enhance the self-esteem of youth through intervention. There are several qualifications, however, to this conclusion. In particular, the effects that are evident are modest in size and do not necessarily generalize to the much larger number of esteem-enhancement interventions that have not received formal evaluation. Relatedly, the extent to which interventions can be effective in enhancing self-esteem during specific developmental periods when this might be especially needed (e.g., early adolescence) remains in need of further clarification. That youth who can be considered to be "at risk" on the basis of either individual vulnerabilities (e.g., low self-esteem) or environmental circumstances show greater responsiveness to programs is, nevertheless, an encouraging trend in this regard. Of additional concern is the limited amount of documentation to indicate that programs can produce gains in self-esteem that are sustained over significant periods of time after participation has ended. Notably, there also is little research available to address the potential of interventions to effect desirable change either in multiple, distinct facets of self-esteem (e.g., stability) or in the processes that are relied on to acquire and maintain feelings of self-worth.

The content of programs and interventions used to enhance self-esteem is quite diverse, ranging from prepackaged curricula to relatively broadly encompassing environmentally focused initiatives (e.g., school reform). The most well-established trend is for interventions, whatever their specific content, to be substantially more effective in promoting increased levels of self-esteem when their design is informed by relevant theory and research (Haney & Durlak, 1998). A single integrated framework to provide a basis for more consistent design of programs with a theoretical and empirical foundation is not currently available. There are, however, promising indications of enhanced effectiveness for certain types of programs that reflect this orientation. These include interventions that seek to enhance the opportunities of youth to derive self-esteem through normative developmental processes in real-world settings over extended periods of time. Also associated with favorable results are strategies geared toward promoting relevant, domain-specific views or feelings about the self in accordance with a multidimensional conceptualization of self-esteem. The following section builds on the foregoing conclusions to consider the question of whether gains in self-esteem that youth experience as a result of participation in interventions, in turn, have beneficial effects on their functioning in other areas.

Do Gains in Self-Esteem in Esteem-Enhancement Interventions Have Positive Effects on Other Areas of Adjustment?

Effects of Esteem-Enhancement Interventions on Youth Adjustment

In their meta-analysis, Haney and Durlak (1998) examined whether changes in self-concept/self-esteem experienced by youth in programs were associated with positive changes in each of several other domains of adjustment. These included behavior (usually as determined by direct observation or teacher rating scales), personality/emotional functioning (typically reports by youth of their levels of anxiety or depression), and academic performance (grades and performance on standardized tests). Positive outcomes were evident in all of these areas for the programs included in their review. Of greatest significance is that desirable adjustment outcomes were most apparent for the programs indicated to produce the largest increases in self-concept/self-esteem (Haney & Durlak, 1998). This result establishes a direct association between effective esteem-enhancement activities (i.e., those that are successful in raising levels of self-esteem) and overall improvements in youth adjustment. It also was found that programs in which enhancement of self-esteem or self-concept was a primary goal (i.e., SE/SC interventions) tended to be associated with better overall adjustment outcomes than those without this emphasis (Haney & Durlak, 1998).

In other programs, gains in specific areas of self-concept or self-esteem have been found to be associated with co-occurring positive changes in related aspects of functioning. Physical fitness training (Marsh & Peart, 1988) and outdoor adventure programs (Hattie et al., 1997), for example, have been found to produce gains in physical dimensions of self-concept as well as actual levels of physical fitness. Educational interventions similarly have been indicated to affect scholastic self-esteem or self-concept in conjunction with demonstrable improvements in academic performance (Cauce et al., 1987; Felner et al., 1993).

Limitations of Research

The preceding results do not indicate unequivocally that gains in self-esteem achieved through interventions have a significant role in promoting better functioning in other areas (Haney & Durlak, 1998; Harter, 1999). Findings from longitudinal nonintervention studies referred to previously provide support for this possibility, but do not address the issue of whether higher levels of self-esteem established through intervention can have similar benefits. Alternatively, positive changes in both self-esteem and other areas of functioning observed for youth participating in programs could be the result of improvements in indicators of adjustment (e.g., grades in school) leading to gains in self-esteem rather than vice versa. Or, as still another possibility, changes in some other area targeted by a program (e.g., quality of parent-child relationship) could be a source of improvements in both self-esteem and indices of adjustment. To differentiate among these alternatives, changes in self-esteem and relevant aspects of adjustment could be assessed at regular intervals during an intervention and then examined with regard to their sequencing (i.e., do changes in self-esteem tend to precede those for adjustment or vice versa) while controlling statistically for other potential influences. Unfortunately, existing evaluation studies have not used the more refined type of research design and statistical analyses necessary for implementation of this approach.

As already noted, with relatively few exceptions, interventions also have been limited by an exclusive focus on promoting and tracking gains in overall levels of self-esteem. Consequently, the potential for desirable patterns of change in more specific aspects of self-esteem (e.g., stability) to have a positive effect on functioning in other domains has not been sufficiently investigated. This is a noteworthy omission given research reviewed previously in which multiple, distinct facets of self-esteem have been found to be significant predictors of several differing aspects of youth adjustment. Similar considerations apply to beneficial modifications in processes involved in acquiring and sustaining self-esteem that also could be instituted through program involvement.

Follow-Up Effects

As with gains in self-esteem, there is a need to understand whether any improvements in other areas of functioning associated with such gains are sustained over significant periods of time. There is only limited research addressing this concern. Similar to findings for measures of self-concept, Outward Bound and Adventure Education programs were found to produce benefits in other areas of functioning (e.g., academic achievement) that not only were sustained but actually increased during follow-up periods (Hattie et al., 1997). It will be recalled in this regard that positive changes in self-esteem or self-concept and other aspects of functioning have the potential to be mutually reinforcing over time, thus amplifying effects of programs on each area beyond initial levels (DuBois & Tevendale, 1999). Illustratively, gains in self-esteem resulting from participation in an intervention such as Outward Bound could facilitate improvements in school performance that, in turn, further increase self-esteem and hence set the stage for additional similar cycles of influence. Initiation of these types of self-sustaining processes could be important in determining whether esteem-enhancement interventions produce long-term improvements in overall youth functioning.

Summary

Interventions enhancing self-esteem successfully tend also to produce significant improvements in other areas of youth adjustment. Whether increased levels of self-esteem are actually responsible for (or at least contribute to) such changes is not yet established. More sophisticated research designs and statistical analyses when evaluating programs will be needed to address this issue. Modifications in specific facets or dimensions of self-esteem and in processes underlying the formation and maintenance of feelings of self-worth merit investigation as further factors that may facilitate improvements in youth adjustment. Changes that programs initiate in self-esteem and other aspects of functioning also have the potential to be mutually reinforcing, thus promoting gains in adjustment that extend significantly beyond the period of actual program involvement and perhaps even increase over time. Relatively little in either the design or evaluation of interventions to date, however, has addressed these possibilities.

Should Esteem-Enhancement Interventions Be Disseminated and, If So, How?

Rationale for Dissemination

The issues addressed thus far partially address the question of whether esteem-enhancement interventions should be disseminated on a wide-scale basis. The indicated need for such interventions and their demonstrated potential to produce gains in self-esteem and related areas of adjustment both are clearly important in this regard. Several further issues also require attention, however, to establish a strong rationale for large-scale implementation of programs and policies in which increasing or otherwise strengthening the self-esteem of youth is a primary goal.

One important consideration is the distinction between *efficacy* and *effectiveness* (Institute of Medicine [IOM], 1994). Efficacy refers to "'the extent to which a specific intervention, procedure, regimen, or service produces a beneficial result under ideal conditions'" (Last, 1988, cited in IOM, 1994, p. 365). Efficacy trials typically are carried out by the same researchers who developed the program or intervention. A great deal of care usually is taken to ensure that all components of the intervention are implemented as planned by individuals who are well trained for this purpose (often these persons are themselves members of the research team).

Effectiveness, by contrast, involves "'the extent to which a specific intervention, procedure, regimen, or service, *when deployed in the field*, does what it is intended to do for a defined population'" (Last, 1988, cited in IOM, 1994, p. 372). Effectiveness is sought after efficacy has been demonstrated; researchers must turn an intervention program over to an outside organization that they hope will implement it in a manner that is consistent with their original intentions and, in so doing, continue to find positive results for the program. One of the major goals of effectiveness research, in addition simply to demonstrating that an intervention can produce desirable results when used by others, is to distinguish those aspects of an intervention that are core elements required for continued efficacy and those instead that can be adapted or changed as needed to fit the needs and interests of a particular organization or community. A school district, for example, could be asked to implement an intervention to increase self-esteem that researchers have found to produce favorable results when they implemented and evaluated it in an initial study of its efficacy. To help evaluate whether it is essential to have individuals with mental health expertise deliver the intervention in the field, different classrooms could be assigned randomly to receive the intervention from either a counselor or teacher.

Effectiveness generally has not been demonstrated for intervention programs designed to promote positive youth development (IOM, 1994). Esteem-enhancement interventions are no exception in this regard. The absence of this type of support necessarily undermines the rationale for widespread dissemination of programs, even those for which promising results have been obtained in efficacy trials.

Another key consideration is the magnitude of impact that esteem-enhancement interventions can be expected to have on youth relative to that which can be anticipated for alternative types of intervention. In the context of a myriad of competing types of programs designed to promote positive youth development, it is not enough simply to demonstrate that programs oriented toward esteem-enhancement typically produce some degree of desirable results. Rather, ideally, there should be evidence that they are likely to yield positive outcomes that compare favorably with those that would be possible with other available approaches to intervention. Returning to the preceding example, the school district involved could be faced with having to make a decision regarding how much (if any) resources should be devoted to implementation of the esteem-enhancement program within the context of a fixed budget and a wide array of other programs being considered for funding. The "competition" might include interventions seeking to promote other aspects of positive youth development such as social competence or prosocial values/morals (i.e., character education). It also might well include more problem-focused programs that are geared toward preventing specific types of negative outcomes such as school drop-out, substance use, teen pregnancy, or school violence. How can esteem-enhancement interventions be expected to fare in these kinds of comparisons? One useful approach would be to consider the results obtained in interventions that have had increasing self-esteem as one of their primary goals—that is, those identified as SE/SC programs by Haney and Durlak (1998) in their meta-analysis. It will be recalled that these programs were found to achieve notably more positive results than non-SE/SC programs (i.e., those in which changes in self-esteem or self-concept were measured but were not a specific goal of the intervention). From a comparative standpoint, the effects of SE/SC programs on various areas of youth adjustment (other than self-esteem) as reported by Haney and Durlak (1998) are quite similar in size to those demonstrated for other types of psychological, educational, and behavioral treatments (Lipsey & Wilson, 1993). Furthermore, when considering benefits relating specifically to prevention (i.e., reducing risk for adjustment difficulties among youth not yet exhibiting problems), the assessed impact of SE/SC interventions is well within the range achieved by other successful prevention programs for children and adolescents (Haney & Durlak, 1998).

A final concern is the need to assess the expected value of program outcomes relative to the costs of implementing the program (IOM, 1994). That is, are the benefits that can be anticipated substantial and important enough to justify the time and expense that will be required to achieve them or are there more cost-efficient means of attaining similar outcomes? It is difficult, if not impossible, to agree on the value that should be attached to youth having high (or otherwise healthy) self-esteem (Beane, 1994). It is feasible, however, to estimate the benefits (in financial terms) to both youth and society more generally that would be associated with various more "tangible" outcomes that might be facilitated by enhancements in self-esteem such as completing high school, reduced reliance on mental health care, increased employment, fewer arrests, and so forth (Felner, DuBois, & Adan, 1991). Given the skepticism expressed regarding esteem-enhancement interventions in recent years, establishing that such programs actually can "pay for themselves" and perhaps also return dividends in monetary terms would be a significant accomplishment. This could be particularly useful for early adolescents in view of the increasing popularity of more "hard line" approaches to dealing with troubled youth in this age group (e.g., "boot camps" for juvenile offenders). Despite such considerations, a review of the current literature unfortunately fails to reveal any instance in which a cost-benefit analysis has been incorporated into the evaluation of an esteem-enhancement program.

Methods of Dissemination

Even when effectiveness and favorable cost-benefit ratios can be demonstrated, several additional factors may influence the success of efforts to disseminate esteem-enhancement interventions. One concern is simply awareness of effective programs. Most program evaluations are published in academic journals or made available through other scholarly outlets (e.g., professional conferences). This process is not likely to be sufficient for informing practitioners and potential host organizations about promising esteem-enhancement interventions. Just as with any "product," successful intervention programs need to be advertised to the appropriate target audiences and marketed to their needs and preferences as potential "consumers" of the intervention (Winett, 1995). For esteem-enhancement interventions, this process might include mailings to relevant practitioner groups, parent organizations, and so forth, judicious use of available media (e.g., Internet), and in-service presentations or demonstration workshops for the staff of possible host organizations.

In marketing esteem-enhancement programs, another key issue is likely to be their acceptability to differing "consumer" groups (Winett, 1995). Consider, for example, that in a socially or politically conservative community, a proposed program could face criticism for seemingly encouraging youth to feel good about themselves regardless of the appropriateness of their actions from a moral or religious perspective. Such concerns raise the larger issue of the role of values in esteem-enhancement interventions (Beane, 1994; Dodd, Nelson, & Hofland, 1994). Researchers and others involved in the dissemination of programs must take the time and effort to work with all relevant "stakeholders" in a given organization or community to ensure that there is a mutually agreed upon approach and rationale for enhancing the self-esteem of youth. One area of consensus could be the value of positive outcomes potentially resulting from esteem-enhancement activities, such as gains in school achievement or reductions in problem behavior. This is just one of several reasons, however, that could be important in the decision of a particular community or organization to support implementation of an esteem-enhancement intervention. Others might include a perceived moral obligation to equip youth with the personal resources needed to cope with life's challenges, the belief that all individuals have an entitlement to a sense of personal dignity, and the prospect of a collective esteem being fostered that enhances the overall quality of life within the surrounding community (Beane, 1994).

To be readily adopted, interventions also need to be "user-friendly" for those who will be responsible for delivering them in differing organizations such as teachers or counselors in the school setting. A clear, detailed, and engaging set of manualized instructions for implementation is an essential requirement in this regard (IOM, 1994). Programs similarly need to address issues of concern to the end-point consumers of programs, youth themselves, using developmentally appropriate strategies. For early adolescents, this might entail efforts to address the broad range of biopsychosocial challenges that characterize the day-to-day experiences of this age group (i.e., pubertal changes, exploration of personal identities, negotiating positive relations with parents and peers, entry into new school environments, and so on). From a process standpoint, it also would be consistent with the developmental needs of young adolescents to take care to avoid a "childish" or patronizing tone in intervention materials and to provide ample opportunities for individual choice within interventions.

Focus groups could be a particularly valuable tool in seeking to address concerns relating to the acceptability and interest level of programs to different constituency groups (Krueger, 1994). Focus groups also offer the added potential benefit of providing researchers with novel ideas or innovations for the content and design of programs from diverse individual, organizational, and community perspectives.

Procuring necessary resources for implementation. As noted previously, esteem-enhancement programs are likely to compete against a wide variety of other types of programs for funding within any given organization or community. Such programs have the potential to be at a relative advantage in this process for at least two reasons. First, as an approach to intervention that reflects a general health promotion orientation, esteem-enhancement lacks direct targeting of the types of specific problems that often are of most pressing concern to organizations and communities such as school dropout, violence, or substance abuse (Felner, 1999). Second, available funding mechanisms often are geared toward efforts to prevent or treat specific types of youth problems rather than approaches such as esteem-enhancement that are aimed at reductions in levels of problems in a wide range of areas.

One useful strategy for addressing these obstacles could be to emphasize the potential efficiencies and greater flexibility inherent in esteem-enhancement as a general rather than problem-specific approach. During early adolescence, the relative advantages of a more general approach may be especially noteworthy. This is because many of the problems of greatest concern for adolescents (e.g., substance use) still often are in an incipient stage of development at this age and thus difficult to focus on directly within either a treatment or prevention framework. Creative combining of requests for resources from multiple problem-specific funding sources represents a further possible strategy to support implementation and dissemination of esteem-enhancement interventions.

Even with adequate initial funding, youth programs often fail to thrive on a long-term basis in the settings and communities in which they have been implemented. Sustainability can be increased by implementing programs in ways that are integrated with the practices and organizational structure of existing organizations within host communities. For early adolescents, advisory groups represent a promising vehicle for the sustained implementation of esteem-enhancement programs within the school setting. Advisory groups provide students with the opportunity to meet regularly with a teacher or other member of the school staff as a means of addressing their developmental needs and concerns and already are a standard component of effective middle school practices (Alexander & George, 1993). Integration of esteem-enhancement activities into community-based organizations (e.g., Boys & Girls Clubs) that seek to promote the positive development of young adolescents during afterschool hours could prove similarly advantageous (Hirsch, Roffman, Deutsch, et al., 2000).

Summary

Esteem-enhancement programs have demonstrated efficacy comparable to that of other treatments and preventive interventions. Currently, however, data is lacking on the effectiveness of programs (i.e., their ability to produce desirable results when implemented by others on a large-scale basis) and the extent to which they are associated with favorable cost-benefit ratios relative to other interventions. To be successful, implementation and dissemination efforts should include strategies designed to increase awareness of programs, ensure their acceptability to potential participants and other stakeholders, and procure resources required for both initial and sustained program operation.

Integrative Model for Esteem-Enhancement

Need for Integrative Model

Substantially greater positive changes in self-esteem, it will be recalled, have been obtained in interventions that are theoretically or empirically based (Haney & Durlak, 1998). Reliance on theory and research also can be expected to be necessary to address currently unresolved issues of achieving sustainable effects on self-esteem, establishing direct contributions of gains in self-esteem to improvements in youth functioning within interventions, and documenting large-scale effectiveness and favorable cost-benefit ratios for programs. Despite these considerations, there has been a surprising lack of utilization of available theory and research in existing esteem-enhancement interventions for youth. In their meta-analysis, Haney and Durlak (1998) found that a theoretical or empirical rationale was evident for approximately only one third of the programs studied.

Overview of Model

A conceptual framework designed to facilitate greater incorporation of theory and research into esteem-enhancement interventions for youth is depicted in Figure 1. In accordance with this aim, all aspects of the model have an empirical and/or theoretical basis.

Major components. The proposed framework includes four principal components: (1) contextual opportunities for self-esteem; (2) esteem formation and maintenance processes; (3) self-esteem; and (4) adjustment. The subcomponents identified within each of these differing portions of the model are derived from theory and research discussed previously. Accordingly, contextual opportunities for self-esteem are conceptualized as consisting of both acceptance/recognition/support from others and competence-building/success experiences (Harter, 1999)

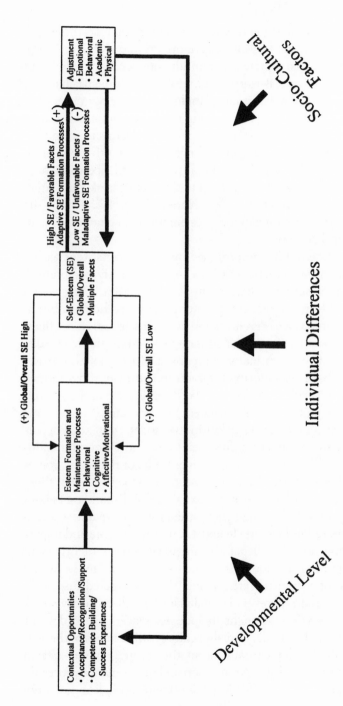

Figure 1. Integrative model for self-esteem enhancement.

and esteem formation and maintenance processes include those that are behavioral, cognitive, and affective/motivational (Kaplan, 1986). Self-esteem, in turn, is depicted as multidimensional, including not only overall feelings of self-worth (i.e., global self-esteem), but also multiple other facets. The latter facets include (but are not necessarily limited to) feelings about the self relating to specific domains or areas of experience (e.g., school), stability of self-esteem across time and situations, and presented aspects of feelings of self-worth evident in behavior (DuBois & Hirsch, 2000). Finally, in accordance with theoretical interest in the role of self-esteem in diverse areas of youth functioning (DuBois & Tevendale, 1999; Haney & Durlak, 1998), the adjustment portion of the model includes emotional, behavioral, academic, and physical components.

The factors addressed in the proposed model are consistent with a need for esteem-enhancement programs to be relatively comprehensive and encompassing in their content and design. This would include consideration of both environmental and psychological/individual sources of influence on self-esteem as well as attention to effects of programs on several differing domains of youth adjustment. The distinctions made within each major component of the model, furthermore, provide a basis for tailoring intervention strategies in a refined manner to address specific sub-facets of both self-esteem and other relevant processes (e.g., esteem enhancement) in programs.

Interrelations among components. Within the model, contextual opportunities for self-esteem directly influence esteem formation and maintenance processes. To the extent that conventional or normative routes to attaining self-esteem are available to youth, it is expected that these will facilitate their involvement in prosocial and skill-building behaviors, encourage them to evaluate their strengths and weaknesses in a reasonably accurate manner, and lead them to attach value and importance to meeting adaptive demands and expectations of others in developmentally relevant domains such as school and family. When such contextual opportunities are lacking, this is expected instead to encourage reliance on potentially maladaptive self-protective–self-enhancing responses. These might include associations with deviant peers, the adoption of inflated, unrealistically positive views of the self, and devaluing of developmentally normative sources of self-esteem such as success in school. Esteem formation and maintenance processes, in turn, are represented as affecting self-esteem, including not only global/overall feelings of self-worth, but also the types of differing facets of self-esteem referred to previously. As shown in Figure 1, multidimensional aspects of self-esteem then influence youth adjustment. These include effects of self-esteem on susceptibility to indicators of disorder and negative functioning (e.g., depression, problem behavior involvement, academic failure) as well as its role in promoting various facets of positive mental health and adjustment (e.g., life satisfaction, prosocial behavior, physical health and fitness). As shown in Figure 1, the most desirable effects on adjustment are expected to occur when youth exhibit a high overall level of self-esteem and when specific facets of self-esteem are favorable as well.

As can be seen in Figure 1, the proposed model also includes several relations among components that are bidirectional (i.e., recursive). Specifically, in accordance with the self-esteem motive (Brown, 1993; Kaplan, 1986), esteem formation and maintenance processes are expected to be more likely to be continued (or discontinued) by youth to the extent that they are (or are not) successful in allowing them to achieve and maintain a desirable level of self-esteem. Illustratively, if a youth finds that placing importance on success in school is instrumental in allowing her to maintain positive feelings about herself, this would encourage her to maintain such an orientation. By contrast, if another youth were to find, for example, that efforts to form friendships with prosocial peers is not effective as a means of achieving a desired level of self-esteem, he would be expected to show an increased disposition to seek out affiliations with alternative and potentially deviant peer groups (Gold, 1994; Kaplan & Lin, 2000). A similar type of feedback loop links self-esteem and youth adjustment. Thus, in addition to the influence of self-esteem on adjustment, positive and negative patterns of functioning are expected to have a reciprocal effect on self-esteem. Favorable adjustment is presumed to strengthen self-esteem, thus setting the stage for it to make further contributions to healthy adaptation, whereas problematic adjustment is expected to weaken self-esteem and thereby create the potential for further deterioration in adaptive functioning. Finally, in a reciprocal feedback loop that serves to connect the two end points of the model, youth adjustment can be seen to also influence contextual opportunities for self-esteem. This aspect of the model reflects the manner in which positive adjustment (e.g., good grades in school) may open up access to new competence-building/success experiences and strengthen relationships with others, whereas adjustment difficulties (e.g., conduct problems) may instead have the opposite effect (DuBois, Felner, Brand, Adan, & Evans, 1992; DuBois, Felner, Meares, & Krier, 1994).

In addition to the foregoing types of recursive linkages, it can be seen in the figure that effects of self-esteem on youth adjustment in the proposed framework are conceptualized as being dependent on esteem formation and maintenance processes. That is, whether or not self-esteem contributes positively or negatively to youth adjustment is expected to be a function not only of the level of overall/global self-esteem and its differing facets, but also whether or not the processes involved in forming and maintaining self-esteem themselves are adaptive. One important consideration in this regard may be the extent to which esteem formation and maintenance processes represent a good fit with the adaptive demands and associated views and expectations of others that characterize the youth's surrounding environment (DuBois et al., 1998; Lerner & Lerner, 1994). Thus, even if self-esteem is high and its various facets are favorable, implications for adjustment may not be desirable if the esteem formation and maintenance processes involved are at odds with salient features of the youth's environment. This might occur, for example, when a youth adopts an unrealistically positive self-image and thus fails to acknowledge significant personal limitations that are perceived by others such as parents, teachers, or peers. A tendency to bolster self-esteem by devaluing success in school or other developmentally important areas would be another possible example.

The interrelations among model components just described have significant implications for program design. The recursive (i.e., bidirectional) linkages among components highlight a potential for interventions to initiate mutually reinforcing and thus self-sustaining patterns of positive change involving self-esteem and other relevant areas of functioning and experience. Consider, for example, a program that produces favorable change in both self-esteem and one or more areas of youth adjustment. The latter gains could help to fuel sustained growth in feelings of self-worth at the same time that the progression toward a more desirable pattern of self-esteem facilitates continuation of trajectories of healthy adjustment. These types of recursive processes could be of key importance in establishing long-term positive effects of interventions. From a practical standpoint, they would seem most likely to be initiated by interventions that target change in multiple components of the proposed model. The manner in which observed effects of self-esteem on youth adjustment are expected to be dependent on associated esteem formation and maintenance processes points further toward the value of a comprehensive approach to targeting model components within interventions. Failure to take into account this type of interdependency presents the risk of gains in self-esteem accruing through maladaptive self-protective–self-enhancing strategies and thus offering few, if any, benefits for overall youth adjustment (and perhaps even affecting some aspects of adjustment adversely).

Developmental, individual, and sociocultural differences. A final key aspect of the model is the allowance made for influences relating to developmental level, individual differences among youth, and sociocultural factors. The proposed model is intended to have general applicability. Nevertheless, it is assumed that the specific patterns of relations among its components can be affected by factors such as, for example, whether youth are in early adolescence, have a distinguishing individual characteristic such as a physical or learning disability, or belong to a given gender or ethnic minority group. To achieve optimal effectiveness it is thus expected that esteem-enhancement interventions likely will need to include not only "generic" or core components experienced by all participants, but also more customized elements geared to the specific needs of youth with differing backgrounds and characteristics.

Illustrative Application to Early Adolescents

Because of the demonstrated need for effective esteem-enhancement interventions during early adolescence, application of the proposed model to this developmental period is of particular interest.

Contextual opportunities for self-esteem. Contextual opportunities for self-esteem during early adolescence could be enhanced through a variety of intervention components designed both to foster strong social ties and to strengthen emerging competencies for this age group. Given that early adolescence can be a time of heightened parent-child conflict (Laursen, Coy, & Collins, 1998), intervention strategies for improving parent-child communication and problem-solving skills for resolving disagreements (Robin & Foster, 1989) could prove beneficial to include as a core element in programs. Other core elements might include activities designed to facilitate adjustment to school transitions experienced by this age group (e.g., elementary school to middle or junior high school; Hirsch, DuBois, & Brownell, 1993). Efforts to involve young adolescents in appropriate extracurricular activities also could offer an important means of helping to ensure adequate exposure to esteem-building experiences both in and outside of school during this period of development. Additional components could be included in programs as necessary to address the needs of specific youth. Examples of these include mentoring relationships for youth likely to benefit from more intensive forms of adult guidance and support during the transition to adolescence (Rhodes, 1994) as well as family support services to increase opportunities for esteem-enhancement among youth from troubled home environments at this age (Friedman, 1994). Skill-building activities such as tutoring or social skills training also could prove useful for those youth found to be lacking in personal competencies necessary to take full advantage of contextual opportunities for self-esteem enhancement (DuBois & Felner, 1996).

Esteem formation and maintenance processes. Intervention components targeting esteem formation and maintenance processes during early adolescence could be designed to encourage responsible use of both the increased opportunities for independence and growing psychological sophistication that are characteristic of this age group (cf. Harter, 1999). Core intervention elements in this area could emphasize a psychoeducational approach in which youth are made aware of the self-esteem motive and how it can influence their patterns of thinking, behavior, and values. Special consideration could be given to the risks associated with over-reliance on various types of self-protective–self-enhancing strategies in seeking to acquire or sustain feelings of self-worth (Tennen & Affleck, 1993). Based on an inventory of each youth's prevailing tendencies in this area, more individualized interventions could be designed to promote modification and changes as needed. These might include efforts designed to increase accuracy in self-perceptions, encourage change in peer group affiliations, or modify the extent to which importance or value is attached to certain areas (e.g., school) as sources of feelings of self-worth. Such intervention strategies could be pursued within a general goal-setting framework (Danish, 1997). In doing so, it likely would be important to gear the strategies employed for any given process to the differing needs of young adolescents who are found to currently exhibit relatively high or low self-esteem. Approaches that could be used to improve accuracy in self-perceptions are illustrative in this regard. For youth with this concern who are reporting a very high level of self-esteem, efforts might be best directed toward minimizing positive distortions or bias in how they view themselves. By contrast, for those lacking in feelings of self-worth, it might instead be most useful to focus on goals such as increasing awareness of personal strengths or reducing tendencies toward excessive self-criticism.

Self-esteem. Intervention components designed to address the self-esteem of young adolescents directly also might be useful. One useful approach could be to simply increase the level of awareness and understanding that youth at this age have of the adaptive significance of multiple facets of their self-esteem beyond overall feelings of self-worth. This could occur in conjunction with implementation of strategies geared toward strengthening facets of self-esteem that exhibit vulnerability to negative change during early adolescence. Illustratively, training in coping skills might be used to help reduce susceptibility to fluctuation and instability in self-feelings during this stage of development and associated risk for problems in adjustment (e.g., aggressive behavior). Youth similarly could be given assistance establishing well-balanced multidimensional profiles of self-evaluation across differing areas of importance in the lives of young adolescents. Such efforts would be expected to lessen the potential for deficits in one or more key content areas of self-esteem (e.g., body image) to contribute to negative adjustment outcomes at this age. It seems likely that these types of intervention components often would benefit from an individualized orientation. Nevertheless, based on available research (DuBois, Felner, Brand, Phillips, & Lease, 1996; DuBois et al., 1999; Harter, 1999), enough commonality exists in the structure and patterning of self-esteem during early adolescence to also justify providing all youth in this age group with at least a core set of basic principles and strategies for developing healthy, well-rounded self-esteem.

Adjustment. The likely bidirectional relation between self-esteem and youth adjustment suggests that it could be of further benefit for esteem-enhancement interventions targeting young adolescents to include components that are geared toward promoting relevant aspects of their adaptive functioning directly (as opposed to relying solely on achieving this goal via enhancements in self-esteem). These might take the form of a general health education format in which youth are helped to acquire skills and information relating to such concerns as managing mood (Lewinsohn, Clarke, Rohde, Hops, & Seeley, 1996), use of effective organizational and study habits in school work (Biggs, 1987), avoiding involvement in high-risk behaviors (Dryfoos, 1998), and engaging in proper nutrition and exercise (Perry, Story, & Lytle, 1997). Referrals for more intensive or specialized services (e.g., psychotherapy or counseling) could be provided on an individualized basis as needed.

Summary

A strong rationale exists for developing a theoretically and empirically based integrative framework to guide esteem-enhancement interventions for youth. The model proposed herein has several distinguishing features. These include: (a) a broad conceptual perspective in which not only overall feelings of self-worth, but also multiple, distinct facets of self-esteem and underlying esteem formation and maintenance processes are highlighted as targets for intervention; (b) major components that underscore a need for consideration of both individual/psychological and environmentally oriented strategies for enhancing self-esteem; (c) recursive and interdependent linkages among model components that have significant implications for program design; and (d) sensitivity to sources of differences among youth that direct attention toward a need for not only general, but also individualized intervention strategies. As demonstrated, the model has potentially useful applications to esteem-enhancement interventions during early adolescence specifically.

Conclusions

Overall, there is promising support for continued use of esteem-enhancement interventions. A majority of youth report positive overall feelings about themselves in the absence of intervention. Nevertheless, for the significant minority who do not, low levels of self-esteem tend to persist and are associated with the emergence of problems in a wide array of areas of functioning. A substantial proportion of youth, moreover, perhaps even a majority, exhibit noteworthy liabilities either in one or more distinct facets of self-esteem or in esteem formation and maintenance processes. These types of limitations in underlying bases for self-esteem can be expected to restrict opportunities for healthy adjustment outcomes even among those youth who when asked report relatively favorable overall feelings of self-worth. Notably, it also appears to be the case that the need for esteem-enhancement interventions is accentuated during particular stages of development, including specifically the period of early adolescence.

There is, in turn, strong evidence that the self-esteem of youth can be increased successfully through intervention and that these gains are associated with positive change in their overall adjustment. Notably, it is when programs focus specifically on the aim of strengthening self-esteem or self-concept that such benefits are most apparent. Under these circumstances, the outcomes obtained in esteem-enhancement interventions closely resemble those achieved in other types of proven therapeutic and preventive interventions.

Despite these favorable trends, there currently are numerous limitations and unresolved concerns pertaining to esteem-enhancement interventions for youth. Several key issues relate to program content and design. To date, for example, interventions typically have sought only to increase global or overall feelings of self-worth. Priority therefore should be given to expanding programs to also incorporate efforts to modify multiple, distinct facets of self-esteem as well as processes involved in esteem formation and maintenance with the goal of facilitating stronger and more enduring program outcomes. A further concern is that many programs presently rely exclusively on individually oriented modes of intervention that tend to reflect only a direct, time-limited approach to esteem-enhancement (e.g., structured educational curricula). Greater consideration needs to be given to broadening this type of design through the introduction of components that involve environmentally oriented approaches to promoting healthy self-esteem (e.g., mentoring). Such strategies offer the promise of creating sustained change in the day-to-day experiences of youth as a relatively indirect, but potentially more powerful ecologically driven route to achieving long-term positive outcomes in programs. Increased attention to adapting and "customizing" program content in ways that are responsive to individual differences among participating youth is an additional important concern. Factors meriting attention in this regard include variability in levels, facets, and processes of self-esteem across individual participating youth as well as differences pertaining to developmental level and sociocultural background.

The proposed model for guiding the design of esteem-enhancement interventions with youth provides a framework for addressing the preceding types of concerns. The validity and practical value of the model itself, however, is in need of study. Can it be used, for example, to successfully predict and thus help understand differences in the extent to which youth benefit from participation in esteem-enhancement interventions? Furthermore, do interventions developed explicitly in accordance with the model produce superior outcomes?

Finally, the research designs used to evaluate esteem-enhancement interventions also are in need of innovation. This will be necessary both for increasing understanding of the causal contribution of enhancements in self-esteem to improvements in other areas of functioning and for better assessing the long-term durability of program effects (Haney & Durlak, 1998). To strengthen the rationale for dissemination of programs, it similarly will be important for tangible benefits of participation to be assessed relative to costs and for initial demonstrations of efficacy to be followed by efforts to establish effectiveness when implemented by practitioners under less controlled conditions. Relatedly, strategic methods of dissemination also need to be developed and evaluated. This step will be critically important to ensure both optimal receptivity to self-esteem programs and the creation of sustained infrastructures of support for them within host organizations and communities.

In summary, the agenda for the future development of esteem-enhancement interventions is both multifaceted and challenging in the tasks that need to be accomplished. This agenda is likely to be advanced upon most successfully through an ongoing and mutually informing process of basic research, innovations in program design and evaluation, and strategic dissemination efforts. Early adolescence represents a promising focal point for the efforts of all those who are willing to help pursue this important endeavor.

References

Adams, G. R. (1992). Introduction and overview. In G. R. Adams, T. P. Gullotta, & R. Montemayor (Eds.), *Adolescent identity formation* (pp. 1-8). Newbury Park, CA: Sage.

Alexander, W. M., & George, P. S. (1993). *The exemplary middle school* (2nd ed.). New York: Holt, Rinehart, & Winston.

Arnett, J. J. (1999). Adolescent storm and stress reconsidered. *American Psychologist, 54*, 317- 326.

Attie, I., & Brooks-Gunn, J. (1989). Development of eating problems in adolescent girls: A longitudinal study. *Developmental Psychology, 25*, 70-79.

Beane, J. A. (1994). Cluttered terrain: The schools' interest in the self. In T. M. Brinthaupt & R. P. Lipka (Eds.), *Changing the self: Philosophies, techniques, and experiences* (pp. 69-87). Albany: State University of New York Press.

Beane, J. A., & Lipka, R. P. (1980). Self-concept and self-esteem: A construct differentiation. *Child Study Journal, 10*, 1-6.

Biggs, J. (1987). *Student approaches to learning and studying*. Melbourne, Australia: ACER.

Blaine, B., & Crocker, J. (1993). Self-esteem and self-serving biases in reactions to positive and negative events: An integrative review. In R. F. Baumeister (Ed.), *Self-esteem: The puzzle of low self-regard* (pp. 55-85). New York: Plenum.

Blyth, D. A., & Traeger, C. M. (1983). The self-concept and self-esteem of early adolescents. *Theory into Practice, 22*, 91-97.

Bracken, B. A. (1996). Clinical applications of a context-dependent multidimensional model of self-concept. In B. A. Bracken (Ed.), *Handbook of self-concept* (pp. 463-503). New York: Wiley.

Brinthaupt, T. M., & Erwin, L. J. (1992). Reporting about the self: Issues and implications. In T. M. Brinthaupt & R. P. Lipka (Eds.), *The self: Definitional and methodological issues* (pp. 137-171). Albany: State University of New York Press.

Bronfenbrenner, U. (1977). Toward an experimental ecology of human development. *American Psychologist, 32*, 513-531.

Brown, J. D. (1993). Motivational conflict and the self: The double-bind of low self-esteem. In R. F. Baumeister (Ed.), *Self-esteem: The puzzle of low self-regard* (pp. 117-130). New York: Plenum.

Byrne, B. M. (1996). *Measuring self-concept across the life span*. Washington, DC: American Psychological Association.

Cairn, R. M. (1996). The influence of age, race, and gender on child and adolescent multidimensional self-concept. In B. A. Bracken (Ed.), *Handbook of self-concept* (pp. 395-420). New York: Wiley.

California Department of Education (1990). *Toward a state of esteem: The final report of the California Task Force to Promote Self-esteem and Personal and Social Responsibility*. Sacramento, CA: Author.

Cassidy, J. (1990). Theoretical and methodological considerations in the study of attachment and the self in young children. In M. T. Greenberg, D. Cicchetti, & E. M. Cummings (Eds.), *Attachment in the preschool years:*

Theory, research, and intervention (pp. 87-119). Chicago: University of Chicago Press.

Cauce, A. M., Comer, J. P., & Schwartz, D. (1987). Long-term effects of a systems-oriented school prevention program. *American Journal of Orthopsychiatry, 57*, 127-131.

Colvin, C. R., & Block, J. (1994). Do positive illusions foster mental health? An examination of the Taylor and Brown formulation. *Psychological Bulletin, 116*, 3-20.

Colvin, C. R., Block, J., & Funder, D. C. (1995). Overly positive self-evaluations and personality: Negative implications for mental health. *Journal of Personality and Social Psychology, 68*, 1152-1162.

Combs, A. W., Soper, D. W., & Courson, C. C. (1963). The measurement of self-concept and self-report. *Educational and Psychological Measurement, 23*, 493-500.

Connell, J. P., & Ilardi, B. C. (1987). Self-system concomitants of discrepancies between children's and teachers' evaluations of academic competence. *Child Development, 58*, 1297-1307.

Cooper, H. (1998). *Synthesizing research: A guide for literature reviews* (3rd ed.). Thousand Oaks, CA: Sage.

Coopersmith, S. (1967). *The antecedents of self-esteem.* San Francisco: Freeman.

Covington, M. V. (1989). Self-esteem and failure in school: Analysis and policy implications. In A. M. Mecca, N. J. Smelser, & J. Vasconcellos (Eds.), *The social importance of self-esteem* (pp. 72-124). Berkeley: University of California Press.

Damon, W. (1995). *Greater expectations: Overcoming the culture of indulgence in America's homes and schools.* New York: Free Press.

Damon, W., & Hart, D. (1982). The development of self-understanding from infancy through adolescence. *Child Development, 53*, 841-864.

Danish, S. J. (1997). Going for the Goal: A life skills program. In G. W. Albee & T. P. Gullotta (Eds.), *Primary prevention works* (pp. 291-312). Thousand Oaks, CA: Sage.

Demo, D. H. (1985). The measurement of self-esteem: Refining our methods. *Journal of Personality and Social Psychology, 48*, 1490-1502.

Dodd, J. M., Nelson, J. R. , & Hofland, B. H. (1994). Minority identity and self-concept: The American Indian experience. In T. M. Brinthaupt & R. P. Lipka (Eds.), *Changing the self: Philosophies, techniques, and experiences* (pp. 307-336). Albany: State University of New York Press.

Dryfoos, J. G. (1998). *Safe passage: Making it through adolescence in a risky society.* New York: Oxford University Press.

DuBois, D. L., Bull, C. A., Sherman, M. D., & Roberts, M. (1998). Self-esteem and adjustment in early adolescence: A social-contextual perspective. *Journal of Youth and Adolescence, 27*, 557-583.

DuBois, D. L., & Felner, R. D. (1996). The quadripartite model of social competence: Theory and applications to clinical intervention. In M. Reinecke, F. M. Dattilio, & A. Freeman (Eds.), *Cognitive therapy: A casebook for clinical practice* (pp. 124-152). New York: Guilford.

DuBois, D. L., Felner, R. D., Brand, S., Adan, A. M., & Evans, E. G. (1992). A prospective study of life stress, social support, and adaptation in early adolescence. *Child Development, 63*, 542-557.

DuBois, D. L., Felner, R. D., Brand, S., & George, G. R. (1999). Profiles of self-esteem in early adolescence: Identification and investigation of adaptive correlates. *American Journal of Community Psychology, 27*, 903-936.

DuBois, D. L., Felner, R. D., Brand, S., Phillips, R. S. C., & Lease, A. M. (1996). Early adolescent self-esteem: A developmental-ecological framework and assessment strategy. *Journal of Research on Adolescence, 6*, 543-579.

DuBois, D. L., Felner, R. D., Meares, H., & Krier, M. (1994). Prospective investigation of the effects of socioeconomic disadvantage, life stress, and social support on early adolescent adjustment. *Journal of Abnormal Psychology, 103*, 511-522.

DuBois, D. L., & Hirsch, B. J. (2000). Self-esteem in early adolescence: From stock character to marquee attraction. *Journal of Early Adolescence, 20*, 5-10.

DuBois, D. L., & Tevendale, H. D. (1999). Self-esteem in childhood and adolescence: Vaccine or epiphenomenon? *Applied and Preventive Psychology, 8*, 103-117.

DuBois, D. L., Tevendale, H. D., Burk-Braxton, C., Swenson, L. P., & Hardesty, J. L. (2000). Self-system influences during early adolescence: Investigation of an integrative model. *Journal of Early Adolescence, 20*, 12-43.

Faunce, W. A. (1984). School achievement, social status, and self-esteem. *Social Psychology Quarterly, 47*, 3-14.

Felner, R. D. (1999). An ecological perspective on pathways of risk, vulnerability, and adaptation: Implications for preventive interventions. In S. W. Russ & T. H. Ollendick (Eds.), *Handbook of psychotherapies with children and adolescents: Issues in clinical child psychology* (pp. 483-503). New York: Kluwer Academic/Plenum.

Felner, R. D., Brand, S., Adan, A. M., Mulhall, P. F., Flowers, N., Sartain, B., & DuBois, D. L. (1993). Restructuring the ecology of the school as an approach to prevention during school transitions: Longitudinal follow-ups and extensions of the School Transitional Environment Project (STEP). *Prevention in Human Services, 10*, 103-136.

Felner, R. D., DuBois, D. L., & Adan, A. (1991). Community-based intervention and prevention: Conceptual underpinnings and progress toward a science of community intervention and evaluation. In C. E. Walker (Ed.), *Clinical psychology: Historical and research foundations* (pp. 459-510). New York: Plenum Press.

Friedman, R. M. (1994). Restructuring of systems to emphasize prevention and family support. *Journal of Clinical Child Psychology, 23*(Suppl.), 40-47.

Gold, M. (1994). Changing the delinquent self. In T. M. Brinthaupt & R. P. Lipka (Eds.), *Changing the self: Philosophies, techniques, and experiences* (pp. 89-108). Albany: State University of New York Press.

Grossman, J. B., & Rhodes, J. E. (in press). The test of time: Predictors and effects of duration in youth mentoring relationships. *American Journal of Community Psychology*.

Gurney, P. W. (1987). Self-esteem in the classroom II: Experiments in enhancement. *School Psychology International, 8*, 21-29.

Hales, S. (1979, March). *A developmental theory of self-esteem based on competence and moral behavior.* Paper presented at the Society for Research in Child Development, San Francisco, CA.

Hamachek, D. (1994). Changes in the self from a developmental/psychosocial perspective. In T. M. Brinthaupt & R. P. Lipka (Eds.), *Changing the self: Philosophies, techniques, and experiences* (pp. 21-68). Albany: State University of New York Press.

Hamburg, B. (1974). Early adolescence: A specific and stressful stage of the life cycle. In G. Coelho, D. Hamburg, & J. Adams (Eds.), *Coping and adaptation* (pp. 101-124). New York: Basic.

Haney, P., & Durlak, J. A. (1998). Changing self-esteem in children and adolescents: A meta-analytic review. *Journal of Clinical Child Psychology, 27*, 423-433.

Harter, S. (1986). Processes underlying the construction, maintenance and enhancement of the self-concept in children. In J. Suls & A. Greenwald (Eds.), *Psychological perspectives on the self* (Vol. 3, pp. 137-181). Hillsdale, NJ: Erlbaum.

Harter, S. (1987). The determinants and mediational role of global self-worth in children. In N. Eisenberg (Ed.), *Contemporary topics in developmental psychology* (pp. 219-242). New York: Wiley.

Harter, S. (1990). Adolescent self and identity development. In S. S. Feldman & G. R. Eliot (Eds.), *At the threshold: The developing adolescent* (pp. 352-387). Cambridge, MA: Harvard University Press.

Harter, S. (1993). Causes and consequences of low self-esteem in children and adolescents. In R. F. Baumeister (Ed.), *Self-esteem: The puzzle of low self-regard* (pp. 87-116). New York: Plenum.

Harter, S. (1999). *The construction of the self: A developmental perspective.* New York: Guilford.

Harter, S., Marold, D. B., & Whitesell, N. R. (1992). A model of psychosocial risk factors leading to suicidal ideation in young adolescents. *Development and Psychopathology, 4,* 167-188.

Hattie, J. (1992). *Self-concept.* Hillsdale, NJ: Lawrence Erlbaum.

Hattie, J., Marsh, H. W., Neill, J. T., & Richards, G. E. (1997). Adventure Education and Outward Bound: Out-of-class experiences that make a lasting difference. *Review of Educational Research, 67,* 43-87.

Henggeler, S. W., Schoenwald, S. K., Borduin, C. M., Rowland, M. D., & Cunningham, P. B. (1998). *Multisystemic treatment of antisocial behavior in children and adolescents.* New York: Guilford.

Hirsch, B. J., & DuBois, D. L. (1991). Self-esteem in early adolescence: The identification and prediction of contrasting longitudinal trajectories. *Journal of Youth and Adolescence, 20,* 53-72.

Hirsch, B. J., DuBois, D. L., & Brownell, A. B. (1993). Trajectory analysis of the transition to junior high school: Implications for prevention and policy. *Prevention in Human Services, 10*(2), 83-101.

Hirsch, B. J., Roffman, J. G., Deutsch, N. L., Flynn, C. A., Loder, T. L., & Pagano, M. E. (2000). Inner-city youth development organizations: Strengthening programs for adolescent girls. *Journal of Early Adolescence, 20,* 210-230.

Hirsch, B. J., Roffman, J. G., Pagano, M. E., & Deutsch, N. L. (2000, April). Inner city youth: Ties to youth development staff and adult kin. In B. Sanchez (Chair), *Natural and volunteer mentoring relationships of adolescents.* Symposium conducted at the Biennial Meeting of the Society for Research on Adolescence, Chicago.

Hughes, J. N., Cavell, T. A., & Grossman, P. A. (1997). A positive view of self: Risk or protection for aggressive children? *Development and Psychopathology, 9,* 75-94.

Institute of Medicine (1994). *Reducing risks for mental disorders.* Washington, DC: National Academy Press.

James, W. (1950). *The principles of psychology* (Vol. 1). New York: Henry Holt. (Original work published 1890).

Kaplan, H. B. (1986). *Social psychology of self-referent behavior.* New York: Plenum.

Kaplan, H. B., & Lin, C. (2000). Deviant identity as a moderator of the relationship between negative self-feelings and deviant behavior. *Journal of Early Adolescence, 20,* 150-177.

Kernis, M. H. (1993). The roles of stability and level of self-esteem in psychological functioning. In R. Baumeister (Ed.), *Self-esteem: The puzzle of low self-regard* (pp. 167-182). New York: Plenum.

Kohn, A. (1994, December). The truth about self-esteem. *Phi Delta Kappan,* pp. 272-283.

Krueger, R. A. (1994). *Focus groups: A practical guide for applied research* (2nd ed.). Thousand Oaks, CA: Sage.

Larson, R. W. (1997). The emergence of solitude as a constructive domain of experience in early adolescence. *Child Development, 68,* 80-93.

Laursen, B., Coy, K. C., & Collins, W. A. (1998). Reconsidering changes in parent-child conflict across adolescence: A meta-analysis. *Child Development, 69,* 817-832.

Lerner, J. V., & Lerner, R. M. (1994). Explorations of the goodness-of-fit model in early adolescence. In W. B. Carey & S. Conway (Eds.), *Prevention and early intervention: Individual differences as risk factors for the mental health of children: A festschrift for Stella Chess and Alexander Thomas* (pp. 161-169). New York: Brunner/Mazel.

Lewinsohn, P. M., Clarke, G. N., Rohde, P., Hops, H., & Seeley, J. R. (1996). A course in coping: A cognitive-behavioral approach to the treatment of adolescent depression. In E. D. Hibbs & P. S. Jensen (Eds.), *Psychosocial treatments for child and adolescent disorders* (pp. 109-135). Washington, DC: American Psychological Association.

Lipsey, M. W., & Wilson, D. B. (1993) The efficacy of psychological, educational, and behavioral treatment: Confirmation from meta-analysis. *American Psychologist, 48,* 1181-1209.

Marsh, H. W. (1990). A multidimensional, hierarchical self-concept: Theoretical and empirical justification. *Educational Psychology Review, 2,* 77-172.

Marsh, H. W., & Peart, N. D. (1988). Competitive and cooperative physical fitness training programs for girls: Effects on fitness and on multidimensional self-concepts. *Journal of Sports Psychology, 10,* 390-407.

Marsh, H. W., Richards, G. E., & Barnes, J. (1986). Multidimensional self-concepts: A long-term follow-up of the effect of participation in an Outward Bound program. *Personality and Social Psychology Bulletin, 12,* 475-492.

Marsh, H. W., & Yeung, A. S. (1997). Causal effects of academic self-concept on academic achievement: Structural equation models of longitudinal data. *Journal of Educational Psychology, 89,* 41-54.

Meggert, S. S. (1996). Who cares what I think: Problems of low self-esteem. In D. Capuzzi & D. R. Gross (Eds.), *Youth at risk: A prevention resource for counselors, teachers, and parents* (2nd ed., pp. 81-103). Alexandria, VA: American Counseling Association.

Moore, C. W., & Allen, J. P. (1996). The effects of volunteering on the young volunteer. *Journal of Primary Prevention, 17*, 231-258.

Offord, D. R. (1987). Prevention of behavioral and emotional disorders in children. *Journal of Child Psychology and Psychiatry, 28*, 9-19.

Perry, C. L., Story, M., & Lytle, L. A. (1997). Promoting healthy dietary behaviors. In R. P. Weissberg & T. P. Gullotta (Eds.), *Healthy children 2010: Enhancing children's wellness* (pp. 214-249). Thousand Oaks, CA: Sage.

Pope, A. W., McHale, S., & Craighead, W. E. (1988). *Self-esteem enhancement with children and adolescents.* New York: Pergamon.

Rhodes, J. E. (1994). Older and wiser: Mentoring relationships in childhood and adolescence. *Journal of Primary Prevention, 14*, 187-196.

Robin, A. L., & Foster, S. L. (1989). *Negotiating parent adolescent conflict: A behavioral-family systems approach.* New York: Guilford.

Rosenberg, M. (1979). *Conceiving the self.* New York: Basic Books.

Rosenberg, M. (1985). Self-concept and psychological well-being in adolescence. In R. L. Leahy (Ed.), *The development of the self* (pp. 205-246). Orlando, FL: Academic Press.

Savin-Williams, R. C., & Demo, D. H. (1983a). Conceiving or misconceiving the self: Issues in adolescent self-esteem. *Journal of Early Adolescence, 3*, 121-140.

Savin-Williams, R. C., & Demo, D. H. (1983b). Situational and transituational determinants of adolescent self-feelings. *Journal of Personality and Social Psychology, 44*, 824-833.

Savin-Williams, R. C., & Demo, D. H. (1984). Developmental change and stability in adolescent self-concept. *Developmental Psychology, 20*, 1100-1110.

Savin-Williams, R. C., & Jaquish, G. A. (1981). The assessment of adolescent self-esteem: A comparison of methods. *Journal of Personality, 49*, 324-336.

Seligman, M. E. P. (1993). *What you can change and what you can't: The complete guide to successful self-improvement.* New York: Fawcett.

Simmons, R. G., & Blyth, D. A. (1987). *Moving into adolescence: The impact of pubertal change and school context.* Hawthorne, NY: Aldine.

Strain, P. S., Kerr, M. M., Stagg, V., Lenkner, D. A., Lambert, D. L., Mendelsohn, S. R., & Franca, V. M. (1983). Relationships between self-concept and directly observed behaviors in kindergarten children. *Psychology in the Schools, 20,* 498-505.

Strein, W. (1988). Classroom-based elementary school affective education programs: A critical review. *Psychology in the Schools, 25,* 288-296.

Tennen, H., & Affleck, G. (1993). The puzzles of low self-esteem: A clinical perspective. In R. Baumeister (Ed.), *Self-esteem: The puzzle of low self-regard* (pp. 241-262). New York: Plenum.

Tevendale, H. D., DuBois, D. L., Lopez, C., & Prindiville, S. L. (1997). Self-esteem stability and early adolescent adjustment: An exploratory study. *Journal of Early Adolescence, 17,* 216-237.

Turner, S., & Scherman, A. (1996). Big brothers: Impact on little brothers' self-concepts and behaviors. *Adolescence, 31,* 875-882.

Verkuyten, M. (1995). Self-esteem, self-concept stability, and aspects of ethnic identity among minority and majority youth in the Netherlands. *Journal of Youth and Adolescence, 24,* 155-175.

Weinstein, R. S., Soule, C. R., Collins, F., Cone, J., Mehlhorn, M., & Simontacchi, K. (1991). Expectations and high school change: Teacher-researcher collaboration to prevent school failure. *American Journal of Community Psychology, 19,* 333-363.

Whaley, A. L. (1993). Self-esteem, cultural identity, and psychosocial adjustment in African American children. *Journal of Black Psychology, 19,* 406-422.

What caused Columbine? (1999, June). *The Phyllis Schlafly Report, 32*(11).

White, R. W. (1960). Competence and the psychosexual stages of development. In M. R. Jones (Ed.), *Nebraska Symposium on Motivation* (Vol. 8, pp. 97-141). Lincoln: University of Nebraska Press.

Winett, R. A. (1995). A framework for health promotion programs and disease prevention programs. *American Psychologist, 50,* 341-350.

Wylie, R. C. (1989). *Measures of self-concept.* Lincoln: University of Nebraska Press.

Zimmerman, M. A., Copeland, L. A., Shope, J. T., & Dielman, T. E. (1997). A longitudinal study of self-esteem: Implications for adolescent development. *Journal of Youth and Adolescence, 26,* 117-141.

Author Note

The writing of this chapter was supported by a grant to the first author from the National Institute of Mental Health (DHHS 5 R29 MH55050). Correspondence should be addressed to David L. DuBois, 210 McAlester Hall, Department of

Psychology, University of Missouri-Columbia, Columbia, MO 65211. Electronic mail can be sent via the Internet to DuBoisD@missouri.edu.

Endnote

1. Numerous theorists have argued for the importance of distinguishing between self-concept and self-esteem (Beane & Lipka, 1980; Blyth & Traeger, 1983; Brinthaupt & Erwin, 1992; Cassidy, 1990; Damon & Hart, 1982; Pope, McHale, & Craighead, 1988; Rosenberg, 1979). In general, they have proposed that self-concept should be regarded as referring primarily to descriptive views of self-attributes, whereas self-esteem should be viewed as more of an affective and evaluative assessment of the adequacy of the content of the self-concept in the context of one's personal standards and self-expectations. This distinction has received some support in recent research, including studies conducted with young adolescents specifically (DuBois, Tevendale, Burk-Braxton, Swenson, & Hardesty, 2000). Yet the terms self-concept and self-esteem often have been used interchangeably by researchers and there generally has been little agreement as to whether particular instruments assess one or the other (or both) of these constructs (Byrne, 1996). For these reasons, researchers conducting both of the meta-analyses of esteem-enhancement interventions (Haney & Durlak, 1998; Hattie, 1992) made the decision to include studies using either type of outcome measure in their reviews. Hattie (1992) found comparable estimates of effect size across studies regardless of whether self-concept or self-esteem was stated to be the self-construct of interest. This finding notwithstanding, the issue of possible differential effects of interventions on self-esteem versus self-concept remains an important concern in need of further investigation.

SUBJECT INDEX

Author Index

Cuban, L., 112–113
Cunningham, P. B., 336
Curran, P. J., 229
Curry, C., 148
Cutting, L., 184

Damon, W., 4, 27, 35, 169–170, 321, 371
Danish, S. J., 358
Davidson, K. C., 229, 232
Davis, G. A., 150–151, 153–156
Davis, S. M., 275
Deci, E. L., 60, 63–64, 74–76, 78, 80–81, 92, 98–101, 104, 106–109, 117
Deckner, C. W., 275
DeLevita, D. J., 26, 29
Delucchi, K., 109–110, 118
Demo, D. H., 4, 12, 59, 68, 158, 167, 170–171, 174, 329–330
DeNeve, K., 66
DeRosier, M. E., 41
DeSimone, A., 227
Deutsch, N., 293, 295, 303, 313, 338, 351
Dewey, J., 114
Diana, M. S., 33
Diaz, T., 227, 229, 234–237, 250, 254
Dielman, T. E., 227, 326–327
DiMatteo, M. R., 252
Dishion, T. J., 4, 177
Dodd, J. M., 349
Dolcini, M. M., 250
Donohew, L., 276
Donovan, J. E., 228
Dornbusch, S., 293
Douglas, K. A., 268
Dow y Garcia Velarde, L. A., 268, 280, 285
Dressler, W. W., 275
Dryfoos, J. G., 104–105, 120, 275, 360
DuBois, D. L., 1, 57–58, 73, 109, 119, 137, 145, 152, 227, 253, 321, 326–329, 332, 338, 344–345, 348, 354, 356, 358–359, 371
Dow, L. A., 273
Duff, J. L., 167, 175
Duncan, G., 255
Duncan, S. C., 229
Duncan, T. E., 229

Dunn, P., 36
Dunning, D., 62
Durlak, J. A., 104, 334–341, 343–344, 352, 354, 362, 371
Dusenbury, L., 234–235, 254, 274–276
Duval, S., 40
Dweck, C., 77, 102–103
Dwyer, J. H., 254, 275

East, P. L, 57, 227
Ebata, A., 143
Eccles, J. S., 10, 29, 31–32, 38–39, 92–93, 95, 102–103, 105, 107–114, 117–120, 122, 137, 139–141, 143–147, 149, 172, 175, 226, 229, 248, 294, 299, 313
Eckert, P., 173–174
Eddy, J. M., 177
Edelbrock, C. S., 226
Edelin, K. C., 110–111, 151
Edelstein, W., 167
Eder, D., 174–175, 178
Edwards, V. B., 154
Ehrhardt, A. A., 36
Elias, M., 143
Elkind, D., 299
Ellickson, P. L., 254, 274
Elliott, G. R., 229
Ellis, B. J., 6
Ellsworth, R., 137
Endler, N. S., 195
Enke, J., 178
Ennett, S. T., 274
Epstein, D., 229, 232
Epstein, J. L., 117, 120, 138
Epstein, S., 60, 193, 195, 199
Erbaugh, J., 211
Erikson, E. H., 25–28, 33, 91–95, 99–104, 123–124, 131, 135, 167, 171, 229, 299
Erwin, L. J., 226, 371
Espinoza, R., 268, 275–276
Evans, E. G., 356
Eysenck, H. J., 211
Eysenck, S. B. G., 211

Fabian, A. K., 296
Faiman, C., 31

Falco, M., 276
Farnham, S. D., 60–61
Fashola, O. S., 114–115, 120
Faunce, W. A., 331
Favazza, A., 110–112, 119
Feinman, J., 143–144, 171
Feldlaufer, H., 140
Feldman, R., 298
Feldman, S. S., 229
Felner, R. D., 43, 108–114, 119, 137, 151–152, 253, 328–329, 338, 344, 348, 351, 356, 358–359
Felson, R. B., 61
Felts, M., 36
Fenzel, L. M., 144
Ferrarese, M. M., 225
Feshbach, S., 61
Festinger, L., 38
Finders, M. J., 173–174
Fine, M., 301
Finn, P., 281
Finnegan, J. R., 275
Fisher, G. A., 217
Flanagan, C. A., 29, 31, 39, 107–111, 137, 143–144, 294, 299, 313
Flannery, D. J., 294
Flasher, J., 285
Flay, B. R., 254, 274–275
Fletcher, J. M., 229, 232
Flewelling, R. L., 274
Flowers, N., 109, 119, 137, 151–152, 338, 344
Ford, A. B., 218
Ford, V. L., 275
Forster, J. L., 274–275
Fowler, W. J., 137
Flynn, C., 293, 295, 303, 313, 351
Flynn, H. A., 70
Ford, M. E., 96–97, 99, 101–102, 104, 106, 115
Fordham, S., 306
Forster, E. M., 175
Foster, C. L., 104
Foster, S. L., 226, 357
Foster, W., 293
Franca, V. M., 330

Francis, D. J., 229, 232
Frankel, B. S., 69–70, 77
Freimuth, V. S., 276
Freire, P., 275
French, S., 143, 147, 149
Freud, S., 313
Friedman, M. A., 35
Friedman, R. M., 358
Frost, R., 295
Fujioka, T., 28
Funder, D. C., 330, 332
Furman, W., 4, 41, 43
Fuzhong, L., 177

Galambos, N. L., 36
Gallion, K. J., 268, 275–276
Gamoran, A., 139
Ganellen, R. J., 70
Garber, J., 6, 92, 145–146
Gargiulo, J., 31
Garmezy, N., 225, 228
Gavin, L.A., 4, 41
Gecas, V., 135
Gee, M., 274
George, G. R., 328–329, 359
George, P. S., 351
George, T. P., 175
Gest, S. D., 225, 228
Gil, A. G., 227
Gilligan, C., 299, 310
Girgus, J. S., 172
Goetz, T. E., 77
Gold, M., 355
Goldman, B., 60–61, 65, 73, 80
Goldstein, H., 209
Good, T. L., 117, 120
Goodenow, C., 108–109
Gordon, A. S., 250
Graber, J. A., 1, 6, 36, 143
Graafsma, T. L. G., 26
Graham, J. W., 274
Gramzow, R., 67
Grannemann, B. D., 61,68, 73
Greene, A. L., 148
Greenberg, L. S., 46
Greenier, K. D., 69–70, 73, 77, 80–81, 227

Meyer-Bahlburg, H. F. L., 36
Mewborn, C. R., 275
Midgley, C., 10, 29, 92, 95, 105,
107–113, 117–118, 122, 137, 139–142,
147, 149, 151, 229, 294,
299, 313
Miller, C., 31, 143–144
Miller, J. W., 137, 310
Miller, P. H., 299
Millstein, S. G., 92, 114
Mischel, W., 195, 199, 226
Misukanis, T. M., 79
Mitchell, C., 143–144, 171
Mitic, W. R., 227
Mizell, M. H., 151–152
Mock, J., 211
Mohr, T., 67
Mone, M. A., 226
Mongillo, J. M., 279
Monroe, s. M., 70
Monsour, A., 170
Montemayor, R., 1
Moore, C. W., 338
Moos, R., 294, 297
Moretti, M., 45
Morling, B., 60
Morrocco, J. C., 137
Moser, A., 35
Mortimore, P., 137, 311
Mounts, N., 28
Mueller, R. A., 79
Mulhall, P. F., 109, 119, 137, 151–152,
338, 344
Murphy, M. R., 227
Murray, L., 293
Murray, P., 227
Musick, J., 293

National Center for Educational
Statistics, 104
National Research Council, 293
Neemann, J., 225, 228
Neill, J. T., 342, 344–345
Nelson, J. R., 349
Newbegin, I., 39
Newcomb, M. D., 14, 228

New Mexico Selected Health Statistics
Annual Report, 271
Nightingale, E. O., 92
Nolen-Hoeksema, S., 172
Nomura, C., 250
Nottlemann, E. D., 225
Nurius, P., 11, 41, 148, 300, 306, 308

Oakes, J., 139
Obeidallah, D., 299–300
Offer, D., 29
Offord, D. R., 334
Ohannessian, C. M., 227
O'Heron, C. A., 37
Olmstead, R. E., 227
Olweus, D., 61, 195–197, 199–203,
205–206, 208–211, 214, 217
O'Malley, P. M., 227–228, 236, 251
Oppenheimer, L., 28, 40–41
Orenstein, P., 172
Orlandi, M. A., 275
Orlofsky, J. L., 26, 37
Osterwegel, A., 27, 40–41
Ouston, J., 137, 311
Owens, A., 39
Oxley, D., 298

Pagano, M., 293, 295, 303, 313, 338, 351
Page, R. N., 139
Pandina, R. J., 250
Paradise, A. W., 60–61, 65–66, 69, 73, 80
Parker, J., 226
Parker, J. G., 12, 41, 102
Parmalee, P. A., 296–297
Parsons, J. E., 32
Pastor, J., 301
Patterson, S., 276
Paul, E. L., 32
Paulhus, D. L., 236
Peart, N. D., 344
Peck, S., 105
Pelham, B. W., 59
Pellegrini, D. S., 225
Pentz, M. A., 254, 275
Perry, C. L., 275, 360
Petersen, A. C., 1, 35–36, 92, 143, 175, 200